THE SOCIAL DYNAMICS OF
FAMILY VIOLENCE

THE SOCIAL DYNAMICS OF
FAMILY VIOLENCE

ANGELA HATTERY GEORGE MASON UNIVERSITY

AND EARL SMITH WAKE FOREST UNIVERSITY

WESTVIEW
PRESS

A Member of the Perseus Books Group

Westview Press was founded in 1975 in Boulder, Colorado, by notable publisher and intellectual Fred Praeger. Westview Press continues to publish scholarly titles and high-quality undergraduate- and graduate-level textbooks in core social science disciplines. With books developed, written, and edited with the needs of serious nonfiction readers, professors, and students in mind, Westview Press honors its long history of publishing books that matter.

Published by Westview Press,
A Member of the Perseus Books Group

Find us on the World Wide Web at www.westviewpress.com.

Every effort has been made to secure required permissions for all text, images, maps, and other art reprinted in this volume.

Westview Press books are available at special discounts for bulk purchases in the United States by corporations, institutions, and other organizations. For more information, please contact the Special Markets Department at the Perseus Books Group, 2300 Chestnut Street, Suite 200, Philadelphia, PA 19103, or call (800) 810-4145, ext. 5000, or e-mail special.markets@perseusbooks.com.

Designed by Trish Wilkinson
Set in 11 point Adobe Garamond Pro

Library of Congress Cataloging-in-Publication Data

Hattery, Angela.
   The social dynamics of family violence / Angela J. Hattery and Earl Smith.
      p.   cm.
   Includes bibliographical references and index.
   ISBN 978-0-8133-4463-8 (pbk. : alk. paper) — ISBN 978-0-8133-4562-8 (e-book)
1. Family violence—United States. 2. Families—United States. 3. Abused children—United States. 4. Abused women—United States. 5. Family social work—United States. I. Smith, Earl. II. Title.
HV6626.H325 2012
362.82'92—dc23   2011043297

10 9 8 7 6 5 4 3 2 1

To Travis & Emma: Gandhi said: Be the Change You Want to See in the World. I hope that the work that takes me away from spending time with you will serve as a reminder to be the change YOU want to see in the world.

—Love, Mom

To Earl: As always, as with everything we do, our partnership focuses me on the things that matter, motivates me when the days are long and the work is difficult, and sustains me through it all.

—Angela

To Angela: Perfect
This work underscores all that we have done together examining what sociologists continue to describe as "life chances." As the society we live in becomes better, hopefully there will not be the need for a book of this type again.

—Earl

Contents

Expanded Table of Contents

1 Social Dynamics of Family Violence

Setting the Stage

She died in September by the ugliest means, weighing an unthinkable 18 pounds, half what a 4-year-old ought to. She withered in poverty in a home in Brooklyn where the authorities said she had been drugged and often bound to a toddler bed by her mother, having realized a bare thimble's worth of living. . . . Marchella weighed 1 pound 4 ounces when she was born, prematurely, on April 3, 2006. A relative recalls thinking she was about the size of a one-liter Pepsi bottle. A twin sister, born first, died. Her name was Miracle.

—N. R. KLEINFIELD, "A Bleak Life, Cut Short at 4, Harrowing from the Start"

This chapter will introduce family violence to the reader. In addition to the introduction of definitions, we will also discuss concepts for defining family violence, compare and contrast scholarly approaches to thinking about family violence, and offer a reconceptualized model for considering family violence.

OBJECTIVES

- Provide the latest empirical data on a variety of types of family violence
- Define critical concepts and recognize key issues relevant to the study of family violence
- Identify and introduce the reader to the theoretical paradigms that have been employed to analyze and understand family violence: (1) the family violence approach, (2) the feminist approach, and (3) the race, class, and gender (RCG) approach
- Illuminate the ways in which social structures and institutions, such as the economy, cultural norms, and religious ideologies, shape violence in families
- Illuminate the ways in which social statuses—race, social class, gender, age, and sexuality—shape patterns of violence in families
- Provide an honest discussion of the issues that families living with violence face

KEY TERMS

family	economy
violence	cultural norms
family violence framework	religion
feminist framework	the military
race, class, and gender theory	social status variation

INTRODUCTION

From their earliest formation, families have been complex and dynamic units that have evolved in order to meet the changing needs of both individuals and societies. Although families are inherently private, they are also public. In the United States alone, the government has on many occasions involved itself in family life, most frequently by passing laws or deciding court cases that determine the structure of the family and establish the rules about families and marriage. For example, one of the major issues of the early twenty-first century entails various branches of state and federal governments—legislatures, voting referenda, and courts—engaged in shaping the legal structure of families through the debate on gay marriage.

Although discussions of gay marriage range from the uninterested to the frantic, just like the discussions on interracial marriage were in the 1960s (Smith and Hattery 2009), what most Americans focus on are their personal beliefs about homosexuality rather than the legal aspects of defining family. For example, when we ask students in our classes to conjure up an image of a wedding and share it with the class, most describe a religious ceremony in a church, temple, or mosque. They describe clothes: tuxedos for men and white wedding dresses for women. And, unlike the tuxedo, the white dress has values and norms attached: it denotes that the woman is a virgin. They describe music, dancing, and food rituals. Despite some variation by race, religion, or region of the country, there is a high level of agreement among the students about the necessary elements of a wedding. What students rarely if ever describe is the signing of the marriage license. Yet it is the marriage license that is the most critical part of the wedding, far more important than the selection of the wedding dress, despite what Randy the fashion consultant on TLC's *Say Yes to the Dress* might say, because it is the legal contract that binds two people and their future children together and defines them as a legitimate family.

This legal contract impacts everything from taxes to health insurance to inheritance (Jackman 2011). Furthermore, the legal definition of *family* is an important aspect to the ways in which violence that occurs in families is treated by the criminal justice and legal systems. This will be our major focus in Chapter 13, but we provide an illustration here. For example, though there are likely to be differences in the way judges issue restraining orders to cohabiting couples as opposed to married couples or gay or lesbian couples as compared to heterosexual couples, the sting of a slap, the gasp for air when one is punched, and the frantic desire to be safe from violence do not differ across the individuals in these different types of couples. Whether the *law* recognizes the couple may shape the way individuals are treated, but it does not shape the feelings of hurt and disillusionment that individuals in these families experience. As important as legal definitions are to shaping the response to violence by the criminal justice and legal systems, for individuals living in families, the definitions of family otherwise have little impact on the actual experience of violence. Therefore, other than when necessary, our discussions of family violence will not be limited by legal definitions. Rather, we will operate under the assumption that families can be and often are defined by their members in much broader ways.

Our primary objective in writing this book is to examine the state of violence in families in the United States at the beginning of the twenty-first century. In this book we tackle from a sociological perspective the most important issues that researchers, policy makers, social service providers, and families themselves face. These issues, which are central to the academic discussions of family scholars and germane to discussions of any type of family, include child abuse, both physical and sexual; elder abuse; intimate partner violence (IPV); and violence in subgroups, such as among gay and lesbian families and families in the military. We also include a chapter on the role that social institutions and structures—such as the economy and religion—play in structuring family violence. Last, we explore variations across family groups, including differences across race and ethnicity, social class, and sexuality. We do all of this using a straightforward approach to these issues, many of which have reached the level of crises of epic proportions in families yet remain largely ignored. We begin, as any discussion of a complex phenomenon should, with some basic definitions. This allows us all to "be on the same page" as we begin our discussions.

DEFINITIONS

Family

Family scholars have developed several different definitions of the term *family*. We discuss five:

1. **Family is a set of people with whom you live and with whom you share biological or legal ties or both (Burton and Jayakody 2001).**

    This definition focuses on what many of us refer to as the nuclear family. This definition restricts family primarily to parents (who are married) and their biological or adopted children or both. This is the definition of family that is used by the census, and it is the most common definition of family in use by both scholars as well as the "average" American.

2. **Family is a set of people you may or may not live with but with whom you share biological or legal ties or both (Cherlin 1999).**

   This definition of family is often referred to as the "extended family." As such, it is used to recognize that both in the past and continuing today, many households include extended family members such as grandparents. It also recognizes the continued importance of family once children have permanently moved out of the house.

3. **Family is a set of people you live with but with whom you may or may not share biological or legal ties or both (Landale and Fennelly 1992).**

   This is a much more contemporary definition of family that is designed to recognize several changes in family life, but specifically the rise of cohabiting couples who in the twenty-first century are increasingly likely to be raising children together. Specifically with regards to the African American family, this definition recognizes both higher rates of cohabitation as well as the practice of sharing child rearing with nonrelatives in response to a variety of forces, such as incarceration. Furthermore, with regards to sexuality, this definition recognizes that as of the writing of this book, marriages or legal unions are still limited to "one man and one woman" in the vast majority of states. Six states currently allow gay marriages, a small handful of others (including several in New England) recognize gay marriage, and slightly more offer equal or similar benefits to gay couples as they do to heterosexual couples. Nineteen states ban gay marriage entirely.[1]

4. **Family is a set of people with whom you share social, physical, or financial support or a combination thereof (Sarkisian and Gerstel 2008).**

   This definition is very inclusive and was developed primarily to recognize the existence of gay and lesbian households that, as we note, are still, at the writing of this book, not recognized in legal terms in most states. Furthermore, this definition is designed to emphasize a key feature of families: the fact that members are interdependent. Families generally provide support of various sorts for their members. The flow and direction of this support may change over time—for example, from parent to child during the period of child rearing to one of child to parent during the later years.

5. **Family is a set of people whom you love (Neff and Karney 2005).**

   The most inclusive of all definitions, this one recognizes that increasingly, people create their own "families" that may or may not be based on formal ties (biology or law) and that these important people may or may not live together. The classic example used to illustrate this concept is the popular television program *Friends*. *Friends* represents a set of young men and women who provide support for each other, love each other, but do not necessarily share any biological or legal ties—of course, there are two exceptions to this rule: Ross and Monica are siblings and Chandler and Monica eventually marry. Some of the "friends" lived together, but others did not. Yet they provided for each other most of the very things that have historically been provided by people with formal family ties. In addition, we note that family scholars often refer to this form of family as "fictive kin," and this is especially common when referring to African American family relationships. We note that some may find the term *fictive kin* offensive because it assumes that some relationships (those relationships based on biology or law) are real and that others (those *not* based on biology or law) are "fictive," that is, not real. Thus, we refrain from this kind of distinction and suggest that the initial development of the term carried no such qualifier.

The final two definitions are critical to the focus and discussion of this book because they both highlight what is perhaps the most devastating aspect of family violence: that whatever form it takes, family violence shatters notions of love, respect, interdependence, and mutual support. Whether the violence involves a man beating to death the woman he claims to love, an adult son extracting emotional and financial blackmail from his elderly parents, or an uncle engaging in incest with a young niece or nephew, family violence *always hijacks safety and security*, the very notions on which family is built. Thus, regardless of who is the victim and who is the perpetrator in any specific example, this shattering of the safety and interdependency is universal.

Violence

Often when we think of violence, we think only of physical abuse: hitting, kicking, slapping, beating, and so forth. Yet central to any discussion of **family violence** are acceptance and recognition of the fact that much of the abuse that occurs in families is emotional and psychological as well as sexual. Emotional and psychological abuse often takes the form of name-calling and verbal degradation. For example, battered women we interviewed as part of a larger project (Hattery 2008; Hattery and Smith 2007) reported that their husbands and boyfriends constantly referred to them as "bitch" or "slut" and that they constantly, even incessantly, accused them of sleeping around or nagged them about not keeping up with the housework. Similar types of verbal abuse take place when children are involved as well. The toll that this type of abuse takes can be and often is significant.

Although most of us find the topic revolting and would rather not think about it, a great deal of sexual abuse takes place in families as well. More than a quarter of young girls report that they have been sexually abused by someone they are related to—most often their mother's boyfriend or another male relative—and one in seven boys reports the same (Steese et al. 2006; Tjaden and Thoennes 2000). In fact, as part of another project (Hattery and Smith 2010), we interviewed two sex offenders who were returning home after periods of incarceration, and in the course of the interviews, both revealed that they were themselves victims of child sexual abuse. The impact of sexual abuse, especially when the victims are children, is severe, long lasting, and often nothing short of devastating (Hattery 2009; Kaiser Family Foundation 2003; Tresniowski 2011).

Violence in families can also take the form of financial abuse. This is most common in battering relationships and in cases of elder abuse. In these situations the abuser typically denies the victim access to financial resources—which among other things prevents them from leaving the abusive situation. In the case of elder abuse, adult children often trick vulnerable parents—who are often suffering from some form of dementia—into changing their will or giving them power of attorney that allows them to drain their parents' financial assets from bank accounts, investments, and so on. This is nothing short of embezzlement, only the victim is one's parent, not one's boss (Fox et al. 2002)

It is also important to recognize, based on the definitions of family we offered above, that family violence is not limited to individuals whose relationships meet the legal definitions of family—for example, the most common perpetrator of child sexual abuse is the new boyfriend of the victim's mother. Nor is family violence limited to people who live together. In fact, the most common time for domestic violence homicide to occur is after a battered woman has already physically separated from her abusive partner. And intimate partner violence is equally present in cohabiting relationships and legal marriages. Thus, unless there is some reason to do so, we will not utilize a single definition of family, but rather will report on the violence that takes place between people who love each other—or claim to—and who consider themselves to be part of an intimate relationship or family.

THEORETICAL APPROACHES

Our second objective in this book is to provide a theoretical framework for understanding family violence. Chapters 3 and 4 will be devoted to a lengthy and in-depth discussion of the theoretical and methodological approaches to the study of violence in families. That said, we would like to take the opportunity here to briefly introduce the reader to some of the theoretical frameworks that are employed to study violence in families. There are essentially three main approaches: (1) the family violence framework, (2) the **feminist framework,** and (3) the race, class, and gender paradigm.

Family Violence Framework

The **family violence framework** was developed largely by Murray Straus and Richard Gelles (1995). Straus and Gelles were among the theory's early pioneers, and their work has shaped the field of family violence for the past thirty-plus years. As family sociologists, they conceptualized families as a set of interconnected relationships, and they looked for commonalities among the various types of family violence, from incest to elder abuse. In short, they recognized that families are constructed around relationships that, among other things, involve obligations and responsibilities but also status and power. For example, their perspective identifies a key pattern in family violence: the tendency for it to be perpetrated by people with power against those without power, that is, stronger, older people abuse younger, weaker people. Of course, this trend reverses when parents reach an elderly status and become vulnerable to their adult children. People with more resources (parents, adult children, husbands) are more likely to be abusive toward those without resources (children, elderly adults, wives) than the reverse. Last, they suggest that people engage in abusive behavior because they can and because it works. When a parent spanks a child, there are generally no consequences ("they can"), and it generally changes a child's behavior in the desired direction ("it works"). Building on these basic tenets, family violence theory is the most widely accepted theoretical framework among scholars of the family who study violence.

Feminist Theory

Feminist theory approaches the analysis of any social phenomenon by assuming first and foremost that gender stratification or patriarchy is universal and that it produces a system of inequality that creates opportunities and offers rewards that privilege men and disadvantage women. Thus, the approach of feminist theory to the study of family violence is focused on the ways in which family violence is a *gendered phenomenon*. In other words, more often than not, the victims of family violence are female and the perpetrators are male. Feminist theorists expand the work of family violence theorists by suggesting that it is not random who "can hit," that is, the ability to access the power necessary to engage in physical, emotional, psychological, and sexual abuse is structured by the system of gender stratification. Thus, although there are exceptions to the rule, as we will explore in Chapter 3, even when women make more money than men or have access to other types of power, they are rarely the perpetrators of violence in families, even when males are the victims. Family violence, feminist theorists argue, should be understood as an extension of other types of gender-based violence, such as rape and sexual harassment, rather than being understood inside of the various configurations of the institution of the family.

Race, Class, and Gender Theory

Race, class, and gender theory is an extension of feminist theory in two key ways: it was developed by a subset of feminist scholars—African American feminists such as Bonnie Thorton Dill and Patricia Hill Collins—and it builds on the idea of structured inequality and power. Distinct from feminist theory, race, class, and gender theory is built on the assumption that there are *multiple systems* of oppression that independently and collaboratively create complex systems of stratification that produce interlocking systems of inequality.

Sometimes it is useful to consider an illustration that is disconnected from the topic we are considering. This strategy prevents us from conflating the theory from what we know about the issue. Let's consider an example from the area of health care. A core tenet of race, class, and gender theory is the assumption that every system of domination has a countersystem of privilege. In other words, oppression is a system of both costs and benefits; when one person receives a "benefit" (such as a lower probability for experiencing intimate partner violence or a higher probability of getting an education), someone else experiences a "cost" (such as a higher probability of experiencing food insecurity or a lower probability of delivering a healthy baby). In other words, the benefit does not accrue from an infinite pool of resources; it is extracted at a cost to someone else. For example, we know that African American men die prematurely: seven or eight years earlier than their white counterparts (Hattery and Smith 2007). Generally, a discussion of this gap in life expectancy focuses on the reasons African American men die early: for example, because they are more likely to hold jobs that involve physical labor, they are more likely to live in poverty, they are more likely to lack access to health care, and they are more likely to experience racial discrimination and the stresses associated with being an African American man. Yet a race, class, and gender framework forces us to ask the opposing question: why is it that white men live so much longer? When we pose the question this way, we realize that the gap is also created by the fact that white men tend to have more access to white-collar employment and the best-quality health care, and their affluence affords them the ability to pay for the "dirty" work in their lives to be taken care of by others, mostly African American men and women. Thus, the intersection of race and social class creates *simultaneously* a disadvantage for African American men and an advantage for white men. Furthermore, when we dig deeper into this question of life expectancy, we see that there are significant gender differences as well. Specifically, not only do women live longer than men, but the racial gap is significantly smaller for women than for men. In short, our understanding of racial disparities in health and illness is improved when we layer these explanations together, focusing not only on gender or race, but also on the ways in which they interact to produce outcomes that vary by both statuses.[2] In terms of family violence, the race, class, and gender paradigm allows us to better understand the fact that African American children are at a higher risk for experiencing child abuse, because they are more likely to live in families that are at higher risk for child abuse, including single-parent families and poor families, as well as because they are seven times more likely to be placed in foster care, where they face a substantially higher risk for child abuse.

SOCIAL STRUCTURES

One of the most important aspects of this book is the time we dedicate to understanding the social and institutional forces that shape family violence. As sociologists our focus is less on the individual him- or herself—we leave those discussions to our colleagues in psychology and social work—and more on the role that social structures such as the economy and religion play in shaping both the risk for family violence as well as the ways in which it is perpetrated and experienced.

The Economy

It will come as no surprise to the reader that money is a major point of contention in any household. Couples fight about money—how to spend it, whose responsibility it is to bring it into the household, and so forth. Parents and their children fight about money—how much allowance should be paid for how many chores, whether one will have access to a car when turning sixteen and what kind of car that should be, how much money the family is willing to invest in paying college tuition, and so forth. Adult sons and daughters fight with each other and with their aging parents over "the inheritance." Money is a site of contest no matter which relationships we are discussing and how they are configured. And it will probably come as no surprise to the reader that as one might predict, some types of family violence—specifically, violence between intimate partners—has increased substantially since the beginning of the recession in late 2007. This point brings us to the role of the larger economy.

In addition to examining the ways in which money becomes a source of stress and conflict in families, in Chapter 8 we explore the ways in which the role and structure of the **economy** itself shape patterns of family violence. In addition to exploring the ways in which individual couples fight about money, we will look carefully at the ways in which wages, discrimination, the definition of the term *worker*, and so on shape the patterns of family violence that we see. For example, we will argue that one of the reasons women are the vast majority (85 percent) of the victims of intimate partner violence is because they are economically vulnerable and dependent upon their male partners. As a result of the static and persistent wage gap, women continue to earn only 75 percent of what men earn. Thus, because money is often linked to power, intimate partner violence takes the shape of men placing expectations on women in exchange for providing for their financial needs. When women fail to meet these expectations—which might be as insignificant as not having dinner on the table at the "proper" time—violence may erupt. When women attempt to leave these types of abusive relationships, the critical factor that prevents them from doing so is often their lack of access to money and their inability to earn a living wage with which to support themselves and their children. In Chapter 8 we explore these issues as well as the recent data on the role the recession has played in shaping intimate partner violence.

Cultural Norms

Just as women's economic vulnerability sets them up as potential victims of intimate partner violence, our beliefs about appropriate male and female roles set men up as potential batterers. Specifically, as we will explore in Chapter 9, **cultural norms**—the rigid expectation that men be the primary breadwinners in their families—create ground that is fertile for intimate partner violence. As we will demonstrate using both the work of other scholars and our own interviews, when men feel their masculinity is threatened, they often respond with violence. One of the primary "triggers" to this violence is a threat to their identity as the family breadwinner. This response can be triggered interpersonally—for example, when a wife complains to her husband that he does not make enough money for them to pay their bills or when she "nags" him about being laid off. This response can also be triggered by the structure of the economy itself, whereby men of color, in particular, face hiring and wage discrimination and whereby men in certain sectors—such as manufacturing—face high levels of layoffs in times such as those years beginning in late 2007 when the overall economy is in recession, making it difficult for these men and their families to achieve and maintain financial success.

In our discussions about the current economy, we will examine the changes the recession has wrought in family structure as well. For example, the most recent data presented by the Pew Foundation indicate that for the first time ever, as many as 20 percent of two-parent households have *women* as their primary breadwinners. We will examine the ways in which these kinds of changes—and their impact on masculine identities—as well as the recession in general have shaped the levels of intimate partner violence we see at the end of the first decade of the twenty-first century.

Religion

A primary source of cultural information regarding appropriate roles in families comes to us from **religion**. In Chapter 10 we examine specifically the role that religion has played in shaping expectations for family roles and in creating a terrain that is ripe for family violence. In addition to the rigid expectations that many religions have for female submission, they also have expectations for the behavior of children and parents, particularly fathers. In all of the major religions across the globe, and indeed in the United States, religious doctrines—holy books and official decrees—as well as beliefs by religious leaders reinforce the notion that men are to be the heads of households and both women and children are supposed to be submissive to them. This ideology contributes to the cultural beliefs about masculinity and femininity, which, as we note above, lay the groundwork for intimate partner violence as well as child abuse. For example, when discussing the role that parents, particularly fathers, play in disciplining their children, Proverbs 13:24 is often cited: "Whoever spares the rod hates his son, but he who loves him is diligent to discipline him." This teaching, especially when coupled with the adage "Spare the rod, spoil the child," is part of the landscape in which corporal punishment occurs. In fact, some cases of child abuse can best be understood as parents, usually fathers, taking this belief to the extreme.

Additionally, most, if not all, major religions are built around the belief that religious leaders are distinct from and superior to "regular" believers. This belief lays the groundwork for the abuse of women and children inside the institution of religion—for example, the Catholic sex scandal that has plagued the United States for the past ten years. Although the sex scandal will not be the sole focus of our subsequent discussion, we will explore the ways in which institutionalized sexism and violence can contribute to the perpetration and perpetuation of family violence. For example, in a survey of battered women, more than 70 percent said that when they consulted religious counselors about the abuse they were experiencing at home, they were told to go home and be better wives. Thus, we devote Chapter 10 to the role that religion plays in family violence.

The Military

A sex-segregated institution that shares much in common with religion, the **military**, along with the current state of war in which the United States finds itself, also contributes in various ways to family violence. The role that the military plays in shaping family violence is complex and ranges from the sex-segregated, hypermasculine nature of the military to the stresses associated with separation of families and experiences of war, posttraumatic stress, and injury. Although for a variety of reasons it is difficult to produce precise estimates of violence in military families, we do know that the rate of homicide, specifically domestic violence homicide, is much greater in military families, especially those in which the husband or father has served in a war zone, than in the general population. Therefore, we devote a special section to this discussion in Chapter 9.

SOCIAL STATUS VARIATION

Our discussion of **social status variation** in family violence is unique compared to the way in which it is typically approached. Unlike the majority of texts that include separate chapters on family violence in different racial or ethnic groups, for example, we will weave discussions of the ways in which two key statuses—race or ethnicity and social class—shape family violence into each chapter. For example, in the chapter on child sexual abuse we examine the disproportionate risk that low-income African American girls face as a result of the prevalence of houses of liquor and prostitution—a form of local sex trafficking—in low-income African American neighborhoods. Similarly, in the chapter on cultural norms, though we will not explore it in depth, we note the disproportionate risk that immigrant women face for intimate partner violence related to a series of factors, including their citizenship status, which is often linked to their husbands'; their lack of English-language proficiency; strong cultural norms of female submissiveness and even polygyny; and their relative isolation. We take this approach because we believe that there is nothing distinct about either racial and ethnic or class groups with regards to family violence. In other words, no group is inherently more or less violent than another. However, because various racial or ethnic and class groups have different lived realities, with differential access to resources and different experiences with discrimination in the labor market, for example, it is critical to examine the ways in which social status—specifically, race or ethnicity and social class—shapes one's risk for and experiences with family violence. Thus, variations will be explored in the context of discussions of the structures—the economy, culture, and religion—that shape family violence.

There are two exceptions to this approach: age and sexuality. Although, when appropriate, we weave discussions of age and sexuality into each chapter, we intentionally dedicate separate chapters to age (Chapter 5 focuses on elder abuse and Chapter 6 focuses on child abuse) and sexuality (Chapter 11) because we believe there are some distinct differences in family violence with regards to age and sexuality that merit focused and intentional discussions. For example, although the vast majority of victims of intimate partner violence are women, and although the strongest case for understanding why is rooted in discussions of male power and privilege, the same patterns do not necessarily apply with regards to either age or sexuality. The majority of victims of elder abuse, for example, are women, which may have more to do with the fact that women outlive men, and thus the proportion of the elderly who are women is significantly greater. Another indication of this type of difference is the fact that whereas men are by far the perpetrators of the majority of intimate partner violence, this is not necessarily the case with elder abuse. Women, too, abuse their aging parents, and in fact because women are far more likely to be the caregivers for aging parents with dementia or Alzheimer's, the risk that they will perpetrate the abuse is increased.

Similarly, although the majority of child physical and especially sexual abuse is perpetrated by men, women also engage in child abuse, especially physical abuse and neglect. With regards to physical abuse, young men are in some cases more likely to be the victims than their sisters, though the reverse is true for sexual abuse. Therefore, although the underlying principles of power and privilege that permeate intimate partner violence also permeate elder and child abuse, the gender dynamics are somewhat different. Rather than gender being the predominant factor, age is as important, and abuse patterns occur at the intersection of gender and age.

Similarly, although there are many things about intimate partner violence in homosexual relationships that are identical to the patterns in heterosexual relationships—and we will highlight these parallels as they arise—gender is a critical distinction. Obviously, in lesbian relationships there is no male partner and in gay male relationships there is no female partner. As with child and elder abuse, the dynamics of power and privilege remain the same, but they break down on lines other than gender. Sometimes the lines of demarcation are masculinity and femininity—with the more "feminine" partner more often the victim. But this is not always the case. Sometimes abuse in homosexual relationships is structured by each partner's risk for being "outed," his or her status as a parent, and a variety of other ways in which vulnerability can be created. Additionally, because there are many ways in which homosexual relationships are unique—they are typically not legal unions, individuals may face discrimination, they are often taken less seriously by the police or emergency room staff—we devote Chapter 11 to discussions of the experiences of violence in homosexual families.

A NOTE ABOUT DATA SOURCES

We rely on a variety of data sources in order to tell the story of family violence. Of particular note, however, and part of what make this book unique is that we personally conducted interviews with nearly one hundred men and women—African American and white, middle class and poor—who live with violence, and this forms the basis of our research. Throughout the book we use these interviews (qualitative data) to provide empirical support for our arguments. We include descriptions of particular people we interviewed, and we present their stories as direct, unedited quotes. Qualitative interviews are an important and rich data source: for sociologists, the quotes that are generated by qualitative interviews are the "statistics" in much the same way as photographs enhance written descriptions or text. We use the qualitative interviews to paint pictures of violence in family life. Because we believe that understanding a phenomenon like family violence depends upon understanding the science used to generate the theories and analyses, we devote an entire chapter, Chapter 4, to a discussion of the methods that family violence scholars use and the strengths and weaknesses of the various data collection techniques that build our scientific understanding of this complex social issue.

Although the interviews that we and others have conducted help to paint a picture of family violence, in order to truly understand the broader implications of that picture, we also need to examine statistics. Statistics provide the kind of empirical data that are needed to make broad, sweeping generalizations about a particular phenomenon. So, for example, reading about what it feels like to be hit in the head with a ball-peen hammer provides the illustration of intimate partner violence. But it does not tell the researcher anything about how common this experience is. Thus, in each chapter, for each topic, we provide statistical data so that the reader can understand the likelihood of an event occurring within a population. Although we are careful to make citations for the statistical evidence we include (both in the text and in tables), we note here that most of the statistical evidence comes from a few sources: the US Census, conducted in 2000 and 2010, the Center for Disease Control (CDC), and the Violence Against Women Act (VAWA), all of which collect data continuously and produce both monthly and annual reports. All of these data sources are the "official" sources and collect data from the entire US population (or appropriate samples based on the US population). Thus, this book is based on combining the best of both qualitative and quantitative data to help improve our understanding of contemporary family violence.

ORGANIZATION OF THE BOOK

The Contents makes clear the topics that will be covered in this book. However, we want to expound on them, as several are somewhat different from what is typically found in a text on family violence. We begin the book with an overview of the history of family violence in the United States. Our third chapter provides an in-depth discussion and review of the various theoretical frameworks that have been employed in studies of family violence along with a description of the theory framing our analysis: the race, class, and gender paradigm. This allows the reader to examine for him- or herself the analytical power and shortcomings of the various perspectives. In Chapter 4 we provide an in-depth discussion and review of the methods that are typically used to study family violence. In particular, we identify the problems inherent in studying family violence and how these barriers shape what we know about violence in families.

As noted above, we devote Chapters 5 and 6 to discussions of age-based violence: elder abuse and child abuse, respectively. Chapter 7 is designed as a transition or bridge chapter, moving us from age-based violence to the most common form of violence: intimate partner violence; specifically, Chapter 7 will examine perhaps the most tragic outcome of child abuse: an increased risk for experiencing violence—either as a perpetrator or as a victim—in adulthood. We devote the middle chapters (8–10) to a discussion of intimate partner violence. Each chapter will take a distinct social structure or institution as its main focus, including the economy, the culture and the military, and religion. Rounding out our discussion of intimate partner violence, Chapter 11 is devoted, as noted above, to an exploration of violence in homosexual families.

The final section of the book, Chapters 12–14, focuses on prevention and avoidance strategies (Chapter 12), the criminal justice and social service and legal responses to family violence (Chapter 13), and our conclusions and recommendations for future research and policy recommendations (Chapter 14).

SUMMARY OF OUR APPROACH IN THIS BOOK

There are several key features to our book that are unique. First and foremost, not only does our book explore the myriad of ways in which violence in families is shaped and perpetuated, but our focus on structural and institutional factors is unique. As noted, the majority of textbooks on family violence focus on the experiences of individual people. As sociologists, we recognize the need, especially for courses on family violence taught in sociology departments, for a book that is organized around and explores the role that institutions such as the economy, religion, the military, and ideologies play in structuring the prevalence and experiences of family violence. Additionally, this approach allows us to consider the reasons that not all families or individuals are at equal risk for victimization or perpetration as well as the reasons certain forms of family violence are more common than others. For example, men who grew up witnessing domestic violence are three times more likely to grow up to batter their wives and girlfriends than men who did not. Last, this approach takes the focus away from "bad people" and examines the ways in which we are all at risk—though differentially—for family violence; any of us can experience the kinds of stresses associated with caregiving that are the cause of a significant portion of both child and elder abuse. In short, we all have a stake in reducing family violence by disrupting the messages of support created and provided by institutional entities such as religion and the military and by increasing the support for caregivers and families at risk.

Our book is also unique in its reliance on the race, class, and gender theoretical framework as the lens for analyzing and interpreting the empirical data on family violence. This approach rests on the assumption that systems of oppression (specifically, race, class, and gender) intersect to create a web that shapes access to opportunities and experiences that vary depending on the actor's position in the social hierarchy (his or her race, class, and gender). Because the theoretical framework that underlies our discussion is based on an intersectional approach, the organization of our book will reflect this fact. In other words, in most textbooks the assumption is that each topic—child abuse, sexual abuse, intimate partner violence—is written from the perspective of and with a focus on the experiences of white people, the default category of citizens, and separate chapters are devoted to the "unique" experiences of individuals of various other races or ethnicities. In each of these "special" chapters, it is assumed that the experiences of nonwhites are unique and that all family violence experienced by nonwhites is the same. In other words, the assumption is that all family violence that African Americans experience—child abuse, sexual abuse, elder abuse—is the same across type and distinct from every type of abuse that white people experience. Rather than taking this approach, we assume that for the most part, with small variations that we will address, family violence is shaped not so much by race or ethnicity or social class as by the relationship between the perpetrator and the victim. Thus, we organize our book around types of violence—child abuse, elder abuse, intimate partner violence—and discuss racial or ethnic and class variation within each type. This novel approach turns the typical assumptions made by scholars of family violence on their heads.

Last, our approach is unique because we are scholars of family violence who have studied it rigorously through employing both qualitative methods (interviews) and quantitative methods (analysis of large-scale data sets). Our book is not simply a review of other people's research; it utilizes our own research to explore the complexities and tragedies of family violence. Because social science research is rigorous, it takes a long time, from start to finish. Thus, the greatest sources of trends in virtually any social phenomenon are often news accounts, and we employ such sources to illustrate contemporary trends—especially with regards to the recession and the war—on family violence. We are also classroom teachers and bring to this textbook combined decades of teaching students about the darker side of family life.

We move now to Chapter 2, in which we provide an overview of the history of family violence—and family more generally—in the United States. Although family violence has always existed, it has been ignored by researchers and the legal system until relatively recently. Our responses to family violence today are thus largely shaped by this history of sweeping it under the rug, and thus a discussion of this history is critical to understanding the phenomenon of family violence today.

NOTES

1. As those who follow the news are aware, any discussion of gay marriage in a book that takes months if not years to move from the writing through the production phase to the shelf is tentative at best because the laws and ordinances on gay marriage are constantly changing. Most recently, in late June 2011, New York State passed legislation allowing gay and lesbian couples to marry. However, as the reader is aware, this has happened in other states, only to see the legislation overturned by court orders or

voter referenda. Gay marriage is a moving target, and our discussion of it as a legal matter is limited by the information available at the time of the writing.

2. Deborah King refers to this concept as "double jeopardy" (1988), and Maxine Baca Zinn and Bonnie Thorton Dill refer to it as the "matrix of domination" (2005).

BIBLIOGRAPHY

Burton, Linda, and Rukmalie Jayakody. 2001. "Rethinking Family Structure and Single Parenthood: Implications for Future Studies of African-American Families and Children." In *The Well-Being of Children and Families: Research and Data Needs*, edited by A. Thorton, 125–153. Ann Arbor: University of Michigan Press.

Cherlin, Andrew. 1999. *Public and Private Families*. New York: McGraw-Hill.

Fox, Greer Litton, Michael L. Benson, Alfred A. DeMaris, and Judy Van Wyk. 2002. "Economic Distress and Intimate Violence: Testing Family Stress and Resources Theories." *Journal of Marriage and the Family* 64: 793–807.

Hattery, Angela J. 2008. *Intimate Partner Violence*. Lanham, MD: Rowman and Littlefield.

_____. 2009. "Sexual Abuse in Childhood and Adolescence and Intimate Partner Violence in Adulthood Among African American and White Women." *Race, Gender, and Class* 15: 79–97.

Hattery, Angela J., and Earl Smith. 2007. *African American Families*. Thousand Oaks, CA: Sage.

_____. 2010. *Prisoner Reentry and Social Capital: The Long Road to Reintegration*. Lanham, MD: Lexington Books.

Jackman, Tom. 2011. "Gene Upshaw's Dramatic Death-Bed Scene: The Rest of the Story." *Washington Post*, May 5. http://www.washingtonpost.com/blogs/the-state -of-nova/post/gene-upshaws-dramatic-death-bed-scene-the-rest-of-the-story/2011 /05/04/AFSF86tF_blog.html.

Kaiser Family Foundation. 2003. "National Survey of Adolescents and Young Adults: Sexual Health Knowledge, Attitudes, and Experiences." http://www.kff.org.

King, D. 1988. "Multiple Jeopardy, Multiple Consciousness: The Context of a Black Feminist Ideology." *Signs* 14, no. 1.

Kleinfield, N. R. 2011. "A Bleak Life, Cut Short at 4, Harrowing from the Start." *New York Times*, May 8.

Landale, Nancy, and Katherine Fennelly. 1992. "Informal Unions Among Mainland Puerto Ricans: Cohabitation or an Alternative to Legal Marriage?" *Journal of Marriage and the Family* 54: 269–280.

Neff, Lisa, and Benjamin R. Karney. 2005. "To Know You Is to Love You: The Implications of Global Adoration and Specific Accuracy for Marital Relationships." *Journal of Personality and Social Psychology* 88: 480–497.

Sarkisian, Natalla, and Naomi Gerstel. 2008. "Till Marriage Do Us Part: Adult Children's Relationships with Their Parents." *Journal of Marriage and Family* 70: 360–376.

Smith, Earl, and Angela Hattery. 2009. *Interracial Intimacies: An Examination of Powerful Men and Their Relationships Across the Color Line*. Durham, NC: Carolina Academic Press.

Steese, Stephanie, Maya Dollette, William Phillips, and Elizabeth Hossfeld. 2006. "Understanding Girls' Circle as an Intervention on Perceived Social Support, Body Image, Self-Efficacy, Locus of Control, and Self-Esteem." *Adolescence* 41: 55–75.

Straus, Murray A., and Richard J. Gelles. 1995. *Physical Violence in American Families*. New Brunswick, NJ: Transaction.

Tjaden, Patricia, and Nancy Thoennes. 2000. *Full Report of the Prevalence, Incidence, and Consequences of Violence Against Women: Findings from the National Violence Against Women Survey*. Washington, DC: US Department of Justice.

Tresniowski, Alex. 2011. "5 Browns: A Family Shattered." *People*, March 21. http://www.people.com/people/archive/article/0,,20472972,00.html.

Zinn, Maxine Baca, and Bonnie Thornton Dill. 2005. "Theorizing Differences from Multicultural Feminism." In *Gender Through the Prism of Difference*, edited by M. B. Zinn, P. Hondagneu-Sotelo, and M. A. Messner, 23–28. Oxford: Oxford University Press.

2 Historical Perspectives on Family Violence

This chapter will trace the history of family violence and its study in the United States. We will review trends in family violence and changes in the laws that govern family violence. In addition to noting the changes in the laws, we will identify the social changes that precipitated the changes in the law.

OBJECTIVES

- To examine the historical definitions of each type of family violence, including child abuse, sexual abuse, elder abuse, and intimate partner violence
- To examine the history of the legal treatment of each type of family violence
- To explore the social and environmental changes that led to changes in definitions and legal treatments of each type of family violence
- To demonstrate the role that the historical construct and legal treatment of family violence play in the contemporary definitions and legal responses

KEY TERMS

Child Protective Services (CPS)
child welfare services/laws
Personal Responsibility Work
    Opportunity Act (PRWORA)
Temporary Aid for Needy Families (TANF)
"cap" babies
battered child syndrome
special populations
medical neglect
anti-immunization movement
child sexual abuse (CSA)
age of consent

incest
patrilineal
cross-cousin marriage
parallel cousin
statutory rape
Megan's Law
Amber Alert
"rule of thumb"
mandatory arrest
Violence Against Women Act
restraining order

INTRODUCTION

As with many social phenomenon, the ways in which that phenomenon is constructed and interpreted at a specific moment in time are shaped by the history of that phenomenon. So, for example, the belief that people of African descent were less than fully human shaped both beliefs and laws about interracial marriage well into the early twentieth century. By the late 1960s, after decades of the civil rights movement and historic legal decisions such as the landmark US Supreme Court decision *Brown v. Board of Education*, which opened the door to integration in schools and other public settings, beliefs about interracial marriage had moderated to the point that laws prohibiting them were declared unconstitutional in the 1967 US Supreme Court ruling *Loving v. Virginia* (Smith and Hattery 2009). Such is the case with the evolution of beliefs about discipline versus abuse, children and wives as possession as opposed to independent beings, and the role of corporal punishment in the socialization of both. Understanding the evolution of both beliefs and the legal treatment of phenomenon helps us to understand the current climate with regards to all forms of family violence. In this chapter we will explore the evolution of these beliefs and practices for each of the types of family violence. We will conclude this chapter by examining the degree to which there are parallel and overlapping evolutions, the ways in which evolution in thinking around one type of family violence influenced beliefs about other forms, and the ways in which various types of family violence are unique with regard to their history and evolution. We will also examine the ways in which recognizing "**special populations**"—minorities, "at risk" youth, the disabled, children of parents who are incarcerated, and so forth—shapes the development and implementation of unique policies, moving us beyond a "one size fits all" approach to dealing with family violence. We begin with a discussion of child abuse.

CHILD ABUSE

Most readers are probably familiar with the notion that beliefs about child abuse have developed and evolved and that the legal response to it changed significantly across the last half of the twentieth century. Both of the authors remember the days when corporal punishment could be and was used in schools, when spanking was not a topic of conversation among parents of young children, and when grandmothers used phrases like "Spare the rod, spoil the child." And when we look back even further we see that there is a long and complex history surrounding child discipline and child abuse. Of course, the reader will also recall from our discussions in Chapter 1 that child abuse can be physical, but it can also be sexual. Because these types of abuse have very different histories and trajectories, we will discuss them separately. We begin with a review of the history of what is routinely referred to simply as "child abuse"—the physical abuse of children.

CHILD PHYSICAL ABUSE

Child abuse has existed for all of recorded history, and in fact only recently, at the beginning of the twentieth century, did commonly held beliefs about it begin to change. Child abuse can take many forms, including the physical beating of a child, infanticide and child murder, neglect, abandonment, and selling a child into slavery. As we shall see throughout this chapter, the customs, norms, and laws in the United States have their roots in the British system—which drew significantly on Roman and Greek law—and thus an examination of the state of children in Britain and across "civilized" Europe prior to the birth of the United States is helpful.

An examination of the assumptions and laws in the early Greek and Roman societies is revealing. "In Roman society the father had complete control over the family, even to the extent that he could kill his children for disobedience" ("Child Abuse—An Overview" n.d.).

Furthermore, fueled in large part by religion, and Catholicism in particular, fathers were charged with the proper socialization of their children. Because children were defined as being unable to engage in rational thought and abstract reasoning (the same notions were applied to women as well), it was believed that physical punishment was often necessary and appropriate as a strategy for the proper training of children. A British law from the thirteenth century declared, "If one beats a child until it bleeds, it will remember, but if one beats it to death, the law applies" (Albrecht Peiper, *Chronik der Kinderheilkunde* [Leipzig: Georg Thieme, 1966], cited in "Child Abuse—An Overview" n.d.).

This notion that children were the property of their parents pervaded beliefs, norms, and practices across Europe throughout the Middle Ages, Renaissance, and early modern period and arrived with immigrants to the colonial United States. While families remained patriarchal, both mothers and fathers were expected to socialize their children through discipline. Some colonial legislatures even passed "stubborn children laws," giving parents the legal right to kill unruly children. According to journalist Roger Rosenblatt (1995), Massachusetts enacted a law in 1646 that allowed the death penalty for a rebellious child, though the law was never enforced.

Abandonment was a common strategy for dealing with unwanted or unruly children, and it was practiced extensively in Europe through the apprenticeship system. Parents could deposit an unwanted or unruly child, usually a male child, to apprentice. Obviously, the child then gained a skill, but the "winner" in this system was typically the "master" who was able to extract free labor for a number of years from a child who had no other recourse or way to escape. Similar to the situation in sweatshops in the late eighteenth and nineteenth centuries, the treatment children received as apprentices could often be characterized as abusive.[1]

By the dawn of the Industrial Revolution, the factory replaced the apprenticeship as a site for abandoning unwanted or unruly children. According to historical records, it was not unusual for children as young as the age of five to be literally turned over to factories who were free to exploit their labor. Children were forced to work sixteen hours a day, and not uncommonly they were shackled to the machines. These children were housed in public poorhouses and almshouses alongside indigent adults ("Child Abuse—An Overview" n.d.). One can only imagine that the living conditions alone constituted abuse by modern standards.

Child neglect, a common experience in the modern era, was not even a concept in the United States until the turn of the twentieth century. As the United States transitioned out of an agricultural economy where food was perhaps plentiful but other necessities were often lacking—including shoes, access to an education, and so forth—into an industrial economy where food became far more scarce and living conditions were deplorable in the rapidly growing urban centers created by industrialization, the conditions most people lived under would be considered substandard by modern standards. Imagine for a moment a charge of neglect during the Great Depression. The inability to adequately feed and clothe a child during a decade when many adults relied on soup and bread lines for their only meal of the day would have been disregarded in light of the overall standards most adults lived under. Thus, it was not until the plentiful period after World War II that child neglect—other than the most severe (see Gordon 1988 for a lengthy discussion of the status of children during the Great Depression)—was a matter of public concern.

Today, despite a dramatic revision to our beliefs, norms, and practices, child abuse, abandonment, and neglect not only are common, but frequently reach devastating conclusions because of our reluctance to intrude on the private sphere of the family.

LEGAL RESPONSE

The primary agency charged with the protection of children is the Department of Health and Human Services (DHHS). Additionally, most jurisdictions have an office of **Child Protective Services (CPS)** that has the legal authority to remove children from their homes and put them into foster care.

As noted above, it was not until the twentieth century that child abuse, abandonment, and neglect became something of public concern. In response to both the dire circumstances of the Depression as well as the dawn of the New Deal programs begun under President Franklin D. Roosevelt, it is not surprising that the first child welfare laws were enacted in the mid-1930s.

The federal government first provided **child welfare services/laws** with the passage of the Social Security Act of 1935 (49 Stat. 620). Under Title IV-B (Child Welfare Services Program) of the act, the Children's Bureau received funding for grants to states for "the protection and care of homeless, dependent, and neglected children and children in danger of becoming delinquent." Prior to 1961, Title IV-B was the only source of federal funding for child welfare services.

The laws to protect children and provide for their welfare were greatly expanded during the next era that enlarged the safety-net programs that began under President John F. Kennedy and reached their peak during the Johnson administration. The 1962 Social Security Amendments (Public Law 87-543) required each state to make child welfare services available to all children. It further required states to provide co-ordination between child welfare services (under Title IV-B) and social services (under Title IV-A, or the Social Services program), which served families on welfare. The law also revised the definition of "child welfare services" to include the prevention and remedy of child abuse. Finally, in 1980 Congress created the separate Foster Care program under Title IV-E. Title IV-A became Title XX (Social Services Block Grant) in 1981, giving states more options regarding the types of social services to fund. Today child abuse prevention and treatment services have remained an eligible category of service. The expansion of child welfare legislation, though partly a response to changing attitudes about children, was more about changing attitudes about the poor. The period immediately following World War II can be characterized as one of the periods in US history that experienced some of the biggest changes in family life, including a reversal in the trend toward later marriages and childbearing as well as a reversal in the trend toward lower fertility rates. Women began marrying earlier, and they started having children earlier as well and having more children than their mothers did; as a result, the children born between 1945 and 1965 are referred to as the "Baby Boom generation." This period also saw a reversal in the trend for women to be employed outside the home. During World War II, with so many men off in the various war theaters, women went to work in factories building the "war machine." After the war, when veterans returned, they went back to their jobs in the factories, and women went home. Veterans also had access to the GI Bill, which greatly expanded home ownership. Thus, the era of the "stay-at-home mom"—the *Leave It to Beaver* era—was ushered in. These changes in the family led to a greater appreciation for the welfare of children.

That said, the most significant force that influenced the expansion of child welfare legislation was an overall focus on the poor. Beginning in the late 1950s, through Democratic leaders, including John F. Kennedy and Lyndon B. Johnson, and public figures like Martin Luther King Jr., along with the social upheaval created by the civil rights movement, the plight of the poor, in the Deep South, in Appalachia, and in urban centers, was exposed nationally. In response, the government substantially expanded all social welfare, including programs that were designed to provide for the welfare of children.

As is the case with the majority of social welfare programs—with the exception of the largest one, Social Security—the vast majority of programs are actually administered at the state and local levels, even though the rules governing them and the money funding them are provided by the federal government. Therefore, it is instructive to examine state-level programs.

There are two distinct types of programs that are designed to address issues of children: welfare and protective services. With regards to welfare, the qualification process is handled individually and at the local level. Thus, children themselves are required to endure a process of qualification before their custodial parent(s) or guardian(s) is awarded access to programs on the part of these children. In other words, if a low-income woman goes to the welfare office to apply for "welfare," her award will be based on the number of people in her household who qualify for welfare. Though one might assume that that all of her minor children (those under age eighteen) are automatically covered, in fact, one of the more troubling aspects of the welfare reform laws of 1996, which "reformed" welfare into the **Personal Responsibility Work Opportunity Act (PRWORA)**, established guidelines that prohibit babies born after a mother has begun receiving **Temporary Aid for Needy Families (TANF)** from being eligible for TANF. Referred to as **"cap" babies** (Hays 2003), these children *do not qualify* for welfare and thus *are not covered by the child welfare laws designed specifically to protect them, in this case from the severest poverty.* (The authors of this legislation developed the notion of "cap babies" in order to disincentivize women already receiving welfare from having more children. This sentiment can be attributed to the stereotype of the "welfare queen" made popular in the 1980s by President Ronald Reagan.)

The second goal of child welfare laws is to protect children from neglect and abuse. Under the Title IV-B Child Welfare Services (Subpart 1) and Promoting Safe and Stable Families (Subpart 2) programs, families in crisis receive preventive intervention so that children will not have to be removed from their homes. If this cannot be achieved, children are placed in foster care temporarily until they can be reunited with their families. If reunification is not possible, parents' rights are terminated and the children are made available for adoption. Practically speaking, this is the law that allows social services to investigate accounts of child neglect and abuse and, if necessary, to remove children temporarily from their homes and even revoke parental custody.

As noted, for a variety of reasons, including a long history of not only tolerating but also advocating the use of physical force on children—defined conveniently as "punishment"—and the long-held belief that family life is "private," one of the barriers to protecting children from neglect and abuse is the simple fact that it is almost always hidden. One important change that has impacted this barrier—though it is difficult to quantify how much—was the development of the notion of "mandatory reporters." The impetus for the development and implementation of a mandatory reporting law came, interestingly, from a pediatric radiologist. In 1961 Dr. C. Henry Kempe first coined the term "**battered child syndrome**" at the annual meeting of the American Academy of Pediatrics, and a year later his findings were published (Kempe 1962). Kempe's research focused on the specific collection and pattern of injuries among children who were being physically abused or neglected or both. Relatively rapidly, by 1967, there was widespread acceptance among health care and welfare workers such that Kempe's findings were expanded to include not just physical abuse and neglect but also sexual and emotional abuse as well as maltreatment, malnourishment, **medical neglect**, and failure to thrive. This expanded definition was critical in shaping current beliefs about and treatment of child abuse. Additionally, Dr. Kempe felt strongly that physicians should be required by law to report abuse when they observed it. By 1967 forty-four states had implemented mandatory reporting laws for a series of occupations, including health care providers, teachers, coaches, and others who frequently interact with, observe, and supervise children. The majority of cases that are referred to Child Protective Services come through the channels created by the mandatory reporting laws.

Definitions of child abuse have continued to expand, and beginning in the mid-1980s and continuing today, modifications have been made to the child welfare statutes, largely in response to changes in social pressures, research that demonstrated gaps, or both. After ignoring child abuse for centuries, there was a push following the initial legislation designed to protect children, and by 1980 there was concern among both the public and social workers that the foster care system was overwhelmed with children. As a result, with the goal of promoting family reunification, Congress passed the Adoption Assistance and Child Welfare Act of 1980 (Public Law 96-272). Less than two decades later, based on research and the reports of social workers, it became apparent that reuniting abused children with their families did not always work in the best interests of the children. Congress revisited the "reasonable efforts" for family reunification originally mandated by the 1980 Adoption Assistance and Child Welfare Act. Under the 1997 Adoption and Safe Families Act (Public Law 105-89), "reasonable efforts" was clarified to mean that the safety of the child comes first. States were directed to indicate circumstances under which an abused child *should not* be returned to the parents or caretakers.

Special Populations

In order to address the needs of children in special populations, a series of laws were passed. In 1994 Congress passed the Multiethnic Placement Act (Public Law 103-382), directing states to actively recruit adoptive and foster families, especially for minority children waiting a long time for placement in a home. The Promoting Safe and Stable Families Amendments of 2001 (Public Law 107-133) were enacted partly to address the rising number of children with incarcerated parents. Currently, 5 million children have a father in prison, and an additional 1 million are the children of incarcerated mothers (Hattery and Smith 2010). The majority of children whose fathers are incarcerated live with and are cared for by the mothers. However, when mothers are incarcerated, the probability that the children will live with their fathers is low, only around 10 percent. About half are cared for by their grandmothers or another female relative, but nearly 25 percent are placed in foster care. Thus, there is a great need for services for children whose mothers are incarcerated.

In 2003 the Child Abuse Prevention and Treatment Act received reauthorization through 2008 under the Keeping Children and Families Safe Act (Public Law 108-36). The law, among other things, directed more comprehensive training of Child Protective Services personnel, including a mandate that they inform alleged abusers, during the first contact, of the nature of complaints against them. The law called for child welfare agencies to coordinate services with other agencies, including public health, mental health, and developmental disabilities agencies. In some states, this coordination has been utilized in order to address another special population: children who witness the abuse between their parents. In Minnesota, for example, when an officer arrives on a domestic violence call, if there are children "within sight or sound" of the domestic violence, the officer is required to refer the children to CPS. This launches a series of services, including counseling and the development of safety plans, especially if the parents decide to continue living together. This progressive law recognizes that children who witness abuse are themselves victims. This notion will be a central part of our discussion in Chapter 7. The law also directed the collection of data for the fourth *National Incidence Study of Child Abuse and Neglect*, the first of which was initiated in 1988 with the Child Abuse Prevention, Adoption, and Family Services Act (Public Law 100-294), which mandated, among other things, the establishment of a system to collect national data on child maltreatment.

Medical Neglect and the Anti-Immunization Movement

Medical neglect, which is a very new phenomenon, refers to the fact that because parents have the legal right to make all of the medical decisions for a child, children may be denied medical care that they need if receiving such care violates an ideological or religious belief held by the parents.

Recently, a case of medical neglect arose around a young cancer patient named Daniel Hauser of New Ulm, Minnesota. Daniel, who is thirteen years old, suffers from Hodgkin's lymphoma. His mother believes that natural, homeopathic remedies are appropriate for Daniel and that the chemotherapy he has been prescribed— which was administered previously—is killing him. Despite the diagnosis that chemotherapy is the only way to treat Daniel's tumors, his mother refused to allow him to be treated. In the spring of 2009 a medical exam revealed that his tumors had returned, and he was court-ordered to receive chemotherapy. With no more legal remedies for resistance, his mother, Colleen, fled with her son. In May 2009 mother and son returned to Minnesota, and a judge took control of Daniel's "medical custody" and ordered him to return to his treatment protocol. In November 2009 he received his last treatment, and his medical report suggests he is now in remission. This controversial case raises the question of who has the right to determine a child's medical needs. In this instance, the court argued that because the probability of remission was high if Daniel received chemotherapy—around 85 percent—and the cost of death was nearly certain if he did not, then the court had the right to protect the medical needs of the child, and this right superseded his parent's rights to restrict his access to medical care.

One of the most recent controversies surrounding medical neglect is the **anti-immunization movement**. The immunization goals of public health programs rely heavily on widespread immunization; ideally, nearly the entire population would be immunized. This strategy is central to the public health movements designed to eradicate disease because the belief is that over a period of time, if the vast majority of a population is immunized, not only will cases diminish, but the diseases themselves may be eradicated entirely from the human population. The case of smallpox is often cited as one of the biggest success stories for immunization.

Beginning in the mid-1900s, parents began to question the role of immunizations in the health of their individual children. Separate from the case in which parents without health care or easy access to clinics simply cannot get their children to the well-baby checkups where immunizations are provided, this movement is based on the individual right of a parent to decide whether to have a child immunized. Though parents in this movement clearly articulate the overall benefits to the population when children are immunized, they believe that in some individual cases children may be harmed by immunizations, and they believe that their children should not be forced to be immunized because they believe it poses a risk to their individual health. Central to this movement is the belief that at least some proportion of cases of autism are caused by vaccinations given to children. Public health officials worry that as a result, we will see the resurgence of devastating childhood diseases that we now consider to be "extinct" in the developed world, including whooping cough, measles, mumps, and diphtheria. There has in fact been a rise in the past decade of these diseases, though there is no evidence that smallpox has returned to the scene. At the time of this writing, refusing to have one's child immunized does not constitute medical neglect. It will be interesting to watch the development of this movement in light of recent medical research, some of which links immunizations to autism and some of which does not, as well as with regards to the potential threat to public health that failing to immunize creates.

Child Sexual Abuse

As was the case with the physical abuse of children, the history of **child sexual abuse (CSA)** is complicated by the fact that definitions and norms have changed significantly over time. Specifically, definitions of both family and the appropriate age for marriage—which generally signals the age one is considered old enough to freely consent to have sex—have changed historically and continue to vary dramatically from place to place. That said, there are some aspects of this phenomenon that are so nearly universal that we can examine them in order to establish some common understanding of the history of CSA. Last, it is important to recognize that even more so than physical abuse, sexuality has always been considered something that is private and belongs inside the family. Only when sexual expression was perceived as threatening did it ever receive public attention. For example, when the open expression of homosexuality raises concerns in a local community or in the wider public, then public attention—including the enforcement of archaic sodomy laws that remain on the books in most US states—focuses on what is otherwise a private matter. Rarely has child sexual abuse been considered a public matter—the only exceptions being when sex offenders kidnap, sexually abuse, and murder a child—or in cases involving the widespread abuse of many children by a single public figure (for example, a teacher, coach, or Catholic priest), and thus there is very little in the historical record of individual cases of CSA. Sex between family members, even if they are of the **age of consent**, is considered abuse. Thus, one of the complexities of defining child sexual abuse involves defining who is in the family.

Definitions of Family

The majority of child sexual abuse occurs inside of the family, and there is every reason to believe that this has always been the case. **Incest**, or the sexual contact between relatives, depends upon how family is defined. For example, in the majority of states in the United States, marriage and sex are illegal between any relatives closer than second cousins. As a result, sex with a child by a parent, grandparent, uncle, aunt, sibling, or first cousin is defined as incest. However, recent attention has focused on the fact that in a handful of US states, marriage—and by definition sexual behavior—is allowed between first cousins. Thus, sex between married first cousins in Florida would be legal, whereas the same sex between the same first cousins in Minnesota would be illegal. The mention that in some states marriage between first cousins is allowed only when one of the potential spouses is infertile is indicative of the concerns surrounding sexual behavior in families and its potential outcomes: children.[2]

In order to better understand the ways in which definitions of family are malleable and thus definitions of incest are variable, it is instructive to look at other cultures. For example, highly **patrilineal** and rural communities, such as the Cree—an

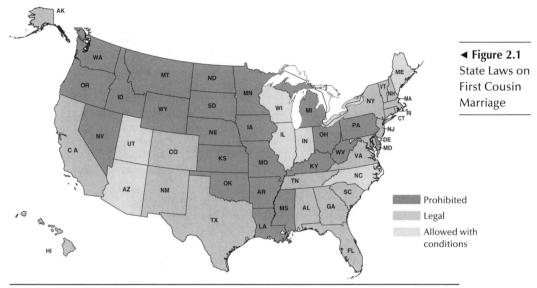

◀ **Figure 2.1**
State Laws on
First Cousin
Marriage

In 24 states (dark gray), such marriages are illegal. In 19 states (medium gray), first cousins are permitted to wed. Seven states (light gray) allow first-cousin marriage but with conditions. Maine, for instance, requires genetic counseling; some states say yes only if one partner is sterile. North Carolina prohibits marriage only for double first cousins.

Source: Based on http://www.cousincouples.com/?page=states.

American Indian culture that thrived in what is now Canada and Minnesota, and who now live on reservations in Montana—practiced **cross-cousin marriage** (Flannery 1938). Cross-cousin marriage, particularly the form in which a son marries his mother's brother's daughter, developed as a strategy for concentrating wealth and power based on a patrilineal structure of inheritance—all wealth is passed down through the males—as well as for alleviating concerns about paternity. The latter was accomplished by ensuring that all sexual access would take place among brothers, and thus even if an individual man was not the father to the children his wife bore, his brother would be, and thus his investment in the children was still an investment in passing on his family's genes.

Cross-cousin marriage is coupled with beliefs about incest and is built on preestablished notions of family. In a highly patrilineal culture, one's family is traced through one's father, not one's mother. Thus, one's father's family is one's family—for example, one's father's brother is one's uncle—but one's mother's family is not one's family. Thus, marriage and sex with one's father's family is incest, but marriage and sex with one's mother's relatives are not defined as incest and are actually preferred to marriage with other nonrelated members of the community, as illustrated in Figure 2.2.

In this case, a boy's (ego is male) "relatives" are his father's brother's children and his mother's sister's children. His ideal marriage partners are his female cross-cousins, his father's sister's daughter and his mother's brother's daughter.[3] Rather than focusing on the intricacies of the patterns, the most important point here is that genetically, parallel and cross-cousins share the same amount of genetic material, yet sex with a

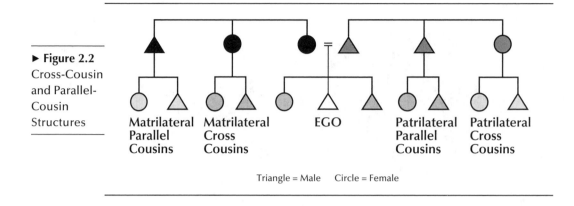

► Figure 2.2
Cross-Cousin
and Parallel-
Cousin
Structures

| Matrilateral Parallel Cousins | Matrilateral Cross Cousins | EGO | Patrilateral Parallel Cousins | Patrilateral Cross Cousins |

Triangle = Male   Circle = Female

parallel cousin would violate the incest taboo, whereas cross-cousins are defined as ideal marriage—and by default sexual—partners. Thus, defining incest is not always determined by shared genetics but may be determined by other social forces as well.

Changing Definitions of the Age of Consent

Currently in the United States the age of consent for marriage is eighteen with two exceptions: Nebraska's age of consent is nineteen, and Mississippi's age of consent is set at twenty-one years of age. With parental consent teenagers in most states can marry at age sixteen, with some states allowing children as young as fourteen (Texas) and twelve (Massachusetts) to marry with parental consent. The majority of states allow for teenagers between the ages of fourteen and sixteen to marry when the girl is pregnant, in some cases even without parental consent.

In contrast, the rules that surround **statutory rape** are somewhat different. For example, the age of consent to sex in most states is sixteen years of age. However, in response to several tragic cases, including that of Genarlow Wilson in Georgia, who was convicted of statutory rape and spent two years in prison after he had consensual oral sex with a fifteen-year-old when he was seventeen, many states have modified their laws to require that there must be an *age difference* of more than two years between the parties when either party is under the age of consent in order for statutory rape to be applicable.[4]

One aspect that makes defining child sexual abuse complex is that the age of consent has changed dramatically over time and especially across space, and just as is the case with cross-cousin marriage, a situation that would be categorized as CSA in the United States at the beginning of the twenty-first century might not be in another culture. For example, Kristoff and WuDunn (2009) chronicle the pattern of child marriage, especially for girls, that continues to persist across rural regions of the Middle East, the Far East, Southeast Asia, and Africa. UNICEF reports on its website that more than 64 million women between the ages of twenty and twenty-four were married as children—under the age of eighteen years old. In Southeast Asian countries and the majority of African countries, more than 65 percent of women were child brides, and in countries in central Asia and the Middle East, rates hover just below 50 percent (http://www.childinfo.org/marriage.html). Though these marriages are technically illegal—most countries worldwide raised the formal age of consent to eighteen after pressure from the United Nations—because cultural beliefs and practices, not legal practices, dominate the lives of rural citizens, there has been very little change in the rate of child marriage in the developing world. We argue that all of these women are victims of child sexual abuse, regardless of the cultural traditions under which they live, yet, as one can see, defining child sexual abuse is problematic when ages of consent, cultural practices, and variations in definitions of family vary across time and place.

Child Sexual Abuse Laws in the United States

Though incest and child sexual abuse have always existed in the United States, and there has likely been little change in the rates across time, the primary motive for changing the laws around CSA was the dramatic increase in *stranger abductions* that typically involved sexual abuse and often murder.

Beginning in the early 1980s, the nation's attention was piqued and focused on several tragic child abduction cases, including that of Adam Walsh in 1981 and Jacob Wetterling in 1989. Adam's decapitated head was found a month or so after his abduction, and Jacob has never been found. These cases, though a tiny minority of all CSA, were so horrific and the parents, especially John Walsh, so vocal that national attention began to be focused on child sexual abuse—at least that which is perpetrated by strangers.

BOX 2.1   "MY BABY IS MISSING"

My Baby Is Missing
By Mark Gado
TruTV Crime Library

Adam Walsh was a happy six-year-old boy living in Florida with his parents, John and Reve Walsh. On July 27, 1981, Adam and his mother went to a mall in Hollywood, Florida on a shopping expedition. They went into a Sears's store where Adam took an interest in a video game display. Mrs. Walsh continued shopping while Adam played the game. With the exception of several minutes, they were within eyesight of the child nearly the entire time. When the mother returned for Adam, he was not where she left

continues

BOX 2.1   "MY BABY IS MISSING" *continued*

him. Reve Walsh asked around and called out in the store for her son. No one answered. Soon, the father joined in the search but still Adam could not be found. Apparently, a few minutes before, several teenagers had been ejected from the store for being disorderly. It was thought that perhaps Adam had inadvertently gone with them. That theory later proved to be false. After nearly two hours of searching throughout the mall, the police were finally notified.

Posters with Adam's image were widely distributed throughout the southern Florida area. Local television stations broadcast Adam's smiling, freckled face wearing a baseball cap, hoping for some sort of lead. But no new information was developed. Two weeks later, Adam's severed head was found in a canal at Vera Beach, some 120 miles away from the mall where he was kidnapped. Adam's body was never recovered. John and Reve Walsh nearly went insane from grief. A ferocious serial killer named Ottis Toole became a suspect in 1983 and confessed to the killing on two separate occasions. He later recanted both confessions. Toole died in prison without ever being charged in the crime. "I believe he killed Adam," John Walsh told reporters at the time of his death.

Source: http://www.trutv.com/library/crime/criminal_mind/psychology/child_abduction /9.html.

In December 1995, with growing acknowledgment of and concern about sex crimes against minors, Congress passed the Sex Crimes Against Children Prevention Act of 1995 (Public Law 104-71). The act increased penalties for those who sexually exploit children by engaging in illegal conduct, or for exploitation conducted via the Internet, as well as for those who transport children with the intent to engage in criminal sexual activity.

In 1996 the US Congress passed **Megan's Law** as an amendment to the Jacob Wetterling Crimes Against Children Act. It required every state to develop some procedure for notifying the public when a sex offender is released into their community. Different states have different procedures for making the required disclosures. Megan's Law was inspired by the case of seven-year-old Megan Kanka, a New Jersey girl who was raped and killed by a known child molester who moved across the street from her family. The Kanka family fought to have local communities warned about sex offenders in the area. The New Jersey legislature passed Megan's Law in 1994. Since the passage of the federal law in May 1996, all states have passed some form of Megan's Law.

Two years later, Congress enacted the Protection of Children from Sexual Predators Act of 1998 (Public Law 105-314), which, among other things, established the Morgan P. Hardiman Child Abduction and Serial Murder Investigative Resources Center (CASMIRC). The purpose of CASMIRC, as stated in the text of the act, is "to provide investigative support through the coordination and provision of federal law enforcement resources, training, and application of other multidisciplinary expertise, to assist federal, state, and local authorities in matters involving child abductions, mysterious disappearance of children, child homicide, and serial murder across the country."

Congress passed the Prosecutorial Remedies and Other Tools to End the Exploitation of Children Today (PROTECT) Act (Public Law 108-21) on April 30, 2003. Among other things, the act established a national **Amber Alert** Program for recovering abducted children and provided that there will be no statute of limitations for sex crimes and abduction of children. (Under previous laws, the statute of limitations expired when the child turned twenty-five.) The law also provided for severe penalties for sex tourism and the denial of pretrial release for suspects in federal child rape or kidnap cases. (The Amber Alert program is named after Amber Hagerman of Texas, who was abducted and murdered in 1996. She was nine years old. A witness notified police, giving a description of the vehicle and the direction it had gone, but police had no way of alerting the public.)

The fact that the majority of child sexual abuse laws are named for victims is not serendipitous. As with the first case—Adam Wash's murder—the legal response to child sexual abuse is driven almost entirely by high-profile, horrific, individual cases. This reactive rather than proactive approach is largely the reason there has been significantly less progress with regards to the laws involving incest—which is by far the most common form of CSA. Incest, as with other forms of family abuse, remains largely hidden behind the privacy of the family, and though we have better estimates of its prevalence—which we will discuss in Chapter 6—there has been little change in the legal approach such that the majority of convicted child molesters serve less than three years in prison, and most return to their abusive behavior within a year of their release. In order to truly understand the impact of CSA on its victims, we need to focus our attention on cases of incest rather than the high-profile cases that though horrific are extremely rare.

ELDER ABUSE

Elder abuse commonly refers to the physical abuse of an adult by his or her younger relatives, usually children, though it may also include other forms of abusive behavior, especially financial abuse, and fits under the larger rubric of "adult abuse" (Bonnie and Wallace 2003). The term *elder abuse* did not enter the national vocabulary until the 1970s (Bonnie and Wallace 2003). Though awareness about elder abuse is relatively recent in comparison to some other forms of abuse, the reader will recall that attempts to address child abuse and neglect began in the 1930s, and there are a variety of reasons for the timing. Perhaps obvious but not often considered, the elderly population in the United States did not make up a substantial part of the overall population until around 1970, when those over age sixty-five made up 10 percent of the US population (as of 2009 that figure had risen to nearly 13 percent). As a result, it is not surprising that the early 1970s marks the beginning of a national focus on elder abuse.

As we will discuss at length in Chapter 5, elder abuse—like all forms of family violence—can take many forms, including physical abuse, sexual abuse, emotional and psychological abuse, as well as neglect. Unique to elder abuse, and one of the most common forms, is financial abuse.

BOX 2.2	DOROTHY MULKEY

When prominent Mid-Michigan rheumatologist Dr. Dorothy Mulkey, 73, said she wanted to cash in an IRA worth $898,000 to buy a home in California, one of her employees was incredulous.

"And she said, 'Are you sure? Do you understand you're losing $365,000?'" Genesee County Sheriff Robert recalled, according to ABC12 local news in Michigan. "[S]he appeared incoherent, almost zombie-like."

Authorities later came to believe Mulkey had been drugged by her 30-year-old caregiver, Andrea Neil, who swindled the physician out of as much as $3 million.

Neil, who had worked as an office assistant in Mulkey's private practice, was paid $1,500 a week to care for the doctor in her Flushing, Michigan home after her retirement.

Police found $78,000 worth of Mulkey's precious metals and coins in Neil's home.

Neil was charged with embezzlement and obtaining money under false pretenses.

"Once they got the victim away from this defendant, she became coherent and she became alert and she knew what was going on," said Genesee County Prosecutor David Leyton.

SOURCE: http://abclocal.go.com/wjrt/story?section=news/local&id=7184470.

Second, others who fall under the legal rubric of elder abuse are adults (those over eighteen years old) who are vulnerable in some way as the result of a disability. This includes adults with mental and physical impairments or chronic diseases or injuries that require more or less constant supervision. Prior to the early 1980s this population was unlikely to survive into adulthood, and those individuals who did were institutionalized. Certainly, there is no question that abuse of these individuals existed, but it was hidden far from view as long as this population remained locked in state hospitals and private facilities. Once this population began to be deinstitutionalized and cared for at home, the abuse that this population experienced entered the mainstream consciousness as well.

This deinstitutionalization led not only to an increased awareness of elder abuse, but also additional factors that contributed to it, namely, the fact that care was increasingly provided by relatives rather than paid staff. This shift changed elder abuse in two ways: it moved it under the rubric of "family violence," which meant that it came to the attention of scholars of family violence, and it spawned a new set of theories for explaining it (Bonnie and Wallace 2003). We will return to a discussion of the theoretical explanations in the next chapter. As with all other forms of abuse, it also generated legislation designed to protect this vulnerable and increasingly growing population.

Legal Response to Elder Abuse

About twenty years before the term *elder abuse* became mainstream, Congress became aware of an increasing number of aging adults who could not take care of their daily needs. In response, in the 1950s, as part of the Social Security Act, Congress provided funds to states on a three-to-one matching basis to set up protective service units for the elderly. Interestingly, in several matched sample studies—comparing adults receiving services via protective units and those who were not—those receiving services had both higher mortality rates and higher rates of institutionalization in nursing homes (Bonnie and Wallace 2003). *Despite increasing evidence that protective service units were in fact detrimental to the health and well-being of aging Americans,* in 1974 the US Congress amended the Social Security Act to provide funding to set up protective units in each of the fifty states and extended the services to all individuals over the age of eighteen (Bonnie and Wallace 2003)!

Attention on elder abuse waned through the 1970s, until the end of that decade when Claude Pepper, US representative from Florida—one of the "grayest" of all US states—held hearings in which the term *granny battering* was introduced. Across the decade of the 1980s, the focus on elder abuse grew beyond the need for protection from neglect and physical abuse to an understanding of the needs elderly Americans had for expanded access to medical services, legal services, financial services, as well as other social services and protective services. The transformation from an *abuse concept* to an *aging concept* paved the way for the 1990 expansion of the Older Americans Act,[5] which, among other things, established a national center for the study of aging and elder abuse (Bonnie and Wallace 2003). By the early 1990s, the then surgeon general of the United States, Louis Sullivan, held a national conference on family violence, and he chose to include elder abuse as a topic under this rubric. This act cemented the notion that elder abuse is one type of family abuse and thus generated and encouraged research by both gerontologists and family violence scholars.

DOMESTIC VIOLENCE

Similar to all forms of family abuse, domestic violence or intimate partner violence can be characterized as being hidden from view and subject to changing definitions and cultural norms. In nearly every culture and across all historical periods, women have been relegated to an inferior status legally as well as socially (Epstein 2007).[6] Scholars who have studied domestic violence historically note that there is significant evidence to conclude that as a result of women's inferior status—as established by both religious doctrine and legal statutes—the physical abuse of women was not only legal but endorsed when it was used as a form of discipline (Graetz 1998; Kelly 1994). Specifically, for most of recorded history, across most cultures, the belief was that women's constitution—their inferior intellect, lack of rationality, tendency to become overemotional—resulted in their needing guidance from their husbands. Thus, the belief was that when a woman behaved inappropriately, it was not only legal but indeed necessary for her husband to discipline her, and often this discipline took the form of physical abuse. And individual men would find support for this behavior from their leaders—both civic and religious. Around AD 300 Roman emperor Constantine burned his wife alive because he no longer had a use for her (Lemon 1996).

For many in the Western world, the inferiority of women was based on and reinforced by biblical references, especially Ephesians 5:22–33, that dictate that wives are to be submissive to their husbands:

> **22** Wives, submit yourselves to your own husbands as you do to the Lord. **23** For the husband is the head of the wife as Christ is the head of the church, his body, of which he is the Savior. **24** Now as the church submits to Christ, so also wives should submit to their husbands in everything. **25** Husbands, love your wives, just as Christ loved the church and gave himself up for her **26** to make her holy, cleansing her by the washing with water through the word, **27** and to present her to himself as a radiant church, without stain or wrinkle or any other blemish, but holy and blameless. **28** In this same way, husbands ought to love their wives as their own bodies. He who loves his wife loves himself. **29** After all, no one ever hated their own body, but they feed and care for their body, just as Christ does the church—**30** for we are members of his body. **31** "For this reason a man will leave his father and mother and be united to his wife, and the two will become one flesh." **32** This is a profound mystery—but I am talking about Christ and the church. **33** However, each one of you also must love his wife as he loves himself, and the wife must respect her husband.

Later in the verse husbands are required to love their wives, but there is no indication that this requires them to refrain from physically abusing them. In fact, as the reader shall see in later chapters, many of the men we interviewed who battered fiercely claimed to love their wives and in fact justified their physical abuse based on this love. One woman's partner proclaimed that he would not beat her if he did not love her so much. Therefore, we argue that it is reasonable to conclude that individual men, religious leaders, and political leaders throughout the Western world and through most of recorded history would have come to the conclusion that the Bible required men to love their wives, but it also required them to demand female submission, and discipline could be utilized to enforce submission when women "forgot their place."

Much like child abuse, domestic violence has a long legal history, the vast majority of which protects men's legal right to beat their wives. The commonly held principle with regards to domestic violence was that it was legal—and tolerable—for a man to beat his wife as long as the rod he used to do so was smaller than the diameter of his thumb (Kelly 1994). This law was referred to as "the **rule of thumb**," though obviously the phrase has a different meaning when used today. In 1824 the Mississippi Supreme Court in *Bradley v. State* (2 Miss. [Walker] 156 [1824]) allowed a husband to administer only "moderate chastisement" in cases of emergency (Lemon 1996; Martin 1976). In 1867 a man in North Carolina was acquitted of giving his wife "three licks with a switch about the size of one of his fingers, but smaller than his thumb." The reviewing appellate court later upheld the acquittal on the grounds that the court should "not interfere with family government in trifling cases" (Martin 1976). And though several states had begun to rescind a man's legal right to beat his wife, again in North Carolina in 1874, the "finger-switch" rule was disavowed when the Supreme Court of North Carolina ruled that "the husband has no right to chastise his wife under any circumstances." However, the court went on to say, *"If no permanent injury has been inflicted, nor malice, cruelty nor dangerous violence shown by the husband, it is better to draw the curtain, shut out the public gaze and leave the parties to forget and forgive"* (Martin 1976; emphasis added). Thus, the message is loud and clear: domestic violence will be tolerated—even as it is becoming illegal—and the best approach to dealing with domestic violence is to consider it a private matter.

This notion that domestic violence is a private matter, as with child abuse and elder abuse, has shaped much of the manner in which the phenomenon continues to unfold in the contemporary United States. Though domestic violence is now illegal in all states, and the marital rape exemption has been removed from all state statutes, it remains very common for domestic violence to either go undetected entirely or be ignored because people continue to perceive it as a private matter. Interviews with battered women reveal that it is commonplace for them to experience a severe beating in an apartment with thin walls, in an apartment complex hallway, in public—often outside of a bar or restaurant—or to be stalked at work or church, and no one intervenes or calls the police. The fact that our public response to domestic violence remains passive is highly indicative of our history of treating it as a private matter between a husband and wife.

A Brief History of the Domestic Violence Movement

The earliest research on "domestic" violence dates to the 1970s. The second wave of feminism with all of its consciousness raising and support groups and public marches and rhetoric brought battering to the mainstream discourse. Women like Susan Brownmiller and Lenore Walker helped to bring battering to the attention of lawmakers, law enforcement agencies, and research scholars. In fact, it was not until 1970 that the index for the *Journal of Marriage and the Family*, the premier journal for sociologists who study the family, included the term *violence*.

During the late 1970s and early 1980s, shelters for battered women began to spring up all over the country, though they are still outnumbered three to one by shelters for abandoned animals (Browne 1989; Koss et al. 1994). More recently, domestic violence advocates and researchers have put together protocols for dealing with domestic violence that have been codified in the form of legal codes such as **mandatory arrest** laws. Yet we still know very little about the inner workings of intimate partner violence, and we are still relatively unsuccessful in reducing its prevalence.

Domestic violence remains a misdemeanor in most states, punishable by probation rather than jail time. In fact, in many communities batterers can opt for a treatment program (as many of those interviewed for this book did) and forego jail time altogether. In these treatment programs batterers learn the rhetoric, but they seldom cease battering. Most of the men whose stories are told in this book admitted openly and freely that they were still in abusive relationships with their partners, and some admitted, or their partners confessed, that battering episodes had occurred within just a day or two of the interview.

Today, the movement around domestic violence has moved toward increasing inclusivity in all forms. Domestic violence advocates now focus on not just the physical and sexual abuse that victims experience but also the emotional and psychological trauma. Domestic violence advocates increasingly recognize the need for prevention and intervention programs that target young people, as dating violence has risen dramatically in the past decade. Additionally, there is a growing awareness of the need for prevention and intervention strategies that are sensitive to racial or ethnic, religious, and other cultural differences. In fact, in our hometown of Winston-Salem, North Carolina, there has been a decadelong attempt to address domestic violence through partnerships between domestic violence advocates and religious leaders. Last, the domestic violence movement has expanded as well to incorporate issues of sexuality, not only violence in gay and lesbian relationships but also violence against transgender individuals.

Legal Response to Domestic Violence

As noted above, by the mid-1880s, some states, Alabama being the first, began to modify their laws by rescinding men's legal rights to beat their wives. However, the enforcement of these laws is highly contested, and in 1886 the North Carolina Supreme Court ruled again that "a criminal indictment cannot be brought against a husband unless the battery is so great as to result in permanent injury, endanger life and limb, or be malicious beyond all reasonable bounds" (Martin 1976, 44).

A significant shift in the enforcement and handling of domestic violence began in 1911 with the establishment of the first "family court," in Buffalo, New York. This movement is significant in that it shifted domestic violence from criminal court to family court. The belief was that family courts would be better suited to handling domestic disputes. Perhaps that is true. But by moving domestic violence out of criminal court, the ability to impose sanctions and require accountability that criminal courts have was diminished. For example, in most states this means that a man convicted of battering will not face the harsher penalties associated with an assault conviction in criminal court. We will return to this point later.

By the 1960s, the dominant belief was that arresting batterers was an inadequate solution to the complexities of domestic violence, and thus police officers were trained in crisis intervention techniques. The most common tactic was to calm the abuser down by walking him around the block. Research on domestic violence demonstrated that this approach tended to intensify rather than reduce the violence. Men who were not arrested believed that they would not be held accountable, and they believed this translated into "free rein" to batter their wives and girlfriends (Browne 1989). Many battered women who have been interviewed for documentaries, including the powerful piece *Defending Our Lives* (Cambridge Films), report this experience as common.

By the late 1980s, based on the recommendations of domestic violence advocates, a return to arresting abusers was implemented on a trial basis in a small number of jurisdictions. In Minnesota, for example, a mandatory arrest law was established that required that officers who were called to domestic violence incidents arrest the perpetrator. This movement was deemed successful, and by the mid-1990s most states had laws that required that batterers be arrested and detained for seventy-two hours. The laws vary from state to state, and various attempts to modify them have taken place in the past decade. For example, in North Carolina, the domestic violence statute is termed *assault on a female*, which indicates that the crime is limited to cases with female victims. This creates serious problems for straight and gay male victims. As noted above, in states like Minnesota, where domestic violence laws are degendered, social workers who saw the traumatic outcomes for children who witness domestic violence advocated for requiring children in these cases to be referred to social services.

As noted earlier, one of the most important decisions to impact domestic violence policy was moving domestic violence cases out of criminal court and into family court, where family matters, including divorce and adoption, take place. Family court operates much more like civil court in the sense that the most common decisions focus on legal relationships—such as child custody or adoption—that have contract implications. Rarely are punishments per se associated with family court. As noted throughout, the specific laws vary from state to state, and we are of course most familiar with our own state, so to use North Carolina as an example, when a man is convicted of "assault on a female"—the charges are dropped more than 50 percent of the time—he is typically offered the opportunity to participate in a batterer intervention program in lieu of jail time or probation. On the one hand, this might seem like a progressive option, especially in light of the fact that by avoiding jail the man can continue to work—if he is employed—and contribute to the financial well-being of his family. However, in practical terms, because family court judges have no ability to require accountability—as is the case when individuals are sentenced to drug or alcohol rehabilitation as part of the terms required to getting a driver's license reinstated after a DUI—the court has no power to enforce his attendance at the program, and as a result, the majority of the men we studied rarely attended the program, and of those who did, few completed more than 25 percent of the program. Whether this influences recidivism rates is still unclear, but what is clear is that the type of assault handled in criminal court is treated very differently from the same type of physical abuse when it occurs between intimate partners.

Another aspect of the criminal justice response to domestic violence is the availability and implementation of a **restraining order** or order of protection that prevents someone who poses a threat from having any contact with the person who files for the order; contact can be defined as physical or via e-mail, telephone, texting, and so forth, which was first made available in California in the late 1970s. As with all other aspects of domestic violence, such orders are obtained and enforced by family courts. Thus, though they may initially make a battered woman feel more secure, in practice they are nothing more than a piece of paper with very little power to protect. More recently, states have developed and implemented a series of stalking laws. In part, these laws developed out of recognition that one aspect of domestic violence is verbal, emotional, or psychological harassment, or a combination. Batterers accomplish a great deal of terrorism of their intimate partners through stalking them—popping up unexpectedly, following them in their cars, calling their phones at all hours of the day and night, a point that we will return to later. However, the need for stalking laws increased substantially as the technology of the late twentieth century began to explode. In an age characterized by cell phone tracking devices, Internet hacking, e-mail harassment, and various forms of harassment associated with social networking—such as posting threats or derogatory comments or pictures on Facebook—the ability a batterer has to harass his victim has increased exponentially. In addition, stalking laws have been a major boost to the prevention and intervention strategies associated with teen violence. Because young men in high school and college often engage in harassing strategies long before they are married to or cohabiting with their partners—indeed, in the case of high school students both parties usually still live with their parents—stalking laws have provided an avenue for early intervention for teens.

One of the most central developments in the overall approach to domestic violence comes from the passage of the **Violence Against Women Act** in 1994. The material for the summary presented here of VAWA was provided by the Faith Trust Institute—a multifaith, multinational organization dedicated to education and the prevention and intervention of gender-based violence:

> VAWA was passed as Title IV, sec. 40001–40703 of the Violent Crime Control and Law Enforcement Act of 1994 HR 3355 and signed as Public Law 103-322 by President Bill Clinton on September 13, 1994. It provided $1.6 billion to enhance investigation and prosecution of the violent crime perpetrated against women, increased pre-trial detention of the accused, imposed automatic and mandatory restitution on those convicted, and allowed civil redress in cases prosecutors chose to leave unprosecuted. VAWA was drafted by Joseph Biden's office with support from a number of advocacy organizations including The National Organization for Women. VAWA was reauthorized by Congress in 2000, and again in December 2005 by President George W. Bush. VAWA was up for reauthorization in 2011, and at the time of the completion of this book it had not been signed into law for the future.
>
> One of the most important outcomes of VAWA was the establishment of an Office within the US Justice Department that deals exclusively with violence against women. Statutorily established following the passage of the reauthorization of VAWA in 2000, the Office on Violence Against Women has the authority to administer the grants authorized under VAWA—which is how many of the shelters, prevention and intervention programs across the nation are funded—as well as develop federal policy around issues relating to domestic violence, dating violence, sexual assault, and stalking. Of course, one of the negative and perhaps unintended consequences of "gendering" laws like this, is that it leaves out male victims—both gay and straight. For example, because many shelters receive the majority of the funding from VAWA they are restricted from providing shelter to men, including teenage boys who arrive with their mothers attempting to escape abusive households. (http://www.faithtrustinstitute.org)

CONCLUSIONS

In this chapter we have reviewed the overall "history" of various types of family violence as they occur in the United States. As we have noted, one of the common principles of family violence—regardless of the form it takes—is that it has been accepted historically and cross-culturally, it has often been endorsed by religious teachings, and the first key to beginning to address it has been to redefine both people and actions. All of these issues are important. For example, as is the case with virtually any practice, attitudes and norms of behavior typically change at a snail's pace compared to changes in the law. Think for a moment about the famous desegregation case *Brown v. Board of Education* decided by the US Supreme Court in 1954. Despite its power, changes to segregated patterns were heavily resisted by those in power (whites) and took decades to achieve any meaningful change. And some fifty-five years *after Brown v. Board*, attitude polls continue to reveal that a strong minority of whites continue to believe that African Americans are less capable, less intelligent, and lazier than whites, all while electing the first African American president of the United States.

So it is with family violence. Recall the many changes in the law and in court cases just in the state of North Carolina during the late nineteenth century. A man's right to beat his wife was rescinded, but that did not necessarily mean that battering was illegal. Once battering was made illegal, that did not necessarily translate into charging individual men with domestic violence. Indeed, as late as 1874 the North Carolina Supreme Court ruled that even if domestic violence was illegal, unless the man killed his wife or abused her so badly that it became a public matter, it should remain "behind the curtain" and treated as any other family problem: that is, it should be ignored. Our current mechanisms for dealing with domestic violence have been largely shaped by the very long history of failing to define it as a problem and tolerating or ignoring it. The same is true for child abuse and elder abuse. Additionally, the fact that Americans continue to attend religious services in which passages from holy books—the Bible, the Talmud, the Qur'an—that endorse female submissiveness are read and "preached" has a profound impact on our attitudes regarding domestic violence and our approach to dealing with it when it occurs. As we will discuss at length in Chapter 10, 70 percent of women who sought counseling from a religious leader—a pastor, rabbi, or iman—reported that they were first told to go home and try to behave "better" so that their husbands would not be tempted to beat them (Nason-Clark 2009). Therefore, understanding something about the history of family violence is the first step in understanding the phenomenon. In the next chapter we examine the theories that are used to explain family violence.

NOTES

1. We argue that any situation that one cannot enter or exit freely is, by definition, abusive. Thus, even in apprenticeship arrangements where the masters were reasonable, the very situation itself constituted abuse.

2. For an interesting discussion of this, see Kershaw 2009.

3. The opposite pattern would apply when ego is a girl.

4. For more on Genarlow Wilson's story, see Dewan 2006.

5. This amendment was sponsored by Claude Pepper.

6. For an excellent examination of domestic violence, including bride burning and dowry murders, see Kristoff and WuDunn 2009.

BIBLIOGRAPHY

Bonnie, R. J., and R. B. Wallace, eds. 2003. *Elder Mistreatment: Abuse, Neglect, and Exploitation in an Aging America*. Washington, DC: National Academies Press.

Browne, A. 1989. *When Battered Women Kill*. New York: Free Press.

"Child Abuse—An Overview." n.d. http://www.libraryindex.com/pages/1360/Child-Abuse-History-OVERVIEW.html#ixzz0eloJmlkd.

Dewan, S. 2006. "Georgia Man Fights Conviction as Molester." *New York Times*, December 19. http://www.nytimes.com/2006/12/19/us/19georgia.html?_r=3&ex=157680000&en=d32f07af9af73a11&ei=5124&partner=permalink&exprod=permalink&oref=slogin&oref=slogin&oref=slogin.

Epstein, C. 2007. "Great Divides: The Cultural, Cognitive, and Social Bases of the Global Subordination of Women." *American Sociological Review* 72: 1–22.

Flannery, R. 1938. "Cross-Cousin Marriage Among the Cree and Montagnais of James Bay." *Primitive Man* 11, nos. 1–2: 29–33.

Gordon, L. 1988. *Heroes of Their Own Lives: The Politics and History of Family Violence*. New York: Penguin.

Graetz, N. 1998. *Silence Is Deadly: Judaism Confronts Wifebeating*. Northvale, NJ: Jason Aronson.

Hattery, A. J., and E. Smith. 2010. *Prisoner Reentry and Social Capital: The Long Road to Reintegration*. Lanham, MD: Lexington Books.

Hays, S. 2003. *Flat Broke on Welfare*. New York: Oxford University Press.

Kelly, H. 1994. "Rule of Thumb and the Folklaw of the Husband's Stick." *Journal of Legal Education* 44, no. 3: 341–365.

Kempe, C. H. 1962. "The Battered Child Syndrome." *Journal of the American Medical Association* 181, no. 17.

Kershaw, S. 2009. "Shaking Off the Shame." *New York Times*, November 25. http://www.nytimes.com/2009/11/26/garden/26cousins.html.

Koss, M. P., L. A. Goodman, A. Browne, L. F. Fitzgerald, G. P. Keita, and N. F. Russo. 1994. *No Safe Haven: Male Violence Against Women at Home, at Work, and in the Community*. Washington, DC: American Psychological Association.

Kristoff, N., and S. WuDunn. 2009. *Half the Sky: Turning Oppression into Opportunity for Women Worldwide*. New York: Alfred A. Knopf.

Lemon, N. 1996. *Domestic Violence Law: A Comprehensive Overview of Cases and Sources*. San Francisco: Austin and Winfield.

Martin, D. 1976. *Battered Wives*. New York: Pocket Books.

Nason-Clark, N. 2009. "Christianity and the Experience of Domestic Violence: What Does Faith Have to Do with It?" *Social Work and Christianity* 36, no. 4: 379–393.

Rosenblatt, R. 1995. "The Society That Pretends to Love Children." *New York Times Magazine*, October 8.

Smith, E., and A. Hattery. 2009. *Interracial Intimacies: An Examination of Powerful Men and Their Relationships Across the Color Line*. Durham, NC: Carolina Academic Press.

3 Theories for Studying Family Violence

This chapter will be a typical textbook chapter that familiarizes students with the three different theoretical frameworks for studying family violence. Each will be reviewed and critiqued on both its strengths and its weaknesses. Additionally, students will be introduced to the key figures associated with each theory, and we will provide examples of their contributions to the field.

OBJECTIVES

- To familiarize the reader with the primary theories that are used to study family violence
- To provide an assessment of each theoretical framework, highlighting both the pros and the cons
- To familiarize the reader with the scholars who have developed each perspective

---

KEY TERMS

grand theories

theories of the middle range

conflict theory

structural functionalism

symbolic interaction theory (SI)

"doing gender"

feminist theory

race, class, and gender theory

criminology theories

strain theory

conformists

rebels and retreatists

ritualists

innovators

social control theory

social bonds

differential association theory (DA)

family violence theory

Conflict Tactics Scale (CTS)

mutual combat

intimate terrorism

situational couple violence

psychological theories

situational theory

exchange theory

social learning theory

THEORETICAL APPROACHES TO FAMILY VIOLENCE

This unique focus on structure and institutions is often less familiar to the nonsociologist. In our own classrooms we find that this framework is very difficult for students to feel completely comfortable with, which stands to reason since the "fathers" of sociology—whose work contributed significantly to our focus on structures and institutions—failed to include the family in their work as their attention was elsewhere.

Lester Frank Ward, for example, whom many consider the "father of American sociology" (Calhoun 2007; Ward 1963), spent his time examining issues related to evolutionary processes, eugenics, as was the case with other early sociologists in the United States and elsewhere. Early on sociologists were concerned with issues such as charities and correction, rural sociology, labor problems, statistics, social reform, social control, personality and social adjustment, and urban and rural sociology.

Urban sociology was big in places like the University of Chicago, but so was the study of immigration, settlement patterns, and ethnicity. We cannot forget, though, that the early sociologists were very interested in putting forth the perspective that sociology was also a science and spent enormous time with these burning issues (Weber 1949).

The family only becomes a central issue in American sociology around the time of the Great Depression. Beginning on Black Tuesday, October 29, 1929, the Great Depression catapulted Americans into a life of despair. The struggles for food, work, living space, and a more normal life did not end until around America's entry into World War II in 1941.

All of this becomes important in terms of family violence. To understand what is happening in the American home, it stands to reason that someone had to be studying it. Family sociologists were at this time those people engaged in chronicling the life chances of American families.

One of the first things that students want to know is why they should care about theory and why they should have to learn it. Most of our own students remark that theory is boring, that it is written by a bunch of dead white men, that in short it has no relevance. In fact, the development and understanding of theory are not only important to the scholars who do the research on family violence or the practitioners who work with families who are experiencing it, but also important for the student of family violence because it provides a sort of road map that helps us to see the patterns in family violence rather than seeing it as a set of disconnected and isolated events.

But first a few caveats! Social theory, we are reminded, has been built upon the same principles as theories of the natural world—the theory of relativity, Boyle's law, Newton's laws—and are all more like guidelines than exact rules. Every young person who has taken a physics or chemistry class with a lab knows that the theories that guide these disciplines provide precise and repeatable "laws" that describe how the physical world works. So, for example, one learns early on that when one applies heat to water, it turns to steam and that the point at which this transformation begins to occur is when the water reaches a temperature of approximately 212 degrees Fahrenheit. Similarly, when water is subjected to cold temperatures, it turns to ice, at approximately 32 degrees Fahrenheit. Yet every meteorologist knows that predicting when a February storm will yield snow, when it will yield ice, and when it will yield rain is difficult at best. And though we often "blame the weatherman," the truth is that predicting the weather—which relies on a variety of complex factors, including air temperature, wind, ground temperature, cloud cover, and so on—is a lot more like developing theories of family violence: it is mushy.

Social and psychological theories are often critiqued for being imprecise, for not being able to explain every variation of a phenomenon, yet just like the problem faced by the meteorologist, individual people are infinitely complex and unique, and when they are combined—as they are in a family—the complexity of possible outcomes grows exponentially. Thus, predicting any one person's behavior, let alone his or her behavior when he or she is acting inside a group or relationship, is difficult at best and impossible at worst. Social and psychological theories then are not designed to predict with certainty the behavior of an individual person; rather, they provide a road map that identifies the patterns that exist and the power that these patterns have in explaining most of human behavior. Social and behavioral scientists make clear that these theories cannot explain or predict every single person's behavior, but they are useful in painting a broad picture of the overall shape of the phenomenon.

Sociological theories come in three types: grand theories, theories of the middle range, and theories that attempt to explain a single phenomenon such as prisoner reentry (e.g., see Hattery and Smith 2010).

GRAND THEORIES

Grand theories, most notably conflict theory, functionalist theory, and symbolic interactionist theory, were developed in order to explain all of the vastness of human behavior. Each is built on the assumption that all types of human behavior—both at the micro or individual level and at the macro or institutional level—will be organized around several key principles.

Conflict Theory

Developed by Karl Marx (Marx, Engels, and Struik 1971), **conflict theory** argues that all of the social world can be understood as a battle over resources. This battle is structured around the antagonistic *class* relationship between those who have access to "the means of production" (the bourgeoisie or capitalists, who own land

and factories) and those who do not (the proletariat, or workers). Marx argued that this fundamental and antagonistic relationship based on class could explain all of human behavior. Marx's conceptualization developed primarily as an economic theory and has been used to explain labor market behavior, wages, the development of unions, and so on. But Marx and his colleagues and more recently neo-Marxist theorists have modified and developed the basic tenets of conflict theory to explain a wide range of phenomenon, from the exploitation of student athletes and the big business of sports (Smith 2007) to the covert and overt goals of the criminal justice system (Wacquant 2001; Wright 1997), the development of social capital networks (Lin 2000), as well as family violence.

Conflict Theory and Family Violence

Frederick Engels, Karl Marx's coauthor of the *Communist Manifesto*, modified their theory of capitalism and exploitation and applied it to the family. Engels argued that the family, as an institution, could be understood and analyzed like the economy. Writing during the height of the Industrial Revolution, when men worked in the public sphere and women stayed at home taking care of the family and doing other home-based work such as piecework for factories, sewing, taking care of small gardens, and so forth, Engels argued that the husband could be compared to the bourgeoisie and the wife to the proletariat. He argued that because men worked for wages, like the bourgeoisie or capitalist he had access to capital, whereas the wife, because her work did not generate wages, was like the proletariat. Under this conceptualization, Engels (1884) argued that women therefore could have their labor exploited because they did not have ownership rights or rights to money, but rather had to rely on the goodness of their husbands who provided for them in exchange for their domestic labor and sexual availability.

Engels extends this argument by suggesting that wives served in a critically important capacity in a capitalist economy: they were responsible for the reproduction of labor. Engels conceptualized this in two ways: the daily reproduction of labor and the generational reproduction of labor. Engels's argument is that women's reproductive capacity and their role as mothers in the family were central to the literal reproduction of the labor force: they gave birth to children who grew up to be the next generation of workers. Additionally, Engels argued that in their capacity as caregivers and caretakers of the home, women's daily cooking, cleaning, and laundry allowed the worker—her husband—to come home to an environment in which, relieved of these responsibilities, he could convalesce and be ready to return to his labor the next day. Though Engels was writing during the peak of the Industrial Revolution when men's labor was often dirty and physically demanding in factories and coal mines, his logic can be applied to today's family as well. In many working-class families, men work more than one job, and though women are often employed as well, they still do the majority of the housework (Bianchi, Robinson, and Milkie 2007), and their commitment to the household labor relieves their husbands or partners of this work and thus eases their ability to work more than one job. In many professional households, men work in jobs that require them to travel or to work extraordinary hours—sixty to eighty per week for many lawyers, physicians, financial consultants, and accountants—and once again it is the household labor done by their wives, who are somewhat less likely to be employed, that "allows" these men to rejuvenate at home and return to work rested.

Conflict theory focuses on the fact that institutions—economies, families—that are built on inherently unequal relationships are thus designed for exploitation, and abuse may be an intended or unintended consequence (Merton 1968). In terms of the economy, for example, the antagonistic relationship between capitalists—or owners of the means of production—and workers centers primarily on wages and working conditions. Owners can increase their profits substantially by paying lower wages. This has always been a core tenet of capitalism, and we see it in the United States as more and more companies outsource manufacturing to developing countries where labor is cheap (Friedman 2006). Owners also seek to limit the benefits they pay for as well as refuse to spend money updating the workplace environment—for example, many institutions including colleges delayed the removal of asbestos in ceiling and floor tiles until the lawsuits for asbestos exposure escalated. In contrast, the worker's self-interests are in earning a fair wage, receiving benefits such as health insurance and retirement funds, and working in an environment that is comfortable, safe, and free from exposure to toxins like asbestos. Because the self-interests of the owners are in direct opposition to the self-interests of the workers, their relationship is inherently antagonistic. Furthermore, when there is a surplus labor force, as exists in the United States in the late 2000s and early 2010s with an unemployment rate hovering between 10 percent and 15 percent, the owner has the power to enforce his or her self-interests and lower wages, reduce benefits, and refuse to improve the environment. Workers are forced to either accept this exploitation of their labor or find themselves unemployed.

Engels argues, as we do elsewhere (Hattery 2008), that one can conceptualize the family in a similar manner. Conflict theorists would argue then that because men tend to make higher wages and have access to other types of power in families, it is not surprising in terms of intimate partner violence that men are more likely to be the perpetrators and women the victims. Comparatively, because similar power dynamics—though even more pronounced—exist between parents and children as well as adult children and elderly parents, the direction of violence tends to be from those with more access to resources toward those who have less access to resources and are thus vulnerable to exploitation and abuse.

The strength of this approach is that it explains the majority of violence in families. The weakness to this approach is that it has difficulty explaining certain patterns of violence, such as violence perpetrated by women against their male partners or violence by adult children who stand to gain a great deal through inheritance or who are benefiting financially from their aging parents. This approach also fails to explain much about sibling abuse and is more difficult to apply in gay and lesbian couples where the power dynamic may not be as obvious, if it exists at all, based on conventional statutes.

Structural-Functionalist Theory

Structural-functionalism was perhaps the most "popular" theoretical approach utilized in sociology across the twentieth century. Many well-known and frequently studied sociologists interpreted the world through the functionalist lens, including Émile Durkheim, Talcott Parsons, and Robert K. Merton. Similar to conflict theory, functionalist theory attempts to explain the entire range of human behavior and has been utilized by the discipline as a whole as well as by criminologists and family sociologists alike.

In sum, functionalist theory was developed in the mid-nineteenth century in response to the claim that sociology was not a "real" science. Early theorists like Durkheim went to great lengths to convince the scientific community of the power of sociology, and apparently he and other early social theorists believed that linking sociology to the natural sciences would yield the most compelling argument for the acceptance of sociology as a bona fide science. Thus, the language and assumptions of functionalist theory look very similar to those that are utilized in the natural sciences. Functionalist theory is built on the core assumption that society is like an organism that has many different parts that all work together to keep the society working in harmony. So, for example, the human body has many different organ systems and individual organs; the organs all have distinct functions that when coordinated with other organs keep the body in equilibrium. Functionalists argue, likewise, that institutions and individuals all serve different functions in society, but it is the coordination of these functions that keeps society running. For example, just as the human body would not work if an individual had two livers and only one kidney, or if organs duplicated functions, similarly in society we designate roles to different institutions because this is more efficient than replication or overlap. We have one system of government, one system of education, one system of health care, and so forth. Schools provide education but do not provide health care, for example. And if they did, or when they do, this is less efficient.

The second core assumption of functionalist theory is that change occurs only in cases of dysfunction. For example, the human body evolved in response to changing environmental pressures, and this response is what kept the human race thriving across many millennia. When things are working properly, according to functionalists, there is no incentive to change, for change might make the system less efficient. In other words, "if it ain't broke, don't fix it."

The recent elections of 2008 and 2010 produced much change, especially in state and federal governments. Then presidential candidate Barack Obama ran on the theme "Change." Dissatisfaction with the Bush administration not only helped Obama attain the presidency but also led to the complete turnover of both houses of Congress. The midterm elections in 2010 saw a reversal of the trends in 2008, due to frustration that the recession has not improved and the United States is still fighting two wars, and political analysts suggest that more upheaval is to be expected. But government was not the only institution to experience pressure to change. The banking institution's dysfunctional practices were blamed for the current recession, and an inordinate amount of time seems to have been spent in the media discussing, proposing, and attempting to force a change in banking practices by the government, especially the Treasury Department. The argument is focused on the fact that poor banking practices led to the collapse of the financial industry, and this created the recession. Though banks and Wall Street firms had implemented these practices a decade ago—in response to the booming economy, especially in real estate—they were not interrogated or forced to change until the crisis hit. This is an example of the type of institutional change described by functionalists. They would argue that when banks and investment firms were making money hand over fist for themselves and their investors there was no incentive to change, even if some foresaw some of the impending doom. Change is not proactive but reactive and is often spurred by a crisis like the recession.

Functionalist Theory and the Family

One of the first functionalists who attempted to analyze the institution of the family through the functionalist lens was Talcott Parsons. Parsons began writing about the family in the early 1950s, and much like Engels did a century earlier, he attempted to transform a "grand theory" and make it applicable to a single institution.

As a functionalist, Parsons began with the assumption that if a family form existed and continued to exist over time, then it must be functional. His logic, built on the assumptions of functionalist theory, is that if the form were dysfunctional, the family would have changed and evolved to a more functional form. Thus, any longstanding form was, by definition, functional. Parsons argued, for example, that the gendered nature of the division of household labor—namely, the fact that regardless of women's hours of paid employment, they do, on average, two-thirds of the household labor (Bianchi, Robinson, and Milkie 2007)—can be traced back to prehistoric times. Specifically, he argues that during the days of the "hunter and gatherer" economies, men needed to be able to range widely to hunt big game, while women—who were often pregnant or nursing small children—were confined to the "home." Over time, these patterns of social behavior evolved into our genetic structure such that in the modern era, men are "wired" genetically to be able to be away from their families for long stretches of time, whereas women are not. In contrast, women, having spent all of these centuries doing the work of the home and family, have evolved skills that make them better at this type of work. For example, it is argued that women can distinguish the needs of a crying baby more easily than men (Parsons and Bales 1955). The notion of sociobiological evolution is at the core of the application of functionalist theory to the institution of the family.

Though there are few if any examples of the strict application of functionalist theory to the study of family violence, we can extend Parson's general thesis and see its influence on family violence theory, namely, through the conduit of gender role theory. Parsons endorses a division of household labor in the family because it is functional, and he believes that the most efficient division is strictly by gender. Though he never approaches the topic of violence, we can see, at least with regards to intimate partner violence, that a strict and rigid construction of gender roles leaves open the possibility for frustrations to occur that may lead to violence. For example, if wives' duties are to please their husbands through maintaining calm and decorated homes, by providing tasty and nutritious meals, by taking care of children, and by being sexually available, then husbands may view any failure at these tasks as an occasion requiring discipline (recall our discussion in Chapter 2). We will return to a lengthier discussion of the role that gender roles and cultural constructions of gender play in intimate partner violence in Chapter 9. With regards to other forms of family violence, we can speculate that functionalist theorists would attribute child abuse and elder abuse to the frustrations that caretakers sometimes feel when they are faced with the difficult and seemingly never-ending task of caretaking. The strength of this approach is that its tenets, were they to be applied, are consistent with the patterns present in the majority of violence in families. The weakness of this approach is that it could be understood as accepting violence as an unintended but unavoidable outcome of the ways in which families are structured. This approach would then leave perpetrators "off the hook" and victims wondering when and how change will occur, much as modern disgruntled wives doing all of the household labor report feeling frustrated (Hattery 2001).

Symbolic Interaction Theory

The fathers of **symbolic interaction (SI) theory** are widely considered to be two social psychologists, George Herbert Mead and Charles Horton Cooley. In contrast to both conflict theory and functionalist theory, SI is a micro-level theory that focuses on the interactions that people have and the ways in which these interactions create reality. Herbert Blumer (1969), a second-generation SI theorist, laid out the following three principles as being central to both Mead and Cooley and SI theory:

1. Human beings act toward things on the basis of the meanings they ascribe to those things.
2. The meaning of such things derives from, or arises out of, the social interaction that one has with others and the society.
3. These meanings are handled in, and modified through, an interpretative process used by the person in dealing with the things he or she encounters.

In sum, SI theorists argue that the interactions that humans have with each other create meaning and that without interaction and interpretation, nothing—relationships, institutions—has any meaning. In contrast to conflict theorists, for example, SI theorists would argue that "work" exists only insofar as we ascribe meaning to it through relationships and interpretation. For example, let us consider the case of cooking. When I cook at home for myself and my family, a task in which I have a great deal of autonomy—I get to decide what to cook, when to cook, what methods to use, and so forth—and for which I am not paid, this is not "work." In contrast, if I go to a local restaurant, put on a white coat and a specific type of white hat, and respond to the directions of the executive chef with regards to what is to be cooked, how, and when, after doing this for forty hours, I am given a paycheck. It is then that my cooking is transformed into "work" (Wilson 1996).

Symbolic Interaction Theory and the Family

Family scholars working from an SI framework developed "role theory" as a way of understanding the forms that families take and the ways in which they operate on a daily basis. For example, when two children are fighting over a toy and a parent interrupts and instructs the children to share the toy, this interaction is reinforcing the roles of both parent and child. Similarly, when a wife greets her husband at the end of the day with the remote control (the modern-day version of the newspaper) and a cocktail and asks about his day at work, the couple is engaging in their roles as husband and wife.

This may sound a lot like functionalist or even conflict theory, but SI is unique in that it does not adhere to the rigid constructions of these roles. Rather, SI focuses on the ways in which the roles are played and reinforced through interaction. For example, the script above could easily be switched, as it may be in modern-day households dealing with the current recession, and the husband may greet his wife at the door with the remote control and her favorite cocktail and inquire about her day at work. The interaction would be analyzed similarly: the two adults are playing out the roles of spouses. What SI theorists would focus on is the degree to which men and women "do spouse" differently (Erickson 2003).

Furthermore, the issue of elder abuse considered from an SI perspective would focus on the ways in which the interaction between child and parent changes over time from the scenario described above to one in which an adult child talks abusively to his or her aging parent. SI theorists would analyze this interaction as an example of how adult children and aging parents "do child-parent interaction" later in life as compared to during childhood.

Specifically with regards to family violence, West and Zimmerman's (1987) work on "**doing gender**" is useful to consider. They argue that when men and women interact in ways that reinforce or challenge gender role stereotypes, they are in fact "doing gender." Thus, a point to which we will return in Chapter 9, intimate partner violence can be understood as an extreme form of "doing gender." When a man responds violently to his female partner, this can be understood as an assertion of his masculinity or an occasion of "doing gender." Similarly, when a battered woman tries to avoid a future incidence of violence by "behaving properly"—being home on time, having dinner on the table on time—she is also "doing gender." Similarly, one could argue that when a parent disciplines a child, which is part of their role as a parent, they are "doing parent," and when abuse occurs, it is a matter, like intimate partner violence, of "doing parent" to an unnecessary extreme (Hattery 2008).

The strength of this approach is that it largely makes intuitive sense. Following a lengthy history in our culture of allowing men to physically discipline their wives and for parents to physically discipline their children, understanding abuse as an extreme form of this behavior that is otherwise central to one's role as a husband or parent makes sense. This approach does not explain well violence that does not follow this pattern (e.g., wives who abuse husbands). The primary weakness of this theory is that it attributes phenomena such as child abuse to individual choices and actions and minimizes the role that institutional structures play in shaping the patterns of violence that we see—for example, the role that patriarchy plays in structuring intimate partner violence as a *gendered* phenomenon.

THEORIES OF THE MIDDLE RANGE

Theories of the middle range are those designed to analyze and predict phenomena in one area or one institution rather than the entirety of human existence. In addition, according to Merton (1968), who coined the term, theories of the middle range, unlike grand theories, require more than abstract arguments but must be supported by empirical support. For example, feminist theory—which feminists would argue is a grand theory but general sociologists consider a theory of the middle range—seeks to explain a wide range of *gendered* phenomena using verifiable empirical evidence. For example, feminist researchers have examined sex segregation in the workplace, the division of household labor, differential treatment in the criminal justice system (feminist criminology), and health behavior as well as differential access to health care, the wage gap, gender stratification in the military and in churches, and of course violence against women—or what is commonly referred to as "gender-based violence."

Each theory of the middle range is built on a set of assumptions. As with the grand theories, we will lay out the assumptions of each theory, summarize the overall position taken by the theory, and provide examples of the ways in which it is used to explain family violence.

Feminist Theory

Feminist theory is built on the assumption that patriarchy—a gender-based hierarchy on which rewards, privileges, and power are distributed—undergirds every human society (Epstein 2007). In her presidential address to the American Sociological Association, Cynthia Fuchs Epstein offers a straightforward summary of feminist theory and its universal applicability: "The divide of biological sex constitutes a marker around which all major institutions of society are organized. All societal institutions assign roles based on the biological sex of their members. The divisions of labor in the family, local and global labor forces, political entities, most religious systems, and nation-states are all organized according to the sexual divide" (2007, 4). Thus, feminist theorists assume that a system of stratification based on gender structures all institutions and thus all human behavior.

Feminist Theory and Family Violence

Because of the fact that a tremendous amount of family violence is gendered, feminist theory, alongside **race, class, and gender theory**, is one of the only theories at the middle range that has been utilized to explain family violence. (Note, none of the grand theories explicitly addresses family violence, though, as we discussed previously, several contribute to specific theories that have attempted to address family violence.) Indeed, one of the earliest areas of examination by feminist scholars was gender-based violence, specifically rape (Brownmiller 1975; Griffin 1979), sexual harassment (MacKinnon 1991), and domestic violence (Walker 1984). These early feminist as well as contemporary feminist scholars, including ourselves (Hattery 2008; Hattery and Smith 2007; Smith 2008), argue that the system of patriarchy that bestows power and privilege on men and oppresses women creates a situation in which men beat their wives *because they can*. Additionally, because institutions are also structured around gender inequality, men beat their wives because there are few consequences for doing so, especially legally. Readers will recall the lengthy discussion of the history of domestic violence in Chapter 2 and the fact that for centuries, domestic violence was legal as long as the perpetrator was a man. Additionally, even once there were laws that made battering illegal, the criminal justice system, including state supreme courts, worked out a sort of "don't ask, don't tell" policy. As long as the woman was not injured severely or killed, then battering was considered a private matter between a man and his wife and was not a matter for the courts. These types of laws along with the statistics reveal that the majority of victims of lethal and near-lethal violence are women—one-third of all homicides of women are the result of domestic violence (*USA Today* 2003)—and are at the core of the feminist argument that battering is a gendered phenomenon. Additionally, the strength of feminist theory is that it focuses on the structural rather than individual nature of gender-based violence. In other words, the focus is less on individual men and more on the role that patriarchy plays in structuring both individual power within households—based on widely held cultural norms about gender relations—as well as institutional power, such as in the criminal justice system, that contribute to or reinforce and support intimate partner violence. Feminist theorists argue that men hit because they can and because they can get away with it. Therefore, one of their solutions to the endemic problem of IPV is the dismantling of patriarchy, or at the very least a change in the way that domestic violence is handled by the criminal justice system. If men were held accountable for domestic violence—if there were a "cost" to engaging in it—then we would likely see a decline in its prevalence.

The weaknesses of feminist theory are several. First, it does not adequately explain the "exceptions to the rule"—the cases in which women beat their male partners. Similarly, it does not address violence in the gay and lesbian communities adequately. Third, feminist theory has much less to contribute to our understanding of child abuse and elder abuse, though it is very powerful in explaining child *sexual* abuse. And last, feminist scholars have a tendency to treat gender-based violence as "violence against women," which keeps the focus on the victims rather than on the perpetrators (see especially Hattery 2008).

Race, Class, and Gender Theory

In many ways **race, class, and gender** theory is an outgrowth of feminist theory. Developed by black feminists including Maxine Baca Zinn, Bonnie Thorton Dill, and Patricia Hill Collins, RCG theory was a response to the alienation that many women of color felt in the feminist movement. Building on the principles of both feminist theory and conflict theory, in essence RCG is built on the assumption that there are multiple systems of oppression—patriarchy, capitalism, racial domination, heteronormativity—that work independently and together to structure both institutional and individual inequality.

RCG assumes that every system of domination has a countersystem of privilege. In other words, oppression is a system of both disadvantages and advantages. For example, we know that African American men die prematurely: seven or eight years earlier than their white counterparts (Hattery and Smith 2007). We remind the reader of our discussion in the first chapter. Generally, a discussion of this gap in life expectancy focuses on the reasons African American men die early, including jobs that involve physical labor, poverty, lack of access to health care, discrimination, and the stresses associated with being an African American man. Yet a race, class, and gender framework forces us to ask the opposing question: why is it that white men live so much longer? When we pose the question this way, we realize that the gap is also created by the fact that white men tend to have more access to white-collar employment and the best-quality health care, and their affluence affords them the ability to pay for the "dirty" work in their lives to be taken care of by others, mostly African American men and women. Thus, the intersection of race and social class creates *simultaneously* a disadvantage for African American men and an advantage for white men. Furthermore, when we dig deeper into this question of life expectancy, we see that there are significant gender differences as well. Specifically, not only do women live longer than men, but the racial gap is significantly smaller for women than for men. In short, our understanding of racial disparities in health and illness is improved when we layer these explanations together: focusing not only on gender or race, but also on the ways in which they interact to produce outcomes that vary by both statuses.[1]

At the structural level, the race, class, and gender framework illuminates the ways in which different systems of domination are mutually reinforcing: patriarchy is woven with racism (or race supremacy), both of which are woven with capitalism. It is critical to point out that the race, class, and gender paradigm requires more than the simple inclusion of individuals of different racial or ethnic groups, social classes, and genders into the sample. The race, class, and gender paradigm requires that the data be analyzed with attention to the inequality regimes that are based in the systems of patriarchy, capitalism, and racial domination (Acker 2006).

Race, Class, and Gender Theory and Family Violence

Compared to feminist theory, RCG not only provides a more complex way of understanding gender-based violence, but has the strength of being able to explain other forms of family violence as well. For example, the ways in which white affluent men feel threats to their masculinity, or beat their wives, or are dealt with at the police station are very different from the experiences of African American men, who may, for example, experience different threats to their masculinity and are certainly exposed to a criminal justice system that can only be characterized as racially unjust (Hattery and Smith 2007; Smith 2008).

RCG would analyze both child and elder abuse as other forms of violence perpetrated by an individual with privilege against an individual who is oppressed. For example, age is a major system of stratification in the United States, as it is in most cultures, with those at both ends experiencing the most oppression and the least power. Though we are a culture of youth, we do not really extend privileges to young people until they are adults. Additionally, recalling both our discussion of the history of child abuse in Chapter 2 as well as the evidence provided by Kristoff and WuDunn (2009), we see that both infanticide (killing a baby before its first birthday) and leaving the elderly to die—in places like sub-Saharan Africa—or engaging in euthanasia suggest that the power and privilege in most cultures belong to those in young and middle adulthood. Thus, RCG theorists would suggest that both child abuse and elder abuse can be explained through this paradigm. RCG theory is also able to explain IPV in gay and lesbian couples by focusing on other status systems, including perceived identity (butch versus femme and "out" versus "closeted"). In the case of the latter, an "out" partner has more power than one who remains closeted, and the "out" partner may use the threat to "out" the closeted partner as part of a system of intimate terrorism.

CRIMINOLOGY THEORIES

Most of the other textbooks on family violence include a discussion of **criminology theories**. Criminology theories are designed specifically to explain all sorts of deviant behavior, including behaviors that are illegal and those that are unusual but not illegal—for example, cheating on a test. We find this interesting because until relatively recently, most family violence was not dealt with as a crime. Therefore, the attempt to retroactively apply theories that were developed when family violence was not on the radar screen of criminologists seems absurd. That said, working under the assumption that family violence is a crime and will be dealt with as a crime—a tentative assumption at best—we review some of the key criminology theories and suggest ways in which they can be utilized to explain family violence.

Robert K. Merton, who was trained as a functionalist theorist by Parsons, developed a theory of social structure and anomie that he then applied to criminal behavior. Merton's basic argument in "Social Structure and Anomie" (1938), which was developed to respond to the critique that functionalist theory did not explain institutional change, explored the way in which changes in social structure—namely, norms—could lead to the alienation of the individual, which could in turn produce a response that would produce structural change. So, for example, Merton argued that as social norms began to change with regards to achieving success, such as the increased focus on and need for education, those who did not have the tools necessary to achieve educational success would feel alienated from the process. In an attempt to deal with this alienation, individuals would develop alternative strategies—other than educational attainment—in order to obtain success. Strategies might include pouring their resources into educating their children (conforming) or seeking avenues for success in the illegitimate economy—for example, through the Mafia or gangs—where education was unnecessary (innovation). This process, an unintended consequence of social change, would then produce additional change in the social system (Merton 1938; Zuckerman 1998).

It is relatively easy to see how Merton transformed his general theory into one that could be used to explain crime. He termed this application **strain theory**. Merton (1968) argued that when an individual or a set of individuals experienced anomie, or strain, their responses to this anomie could be analyzed through the lens of deviance: responses are either consistent with traditionally held norms or deviant in terms of these norms. We illustrate with an example of a variety of responses by individuals attempting to achieve the American dream.

Conformists accept the norms of success as well as the pathways toward getting there. Conformists will stay in school, seek more education and training, and work hard in order to achieve the American dream.

Both **rebels and retreatists** reject both the norms of success and the normative pathways. Rebels will establish a different set of norms of success—for example, they might reject the notion of acquiring and building wealth and instead seek the freedom associated with not being beholden to material wealth and tied down by concrete things like a mortgage and car payment. They will also seek alternative ways of getting what they desire, such as engaging in the illegitimate economy or participating in marginal economies. The "beatnicks" and "hippies" of the 1960s are a good example of rebels. In contrast, retreatists more or less "check out" altogether. These individuals tend to be highly alienated and live on the margins. Ted Kaczynski, the "Unibomber," would be an example of a retreatist.

Ritualists are individuals who have rejected the norms of success—usually because they have become uninterested like the rebels or view them as unattainable—yet they continue, usually out of habit, to participate in the pathways to success. An example of a ritualist is someone who continues to go to school despite the fact that they have given up on the idea of graduating, or the employee who continues to work in the factory even though he or she realizes that doing so will never lead to the acquisition of the tenets of the American dream. Ritualists are often very disenchanted people.

Innovators are individuals who continue to accept the norms of success but reject the accepted pathways for achieving it. Examples of innovators are students who cheat rather than study for a test or adults who make their money through the illegitimate economy—by selling drugs, engaging in prostitution, involvement with the Mafia or gangs—rather than work in a legitimate job in order to achieve success and acquire the accoutrements of the American dream.

	Category	Acceptance of Norms	Acceptance of Pathways
▶ **Figure 3.1** Merton's Strain Theory	*Conformist*	ACCEPT	ACCEPT
	Rebel	REJECT	REJECT
	Retreatist	REJECT	REJECT
	Ritualist	REJECT	ACCEPT
	Innovator	ACCEPT	REJECT

Merton's typology has been used to explain criminal behavior. When individuals experience strain, in this case the kind of strain that leaves them feeling alienated from the standard routes to success, they may begin to engage in "deviant" behavior in order either to achieve success or to reject it altogether.

Merton's typology has not been applied to discussions of the family or family violence in particular except by one of the authors. Smith (2008) argues that one way of understanding and explaining the intimate partner violence perpetrated by African American men is to employ Merton's strain theory. In particular, Smith argues:

> My analysis demonstrates that though the "causes" and the "triggers" for violence may not vary across race, the structural inequalities that African American men face—specifically discrimination in the labor market and incarceration—lead to higher levels of alienation, stronger threats to one's masculine identity, and consequently the utilization of more severe violence to alleviate the high levels of strain. In addition, African American men are disproportionately likely to have experienced violence in the families in which they grew up. This exposure to violence puts them at increased risk for battering in adulthood. Merton's framework provides an unique and useful way of thinking about the racial variation evident in the statistics on IPV.

In addition, we would suggest that just as Smith utilizes Merton's framework to deconstruct racial variations in intimate partner violence, other forms of family violence might be analyzed utilizing this framework as well. So, for example, we know that the rate of child abuse is higher in single-parent families. We might conclude that single parents experience strain in child rearing both because they are the only parent engaged in the day-to-day work of child rearing and because the pressures on them to earn a living and provide for the child are greater. The strain produced by these two conditions may result in well-meaning parents engaging in physical discipline that "gets out of control" rather than the more emotionally costly and time-consuming strategies including "time-out," reasoning with children, and so forth.

The strength of Merton's theory is that it takes into consideration the role that institutional pressure and structures play in criminal behavior. Merton's theory is unique among criminology theories in this regard, as the majority focus solely on the individual. And, as Smith has argued, it does have some applicability to some forms of family violence.

The weakness of Merton's theory is that it was not designed to address this kind of "deviant" behavior and thus has not been widely utilized by family scholars in general and family violence scholars in particular. Additionally, though Merton's theory focuses on structure in shaping human behavior, it does not focus on the role of gender, age, or any form of inequality in structuring family violence.

SOCIAL CONTROL THEORY

Social control theory, developed by Travis Hirschi, derives its assumptions largely from both functionalist theory and social psychological theories of socialization. Hirschi (1969) argues that socialization and specifically the development of social bonds lead to the type of social control that is necessary to prevent one from engaging in criminal behavior. A core assumption of Hirschi's theory is that individuals are born without any ability to engage in social control. Additionally, the implied assumption is that engaging in deviant or criminal behavior is more desirable than not, and thus internal mechanisms of social control must be developed. The development of these internal mechanisms occurs through what Hirschi refers to as **social bonds**. The more a child is concerned about the assessment of parents, teachers, and other important adults and the closer the child feels to each of the individuals—the stronger the social bonds—the less likely he or she is to engage in deviant or criminal behavior. Thus, a parent may refrain from hitting a child, a husband may refrain from beating his wife, or a stepparent my refrain from sexually abusing a stepchild because of the embarrassment and shame that would result if another adult found out. For example, a man might refrain from beating his wife because he is worried that his mother and father would think less of him. Or, in a more generalized way, in adulthood, he might fear the embarrassment that would ensue if a police officer arrested him or when his mug shot was taken at the local police department. Though not widely used to examine family violence—primarily, as we noted, because family violence has not been considered an area of interest for criminologists—this approach does offer some insight into behavior at the individual level.

The strength of this approach is that it is intuitive: it makes sense. Second, the solutions that arise from it also make sense: if we can work with parents to develop deep social bonds, we can reduce family violence.

The weakness of this approach, like many criminology theories, including Merton's, is that it assumes that family violence is the same as other acts of deviance or criminal behavior. We will argue in the subsequent chapters that family violence is not like other criminal activity or deviant behavior; rather, building on the historical development of family violence, we will argue that it arises out of constructions of power and privilege, norms of behavior and accountability, as well as ideological distinctions between discipline and abuse. Additionally, social control theory is an individual-level theory and does not consider the role of structures and institutions in shaping any deviant behavior and family violence in particular. Last, applying social control theory to family violence would rely on the assumption that engaging in family violence would bring shame upon the perpetrator. When considering this alongside the history of various forms of family violence, this seems likely to be a stretch. And when we discuss the role of child abuse in the development of batterers, we will see that this assumption is likely false; indeed, much of family violence is "the way things have always been" and would thus not produce shame in the perpetrator.

DIFFERENTIAL ASSOCIATION THEORY

Developed by Edwin Sutherland out of the symbolic interaction perspective, **differential association theory (DA)** is built on the assumption that deviance is learned behavior and that the process for learning it is exposure to others who are engaging in it. Recalling our discussion of SI theory, Sutherland (1924) argues that behaviors take on different meanings based on the groups with which they are associated. Thus, for example, shaking down a "mark" might be considered deviant and criminal under normal circumstances, but inside of a gang or a group of individuals who are engaged in crime, it might be understood as a means of getting the money that is needed for another activity. Similarly, murder, especially among gang members, may be understood as an action necessary to prove allegiance or to avenge the murder of one's own by a rival gang; thus, it is justified and not necessarily defined as a criminal act.

Key to differential association theory is the notion that deviant and criminal behavior is learned by exposure to it. Thus, the likelihood of an individual engaging in deviance or criminal behavior is directly linked to the probability that an individual is exposed repeatedly to it and develops intimate types of relationships with individuals and groups that are engaged in deviance and criminal behavior. This theory is widely used to explain the way in which young children living in housing projects get involved in deviance and crime vis-à-vis their exposure to gangs.

We are unaware of any attempts to apply differential association theory directly to the study of family violence, but where it does makes sense is the process it proposes for learning behaviors. For example, when we discuss the role that boys' exposure to intimate partner violence plays in the likelihood that they will grow up to perpetrate intimate partner violence, the tenets of differential association theory apply. In short, young men who witness domestic violence are three times more likely than their counterparts to grow up to be batterers. Differential association theory would suggest that this is because when a young boy witnesses his father or stepfather beating his mother, he is both learning the "tools of the trade" and also learning that this behavior produces an outcome that his father or stepfather seems to desire. Just like the young boy hanging out on the corner with gangbangers or the suburban youngster hanging out in the basement with older siblings who are smoking pot, the lessons and skills for deviant behavior are transmitted through exposure. This is the main contribution this approach can make to the study of family violence.

As with all of the other criminology theories, differential association theory is an individual-level theory that does not take into account the structural forces that shape family violence. Additionally, as with all types of deviant or criminal behavior, differential association theory does not adequately explain the person who is exposed to deviance but chooses not to engage in it—as is the case for 50 percent of the boys who observe intimate partner violence in the families in which they grew up. Nor does it explain the individual who engages in deviant or criminal behavior yet has not been exposed—or who has been exposed only minimally—to this activity.

THEORIES SPECIFIC TO THE STUFF OF FAMILY VIOLENCE

Last, we turn to a discussion of the theories that are specific to discussions of family violence. We will begin with family violence theory as it was designed to understand, explain, and predict all forms of family violence. Second, we will discuss theoretical approaches that were developed specifically to address one form of family violence and are unlikely to be transformed to discussions of other forms.

Family Violence Theory

The "fathers" of **family violence theory** are Richard Gelles and Murray Straus (Straus, Gelles, and Smith 1990). In addition to developing a general theory of family violence that is based on conflict theory, they also developed an instrument—which we will discuss in Chapter 4—to measure family violence. This instrument is called the **Conflict Tactics Scale (CTS)**. In a discussion of the CTS, Straus summarizes the theory of family violence:

> CTS is based on conflict theory. This theory assumes that conflict is inherent in all human groups, including the family. It is inherent because group members, while sharing many interests, also have different interests. These range from specifics, such as what color to paint the bedroom, to the desire of those in

power to stay in power and of those at the bottom to gain more control of their lives. Conflict is also a key part of the feminist theory of family violence. . . . [T]he version of conflict theory on which the CTS is based assumes that *any* inequality in the family, including dominance by a *female* partner, increases the probability of violence because the dominant partner may use violence to maintain his or her position, or the subordinate partner may use violence to try to achieve a more equitable relationship. Thus, a key feature of the CTS is that it measures violence by both partners in a relationship. (1999, 195)

In short, family violence theory assumes that violence arises out of conflict and that the person perpetrating the violence does so because he or she has the power to do so and because it works: it tends to end the conflict at least temporarily. Additionally, Straus and Gelles and other family violence theorists would argue that violence is a response, albeit an undesirable one, to disagreement or conflict. Family violence theorists would argue that violence erupts in families when individuals lack the skills to make other more appropriate responses, for example. Additionally, they argue that violence may be employed because, as noted above, it is an "easy" response especially for individuals who are otherwise overburdened or stressed—single parents, families living in poverty, or young couples who have not developed the communication skills and patience necessary to address conflict. In short, individuals in families who have power engage in violence because they can and because it works (Gelles and Straus 1988). Gelles and Straus (1988) also note in their theoretical discussion of the CTS that violence may be attempted by a subordinate partner in order to level the playing field and gain status in the relationship.

Family violence theory has much strength and shares some overlap with the other major theory used to examine family violence: feminist theory. Both family violence theorists and feminist theorists agree that violence in families is shaped by inequality and power and that those who engage in it do so because they can. They are not challenged by other family members, and they are not held accountable by the criminal justice system. A second strength of family violence theory is that it is "gender neutral"—in other words, it takes into account the possibility that men can be and are victims of family violence and women can be and are perpetrators of family violence.

There are two major critiques of family violence theory and the CTS in particular. We will discuss the critique of the CTS in the subsequent chapter, which is devoted to methods. Feminists argue that family violence theorists ignore the role of patriarchy in shaping power and inequality in families. As we will document in Chapter 8, though many women in today's households earn more money than their male partners, this rarely translates into "power" in the relationship. And specifically with regards to intimate partner violence, women who outearn their male partners are not only no more likely to be violent toward them but are *actually at increased risk* for being the target of male violence because their economic power upsets the traditional gender roles of the family. This upsetting can be interpreted as a threat to masculinity by male partners who may respond and reassert their masculinity through violence (Hattery 2008; Smith 2008). Additionally, our research (Hattery 2008; Smith 2008) confirms what feminist scholars have noted for decades, that only *rarely* do women—who are subordinate in relationships by virtue of their second-class status rooted in our patriarchal system—use violence against their male partners, and when they do, it is almost always in response to violence they are experiencing (they are fighting back) rather than violence that they instigate in order to "level the playing field," as Straus and Gelles suggest.

Intimate Terrorism Versus Situational Couple Violence

Among scholars of IPV there is a critical debate centering on "**mutual combat**," a term coined by Gelles and Straus (1988), referring to families in which both male and female partners engage in violence against each other. Derived from their findings from studies that utilized the CTS and revealed that in some families both male and female partners engage in violence against each other, Straus and Gelles developed the concept of "mutual combat."

Michael P. Johnson and his colleagues have extended this debate and attempted to distinguish between two different forms of IPV: intimate terrorism and situational couple violence. These corresponding forms of violence against women differentiate themselves in terms of the *lethalness* of the violence—the likelihood that it will produce severe injury or death—and the *level of control* in the relationship.

Intimate Terrorism: Johnson and his colleagues (Johnson and Ferraro 2000) describe **intimate terrorism** as "a partner's attempt to exert control over his partner using a broad range of power and control tactics, which include physical violence" (Leone et al. 2004).

Situational Couple Violence: In contrast, **situational couple violence** "does not exist within a general pattern of controlling behavior. This form of violence is not motivated by a desire to control and over power a partner or a relationship, but rather occurs when specific conflict situations escalate to violence" (Leone et al. 2004).

The strength of Johnson's framework is that unlike other theories, including feminist theory, he creates a framework that allows for the fact that not all violence may be the same. And certainly in our interviews, we met people whose relationships were highly conflictual—they fought, sometimes physically—but their fights could be understood in the context of conflict, and there were none of the other types of abuse present (sexual abuse, emotional abuse, or psychological abuse). Additionally, the violence was rarely severe, and it was generally perpetrated about equally. The weaknesses of Johnson's approach, similar to those associated with the family violence framework, are that, first, this distinction often blurs or hides the ways in which IPV is about gender and power and that when we look at lethality and injury and remove conflict as a required context, women are far more likely to be the victims and men the perpetrators, and, second, in many violent relationships, both types of violence—intimate terrorism and situational couple violence—exist. Last, we note that this approach is limited to attempting to explain only intimate partner violence and not other forms of family violence. This is not a weakness but a distinction.

Psychological Theories

We conclude our discussion of theories of intimate partner violence with a brief overview of psychological theories. Because we are sociologists and this book is rooted in the sociological tradition, we do not feel it is necessary to provide the reader with a strong working knowledge of these theories, but readers should be familiar with them.

Psychological theories of IPV were developed primarily through either experimentation by psychologists or research conducted by therapists whose work is limited to that context. Psychologists have long been interested in understanding why human beings engage in violence. This interest reached a peak in the 1960s following the fallout from World War II and the knowledge of the incredible atrocities perpetrated by the Nazis. One of the landmark studies on the psychology of violence was performed by Stanley Milgram (1974). In sum, Milgram recruited white middle-aged men to participate in a "learning" study. His subjects arrived at his lab and were told that they were part of a study that focused on techniques for improving learning; they would play the role of "teacher." The "student," played by a confederate of Milgram's, was seated in an adjacent room. The teacher could hear but not see the student. As the experiment began, Milgram introduced the teacher and student and showed the teacher that he was hooking the student up to a series of electrodes that would deliver electric shocks every time the student failed a task. He then closed the door and moved the teacher to his station, which included a "shocking" device, labeled from 5 volts to XXX. The experiment involved the teacher reading word pairs to the student. The student intentionally missed, and when he did, Milgram instructed the teacher to administer a shock (which was of course not real), and each subsequent miss required a more severe shock. Unbelievably, Milgram reported that 50 percent of the subjects went all the way up to the end of the scale and delivered the XXX shock. In the film that documents the experiments, we see the incredible anxiety on the faces of the subjects, their verbal resistance to Milgram, their ultimate complicity, and finally their intense relief when they realize that the student is fine and everything was just an act of theater.

The conclusion Milgram reaches is that under certain constrained circumstances, anyone can be propelled to perpetrate violence. Thus, extensions of Milgram's work would theorize that individuals who engage in any kind of family violence are not necessarily mentally ill, but rather are victims of contexts and pressures that lead them to engage in violence. More recently, the work of Philip Zimbardo (2008) confirms these basic findings.

Much of the psychological literature derived from counseling settings focused on batterers clearly identifies two predictors of family violence: mental health—such as the presence of anger and control problems or intermittent explosive disorder—and substance abuse. David Adams, a specialist in batterer intervention in the Boston program Emerge, argues that although battering is not typically a result of mental *illness*, it is a result of a mental health *issue* and must be treated rather than punished. Though we will not discuss interventions here, as these will be reserved for Chapter 13, these intervention models provide insight into the psychology of an individual who engages in IPV. Often batterers have anger management issues, they are unable to take the role of the other (Scully 1990), and their behavior is influenced by the use or abuse of alcohol and drugs. As Adams notes on the Emerge website: "While alcohol and other drugs can certainly escalate abuse, neither cause a batterer to abuse his partner. Substances will lower inhibitions, and many abusers believe they have less responsibility while using substances. Under the influence, abusers may have fewer barriers on how abusive they will be, so the abuse tends to be more violent."

Thus, in summary, psychological theories of violence in general (Milgram) and family violence in particular offer two critical concepts: first, that violence is not limited to individuals who have mental defects or mental illness (in fact, anyone under the right circumstances will engage in violence), and, second, violent behavior can result from mental health issues, including anger management problems and substance abuse, and it should thus be treated rather than criminalized. It is important to point out that both of these imply and psychologists generally agree that violence is *learned behavior*; it is rarely the result of capacities with which people are born and thereby destined.

THEORIES OF ELDER ABUSE AND CHILD ABUSE

The research on child and elder abuse often overlap, as do the theories developed to explain them. This is not surprising because the primary focus of scholars of child abuse and elder abuse is on individual explanations and categorizes most of the abuse as situational or acute rather than chronic. Because these scholars of these two specific types of family abuse have relied so heavily on each others' work, it makes sense for us to treat them together for the purposes of examining specific theories focused on child and elder abuse. A variety of theories have been developed specifically to explain elder abuse (Bonnie and Wallace 2003). One of the most popular is

situational theory. Situational theory is based on the assumption that the abuse itself is situational or acute rather than chronic and arises primarily from the overburdening of a caregiver. Scholars of child abuse have adopted this perspective as well (Gelles and Strauss 1988). Situational theory is appealing because it is based on intuitive assumptions, namely, that the majority of abuse occurs when caregivers are tired, stressed, overcommitted, and generally overburdened. And any of us who have been parents—as both the authors are—know how this feels and can relate to the parent who "loses" it as a result of being stressed and overburdened. This theory is also appealing because the research on both parenting and caregiving for the elder is full of empirical support for the notion that caregivers in either situation often are overburdened as they attempt to balance caregiving with other responsibilities like work. In fact, beginning in the mid-1990s family scholars developed the term *sandwich generation* to refer to adults in their forties (most often women) who were both parenting and caring for aging parents at the same time. Situational theory is particularly useful in thinking about situations such as this where there are simply too many demands on an individual and their frustrations are occasionally expressed through abusive or neglectful behavior or both.

Several additional theories have been used to explain elder abuse and have been adapted to research on child abuse as well. **Exchange theory** focuses on the role that patterns of dependency that exist in families play in abuse. These patterns are developed in family life and often continue across the life course. If these patterns have been unhealthy or harmful, as roles in the family switch from parents caring for children to adult children caring for aging parents, these patterns of abuse may continue in a new form.

Social learning theory is another major theory that has been used to explain both child and elder abuse. Social learning theory is based on the principle that children are socialized to behave in particular ways by socializing agents—parents, teachers, coaches, Scout leaders—and that once these behaviors are learned, they are part of an individual's "tool kit" and guide an individual's behavior. With regards to child abuse and elder abuse, the argument is essentially that when children grow up learning that conflict is resolved through hitting or that physical punishment is appropriate, then they are more likely to use these techniques when they are caregivers themselves—either to children or to their aging parents. Like situational theory, social learning theory is popular because it is intuitive and useful in explaining the high probability of intergenerational patterns of abuse.

The weaknesses of these specific theories are several. First, as with Johnson's typology for understanding intimate partner violence, these specific theories are limited to specific forms of family violence—elder abuse and child abuse—and do not offer a framework for understanding, analyzing, and explaining family violence as a unique phenomenon. Second, as with many of the other theories we have outlined in this chapter, these theoretical perspectives—situational theory, social learning theory, and exchange theory—are all individual-level theories and do not account for structural factors that shape elder and child abuse. So, for example, the focus on overburdened caregivers considers individuals' experiences with stress and treats this as a problem of individuals who are overburdened without attention to the role that status location plays in *structuring who* is overburdened (Hattery 2001); for example, single mothers, low-income families, and women in the sandwich generation are more likely to experience situational abuse caused by being overburdened than women who do not fall into these categories. Additionally, situational theory is of little use in explaining chronic abuse and abuse that is transmitted intergenerationally. Social learning theory suffers from additional weaknesses as well as the tendency to paint abusers as "bad people" rather than understanding the structural and individual forces that shape their behavior. For example, as horrific as the abuse wrought by a sex offender can be, in our interviews with sex offenders, we heard about their own experiences with horrific sexual abuse by their mothers' boyfriends and pimps (Hattery and Smith 2010). This knowledge does not lessen the impact of their abusive behavior, but it provides clues about how it came about.

Taken altogether, even though most scholars adhere to one specific theoretical paradigm and devote decades of research to test it and demonstrate its utility, many also acknowledge that the most effective way in which to understand family violence is to analyze it through a lens provided by taking a comprehensive approach that draws on the strengths of multiple theoretical approaches.

CONCLUSIONS

If the reader comes away with nothing else, we hope he or she finishes this chapter with a few key thoughts. First, the theories used to understand family violence are relatively underdeveloped for several key reasons. As noted in the previous chapter, defining violence in families as something worthy of attention is a relatively new development. As we alluded to here and as we will discuss in the next chapter, measuring family violence is contentious! Because the sociological model of theory and methods relies on the interplay between theory and methods, a lack of well-established theories to guide research will result in an ad hoc approach that will fail to generate the kinds of data necessary to confirm, reject, and advance the existing theoretical frameworks. Instead, these ad hoc approaches to research will result in a tendency to build ad hoc theories.

Second, though there are some scholars who align themselves exclusively with one theoretical paradigm or use only one method (e.g., Straus and the CTS), many scholars, ourselves included, have found that the most powerful and comprehensive explanations of family violence arise when scholars are not afraid to call on many different theoretical traditions and methodological approaches. In our own work, for example, we have found that there are useful aspects to conflict theory—especially that written by Frederick Engels—feminist theory, and the race, class and gender paradigm. The reader will see firsthand how we combine these approaches in subsequent chapters. We turn now to a discussion of the methods used to investigate family violence.

RESOURCES

Emerge: http://www.emergedv.com/
Milgram Experiments: http://www.youtube.com/watch?v=t2PGnHHnRMk

NOTE

1. Deborah King refers to this as "double jeopardy" (1988), and Maxine Baca Zinn and Bonnie Thorton Dill refer to it as the "matrix of domination" (2005).

BIBLIOGRAPHY

Acker, Joan. 2006. *Class Questions, Feminist Answers*. New York: Routledge.

Bianchi, Suzanne, John P. Robinson, and Melissa A. Milkie. 2007. *Changing Rhythms of American Family Life*. New York: Russell Sage Foundation.

Blumer, Herbert. 1969. *Symbolic Interactionism: Perspective and Method*. Berkeley and Los Angeles: University of California Press.

Bonnie, Richard J., and Robert B. Wallace. 2003. *Elder Mistreatment: Abuse, Neglect, and Exploitation in an Aging America*. Washington, DC: National Academies Press.

Brownmiller, Susan. 1975. *Against Our Will: Men, Women, and Rape*. New York: Simon and Schuster.

Calhoun, Craig J. 2007. *Sociology in America: A History*. Chicago: University of Chicago Press.

Engels, Friedrich. 1884. *The Origin of the Family, Private Property, and the State*. Introduction by Eleanor Leacock. New York: International Publishers.

Epstein, Cynthia. 2007. "Great Divides: The Cultural, Cognitive, and Social Bases of the Global Subordination of Women." *American Sociological Review* 72: 1–22.

Erickson, Rebecca. 2003. "The Familial Institution." In *Handbook of Symbolic Interactionism*, edited by L. Reynolds and N. Herman-Kinney, 511–538. Lanham, MD: Rowman and Littlefield.

Friedman, Thomas. 2006. *The World Is Flat: A Brief History of the 21st Century*. New York: Farrar, Straus, and Giroux.

Gelles, Richard J., and Murray A. Straus. 1988. *Intimate Violence*. New York: Simon and Schuster.

Griffin, Susan. 1979. *Rape: The Politics of Consciousness*. New York: Harper & Row.

Hattery, Angela. 2001. *Women, Work, and Family: Balancing and Weaving*. Thousand Oaks, CA: Sage.

_____. 2008. *Intimate Partner Violence.* Lanham, MD: Rowman and Littlefield.

Hattery, Angela J., and Earl Smith. 2007. *African American Families.* Thousand Oaks, CA: Sage.

_____. 2010. *Prisoner Reentry and Social Capital: The Long Road to Reintegration.* Lanham, MD: Lexington Books.

Hirschi, Travis. 1969. *Causes of Delinquency.* Berkeley and Los Angeles: University of California Press.

Johnson, Michael P., and Kathleen J. Ferraro. 2000. "Research on Domestic Violence in the 1990s: Making Distinctions." *Journal of Marriage and the Family* 62: 948–963.

King, D. 1988. "Multiple Jeopardy, Multiple Consciousness: The Context of a Black Feminist Ideology." *Signs* 14, no. 1.

Kristoff, Nicholas, and Sheryl WuDunn. 2009. *Half the Sky: Turning Oppression into Opportunity for Women Worldwide.* New York: Alfred A. Knopf.

Leone, Janel M., Michael P. Johnson, Catherine L. Cohan, and Susan E. Lloyd. 2004. "Consequences of Male Partner Violence for Low-Income Minority Women." *Journal of Marriage and Family* 66: 472–490.

Lin, N. 2000. "Inequality in Social Capital." *Contemporary Sociology* 29: 785–795.

MacKinnon, Catharine. 1991. *Toward a Feminist Theory of the State.* Cambridge: Harvard University Press.

Marx, Karl, Friedrich Engels, and Dirk Jan Struik. 1971. *Birth of the Communist Manifesto, with Full Text of the Manifesto, All Prefaces by Marx and Engels, Early Drafts by Engels, and Other Supplementary Material.* New York: International Publishers.

Merton, Robert K. 1938. "Social Structure and Anomie." *American Sociological Review* 3: 672–682.

_____. 1968. *Social Theory and Social Structure.* New York: Free Press.

Milgram, Stanley. 1974. *Obedience to Authority: An Experimental View.* New York: Harper.

Parsons, Talcott, and Robert Bales. 1955. *Family, Socialization, and the Interaction Process.* Glencoe, IL: Free Press.

Scully, Diana. 1990. *Understanding Sexual Violence: A Study of Convicted Rapists.* Boston: Unwin Hyman.

Smith, Earl. 2007. *Race, Sport, and the American Dream.* Durham, NC: Carolina Academic Press.

_____. 2008. "African American Men and Intimate Partner Violence." *Journal of African American Studies* 12: 156–179.

Straus, Murray A. 1999. "The Controversy over Domestic Violence by Women: A Methodological, Theoretical, and Sociology of Science Analysis." In *Violence in Intimate Relationships*, edited by X. B. Arriaga and S. Oskamp. London: Sage.

Straus, Murray A., Richard J. Gelles, and Christine Smith. 1990. *Physical Violence in American Families: Risk Factors and Adaptations to Violence in 8,145 Families.* New Brunswick, NJ: Transaction.

Sutherland, Edwin. 1924. *Criminology.* Philadelphia: Lippincott.

USA Today. 2003. "Study: Partners Blamed for One-Fifth of Violence Against Women." July 1.

Wacquant, Loic. 2001. "Deadly Symbiosis When Ghetto and Prison Meet and Mesh." *Punishment and Society* 3: 95–133.

Walker, Lenore E. 1984. *The Battered Woman Syndrome*. New York: Springer.

Ward, Lester Frank. 1963. *Lester Frank Ward: Selections from His Work*. New York: Crowell.

Weber, Max. 1949. *The Methodology of the Social Sciences*. Edited by Edward A. Shils and Henry A. Finch. Glencoe, IL: Free Press.

West, Candace, and Don H. Zimmerman. 1987. "Doing Gender." *Gender and Society* 1: 125–151.

Wilson, Williams J. 1996. *When Work Disappears: The World of the New Urban Poor*. New York: Alfred A. Knopf.

Wright, Erik O. 1997. *Class Counts: Comparative Studies in Class Analysis*. New York: Cambridge University Press.

Zimbardo, Phillip. 2008. *The Lucifer Effect: Understanding How Good People Turn Evil*. New York: Random House.

Zinn, Maxine Baca, and Bonnie Thornton Dill. 2005. "Theorizing Differences from Multicultural Feminism." In *Gender Through the Prism of Difference*, edited by M. B. Zinn, P. Hondagneu-Sotelo, and M. A. Messner, 23–28. Oxford: Oxford University Press.

Zuckerman, Harriet. 1998. "Accumulation of Advantage and Disadvantage: The Theory and Its Intellectual Biography." In *Robert K. Merton and Contemporary Sociology*, edited by Carlo Mongardini and Simonetta Tabboni. New Brunswick, NJ: Transaction Books.

4 Methods for Studying Family Violence

This chapter will be devoted to a discussion of the methodological approaches to studying family violence. In addition to outlining each approach, we will critique each, identifying its strengths and weaknesses. We will also provide the reader with examples of the outcomes of each type of research and provide resources—including data sets—where students can go to learn more and even conduct their own analysis.

OBJECTIVES

- To provide an overview of the methodological approaches that have been used to study family violence
- To provide an assessment of the strengths and weaknesses of each approach
- To provide the reader with access to sources of data so that they can explore family violence on their own

KEY TERMS

objectivity
generalizability
repeatability or replicability
experiment
random assignment
manipulation of independent variables
control of third variables
correlational
sampling
qualitative research
face-to-face interviews
ethnography

observational methods
epistemology
quantitative methods
survey research
National Violence Against Women
    (NAWA) Survey
random digit dialing
Bureau of Justice Statistics (BJS)
National Crime Victimization Survey (NCVS)
Uniform Crime Reports (UCR)
ecological fallacy
Conflict Tactics Scale

INTRODUCTION

One of the most important aspects of social science research is the methods that we use to gather empirical data. Whereas theory provides the framework for analyzing and interpreting what we see in the social world, "methods" ensure that when we collect empirical data in order to test hypotheses and determine the utility of theoretical frameworks, these data are collected systematically, rigorously, and in ways that are repeatable.

A BRIEF HISTORY OF SOCIOLOGICAL METHODS

Sociology is one of the youngest "sciences"—perhaps senior only to computer science—and thus draws heavily on the methods utilized by natural and other social

---

OBJECTIVITY, GENERALIZABILITY, AND REPEATABILITY

Objectivity: The absolute core tenet of the scientific method is objectivity. This means nothing short of removing the researcher from the process—much easier said than done in social science research! The reader who has taken even the most rudimentary natural science class at the high school level will be familiar with this core tenet. Objectivity relies on removing the researcher from the process by assigning the measurement or observation to instruments that can be calibrated. For example, disciplines such as chemistry rely heavily on perfectly calibrated titration equipment, and physics relies on perfectly calibrated scales. Measurement tools such as litmus paper, for example, are "responsible" for determining if a chemical reaction produces a base or an acid; this type of analysis is not left up to a human being who might otherwise "eyeball" the results and inaccurately assess the reaction. Fundamentally, objectivity is considered to be important because it prevents the scientist from generating data and results that intentionally confirm his or her hypothesis rather than allow the outcomes of the research to occur "naturally" and without the intent of the scientist being injected.

Generalizability: Another core tenet of the natural science method is the ability to generalize the findings from one sample to another. Simply put, this means that every time a chemist or biologist applies heat to water, it should boil at precisely 220 degrees Fahrenheit. This process should work with any sample of water, in any location, and always at the same temperature, not at 219 degrees or 221 degrees, but at precisely 220 degrees. The assumption is that when a finding is generalizable, then it is "real."

Repeatability: Repeatability or replicability is the notion that a finding can be repeated by any scientist under any condition. Similar to the notion of generalizability, which focuses on the replicability across different samples and conditions, repeatability focuses on the replicability across scientists. This is perhaps the primary test that confirms that a finding is "real"; if a scientist had inserted his or her own biases into the research—the opposite of objectivity—then another scientist, without the same biases, would not be able to replicate the findings.

and behavioral sciences in developing its own set of methods for research. Specifically, sociological methods have attempted to re-create the key tenets of natural science methods—objectivity, generalizability, and repeatability—in the social world.

MENDEL'S ETHICS

Gregor Mendel is probably best known for discovering the laws of inheritance as they relate to dominant and recessive genes. Mendel bred and cross-bred green (dominant) and yellow (recessive) pea plants and discovered that when cross-bred, the dominant gene is always expressed. Recessive traits are expressed only when the "parents" both carry a recessive gene. When both parents express the recessive trait (yellow), 100 percent of the offspring will express the recessive trait. When one parent expresses the dominant trait and both genes are dominant, then 100 percent of the offspring will express the dominant trait, even if the second parent carries a recessive gene.

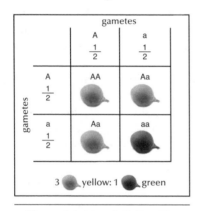

▲ **Figure 4.1** Mendel's Pea Plant Experiments

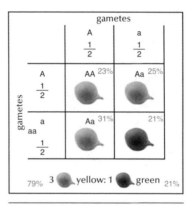

▲ **Figure 4.2** Mendel Revised

However, when both parents express the dominant trait but carry a recessive gene, 25 percent of the offspring will express the recessive trait.

Fisher concludes two important things: first, Mendel's law is right, and, second, Mendel was afraid that people would not believe his experiments unless the findings were "clean," 75 to 25, and thus he "fudged" his data in order to make a real finding more compelling. This is precisely the reason natural science and its younger sibling social science are based on the principle of objectivity.

There are several important issues that distinguish the natural sciences from the social and behavioral sciences that bear on methods. First, because the majority of social science research is conducted on living people, there are many restrictions on the types of research we can conduct relative to the natural sciences. For example, the hallmark of natural science research—the **experiment**—is often difficult to perform in the settings social scientists are the most interested in.

EXPERIMENTAL CONDITIONS

The experiment requires three conditions:

1. **Random assignment:** Random assignment refers to the process by which subjects are assigned to their conditions "randomly" rather than based on some quality or characteristic that they have. For example, in an experiment that involves both male and female subjects, the experimenter might flip a coin to determine which treatment condition each subject would receive. Because a coin flip is a random event, the researcher can be sure that the subject was assigned to the treatment or the control based on the coin flip, not his or her gender. In order to be certain that it is the independent variable and not something else that is causing a change in the dependent variable, two additional requirements must be met:

2. **Manipulation of the independent variable:** In order to isolate the cause of a change, the researcher must be controlling the variation in the independent variable and not allowing it to vary on its own. Recall our discussion of boiling water. In order to be sure that it was heat that was causing water to boil, early scientists had to apply more heat incrementally to the pot of water—and measure the temperature—in order to determine that heat is the cause of boiling water.

3. **Control of third variables:** Control of third variables allows the researcher to isolate the independent variable he or she is changing in order to be certain that it is the single cause of the change in the dependent variable. Again, returning to our discussion of water boiling, early scientists would have applied only heat and not allowed any other factor to vary—such as light or wind—in order to isolate heat as the single factor that causes water to boil.

For example, in order to truly test the intergenerational transmission of violence thesis, social scientists would have to identify hundreds of children at birth, randomly assign them to a condition—either exposure to violence in childhood or no exposure to violence in childhood—and then track their experiences with violence in adulthood. It should be obvious why this research could never be conducted, but for the record, so we can be perfectly clear about the pitfalls to social science research, let's review the concerns.

First, we as a society believe it is unethical to remove children at birth and assign them to live in different families. What parent would agree to this?! Second, it is unethical to *knowingly* expose children to violence. Third, it is unethical to know that adults are perpetrating violence against children or among themselves and not intervene. Thus, the experiment would be impossible to conduct. Yet from a methodological perspective, it is the *only* way to determine if exposure to violence in childhood *causes* children to grow up to perpetrate violence in adulthood. As a result, social science research that investigates this topic is limited to drawing **cor-**

relational conclusions—indications or evidence that events coexist—based on survey and interview research.

A second and important way in which sociological research is distinct from virtually all other sciences is that we believe that individuals that we study are infinitely unique. Whereas a chemist can assume that any sample of hydrochloric acid that he or she utilizes in the lab is chemically consistent, sociologists know that no two human beings—not even twins—are interchangeable. And although much psychological research on the brain assumes that with the possible exception of gender or race all brains work in the same way, sociologists believe that every aspect of one's life, from biology to gender to race to sexual orientation to religion to social class to geography, shapes us and our experiences. Thus, **sampling** is a critically important matter in sociology. Because we assume that none of our subjects are interchangeable, we seek to design sampling techniques that capture as much of the range of human experience as is relevant to our research questions. This is difficult, time-consuming, and very expensive, and these constraints further shape much of the way our research is conducted. And this is what makes sociological research unique from all other disciplines.

The majority of sociological research falls into two categories: interviews and surveys. Though sociologists also conduct experiments, analyze historical records, and engage in other methodological techniques, because the vast majority of research on family violence has relied on the two most common methods, we will focus on both and give examples of each where the reader can go to find original data to analyze.

INTERVIEWS AND QUALITATIVE RESEARCH

Qualitative research includes any of a number of techniques that involve researching phenomena in a natural setting or through interactions with individuals experiencing the phenomenon being researched. Qualitative methods generate descriptive data, rather than numbers, that are analyzed by identifying themes or "qualities" rather than utilizing typical statistical methods.

Researchers may conduct in-depth **face-to-face interviews** with victims and perpetrators of intimate partner violence, as we did (Hattery 2008; Hattery and Smith 2007). The interview method has several advantages over survey methods—which we will discuss below—in terms of understanding family violence. First, a seasoned interviewer can often build rapport with a subject rather quickly, and once trust is established, subjects will often disclose extremely painful and intimate details of their lives that are necessary in order to develop an accurate picture of the phenomenon. For example, often when students read the results of surveys conducted on intimate partner violence they seem able to develop an understanding of the frequency of violence in American society—or any other society—because the reports are based on the percentage of people who answer a question such as: "In the last year did your partner slap or hit you?" In contrast, reports derived from qualitative interviews that provide the details of a violent episode (see Browne 1989 and Hattery 2008 for examples) allow a student to understand the severity of the violence that is typical in violent families as well as provide the student an opportunity to develop sympathy for the victims whom they have grown to "know" through reading the intimate details of their lives. We illustrate with a brief example from our own research. A young African American man we interviewed told us about the violence he grew up with and recounted the day his mother shot his father:

She would go downtown and take out warrants out on him and restraining orders and he'll go back and one night she took and killed him, you know they got into a fight, and one night she took and got it, they got into a fight, and she grabbed a pistol and shot him in the head, and he got killed the day before I had to go to court and go to training school, and uh, I went to training school at the age of fourteen years old. I didn't know where my mother was at, she was going with guys that would sell her drugs, you know, she was doping, you know.

Eddie, fortysomething African American man, North Carolina

This type of thick description (Geertz 1974) paints a picture of the violence and allows the reader to experience—by reading—the violence as it was experienced by the victim. Additionally, presented in the subject's own words, the reader can interpret and analyze the data on his or her own. Last, this type of description is likely to be remembered far longer than a statistic, and this is often useful from the perspective of educating the public about a particular issue such as child abuse or intimate partner violence.

As implied above, another strength of interview data is that the questions posed by researchers are typically open-ended and allow for the subject to interpret the question through his or her own lexicon and respond based on that interpretation and in his or her own words. The challenge for the interviewer is often to guide the subjects, especially if they seem to misunderstand the intent of a question, as well as to generate "data" in the form of quotes that are clear and distinct enough to be published. For example, in our interviews with men and women who have recently been released from prison (Hattery and Smith 2010), the individuals we were interviewing were not terribly articulate, and many of their responses were not only "slang" but peppered with references to aspects of life in prison or drug use that would be meaningless to the reader not familiar with these terms. Thus, whereas the statistician is charged with analyzing complex survey data, the researcher who utilizes interview data must often provide a translation of the interview for the reader that manages to retain the intent and "voice" of the subject. Or, in the case of a battered woman we interviewed who had grown up as a child prostitute and was severely ashamed by it, the researcher must rely on nonverbal clues to be able to accurately interpret and translate the subject's experiences for the reader.

EVIE

The following is a quote from Evie, an African American woman we interviewed in North Carolina. She was in her fifties and was living in the battered women's shelter as she attempted to leave her abusive partner.

You can't imagine what it's like to have to sit on the laps of men when you are a ten-year-old. I hadn't even learned to ride a bike yet.

Analysis:
1. Reading the quote, separate from the remainder of the interview, one might not be struck by the quote and may conclude that it simply suggested that Evie was talking about an unfortunate childhood, one that was void of the simplest childhood pleasures: a bike.
2. Reading the entire interview, the researcher would have a context for the quote that might change the analysis. We provide some of the context here in order to demonstrate the ways in which contextualizing a single quote can significantly alter the interpretation.

Context: Evie grew up in a liquor house, or drink house. Liquor houses are a sort of unregulated social club; usually, they are created in a townhouse-style apartment in the public housing projects. In a typical liquor house, a man allows a woman (and often her children) to live rent free upstairs in exchange for her (and her children) running the liquor house on the main level of the home. And this arrangement usually involves an exchange for sex with the woman whenever he desires it.

When we inquired about the men who frequented the drink houses, Evie told us that the primary customers were white male executives from R. J. Reynolds Tobacco Company (our research was conducted in Winston-Salem, North Carolina). One cannot underestimate the degree to which Winston-Salem (note that two brands of Reynolds's cigarettes bear the names of the town) is a "company town" even today. These men would come during their lunch hour and at happy-hour time (usually four o'clock) to consume alcohol, smoke, and have sex before returning to their quiet, white middle-class neighborhoods.

3. Now that the analyst has a greater context for the original quote, he or she would come to the conclusion that Evie was most likely involved in some level of illegitimate activity. She confirms this with the following quote:

continues

EVIE *continued*

Some of the Reynolds men got paid on Wednesday. They'll come in, maybe, and buy . . . give me a five, and maybe they done bought four drinks and I would have the change. Sometimes they would sell fish in there. And a lot of times, some of the guys would get the cigarettes and change cigarettes for drinks.

4. Evie continues to describe her role in the liquor house:

And it was just like, I wonder that the people that lived out by a car [meaning out in the suburbs]. There was nice section. But they would come in our neighborhood, and drink, and buy women and stuff like that.

When combined with the initial quote, and with our observation of her nonverbal body language—Evie lowered her face, her eyes became dark and teared up, and she turned toward the female researcher and decidedly away from the male interviewer—we, as the researchers, came to the conclusion that Evie was in fact prostituted to the men in the liquor house, the customers. At ten years old, Evie was a victim of childhood prostitution.

In addition to interviewing, other qualitative techniques include ethnography and observational methods. In general, **ethnography**—which frequently involves both observations and interviews—and **observational methods** require the researcher to embed him- or herself in a naturalistic setting and observe behavior. Examples related to family violence would include volunteering at a shelter for battered women and their children and observing the experiences of the women and their children as they attempt to escape the violence or sitting in an emergency room at a local hospital to observe the kinds of injuries that victims of domestic violence or child abuse seek treatment for. Researchers might also observe in family court in order to better understand protective orders and child custody, or they may "ride along" with police officers responding to domestic or family violence calls. The former examples, such as volunteering over a long period of time in a shelter, would likely create opportunities for the researcher to conduct interviews as well. The latter examples, such as observing in an emergency room or courtroom or participating in "ride-alongs" with police offers, would likely not include interviews, primarily because the opportunity to have anything more than a short interaction—if they were allowed to interact at all—with the subjects would preclude the opportunity to develop rapport and conduct a formal interview. Additionally, these environments are not conducive to interviews because the researcher is relying on other parties whose professional concerns are not research—emergency room nurses whose job is to provide medical attention, judges whose job is to approve legal instruments, or police officers whose job is to protect the public—and who would not be willing to allow the researcher the time to conduct an interview. In all of these instances, these professionals' jobs require that they move on to the next case once they have met their professional goals: stabilized a patient, made an arrest, and the like. The only exception to this would be the possibility, if it were the focus of the research, to interview the professionals about their attitudes, observations, and so forth.

Strengths: In all of these cases that utilize ethnographic or observational methods, as with interview methods, the data that are collected and analyzed are rich and thick and provide the reader with a great deal of detail regarding the phenomenon. And though all data are sifted through the lens of the researcher, as demonstrated by the text box on the next page, one of the great strengths of qualitative methods is that the data generated were produced by the subjects themselves rather than their experiences being forced into a set of check boxes that may or may not really capture these experiences accurately. For example, as we shall see below when we discuss the Conflict Tactics Scale in detail, one of the main criticisms waged especially by feminist scholars is that the questions used to solicit experiences with domestic violence include contextualizing language. For example, "During the past year, how many fights with your partner resulted in (you/him/her) hitting, shoving, or throwing things at (you/him/her)?" Scholars, and feminist scholars in particular, who utilize qualitative methods to study family violence note that often the violence seemed to lack a context at all, especially for victims. Thus, questions that include a context may result in underreporting of violence, especially for victims who live in extremely violent households, like those described by Browne (1989), where violence is an almost daily event. Thus, the strengths of qualitative research—interviews, ethnography, and observational methods—are that these methods provide opportunities for researchers to see the violence or to hear about it in the subject's own voice and interpreted through his or her own framework. It also produces the kind of data that are very compelling to consumers—students, policy makers, funders—of the research.

Weaknesses: The primary weaknesses of qualitative methods are directly tied to the development of sociological methods: replicability and generalizability. Interviews, for example, are designed on the premise that questions need not be standardized and that interviewers can rephrase questions, adjust the order in which questions are asked, ask follow-up questions as well as those that seek clarification, or redirect the interviewee. As a result, though most interview schedules—the term we use to describe the flow of questions that will be asked during an interview—are standardized enough to cover the same material with each subject, because of the flexibility of the process of the interview, each interview will also produce data that are not standardized across each interview. Thus, not only are the interviews conducted by one interview team not necessarily standardized across the sample, but the likelihood that they can be reproduced—the key to replication—across samples with different interviewers is very low.

Additionally, a strong literature generated primarily by both feminist and minority scholars illustrates the role that the race and gender of the interviewer and interviewee play in the data that are generated in an interview (Hawkesworth and Hawkesworth 2006; Zuberi and Bonilla-Silva 2008). Specifically, Zuberi and Bonilla-Silva focus on the role that power plays in designing studies, choosing research questions, selecting samples, and interpreting data. They note that race and gender shape every aspect of research. And of importance to our discussion here is the fact that when the phenomenon itself is strongly shaped by power—in this case gender and age—the biases of the researcher can be even more damaging to the integrity of the study. For example, the criticism that feminist scholars have made about the contextualizing nature of survey questions as "conflict" is an example of this overall concern. Another example of a concern is related to the way in which rapport is established in an interview. If subjects feel that the researcher uses his or her power in ways that are coercive and thus blur the lines of consent, then the integrity of the interview itself and the data is compromised. Thus, especially in research with disadvantaged or marginalized populations—women, minorities, and gays and lesbians—researchers who have power need to be aware of this dynamic. One "solution" to dealing with this potential concern is to design diverse teams of researchers. This has both the effect of addressing the concerns about power as well as the potential to ease the establishment of rapport.

ANGELA HATTERY AND EARL SMITH AND AFRICAN AMERICAN WOMEN

Our own experience illustrates the ways in which diversity in the research team can produce better data than teams that are not diverse. As an African American man and a white woman, we often found that rapport developed with subjects based either on race or on gender. And in some cases, rapport would "switch" and "move" during the course of a single interview. For example, we were conducting an interview with an African American woman who was living in the shelter for battered women as a result of the violence in her home. When she talked about the violence she experienced at the hands of the man who claimed to love her or when she described the sexual abuse her stepfather perpetrated against her, she looked almost exclusively at Hattery, and it was as if Smith was not in the room. Later in the interview, when she described her neighborhood and the occasional white person she saw, she looked directly at Smith and said, "The only time white people come through the projects is when they are lost or looking to buy drugs." This example, though perhaps extreme, illustrates the concerns raised by Zuberi and Bonilla-Silva and others and makes a strong case for the importance of diverse research teams, especially when the issues being researched are themselves racialized and gendered.

Hawkesworth and Hawkesworth (2006) raise the more theoretical question of the distinction between methodology and epistemology. As noted above, research methods are a tool for ensuring that data are gathered or generated, analyzed, and reported in a manner that is as objective as possible and reduces the influence of the researcher's own implicit biases. In contrast, **epistemology** refers to "ways of knowing." As Hawkesworth and Hawkesworth argue, the way we "know" things is significantly shaped by our social location—our place in the world. For example, Hattery argues in her work on rape (Hattery and Kane 1995) that women in general have a more complex understanding of sexual abuse because for them it has always been part of their landscape. Parents warn young girls about the evils that lurk in dark alleys and more recently about the risks of date-rape drugs. By their teen years, most young women know of at least one friend who has experienced sexual abuse or rape, for the truth is that by that time perhaps one in five (20 percent) girls have been raped or abused. In contrast, parents, teachers, and other adults such as coaches rarely talk with young boys about sexual abuse or rape. The perception is that they are at no risk. And although this perception is wrong—as many as one in seven boys will be sexually abused by adulthood—the truth is that their risk is significantly less, which is at least part of the reason for the silence. Additionally, they are very unlikely to know about their friends—both boys and girls—who have been sexually abused or raped, in part because the perpetrators are almost always men, and as a result the victims often respond by limiting their relationships with boys and men and rarely disclose such a painful experience to someone who "looks" like the person who hurt and violated them. Thus, the landscape for girls and women is one where rape and sexual abuse are a constant, whereas the landscape for men is such that rape and sexual abuse are rarely visible.

This example illustrates that fact that regardless of their individual experiences, women and men have different "ways of knowing" about sexual abuse and rape. This knowledge is likely to influence every aspect of the research process, including the choice of research questions, the selection of subjects, the methods chosen, and the analysis. For example, especially with regards to questions about gender, feminist scholars are far more likely to employ qualitative methods such as interviewing. This may be in part because they are comfortable and experienced in listening to women talk about their experiences and partly, because of their more complex understanding of these phenomena, they deliberately choose to employ methods that will reveal rather than minimize these complexities. Despite the fact that one might draw the conclusion that this means that one must be an "insider" (Merton 1972) in order to study a phenomenon that is racialized or gendered—such as domestic violence—in fact, scholars such as Hawkesworth and Hawkesworth and Merton, as well as ourselves, use this to advocate for the importance of diverse research teams; we believe strongly that the best "body of research" is generated when a phenomenon is studied by people with various epistemological standpoints. And, we note, generally when issues that are gendered or racialized are studied, it is rarely the case that white men are excluded from studying these phenomena but rather that women and minorities are accused of being "too close" to the subject to be able to be objective. We argue that as long as objective methods are employed that reduce the subjectivity of the scientist, we do not need to worry about the "outsider" or "insider" status of the researcher.

The second key weakness of qualitative methods is generalizability. As we noted above, because sociologists operate under the assumption that all individuals are unique and that their experiences are strongly shaped by their social location and geographic location, we must accept the fact that a study performed on a small sample, typically in one geographic location, may not accurately represent the way in which the phenomenon actually occurs. For example, our interviews with twenty-five men and women who were returning home from prison to a midsize city in the Southeast in 2008 may not represent the experiences of men and women returning to rural South Dakota in 2010. And because qualitative research is very expensive and time-consuming to conduct, the samples are almost always small and almost always limited by geography. Imagine flying around the United States to interview a single person in each of the more than three thousand counties, for example. It would take a long time and be very expensive. In order to counteract this limitation, qualitative researchers often interpret their own data and draw conclusions in the context of other qualitative research with different populations, in different geographic locations, and over time as well as by comparing the "rates" they discover to those generated by studies that utilize national probability samples.

SURVEY RESEARCH AND QUANTITATIVE METHODS

> **Quantitative Methods:** techniques or strategies for collecting numeric data—and usually vast quantities of it—that require statistical techniques in order to analyze it.

The majority of sociological research that is performed, and this holds for family violence as well, is **survey research**. Survey research can be and is performed in many different ways, including the study of family violence, and in this section we will provide a brief overview of survey methods as well as examine several ways in which it has been utilized to generate data regarding family violence.

Most readers have probably taken a survey. The use of surveys begins early in our lives—often in school—and most of us probably do not even realize the extent to which we have participated in survey research. At the time of the writing of this book it is the spring of 2011, and we have just completed the biggest survey ever undertaken: the decennial US Census. The census is a set of survey questions designed to count the population and gather data on relationships, families, and housing that can then be used to create a portrait of the US population. The census allows us to estimate, for example, the racial composition of the US population, and to track trends in marriage rates and fertility, as well as phenomena such as home ownership.

◄ **Figure 4.3**
The 2010 Census Form

Source: http://www.census.gov/schools/pdf/2010form_info.pdf

On the other end of the scale, many or perhaps most of us have completed surveys about who we are likely to vote for in the next election, for example, or how likely we are to buy a new car or some other product in the next six months. These types of surveys—often only a single question—are the hallmark of political science and market research. And college students are certainly accustomed to surveys, as all incoming students are typically surveyed about their social behavior—including their use of alcohol and drugs—and they are often surveyed about potential changes on campus, including dining plans or housing.

Survey research involves two key elements: designing the survey itself so that the questions asked generate data that researchers can use to address larger research questions and sampling. When constructed properly, samples of as few as 1,000 can predict within 2 or 3 percentage points the outcome of national elections. However, in order to produce this level of reliability and generalizability, the measurement and sampling must be extremely well designed, and when they are not, which is often the case, data that are significantly flawed are nonetheless entered into the public discourse and taken as fact. We will illustrate this point later when we critique specific surveys that are used to generate data on family violence.

SURVEYS AND FAMILY VIOLENCE

There are two types of surveys that are used to generate data about various forms of family violence: self-report research and crime reports. Because they have different purposes, they generate different types of data. We begin with an overview of each and then provide information so that interested students and researchers can access this data themselves.

Scholars who are interested in using survey methods to study family violence typically intend to take advantage of the strengths of survey design: replicability and generalizability. Thus, they design surveys with closed-ended questions that require respondents to choose from a fixed number of predetermined responses. By developing measures and pretesting them in different populations, researchers can be sure that the questions they ask will be interpreted nearly the same way by each respondent, and thus if used repeatedly and in different populations, these items should measure the same thing. We illustrate with an example from the **National Violence Against Women (NVAW) Survey** (Tjaden and Thoennes 2000).

In the last twelve months has your partner ever hit you with an object?

Yes   No

As the reader can see, this question seems very straightforward and should elicit the same response from *any person* who has been hit with an object. Thus, the survey meets the standard of replicability that is so heavily valued in the natural sciences. In order to generate responses that are generalizable, a sample must be constructed that is representative of all those people living in the United States. The NVAW Survey utilized one of the most common and powerful sampling designs in order to gather data from a nationally representative sample of men and women. This method is referred to as **random digit dialing**, or RDD. Random digit dialing combines the survey with computer technology that aids in both the sampling and the administration of the survey. In short, the survey is loaded into a computer system, and a trained phone interviewer administers the survey to respondents over the telephone. When the interviewer is ready to conduct an interview, he or she instructs the computer to randomly generate a telephone number, which is then dialed by the computer. This phone number is generated by randomly selecting a number for each of the ten digits. Based on this design the variation of conceivable ten-digit number combinations that can be generated is enormous! And because the phone numbers are generated randomly, any of us has the same probability for having our phone number called as the next person. This is the biggest strength to this design because it ensures that no group of people can be intentionally or unintentionally left out of the study. Additionally, because phone numbers are assigned in a manner that is also "random"— other than the fact that area codes and some prefixes indicate a certain geographic region—and all numbers are equally likely to be generated by the computer, we can be sure that everyone has the *same probability* of being included in the study. An additional strength, which is especially important in the twenty-first century, is the fact that because phone numbers are generated through a random digit process rather than by using phone books or other phone listings, the sample will include unlisted phone numbers as well as cell phone numbers, thus ensuring that young people, for example, who may have cell phones and not "landlines," will be as likely to be surveyed as older folks. The one group that is excluded by this design is people who do not have phones. Thus, there is a social class bias to this design, though in terms of surveying the very poor, sociologists have yet to design something better.

There are a couple of drawbacks to this design that are of varying consequence. First, because the numbers are generated randomly, some percentage of these will not actually be phone numbers, or they may be phone numbers to large institutions or offices—for example, the general phone number for the University of Wisconsin Hospital. Obviously, the interviewer would realize that the operator answering the phone is not an eligible subject, based on this sampling design, and would apologize for taking up her or his time and hang up. This is a not a major concern, but it does mean that time will be spent that fails to generate a usable survey. Though not always the case, this survey in particular—the NVAW Survey—has a Spanish-language option, but it does not offer the administration of the survey in any other language. Thus, non-English- or non-Spanish-speaking individuals, though they will be included in the sample, will not be able to participate in the study. As the population of the United States continues to become increasingly diverse, scientists who develop surveys would be best served by developing Spanish versions of any survey—as Hispanics, according to the 2010 census, now make up nearly 20 percent of the US population—as well as survey options in other languages. When only available in

English, a survey's generalizability is significantly limited to the English-speaking US population.

Last, and of more serious concern to this study—and indeed any study of intimate partner violence—is the possibility that a battered woman is selected, but when the interviewer calls she is unable to participate or participate honestly because she is being carefully watched by her abusive partner. Thus, there is some possibility that underreporting of violence may occur, and it is likely to occur in the most violent and abusive homes that also include a great deal of emotionally controlling behavior. This in turn becomes problematic because it may lead to an underestimate of the most severe violence that is occurring in families in our communities.

The second category of surveys that generate data on family violence is conducted by government and law enforcement agencies. In some instances, these surveys are designed specifically to gather information on family violence, and in others they are part of the larger reporting system in which law enforcement agencies are required to participate. For example, the **Bureau of Justice Statistics (BJS)**, the government clearinghouse for all data related to crime, the criminal justice system, law enforcement, and corrections, conducts the **National Crime Victimization Survey (NCVS)** every six months. The major source of information on all types of criminal victimization, the survey involves contacting one hundred thousand persons aged twelve or over who are surveyed either in person or by telephone about their experiences as victims of crime. Demographic data on the victim and the offender (if known) are collected as well as information about the relationship between the victim and the offender, the victimization itself, and whether the victim reported the crime to law enforcement. Though it focuses on all types of victimization, including being the victim of a robbery or stranger assault, it does contain data on various types of family violence, including domestic violence, sexual abuse, and child abuse.

This type of crime survey suffers from the same type of threats that other surveys do, namely, the exclusion of small pockets in the population who may not have access to a telephone or speak a language in which the survey is being conducted. Additionally, the primary flaw of this type of survey in estimating levels of family violence is that it requires the respondent to conceptualize or frame her or his experience as a "crime." In many cases of family violence, the victims do not frame their experiences as crimes. This can occur for a variety of reasons, including the fact that they simply may not believe the behavior they are experiencing constitutes a crime. For example, a victim of child abuse may believe that his or her parents have a "right" to engage in physical forms of discipline and that his or her experience does not constitute a crime. Second, it is not uncommon for victims of family abuse, both child abuse and domestic abuse, to have reported the violence, sometimes even to a law enforcement agent, only to have the complaint dismissed. Thus, they may assume, usually wrongly, that their experiences do not "qualify" as crimes when in fact they do. Taken together, these design issues will result in under-, rather than over-, reporting of family violence. And often the underreporting leads to severe underestimates that, when used by funding agencies to allocate resources to agencies serving victims of family violence, will result in the underfunding of much-needed resources.

The third type of "survey" involves the reporting that all law enforcement agencies are required by law to perform. The **Uniform Crime Reports** require that all law enforcement agencies, including municipal police departments and county sheriff offices, send a "report" each month directly to the Federal Bureau of Investigation (FBI). Though these reports include "crime counts"—how many crimes of various types were reported in the previous month—they also include data on crimes cleared, data on persons arrested (age, race, gender), characteristics of homicides and assaults, and homicides of police officers. As an aside, as a result of political pressure, these reports also contain data on each and every "stop" an officer makes. These data are used to track racial differences in "stops" and arrests or what we commonly refer to as racial profiling (Hattery and Smith 2007).

STRENGTHS OF SURVEY RESEARCH

As noted above, one of the primary strengths of survey data is the fact that standard questions offer the possibility for replication. For example, the Conflict Tactics Scale (which we will discuss at length below) has been administered to tens of thousands of individuals over a period of thirty or so years. This allows researchers to develop reliable gauges of trends. For example, has the physical abuse of children increased or decreased over time? Have boys become more vulnerable to child sexual abuse since the 1970s? And, if so, does this represent an actual change in the phenomenon or a change in the willingness of boys to report sexual abuse? This is a very important characteristic of survey research that contributes significantly to our understanding of various types of family violence.

Of equal or perhaps even greater importance is the fact that survey research allows scholars and policy makers to estimate the prevalence of various types of family violence both overall and in distinct populations. Having some ability to estimate how often violence is occurring and who the victims and perpetrators are is essential for many reasons. First, just like with disease, it is important to understand the level of violence that is occurring in our families and homes. Second, in order to adequately staff a variety of agencies, from shelters for battered women to emergency rooms to domestic violence units in police departments, we need an estimate of the rate of violence in our local communities. Third, nonprofit agencies that serve victims and provide intervention services for offenders rely on these numbers not only for staffing purposes but also for seeking the funding necessary to provide these services. In order to justify proposals that seek tens of thousands of dollars in both federal and private funding, agencies need to provide an estimate of the need that exists for their services. Last, these types of data are the best way of estimating difference among populations, especially race, gender, age, sexual orientation, religious, and geographic groups. For example, the most recent data on domestic violence indicate that for the first time ever, the rate of domestic violence is significantly higher among African American women than among white women (Violence Policy Center 2008), an issue we will explore at greater length in subsequent chapters.

WEAKNESSES OF SURVEY RESEARCH

Of course, the weaknesses of survey research are the flip side of the strengths of interview data, namely, that numbers tell a different kind of "story" than the stories told by individual men, women, and children. When we read a statistic that one in four women will experience an episode of domestic violence in her lifetime, we may be shocked. But that shock is soon forgotten if we cannot connect that statistic to the actual experiences of battered women. Thus, one of the weaknesses of survey data is that surveys are designed to elicit standard responses to short questions or statements and very rarely include the kinds of questions that will elicit detailed responses. In fact, one critique of many surveys designed to estimate family violence is that they do not include measures of frequency. So, as noted above, we may gather data on how many people have been hit with an object by their partner in the past twelve months, but we cannot distinguish those who were hit only once and those who were hit many times in a single episode let alone in many different episodes. And though violence is violence, it is clear that it can be qualitatively different, and we should be designing survey questions and responses that better capture these qualitative differences. Another way to think about this is the adage that "a picture is worth a thousand words." Qualitative data, though built on words, generate a "picture" in ways that quantitative data rarely can.

As noted above, one of the main potential weaknesses of all types of survey research is the very real possibility of inaccuracies in reporting. And though some types of surveys or survey populations may be predisposed to suffering from overreporting, in all cases of research on family violence, the real concern is in underreporting. There is less to be concerned about when the underreporting is not specifically linked to the phenomenon of family violence, but there is reason to be concerned when it is. So, as noted previously, if the context of the survey itself (as is the case with the NCVS) or the questions (as with the Conflict Tactics Scale) shape the types of incidents that victims and perpetrators report and if this results in underreporting, then the data that are generated will be *less accurate* than we anticipate and in ways that we cannot adjust for. Additionally, as noted with regards to the NVAW Survey, if the design relies on calling household phone numbers, we can assume that the greatest risk for underreporting will be *directly related to the experiences of violence*; namely, the surveillance that many severely battered women experience will prohibit them from responding to the survey. Moreover, when conclusions about the prevalence of violence and the levels of it are based on these reports, then we will be underestimating the problem and underfunding our responses to it.

Last, we simply want to point out a rarely discussed but extremely common error that people make when interpreting and applying survey data. The term **ecological fallacy** describes this error, which involves the attempt to predict individual experiences or outcomes from aggregate-level data. So, for example, just because we know that one in four women will experience an episode of domestic violence in her lifetime, and that this rate increases for women who are poor, are nonwhite, marry young, have more than the average number of children, and live with a partner who abuses alcohol or drugs, we cannot predict the likelihood that an individual with these traits will be abused. So, if you are reading this book and you have these traits, all we know is that people like you have a higher risk for being a victim, but we cannot predict the likelihood that *you as an individual person* will be victimized. Thus, we need to be very cautious when we attempt to generalize these types of findings to individuals in their own lives.

CONFLICT TACTICS SCALE

The **Conflict Tactics Scale** is the most widely utilized and most controversial of the large-scale surveys that have been utilized to measure family violence. Developed by Murray Straus and Richard Gelles in the early 1970s, this was the first attempt to develop a tool that could be used to measure the prevalence of family violence nationally. Straus and Gelles, who are trained as psychologists, have primarily conducted their research on samples of college students. However, according to Straus (1999), the CTS has been administered in more than one hundred empirical studies. We were unable to find any instances in which the survey was administered to a nationally representative sample. Rather, the CTS seems to be utilized most often by psychologists using college samples and therapists who administer it in a therapy setting. Thus, one shortcoming of the actual implementation of the CTS is that any findings generated through its use may not represent the experiences of the majority of adults living in the United States. As we know, college students represent a very small subset of Americans—a subset that is both "whiter" and wealthier than the overall population. Additionally, though dating violence is on the rise and an issue we will be exploring in subsequent chapters, the majority of intimate partner violence is perpetrated and experienced in adulthood, and thus a college student sample will certainly underestimate the prevalence based on the prematurity of the sampling.

As Straus himself points out in response to criticisms of the CTS, it was not designed to measure power or intent but is strictly limited to measuring behavior. On the one hand, this is quite important because it means that the findings are based on things that happened rather than on one person's assessment of why the behavior happened or what caused it. Below are some of the items that are found in the CTS.

When you had an argument with your partner in the past year, how many times have you threatened to hit or throw something at him or her?

Never   Once   Twice   3–5 times   6–10 times   11–20 times   more than 20 times

How many times has he or she threatened to hit or throw something at you?

Never   Once   Twice   3–5 times   6–10 times   11–20 times   more than 20 times

There are many critiques of the CTS. Feminists and others critique the CTS for *not* measuring perceived intent. They argue that although all hits may be the same, a hit in the context of an argument might indicate something different about the couple's relationship than a hit that comes out of nowhere. The former would likely be an indicator of what Johnson and colleagues refer to as situational couple violence, and the latter might indicate a case of intimate terrorism (Leone et al. 2004). Similarly, the CTS includes measures of injury, but it does not measure the extent of an injury. Thus, incidents that require a bandage will be categorized alongside those that involve broken bones, emergency room visits, and even surgery. The same is true of frequency. The CTS does not measure multiple incidents of the same behavior; it measures only if the behavior occurred at all. And, last, as noted above, contextualizing the violence for the respondent by using the term *conflict* or the phrase *when you had an argument* is far more likely to capture situational couple violence—which by definition is violence that occurs during an argument or is the result of conflict—rather than the more serious violence, which seems to "come out of the blue," that is associated with intimate terrorism.

Thus, studies that rely on the CTS alone, by failing to distinguish between certain types of violence, frequency, level of injury, and so on, may tend to overestimate situational couple violence and underestimate intimate terrorism. This is problematic because intimate terrorism is far more likely to result in an escalation of violence that may result in the very real need for a victim to escape, serious injury, and even homicide.

The reader will recall from the discussion of theory in Chapter 3 that feminist theorists make specific critiques of family violence research and the CTS in particular. Here we summarize the feminist critique of the CTS.

The Conflict Tactics Scale (CTS) is a set of questions designed to measure conflict and violence in families (Straus 1999). Yet feminists argue that at least some incidents of intimate partner violence do not occur around a conflict. In interviews with battered women we (Hattery 2008; Hattery and Smith 2007) and our colleagues (Browne and Finkelhor 1986; Browne 1989; Koss et al. 1994) document many incidents of violence—some of it very severe—that seemed, according to the victims, to arise out of nowhere. In these cases women report that their male partners simply came home and started beating on them, for example, and that there was no context of conflict or argument for the violence. Thus, feminist theorists argue that the CTS underreports the intimate partner violence women experience because it focuses the questions only around occasions of conflict. Additionally, feminist theorists argue that much of the violence that is perpetrated by women and reported in the CTS is violence that must be characterized as self-defense. For example, we interviewed a woman who was court-ordered to an intervention program for batterers. Her husband had her arrested after she bit his arm severely, and the judge ordered her to attend the intervention program. In our interview she revealed, and we confirmed this with the staff of the program, that she bit her husband's arm while he was banging her head against the dashboard while he was driving! The CTS would have captured her behavior as an incident of female-perpetrated violence—because it also met the criterion of occurring within the context of an argument—but it would not have captured the fact that this behavior was self-defensive, not an attack. Thus, feminists argue that complete gender neutrality and the limiting of experiences with violence to those that occur in the context of conflict—as opposed to including violence that just seems to come out of nowhere—both arise from the tendency by family violence scholars to ignore the system of gendered inequality (patriarchy) that undergirds most patterns of violence in the United States, and indeed globally (see Acker 2006; Epstein 2007). Additionally, family violence scholars who employ tools like the CTS fail to distinguish acts of self-defense from attacks—thus overestimating both women's violence and situational couple violence—and in doing so they conclude, as Johnson and his colleagues do (Leone et al. 2004), that situational couple violence is the more prevalent type of intimate partner violence and that the more severe form, intimate terrorism, is rare, which contradicts the findings of other quantitative research as well as qualitative, interview-based research. This is an important weaknesses in family violence theory that unfortunately infiltrates both the academic literature on family violence as well as the media—which loves these types of reports—which then shape, inaccurately, the perceptions of the general public, including many of those in professions who deal with intimate partner violence, including police officers, judges, and divorce attorneys (Martin 2005).

CONCLUSIONS

We have always believed in the triangulation of methods: we look to both survey data and interview data in order to better "see" the face of family violence. Because different methods have different purposes as well as different strengths and weaknesses, rather than preferencing one over the other, we believe the best approach is to take the best of each and combine these "bests" in order to create a more complex picture of family violence. This process can be performed by individual scholars—and in subsequent chapters the reader will see how we accomplish this—as well as by scholars working together in the larger field. For example, edited books and journals that take family violence, child abuse, or intimate partner violence as their focus would be best served by including chapters and research essays in such a way as to represent the range of methodological and theoretical approaches. By incorporating the best and most advanced statistical measures of family violence alongside the more compelling "stories" generated by interviews and observation, the academic field, the practitioner, and the student can develop the most comprehensive understanding of family violence.

Last, because of the various ways in which quantitative data on family violence are collected and because of the relative accessibility of much of the quantitative data, we strongly advocate this approach for the student or scholar who wishes to see for him- or herself. We find that, although it may be tedious, the best way to accurately estimate the prevalence of family violence that is *reported* is to build cross-checking tables from all of the sources of data available—the BJS, NCVS, and UCR. Estimates can then be derived from data from survey sources such as the NVAW Survey and the CTS. We note that some websites developed by policy and advocacy groups have done this as well, and some data may be available in a form that is "ready to use." The Appendix contains a review of the data sources that can be accessed by individual researchers and students. These are excellent sources of data for research papers. They can provide the most recent data for funding reports, and because several surveys allow the researcher to conduct his or her own analysis, they can be an excellent source for an honor's or master's thesis.

Studying family violence is a challenging but very rewarding experience, and we look forward to taking the reader through the phenomenon in the next several chapters.

RESOURCES

Inter-University Consortium for Political and Social Research (ICPSR): http://www
.icpsr.umich.edu/icpsrweb/ICPSR/index.jsp
The CTS is available at the following website: http://www.friendsnrc.org/download
/outcomeresources/toolkit/annot/conts.pdf
The Bureau of Justice Statistics: http://bjs.ojp.usdoj.gov/
The UCR data are available at the FBI website: http://www.fbi.gov/ucr/ucr.htm

Intimate Partner Violence

National Coalition Against Domestic Violence: http://www.ncadv.org/
United States Department of Justice Office on Violence Against Women: http://www
.ovw.usdoj.gov/

Many states also have websites for data related to intimate partner violence inside the state.

Child Abuse

National Children's Advocacy Center: http://www.nationalcac.org/
Prevent Child Abuse America: http://www.preventchildabuse.org/index.shtml
National Children's Alliance: http://www.nationalchildrensalliance.org/

Elder Abuse

Center of Excellence on Elder Abuse and Neglect: http://www.centeronelderabuse.org/page.cfm?pgid=7
National Committee for the Prevention of Elder Abuse: http://www.preventelderabuse.org/communities/advocacy.html

BIBLIOGRAPHY

Acker, Joan. 2006. *Class Questions, Feminist Answers.* New York: Routledge.
Browne, Angela. 1989. *When Battered Women Kill.* New York: Free Press.
Browne, Angela, and David Finkelhor. 1986. "Impact of Child Sexual Abuse." *Review of the Research Psychological Bulletin*: 66–77.
Epstein, Cynthia. 2007. "Great Divides: The Cultural, Cognitive, and Social Bases of the Global Subordination of Women." *American Sociological Review* 72: 1–22.
Geertz, Clifford. 1974. *Myth, Symbol, and Culture.* New York: W. W. Norton.
Hattery, Angela J. 2008. *Intimate Partner Violence.* Lanham, MD: Rowman and Littlefield.
Hattery, Angela J., and Emily W. Kane. 1995. "Men's and Women's Perceptions of Non-consensual Sexual Intercourse." *Sex Roles* 33: 785–802.
Hattery, Angela J., and Earl Smith. 2007. *African American Families.* Thousand Oaks, CA: Sage.
———. 2010. *Prisoner Reentry and Social Capital: The Long Road to Reintegration.* Lanham, MD: Lexington Books.
Hawkesworth, Mary E., and M. E. Hawkesworth. 2006. *Feminist Inquiry: From Political Conviction to Methodological Innovation.* New Brunswick: Rutgers University Press.
Koss, M. P., L. A. Goodman, A. Browne, L. F. Fitzgerald, G. P. Keita, and N. F. Russo. 1994. *No Safe Haven: Male Violence Against Women at Home, at Work, and in the Community.* Washington, DC: American Psychological Association.
Leone, Janel M., Michael P. Johnson, Catherine L. Cohan, and Susan E. Lloyd. 2004. "Consequences of Male Partner Violence for Low-Income Minority Women." *Journal of Marriage and Family* 66: 472–490.
Martin, Patricia Yancey. 2005. *Rape Work: Victims, Gender, and Emotions in Organization and Community Context.* New York: Routledge.

Merton, Robert K. 1972. "Insiders and Outsiders: A Chapter in the Sociology of Knowledge." *American Journal of Sociology* 78: 9–47.

Straus, Murray A. 1999. "The Controversy over Domestic Violence by Women: A Methodological, Theoretical, and Sociology of Science Analysis." In *Violence in Intimate Relationships*, edited by X. B. Arriaga and S. Oskamp. London: Sage.

Tjaden, Patricia, and Nancy Thoennes. 2000. *Full Report of the Prevalence, Incidence, and Consequences of Violence Against Women: Findings from the National Violence Against Women Survey*. Washington, DC: US Department of Justice.

Violence Policy Center. 2008. "When Men Murder Women: An Analysis of 2006 Homicide Data." Washington, DC: Violence Policy Center.

Zuberi, Tukufu, and Eduardo Bonilla-Silva. 2008. *White Logic, White Methods: Racism and Methodology*. Lanham, MD: Rowman and Littlefield.

5 Abuse Across the Life Course

Elder Abuse

Santa Clara County
By John Coté, *Chronicle* Staff Writer, March 8, 2008

A Los Gatos doctor was sentenced Friday to a year in jail for falsely telling an 87-year-old patient he had prostate cancer and convincing him to undergo unnecessary therapy in which tiny radioactive rods were inserted into him with needles.

Ali Moayed, 41, was also accused of falsifying pathology reports for two other patients and recommending they undergo the treatment, known as brachytherapy. Moayed's deception was uncovered before those two men had the procedure, Santa Clara County prosecutors said. All three instances were in 2005. . . . Moayed received about $5,000 in insurance payments for the treatment.

—*SAN FRANCISCO GATE,* http://articles.sfgate.com/2008-03-08 /bay-area/17165621_1_prostate-cancer-radioactive-seeds-butler

This chapter will focus on the abuse of the elderly, primarily by their children, but also by nonrelative caregivers in both the home setting and institutional settings. We will review the research on elder abuse and the laws that deal with elder abuse and provide the reader with a conceptual framework for understanding the significance of elder abuse. As will be the case in all chapters, we will not limit our discussion to physical abuse but will include lengthy discussions of psychological abuse—especially of individuals suffering from dementia or Alzheimer's—and financial abuse.

OBJECTIVES

- To familiarize the reader with the changing demographics of the US population, specifically with regards to age
- To familiarize the reader with the trends in life expectancy and health in later life
- To familiarize the reader with trends in caregiving patterns for the aging
- To expose the reader to the abuse of elderly by their children

- To expose the reader to the abuse of elderly by nonrelative caregivers in both home and institutional settings
- To expose the reader to various types of elder abuse, including physical, psychological, and financial
- To examine the ways in which elder abuse is being dealt with by law enforcement and legal and social welfare institutions
- To offer some ideas for the prevention and early intervention of elder abuse

KEY TERMS

age pyramid
life expectancy
sandwich generation
financial abuse
neglect
active neglect
passive neglect
self-neglect
physical abuse
psychological abuse

ageism
sexual abuse
psychological model
social learning theory
symbolic interaction theory
social exchange theory
situational theory
ecological theory
feminist theory

INTRODUCTION

As we noted in our discussion of the history of various types of abuse (Chapter 2), elder abuse is relatively recent: both as a phenomenon and as a social problem. As is the case with all forms of family violence, elder abuse has long been invisible; hidden from view by the fact that it most often occurred in the privacy of one's home—either the caregiver's or the victim's. And though we now have a much greater awareness of elder abuse, our ability to estimate its prevalence is limited by the fact that the majority of elderly victims continue to be cared for and abused in the privacy of the home. That said, it is critical to develop an understanding of both the prevalence of elder abuse and the changing demographics that impact the rate of elder abuse. We begin by discussing the changing demographics.

CHANGING DEMOGRAPHICS

One important dimension of elder abuse, its history, and its current prevalence is the changing age structure of the United States, especially across the twentieth century and into the first decade of the twenty-first century. At the beginning of the twentieth century, the largest portion of the US population were children under the age of eighteen. The second-largest group were people who in 1900 would have been defined as "middle-aged," and by far the smallest proportion of the US population was aging or elderly. In contrast, as birthrates have steadily declined and life expectancy has steadily increased—a matter we will discuss in the next paragraph—the US population of today is more evenly spread across age categories, with just as many young people (under age eighteen) as those over age fifty-five. Largely as a result of the increased life expectancy that most Americans have experienced, it is not until the oldest groups among the elderly, those over age eighty, that we see any major decrease in the size of the population.

An **age pyramid** is an excellent visual way to illustrate the changes in the composition of a population. The age pyramids shown in Figures 5.1 and 5.2, one from 1900 and the other from 2000, illustrate clearly the shifts and trends in the US population by age. In 1900 the pyramid is truly a pyramid, with the base, composed of the youngest members of our population, being the largest, and the top, the elderly, being the smallest. In 2000 the age "pyramid" is not really a pyramid at all but more like an hourglass; the hourglass shape indicates that currently the US population has *nearly* equal proportions of citizens in every age category except at birth and after about age fifty-five, at which point we see the age categories shrinking. Thinking toward the future, as birthrates continue to decline and life expectancy continues to increase, demographers predict that by midcentury or sooner, the US population will be most well illustrated by an inverted pyramid. We note there that the age "pyramid" for the European Union has already begun to shift from an hourglass shape very vaguely toward the shape of an inverted pyramid, and we anticipate a similar shift in the US population as well.

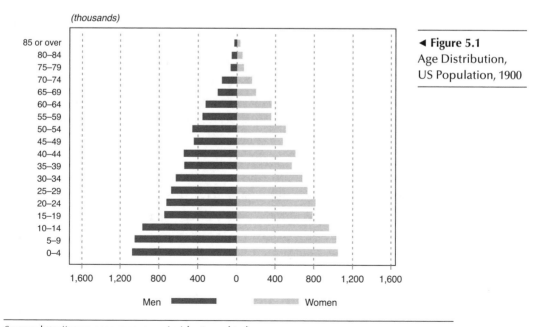

◀ **Figure 5.1**
Age Distribution,
US Population, 1900

Source: http://www.censusscope.org/us/chart_age.html

▶ **Figure 5.2**
Age Pyramid,
2000

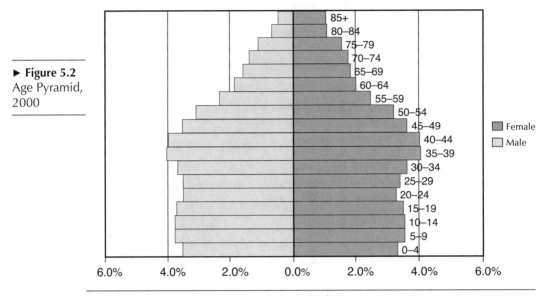

Source: http://www.censusscope.org/us/chart_age.html

What does all of this mean with regards to elder abuse? First, it helps to explain a part of the *history* of elder abuse. As noted in Chapter 2, in addition to the fact that elder abuse had not been defined and that it was largely hidden from public view and considered a private family matter, it is also true that a very small percentage of the population lived to become elderly. And if we assume that only a small fraction of elders will be abused, the prevalence of elder abuse was likely very low for the first half of the twentieth century simply because to live long enough to be considered elderly was indeed a rare event.

Today, as the population of elders continues to grow, the prevalence of abuse will undoubtedly increase. Quite simply, there are more potential victims. Additionally, there are a number of changes that produce key stressors that increase the likelihood of elder abuse, and we will discuss these below. That said, one of the important lessons we can and should draw from the changes in the age pyramids is that as the pyramid transitions from the hourglass shape we see today to eventually—as birthrates continue to decline and life expectancy continues to expand—something resembling an inverted pyramid, the number of people needing elder care will increase, while the number of people available to provide care and pay for it will dramatically decrease. This fact alone suggests that the age structure of a society itself shapes the likelihood of elder abuse and its prevalence. Despite acknowledging elder abuse, educating individuals about it, and the existence of prevention programs, the likelihood that it will continue to increase is high given the limited human resources—family members and potential care providers—that are available for each aging person in the population.

CHANGING LIFE EXPECTANCY

Among the best indicators of the changes in the health and well-being of Americans across the twentieth century is the rapid increase in **life expectancy**—or the number of years the average person can expect to live—rising from 47.3 years in 1900 to 77.8 years in 2009 (Arias 2010). As noted above, though many factors have contributed to the changes in the age pyramid in the United States, the greatest contributing factor is no doubt the incredible rise in life expectancy in such a relatively short period of time: thirty years in a century. As life expectancy has increased, so has the potential for elder abuse.

Race and Gender Variation: It is important to note that both race and gender significantly shape life expectancy. For example, in 1900 the life expectancy for white men was 46.6, and for white women it was 48.7. In comparison, African American men's life expectancy was only 32.5 years, and African American women could expect to live only one year longer: 33.5 years. Interestingly, across the twentieth century the racial gap of more than 10 years narrowed slightly for men and significantly for women, while the gender gap for both racial groups increased. Life expectancy for white men in 2009 was 75.3 years, and for white women it was 80.5 years. In contrast, African American men's life expectancy increased to 69 years (more than double the figure in 1900), and African American women's rose to 76.1—slightly higher than the figure for white men (Arias 2010).

When considering the overall increase in life expectancy, the rise has been driven primarily by a few key factors: public health policies, an increase in the standard of living, and changes in medicine. Consider the factors that continue to depress life expectancy in developing nations—access to clean water and sewage removal, a lack of the widespread use of vaccinations, and access to a nutrient-rich diet—and the reader will understand the types of changes that took place in twentieth-century America.

The increase in the gender gap in life expectancy is a bit harder to explain, but most scholars who study life expectancy point out a few key factors: stress and violence. Men of all racial and ethnic groups live lives that are more marked by stress than their female counterparts. This includes stress at work—both psychological and physical—and a lack of intimate relationships that are believed to reduce stress. For example, men are more likely to work in jobs that generate stress such as medicine and finance, as well as jobs that are difficult or physically demanding, including construction, heavy manufacturing, mining, and road work; quite simply, they are more likely to die "on the job" than women. Second, men are less likely to be married than their female counterparts—a factor that has been shown to enhance overall health and extend life expectancy—and they are less likely to report that they have close personal friendships that involve regular contact (Reis and Franks 1994), a factor that is likely to shape health and life expectancy in many different ways. Also, it is believed that intimate relationships and friendships improve mental health in ways that affect both physical health and life expectancy. One way of measuring the impact of psychologically related stress is that suicide is the eighth leading cause of death for white men (National Center for Health Statistics 2004).

All of the data on violence indicate that although women are far more likely to be victims of lethal and near-lethal intimate partner violence, men are *far more likely* to be victims of violence, especially homicide. And this is exacerbated by race. In fact, homicide is the fifth most common cause of death for African American men (National Center for Health Statistics 2004). Thus, as the health of men and women of all racial and ethnic groups has improved across the twentieth century thanks to advances in public health and sanitation, work-related stress and violence have differentially gendered life expectancy. Differences in race and gender with regards to life expectancy shape patterns of elder abuse, specifically who is at greatest risk for becoming a victim.

RACE AND GENDER AS PREDICTORS OF ELDER ABUSE

According to the Centers for Disease Control (CDC), with the exception of abandonment—which refers to the situation in which a caregiver simply stops providing any care and even stops having any contact with the elderly person, as compared to neglect, in which case the care provider continues to provide care but that care is inadequate—older women are far more likely to be victims of all forms of elder abuse than their male counterparts. In fact, most research, including that reported by the Centers for Disease Control (http://www.cdc.gov/violenceprevention/pub/EM _factsheet.html) as well as scholarly publications (Mouton et al. 2004), indicates that elderly women experience levels of physical abuse that are similar to younger women, and the prevalence of verbal abuse is actually higher among elderly women (44 percent) than among younger women (7.5 percent) (Mouton et al. 2004).

Scholars suggest that just as with other forms of family violence, gender shapes the experiences of elder abuse in similar patterns. Indeed, in some cases the abuse is a continuation of domestic violence that began when the women and their husbands and partners were much younger.

With regards to race, there are significant racial differences. Mouton and colleagues (2004) followed ninety-one thousand postmenopausal women for three years and found that African American women were 2.84 times more likely to report that they had experienced an act of physical violence than their white counterparts. In contrast, white women were more likely than all other women to report verbal abuse. This study, based on functionally independent older women, reflects findings that are more consistent with the literature on intimate partner violence rather than elder abuse. Women's greater life expectancy, regardless of race,

Elderly Women Often Abused

Of 842 women aged 60 or over seen in primary care settings in three states, nearly half had experienced maltreatment of a psychological or emotional nature. Women who encountered one type of mistreatment were often found to have encountered other types as well.

◀ **Figure 5.3**
Rates of
Elder Abuse

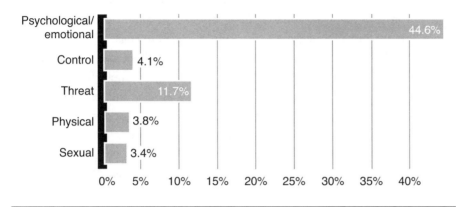

Source: Psychiatric News, June 16, 2006, Volume 41, Number 12, p. 20, http://pn.psychiatry online.org/content/41/12/20.full

and their vulnerability to other forms of violence, namely, sexual abuse and domestic violence, result in the fact that among the elderly, women are far more likely to be the victims of all forms of elder abuse, except neglect, which is experienced more frequently by men.

INDIRECT AND DIRECT CAUSES OF ELDER ABUSE

Because the vast majority of elder abuse is born out of a set of factors, including access to the elderly person, the elderly person's level of physical and cognitive functioning, the elderly person's level of vulnerability, and so forth, the role of race and gender in shaping patterns of elder abuse is an indirect rather than a direct factor. For example, because elderly women are perceived as being less capable and knowledgeable about finances and because white women have the longest life expectancy as well as higher levels of wealth (Hattery and Smith 2007; Shapiro 2003), we can anticipate that white women will constitute the largest segment of the population of victims of financial abuse. It is not so much their gender or their whiteness explicitly that leaves them vulnerable to financial abuse but rather the ways in which their race and gender shape their life expectancy, wealth, and image (not fiscally capable) that render them vulnerable to financial abuse.

Finally, it is important to note that unlike other forms of family violence that we are exploring in this book, elder abuse is unique in that it is often perpetrated by non-relatives. Though family caregivers perpetuate abuse, so do nonfamilial caregivers and strangers. For example, in response to longer life expectancy and the accompanying array of physical and cognitive diseases that often plague those of us who live to advanced old age, during the latter half of the twentieth century the United States experienced a dramatic rise in the number of nursing home facilities, long-term care facilities, Alzheimer's care facilities, and so forth. "Warehousing" the elderly, especially those who are dependent and suffering from physical and cognitive decline, opens up the opportunity for paid caregivers and institutional staff to engage in all of the various types of abuse that the elderly experience. In addition, especially with regards to financial abuse, the elderly are often targets for scams—for example, from being sold home improvements for which cash is exchanged in advance and the work is never completed to the types of pressures from salespeople who earn their money by commission and may sell vulnerable elderly financial services they do not need. That said, family members are most often the perpetrators of elder abuse, perpetrating 90 percent of the abuse, according to the National Center on Elder Abuse (NCEA).

SANDWICH GENERATION

In addition to elder abuse that is really an *extension* of domestic violence that has occurred in a victim's life, often across decades, some scholars of elder abuse point to one significant change in family structure that makes the elderly more vulnerable to neglect and abuse. The emergence of the "**sandwich generation**" of the late twentieth century is a structural change in the institution of the family that creates the types of stresses that some scholars argue may be linked to elder abuse. Specifically, the term *sandwich generation* refers to the concept that many middle-aged women are caring simultaneously for young children and aging parents. Carol Abaya, a syndicated news columnist, coined the term in 1992 when she started a syndicated news column, "The Sandwich Generation."

According to research conducted by the Pew Institute, as many as one in eight Americans have an older relative living with them, and as many as 10 million are part of the sandwich generation, providing daily care, financial assistance, and often supervision to both their own children as well as their aging parents and in some cases grandparents.

The sandwich generation is the result of a number of changes in family structure that have occurred almost simultaneously. Though the focus in this chapter has been on the significant increase in life expectancy that has dramatically extended the lives of older adults, at least three other structural changes have occurred as well: delayed childbearing, the prolonging of the onset of adulthood, and the reduction of retirement opportunities.

Beginning in the late 1960s, more and more young adults deferred adulthood by attending college; today many young adults are further delaying adulthood by pursuing training, professional school, and graduate school that extend until their late twenties and early thirties. Coupled with a tightening job market and the skyrocketing costs of higher education that often lead to students exiting institutions of higher education with student loans in the six digits, many parents find that they are still providing significant financial support to their "children" until they reach their early thirties. Increasingly commonly, they are also providing housing—either by paying rent or by allowing their grown children to live with them—a phenomenon referred to as "boomerang children." Thus, whereas adults may have expected to care for aging parents, few thought they would also have children at home simultaneously!

One significant consequence of both longevity and the deferral of adulthood in the late twentieth century—often in response to involvement in higher education—was a significant delay in childbearing. Whereas at the turn of the twentieth century most American women had their first child in their late teens, today the age of first childbirth is twenty-six years for women and twenty-seven years for men. Thus, most adults who became parents after 1990, in their mid- to late twenties, will be in their forties before their children graduate from high school, and they may be in their early fifties when these children graduate from college. Thus, as adult children defer adulthood until their late twenties and early thirties, their parents find that they are providing significant support for their children until they themselves are in their early sixties and just on the cusp of their own retirement!

The structures of the workplace have also changed in the last quarter century in ways that have significantly shaped retirement. Employees and workers of the mid-twentieth century benefited from both union pressures and government policies that created rather generous retirement benefits. Specifically, most employees of companies and the government could expect a "pension" that they were eligible to collect beginning in their late fifties, or at the latest by age sixty. Pensions of this era, which are collected by a significant number of adults over the age of sixty, provided relatively generous monthly stipends and comprehensive health benefits. Additionally, the prevailing belief was that workers should be able to enjoy the fruits of retirement, and thus benefits commonly "kicked in" by age sixty at the oldest. Today, there are very few businesses that offer the traditional "pension." Pensions have been replaced by retirement plans—which actually vary but fall under the general term *401k*—that generally allow employees to contribute a predetermined percentage of their income, prior to being taxed, into investment accounts that can then be accessed when one retires. Additionally, most employers have some sort of "matching" plan whereby the company also contributes a percentage of the employee's salary—often between 5 percent and 10 percent, depending on the number of years of employment—into the employee's account. The shift away from pension-style retirement to investment retirement is considered by some to be positive for employees. First and foremost it allows individuals to take control of their own retirement funds and if all goes well offers them the opportunity to produce greater gains in their investment accounts than might be possible when pension funds are invested without employee input. The reader may recall that this was an argument made by then president George W. Bush when he proposed a similar change to Social Security. Additionally, CEOs prefer investment retirement accounts because they are far less expensive for companies. Whereas investment retirement accounts give control to the employee, they also rely on the employee to make the bulk of the contributions and determine individually when to retire and how to withdraw the funds. In contrast, the typical pension of the mid- to late twentieth century guaranteed specific payouts at retirement as well as cost-of-living increases over time. Furthermore, the bulk of the money in pension funds was contributed by the employer and current employees. These pension funds operated much more like Social Security, where employees pay "ahead" but are ensured a certain monthly payout at retirement. These funds allowed individuals to retire at age fifty-five and often required retirement by age sixty. In contrast, investment retirement accounts depend entirely on the contributions by the employee, their performance and payout structure is the responsibility of the employee, and they often allow employees to work past age sixty-two. The individual who has not contributed or who has contributed only the minimum to their retirement account, or who has managed the investments poorly, or who plans to retire just when a recession hits and investment accounts suffer significant losses as the stock market "crashes"—in the past few years retirement accounts lost billions of dollars—may find that he or she is unable to retire because there are not enough funds in the account. Additionally, whereas pensions paid out until death, investment accounts pay until they are empty. Thus,

---

CAROL ABAYA

In the late 1980s Carol Abaya, a syndicated news columnist, found herself in what was then considered a unique situation. After her mother suffered a severe and debilitating injury, Carol felt she had no choice but to "take the reins" of her mother's life, including taking over her finances, supervising her health care, and moving her into her own home. Meanwhile, she was raising a teenager. Carol soon began to recognize the stresses associated with not only "elder care" but also providing care and in this case breadwinning for a multigenerational family. And although there are many advantages to having family members of multiple generations in the household, the stresses associated with this arrangement are significant as well, primarily because children (including adolescents and teenagers) require supervision, attention to daily needs, financial support, and often "chauffeuring," all of which significantly constrain the daily lives of the caregiver. Women, and men, of the sandwich generation wonder when, if ever, they will be able to reclaim their lives and focus on themselves—something many Americans assume will happen when they "empty the nest" and in the period prior to as well as during retirement. Though Carol never became neglectful or abusive toward either her son or her mother, one can imagine how the stresses of people—mostly women—living in the sandwich generation create a situation ripe for neglect and even abuse.

individuals may be hesitant to retire until they are sure the funds they have amassed are adequate and the time they have left to live is minimal. These structural changes in retirement policies mean that the majority of caregivers in the "sandwich generation" are also full-time workers. The pressures and costs of elder care may prolong their careers and delay retirement, and simultaneously, this continuation of employment often leads to an additional stress on the day-to-day activities of the caregiver who has one more role and one more set of expectations and requirements to balance.

PREVALENCE OF ELDER ABUSE

Research on the prevalence of elder abuse is scarce, in part because the issue has only recently been defined, but primarily because it is difficult to conduct research on a problem that is hidden and in a population that is often experiencing declining cognitive abilities, which render them unavailable for surveys and interviews. However, the National Center for Elder Abuse estimates that in 2004 between 1 and 2 million people over the age of sixty-five were victims of abuse. Research published by the prestigious medical journal the *Lancet* reports that 2 percent to 10 percent of the elderly have experienced some form of elder abuse (Lachs and Pillemer 2004).

Furthermore, based on qualitative research on injuries that require medical treatment, and calls for assistance, particularly regarding financial abuse, scholars estimate that for every act of abuse that is reported, there are at least five acts that go unreported. Thus, there is a "widely held consensus" that elder abuse is severely underreported and that as many as 2.5 million people over the age of sixty are the victims of abuse each year (Bonnie and Wallace 2003). Last, an additional problem we face in attempting to estimate the prevalence of elder abuse is the fact that there are many different types of elder abuse, and the risks associated with each are not only different but also shaped by factors such as gender, race, and socioeconomic class as well as living arrangements (whether one is living alone, with one's children, or in an assisted living facility), health, and cognitive functioning. We turn now to a discussion of the various types of elder abuse that occur in the United States.

TYPES OF ELDER ABUSE

Scholars of elder abuse and advocates for the elderly identify at least five categories of elder abuse: financial, neglect, physical, psychological, and sexual. Although there are many cases in which an elderly person is the victim of more than one type of abuse, it is also common for abuse to be segmented or not overlapping, and thus the victim may experience abuse of only one type or the abuse may occur discreetly with different types not overlapping and occurring at very different times in the elder's later years. We begin with a discussion of financial abuse.

Financial Abuse

In summary, elder **financial abuse** involves a variety of behaviors—the majority of it is criminal and can be prosecuted—that involve improperly taking money or other financial assets from the elderly. Sometimes the abuse is forceful, sometimes the abuse involves deceit, and frequently the abuse is predicated on the older person's diminished cognitive capacity. Of all reported elder abuse, 12.3 percent is financial abuse, and in 2005 there were approximately 5 million victims of financial abuse, according to the National Center on Elder Abuse. Elder financial abuse spans a broad spectrum of conduct, including:

- taking money or property
- forging an older person's signature
- getting an older person to sign a deed, will, or power of attorney through deception, coercion, or undue influence
- using the older person's property or possessions without permission
- promising lifelong care in exchange for money or property and not following through on the promise
- the use of deception to gain victims' confidence ("cons")
- fraudulent or deceptive acts ("scams"), through the use of deception, trickery, false pretense, or dishonest acts or statements for financial gain
- telemarketing scams, a specific and widespread fraud in which perpetrators call victims and use deception, scare tactics, or exaggerated claims to get them to send money or disclose credit card information, allowing the scammer to make charges against victims' credit cards without authorization

Who Are the Perpetrators?

One of the unique aspects of financial abuse, as opposed to the other types of abuse, is that the abuse, though often perpetrated by family member—according to a recent study reported by National Adult Protective Services, 60 percent of elder financial abuse that involved Adult Protective Services *involved family members*—is also frequently perpetrated by nonfamilial caregivers. Furthermore, unlike any other form of family abuse, the elderly face a high risk of being victimized by scams and swindles that are perpetrated by strangers. The National Committee for the Prevention of Elder Abuse (NCPEA) (see their listing in the "Resources" section) indicates that although financial abuse may be perpetrated by both family members and nonfamily members—both acquaintances and strangers—family members and nonfamily members may have very different motives for perpetrating the abuse. Some of the motives that family members have for perpetrating financial abuse against the elderly include:

- They have substance abuse, gambling, or financial problems and believe that they can "solve" these problems by taking money from an elderly relative. They may even convince themselves that they will make restitution once they get out of their own financial trouble.
- As a person who will eventually inherit from their elderly relative, they may feel justified in taking what they believe is "almost" or "rightfully" theirs already.
- As someone responsible for the care of an elderly relative, they may fear that their older family member will get sick and use up their savings, depriving the abuser of an inheritance or even "costing" them, if they anticipate that they will have to pay some or all of the financial costs of caring for the elderly relative who has exhausted his or her funds.
- They may have had a negative relationship with the older person and feel a sense of "entitlement" but worry that because the relationship is "negative," they have been or will be denied "their fair share" when the elderly person dies.
- They may have negative feelings toward siblings or other family members whom they want to prevent from acquiring or inheriting the older person's assets.

It is important to point out that the types of abuse discussed above may not begin maliciously. For example, an adult son or daughter may begin by paying an elderly parent's bills out of his or her checking account, and only when a stressful event arises does he or she begin stealing from the parent.

In contrast, predatory individuals seek out vulnerable seniors with the intent of exploiting them. They generally come in two categories: those who seek relationships or find means to exploit an existing relationship, similar to the types of motives outlined above, and those who have no particular relationship with the person they exploit and simply identify the most vulnerable senior whom they then victimize. In the first case, they may:

- profess to love the older person—commonly known as "sweetheart scams"— and then often seek a marriage without a prenuptial agreement that allows them to access financial assets while the elderly person is still alive as well as at the time of their death.
- seek employment as personal care attendants, counselors, and so forth to gain access to financial assets or even be written into a will; in some extreme and sophisticated cases, individuals who become trusted attendants "turn" the elderly person against his or her own family members and assist him or her in "writing" these relatives out of the will!

The second type of perpetrator is rarely motivated by a personal relationship with an elderly person and rarely seeks a relationship in order to accomplish the financial abuse. Rather, these are scams that target a large number of people with the hopes of snaring a few. Common techniques include:

- identifying vulnerable persons by driving through neighborhoods (to find persons who are alone and isolated) or contacting recently widowed persons they find through newspaper death announcements
- moving from community to community to avoid being apprehended (transient criminals)
- being unscrupulous professionals or businesspersons, or posing as such, and may:
  - overcharge for services or products
  - use deceptive or unfair business practices
  - use their positions of trust or respect to gain compliance

One of the most common scams of this type is to pose as a repair person at an elderly person's home. The scammer convinces the elderly person that they are desperately in need of home repairs, among the most common being the claim that the senior needs a new roof. They demand payment, often five to ten thousand dollars, in advance. They may show up once or twice, but typically they do not complete any of the work, and they vanish with the money. During the spring and fall it is not uncommon to see billboards on the local roads or public service announcements on television warning the elderly of this type of scam. The following is an example of such a scam, which was reported in the *Houston Chronicle* as both news and a warning to local seniors.

BOX 5.1   SCAM WARNING

Scam Warning Issued to Elderly in Fort Bend County
Zen T. C. Zheng, Houston Chronicle, January 17, 2011

Jan. 17, 2011 (McClatchy-Tribune Regional News delivered by Newstex)—An official with an agency that serves the elderly is urging homeowners not to open their doors to strangers claiming to be financial planners after a Fort Bend County woman's credit card information was stolen and hit with multiple charges.

Curtis Cooper, manager of the Houston-Galveston Area Council's Area Agency on Aging, has advised all the local aid organizations contracted with his agency to warn clients about the incident, which happened Thursday in the Greatwood subdivision near Sugar Land.

Cooper said the incident was brought to his attention by a daughter of the victim. According to the daughter, a woman who claimed to be working for the Area Agency on Aging knocked at her mother's door and identified herself as Cathy.

| BOX 5.1 | SCAM WARNING *continued* |

She talked the older woman into allowing her to access her computer by saying she needed to load software to assist her in managing her finances. The daughter said her mother's credit card was hit with charges after her computer was used.

After the woman informed her daughters of the event, they closed all her bank and credit card accounts, and contacted the Fort Bend County Sheriff's Office, Cooper said.

Manuela Arroyos, chief executive officer of Fort Bend Seniors Meals on Wheels, said her staff is telling their clients about the incident and urging them to report suspicious activity to authorities.

"It is important that clients are reminded not to let unknown people enter their home that they did not invite," Cooper said.

SOURCE: http://www.aarp.org/money/scams-fraud/news-012011/scam_warning_issued_to _elderly_in_fort_bend_county.html.

Who Is at Risk?

According to the National Committee for the Prevention of Elder Abuse, there are certain conditions or factors that increase an older person's risk of being victimized. These include:

- isolation
- loneliness
- recent losses
- physical or mental disabilities
- lack of familiarity with financial matters
- family members who are unemployed or have substance abuse problems

What role do these factors play in increasing the probability for being victimized? The first three factors (isolation, loneliness, and recent losses) are ones that are common to many types of abuse—both of the elderly and of other populations—because they indicate an overall sense of vulnerability. Individuals who are lonely or isolated may be far more "hungry" for interaction with others and thus may be less discriminating in terms of whom they interact with or the types of information they share. These feelings of loneliness are common among adolescent girls who were sexually abused in childhood and often lead them to choose romantic partners who are abusive toward them. We will return to a lengthy discussion of this in both Chapters 7 and 13.

The three other factors (physical or mental disabilities, lack of familiarity with financial matters, or having family members with financial or substance abuse issues) make elderly individuals particularly vulnerable to financial abuse primarily because they can be easily targeted—for example, their lack of familiarity with financial matters may mean that they do not know what kinds of transactions in their bank accounts are normal and which are questionable, or they may be vulnerable to scams like the one highlighted above because they do not have a good understanding of computers—and victimized by family, nonfamilial caregivers, and strangers. Thus, those who have elderly family members with these risk factors or practitioners who work with the elderly should be particularly vigilant about watching for early warning signs—new "friends" and so forth—as these may be indicators that an elderly person is about to be scammed or has already been "groomed" for abuse.

Why Are the Elderly Attractive Targets?

There are many reasons, in addition to the above "risk" factors, that the elderly are "attractive" targets for potential financial crime. According to the Center for American Progress (http://www.americanprogress.org/issues/2008/07/elderly_poverty .html), the poverty rate among the elderly is 9.4 percent, well below the average poverty rate for all Americans, but they note that without Social Security benefits, 44 percent of the elderly would be living in poverty. This is important for two reasons. First, because the majority of elderly qualify for and receive Social Security, scams that target the stealing of these kinds of benefits, once mastered, can likely be applied to a large population. Additionally, the very receipt of benefits such as Social Security makes the elderly vulnerable to exploitation because of the uniformity of the receipt of these kinds of benefits. For example, Social Security checks arrive in every recipient's mailbox on the same day, they must be cashed at the bank, and so on, all of which lead to the elderly developing easily discernible patterns in their movements, making them easier targets.

Second, though as noted many of the elderly are poor, this age group nevertheless controls 70 percent of the nation's wealth, according to the National Committee on the Prevention of Elder Abuse. How can these two things be true at once? The elderly, unlike younger Americans, with the exception of health care costs, tend to have fewer fixed expenses—such as mortgages and college tuition—and thus, if they are healthy or have excellent health insurance, they are likely to have more disposable income per month than their younger counterparts, even after they retire. Second, as with all Americans who strive toward achieving the American dream, the elderly who have managed to work hard and save have simply, over time, accumulated more wealth than those who are younger and have worked fewer years. For those elderly who have investment incomes, time is their asset, and as they age their investments and wealth grow. For all of these reasons, the elderly have access to more wealth than younger Americans, and thus they can be construed as targets, for both scam artists and desperate relatives.

Despite having more wealth, as a group, than younger Americans, many seniors do not recognize the value of their wealth. This can be for reasons related to time, such as the marked appreciation of a home they have owned for forty or fifty years, as well as gender. For example, many elderly women, if they have not managed the family investments, may have no idea how much their investments or even bank accounts are worth. This fact alone puts elderly women at greater risk for financial abuse for several distinct reasons. First, we note that although there is strong evidence that this is changing, historically gender roles were divvied up in such a way that men controlled the household finances; because men were believed to be better at math, men were often the only member of the household earning a wage, and men remain far more likely to own businesses than women, and thus the financial skills they develop and use at work could be translated to the home. Thus, especially among older women, it is not unusual for them to have very little financial experience. Second, because women outlive men in every racial and ethnic group, older women may find that their first experience dealing with financial matters is when they are widowed. Both their inexperience and the loss of their spouse—which as noted above is a major risk factor for being a victim—put them at greater risk. Last, because women are likely to live well into their eighties, when other diseases become more common, especially cognitive decline, this increases their risk for financial abuse in and of itself but also because they are more likely to need assistance at home or move into an assisted care facility—a fact that also increases their risk for financial abuse. Last, as the scam above documents, women, because of historical patterns of the division of household labor, are at greater risk for scams that involve not only finances but also home maintenance because they have less experience in dealing with these matters.

These risk factors for financial abuse are increasing as financial transactions and "markets" have become digitized. Whereas the typical working American in his or her thirties or forties may appreciate the fact that bank accounts, mortgage assets, and investment accounts may be monitored "24/7" through online accounts, many of the elderly who are "afraid" of technology and may have limited, if any, access to computers and the World Wide Web may actually have less access to the value of their wealth and investments than they did ten years ago when they received quarterly paper records in the mail. Again, the scam we included above illustrates this point.

Elderly men and women who have disabilities and are dependent on others for help, including daily care, are "ideal" targets. The "helper"—be he or she a relative or nonrelative—may gain easy access to financial records and after having developed rapport may be able to exert undue influence over an elderly person. Imagine, for example, that a middle-age grandchild or a nonrelative caregiver "offers" to show the elderly person how to set up online banking for their assets. It is quite plausible that during the process the elderly person—who may not realize their own vulnerability—may share passwords, Social Security numbers, and other private information that the "helper" can then use to access the accounts directly and steal money.

Last, and perhaps most insidious, is the fact that many people who engage in financial abuse of the elderly may believe that because their victims are physically frail and dependent and old that they may not live long enough to make a complaint or testify in a hearing should the abuse be discovered. This kind of "cost-benefit" analysis adds to the vulnerability of the elderly and their value as "targets" for abuse.

What Are the Indicators?

The National Committee for the Prevention of Elder Abuse has put together a list of indicators or signs that abuse has occurred. This list was compiled by the NCPEA by examining hundreds of cases of financial abuse of the elderly. They note that some of the indicators listed below can be explained by other causes or factors, and thus no single indicator should be taken as conclusive proof. Rather, one should look for patterns or clusters of indicators that suggest a problem. That said, even one indicator should be explored to be sure that it is not the first sign of the beginning of an abusive process. Finally, we note that many of these "early warning signs" are significant enough that even if they are not caused by abuse, they should be investigated so that problems that may stem from another cause—perhaps the elderly person is not receiving enough benefits to pay his or her bills, or perhaps health costs that have been unclaimed can be filed—can be addressed. The following is a comprehensive list of indicators that should be explored:

- unpaid bills, eviction notices, or notices to discontinue utilities
- withdrawals from bank accounts or transfers between accounts that the older person cannot explain
- bank statements and canceled checks no longer come to the elder's home, or all paper statements have been discontinued and are sent only electronically
- new "best friends"
- legal documents, such as powers of attorney, which the older person did not understand at the time he or she signed them
- unusual activity in the older person's bank accounts including large unexplained withdrawals, frequent transfers between accounts, or ATM withdrawals
- the care of the elder is not commensurate with the size of his or her estate; for example, hundreds of dollars in lawn mowing expenses or house cleaning for a relatively small yard and house
- a caregiver expresses excessive interest in the amount of money being spent on the older person

- belongings or property are missing
- suspicious signatures on checks or other documents
- absence of documentation about financial arrangements
- implausible explanations given about the elderly person's finances by the elder or the caregiver
- the elder is unaware of or does not understand financial arrangements that have been made for him or her

---

BOX 5.2	FLORENCE HARTER

When 86-year-old Florence Harter was hospitalized in 1996, she confided to a hospital employee that she was worried that some of her bills might be missed and go unpaid while she was in the hospital. The aide, Maria Galacia, volunteered to help, and Harter gave Galacia the keys to her apartment so she could bring Harter her checkbook. After being discharged from the hospital, Harter discovered that her apartment had been burglarized. Harter confronted Galacia, who threatened to sue Harter for accusing her of taking her jewelry. Galacia then intimidated Harter into making regular cash payments to Galacia in exchange for Galacia's agreement not to sue Harter. This scheme continued for over a year until one day, Galacia and Harter went together to Harter's bank and Galacia, who claimed to be Harter's caretaker, attempted to withdraw $10,000 in cash. This aroused the suspicion of a bank vice president, who questioned Galacia about the transaction. Galacia left the bank without making the withdrawal, but returned with Harter a week later and attempted again to withdraw $10,000 in cash. This time the bank contacted the Chicago police. Galacia was subsequently convicted of theft by deception and ordered to pay $45,000 in restitution to Harter.

SOURCE: Sneed 2001.

Neglect and Self-Neglect

Neglect is the failure of caregivers to fulfill their responsibilities to provide needed care. There are many different types of abuse that are considered under the general rubric of neglect and self-neglect. We begin with a few distinctions.

Active **neglect** refers to behavior that is willful—that is, the caregiver intentionally withholds care or necessities. The neglect may be motivated by financial gain (e.g., the caregiver stands to inherit) or reflect interpersonal conflicts.

Passive **neglect** refers to situations in which the caregiver is unable to fulfill his or her caregiving responsibilities as a result of illness, disability, stress, ignorance, lack of maturity, or lack of resources.

Self-neglect refers to situations in which there is no perpetrator, and neglect is the result of the older person's refusing care despite his or her need for care. Self-neglect is not technically a form of family violence, but we include the definition here because self-neglect might occur alongside caregiver neglect—either passive or active—and an individual who suspects neglect is taking place may want to explore the possibility of self-neglect occurring as well.

Who Are the Perpetrators?

Unlike financial abuse where the perpetrators may be strangers who are engaged in a scam to swindle money from the elderly, in cases of neglect, the perpetrators are always people who have agreed to—in the case of family members—or been hired to provide care for the elderly person. Thus, in general the perpetrators may be paid attendants, family members, or employees of long-term care facilities, hospital facilities, or nursing homes. We note that unlike parental responsibilities to care for children under the age of eighteen, there are no laws that require a child to care for aging parents, nor is there any law that requires a spouse or any other relative to provide this care. Thus, when relatives do serve as caregivers, this is a voluntary activity—though we can imagine cases in which there is coercion or pressure involved on the part of the elder needing care (financial or inheritance promises) or on the part of other siblings who might in fact offer some compensation to the caregiver.

Often, but not always, the perpetrators are individuals—family members or paid professionals—who lack adequate skills, training, time, or energy. Sometimes the perpetrators are caregivers who are mentally ill or who have alcohol, substance abuse, or other mental health problems. In some cases the perpetrators are spouses who are providing care and who suffer from their own dementia or other cognitive or physical impairments that compromise their ability to give appropriate care.

Who Is at Risk?

Quite obviously, the number-one factor that contributes to the vulnerability of an elderly person for this type of abuse is their mental or physical capacity and subsequent need for care. Individuals who are self-sufficient, intellectually "sharp," and have limited or no physical incapacities are not at risk for this type of abuse.

Though anyone who depends on others for some or all of their care is at risk, there are certain conditions that elevate the likelihood of this type of abuse. For example, individuals with "high" care needs are more likely to experience neglect than those with "low" care needs. For example, elderly who need assistance with tasks like grocery shopping, cooking, and cleaning are at a lower risk for neglect than those who require assistance with all of the aforementioned tasks as well as more personal "daily care" tasks, such as bathing. Those who have particularly challenging needs such as incontinence—and thus must wear diapers—or those with complex medical needs such as the regular delivery of medications, especially suppositories, are more likely to have their needs neglected. And, sadly, those with significant cognitive impairments—especially diseases such as Alzheimer's and advanced stage Parkinson's—

are the most vulnerable to neglect. Elderly patients with Alzheimer's and Parkinson's are particularly vulnerable both because their needs are great and often difficult to meet—they can be belligerent—and because their cognitive impairments may make them less able to detect the neglect when it is occurring in ways that a cognitively intact elderly person with physical impairments would be able to.

The following tragedy involving various types of abuse of multiple patients with Alzheimer's was reported in the *Athens (GA) Banner Herald*:

BOX 5.3   DONNA TOWER

Three Cases Revealed but Elder Abuse Largely Hidden

Donna Tower's uncle told his family that someone was stealing his money, but the family didn't believe him at first because he has Alzheimer's.

In the end, the family learned that he was telling the truth—that the administrator of a Winterville nursing home was taking his money, and his brother's, but no one would believe him.

"(She) had been taking their checks and we didn't realize it," Tower said. "My uncle with Alzheimer's had said someone was stealing his money all along, but we just brushed it off because we thought it was just in his mind."

Sherrye Dianne Huff, former administrator of the Winterville Retirement Center, was arrested Monday on five felony charges—three counts of theft and two counts of exploiting an elderly or disabled person—and one count of misdemeanor theft for stealing from the Alzheimer's patient.

The investigator, Winterville police Sgt. Jimmy Fulcher, discovered while looking into the theft case that elder abuse is more widespread than people realize.

He arrested another Winterville Retirement Center employee on charges she punched another Alzheimer's patient in the face for taking some butter off a food cart in the facility's dining hall.

The 82-year-old resident died a few weeks later and authorities are investigating to see if her death was related to the assault.

Soon after, police say another employee of the Winterville Retirement Center stole drugs that had been prescribed for the patient who died, and police later found out the administrator was stealing money from other residents.

The three cases of abuse and financial exploitation happened in less than three months.

"More than likely, it's (elder abuse) more widespread than we know," said Fulcher, who last week launched a fourth investigation into the possible theft of money from another Winterville Retirement Center resident.

"Most times when a patient reports something it's hard to prove it because when they have Alzheimer's, they will sometimes say something happened to them when it hasn't

continues

BOX 5.3	DONNA TOWER *continued*

happened," he said. "In this (assault) case I consider myself extremely lucky as far as getting cooperation" from other employees who witnessed the assault.

"Elder abuse is one of the most unrecognized and under-reported crimes," said Ravae Graham, a deputy director with the state Department of Human Services. "Many abuse victims don't realize it, don't know what to do about it, or are too afraid to report their abuse or neglect."

The National Center on Elder Abuse estimates that for each documented case of neglect or abuse, five cases go unreported.

Though people place trust in professionals to take care of their loved ones, relatives need to look for signs of abuse, according to an Athens woman, who took her mother out of an area nursing home after only a month when she discovered employees weren't giving her mother the medication she needed.

"When you bring your parent to a nursing home, you think they should be getting the best care possible," said the woman, who asked to not be identified. "Prisoners get better care than people in nursing homes."

After the woman took her 86-year-old mother out of the nursing home to live with her, she discovered a large bed sore because nursing home employees let the dementia patient sit in the same position in a wheelchair for hours.

"It takes a special kind of person to work in a nursing home because they have to deal with people who can become very combative when they don't want to be bathed or take their medicine," she said. "That can become very frustrating, but that's no excuse to abuse or neglect anyone because that's their job and they knew what they were getting into."

Anyone who is looking to place a loved one in a nursing home should do some research to see the facility's track record, experts said.

Source: Joe Johnson, May 8, 2011, http://onlineathens.com/stories/050811/new_8260 20509.shtml.

What Are the Indicators?

Indicators of neglect include the condition of the older person's home (environmental indicators), physical signs of poor care, and behavioral characteristics of the caregiver and the older person. Some of the indicators listed below may not signal neglect but rather reflect lack of resources or mental health problems. However, the presence of any factor should encourage a conversation or mild investigation to be sure there are not deeper underlying problems, and of course when a pattern or cluster of indicators occurs simultaneously, this should raise greater concern that there might be a problem that requires immediate investigation and action. The following are "checklists" of things to look for as evidence that neglect may be a concern.

SIGNS OF NEGLECT

Signs of Neglect Observed in the Home

- absence of necessities including food (an empty refrigerator), water, heat in the winter or air-conditioning in the summer (as dictated by the environment)
- inadequate living environment evidenced by lack of utilities, sufficient space, and ventilation
- animal or insect infestations
- signs of medication mismanagement, including empty or unmarked bottles or outdated prescriptions
- housing is unsafe as a result of disrepair, faulty wiring, inadequate sanitation, substandard cleanliness, or architectural barriers

Signs of Neglect That Are
Related to the Person's Physical Condition

- poor personal hygiene including soiled clothing, dirty nails and skin, matted or lice-infested hair, odors, and the presence of feces or urine
- unclothed, or improperly clothed for weather
- decubiti (bedsores)
- skin rashes
- dehydration, evidenced by low urinary output, dry fragile skin, dry sore mouth, apathy, lack of energy, and mental confusion
- untreated medical or mental conditions including infections, soiled bandages, and unattended fractures or the presence of conditions that should be controlled by medication such as diabetes
- absence of needed dentures, eyeglasses, hearing aids, walkers, wheelchairs, braces, or commodes
- exacerbation of chronic diseases despite a care plan
- worsening dementia

Behavioral Indicators

Observed in the Caregiver or Abuser

- expresses anger, frustration, or exhaustion
- isolates the senior from the outside world, friends, or relatives
- obviously lacks caregiving skills
- is unreasonably critical and dissatisfied with social and health care providers and changes providers frequently
- refuses to apply for economic aid or services for the senior and resists outside help

continues

SIGNS OF NEGLECT *continued*

Observed in the Victim

- exhibits emotional distress such as crying
- exhibits symptoms of depression or despair including being disengaged or despondent, "flat" affect, talking about suicide
- has nightmares or difficulty sleeping
- has had a sudden loss of appetite that is unrelated to a medical condition
- is confused and disoriented (this may be the result of malnutrition or being improperly medicated)
- is emotionally numb, withdrawn, or detached
- exhibits regressive behavior (which may include a sudden inability or lack of interest in performing daily care tasks that were previously manageable)
- exhibits self-destructive behavior
- exhibits fear toward the caregiver
- expresses unrealistic expectations about their care (e.g., claiming that their care is adequate when it is not or insisting that the situation will improve)

All of these indicators can be present in cases of neglect by a caregiver as well as self-neglect. Relatives, care providers, and advocates for the elderly should be aware of these indicators and investigate any situation in which an indicator is present. Because there can be many "causes" of neglect, including poverty, solutions will be highly situationally dependent, and it make take multiple attempts to address a case, especially if the neglect is severe.

Physical Abuse

Because much of this book is about physical abuse, it is not necessary to review the definition of **physical abuse**. We do remind the reader that he or she can find definitions of physical abuse earlier in this chapter as well as in Chapters 1 and 2. Physical abuse of the elderly can occur at the hands of family members or paid caregivers. Most common, as noted above, is physical abuse that is a continuation of domestic violence that has been a part of the victim's life previously and typically began long before they were considered "elderly." Though the source of physical abuse will dictate interventions and solutions, the indicators of physical abuse are not likely to vary by the relationship between the victim and the perpetrator—spouse, adult child, paid caregiver—but rather will be shaped by the individual qualities of both the victim and the perpetrator and may be present in other relationships that involve the same perpetrator. For example, a husband who beats his wife with objects may also beat his children in similar patterns, or a paid caregiver whose abusive behavior involves tying an elderly victim to his or her bed may exhibit the same behavior with other elderly people for whom he or she is providing care.

What Are the Indicators?

As with other types of elder abuse there are multiple types of indicators that physical abuse is taking place. Physical indicators may include injuries or bruises, while behavioral indicators are ways victims and abusers act or interact with each other. As with the indicators of other types of abuse, many of the indicators listed below can be explained by other causes (e.g., a bruise may be the result of an accidental fall), and no single indicator can be taken as conclusive proof. Rather, one should look for patterns or clusters of indicators that suggest a problem. That said, no indicator should be ignored because it likely indicates something. If a bruise is not the result of physical abuse but instead of a fall, then one would need to explore both the health of the elderly person (is their sense of balance declining?) and the overall environment—for example, if they live in a home with stairs, accommodations may need to be made.

INDICATIONS OF PHYSICAL ABUSE

Physical Indicators

- sprains, dislocations, fractures, or broken bones
- burns from cigarettes, appliances, or hot water
- abrasions on arms, legs, or torso that resemble rope or strap marks
- internal injuries evidenced by pain, difficulty with normal functioning of organs, and bleeding from body orifices
- bruises—the following types of bruises are rarely accidental:
  - bilateral bruising to the arms (may indicate that the person has been shaken, grabbed, or restrained)
  - bilateral bruising of the inner thighs (may indicate sexual abuse)
  - "wrap-around" bruises that encircle an older person's arms, legs, or torso (may indicate that the person has been physically restrained)
  - multicolored bruises (indicating that they were sustained in the same location over a period of time)
- injuries healing through "secondary intention" (indicating that they did not receive appropriate care)
- signs of traumatic hair and tooth loss

continues

INDICATIONS OF PHYSICAL ABUSE *continued*

Behavioral Indicators

- when inquiries about injuries are made, they are unexplained or explanations are implausible (they do not "fit" with the injuries observed)
- family members provide different explanations of how injuries were sustained
- a history of similar injuries or numerous or suspicious hospitalizations
- victims are brought to different medical facilities for treatment to prevent medical practitioners from observing a pattern of abuse
- delay between onset of injury and seeking medical care

In summary, physical abuse of the elderly may have "elderly onset"—it begins after someone grows old and requires care and supervision—or it may be a continuation of battering that began decades earlier when the victim was newly married. In the case of violence that is a continuation of abuse, the indicators may be less visible because the perpetrator has had years to "practice" hiding the evidence of the abuse, thus making it more difficult to detect. In either case, our elderly deserve to live lives free of all types of abuse, whether it has only recently begun or has been a part of an elderly person's life for decades.

Psychological Abuse

Psychological abuse is the willful infliction of mental or emotional anguish by threat, humiliation, or other verbal or nonverbal conduct. Cultural values and expectations play a significant role in how psychological abuse is manifested and how it affects its victims. For example, in cultures where the elderly are revered for their cultural and historical knowledge and their sheer survival—this is very typical in developing cultures across Asia and Africa—psychological abuse of the elderly is uncommon. For example, among nomadic peoples who range across sub-Saharan Africa, day-to-day living is very difficult. The infant mortality rate is high, and life expectancy is short. Thus, when someone lives to be "old"—perhaps living forty-five years—they are considered to be special; they have clearly been blessed with such a long life, and because the history of the people and the family is entirely oral, they possess important information. For example, among the !Kung, a nomadic group who live in Botswana, just north of South Africa, an elder not only carries the family and group history, but based on his or her longevity will also possess information about weather and seasonal patterns that are critical to surviving the next weather crisis; he or she may remember that last severe drought and strategies for finding water when the rivers are dry. Thus, to abuse an elder in the !Kung society would be to seriously disrespect and disadvantage the rest of the group.

In contrast, in Western postindustrial cultures like the United States where aging is considered to be negative and the elderly are devalued, psychological abuse of the elderly is more common. Think, for example, of the images of the elderly that we see on television and in the movies. How are they depicted? In our economy, people who are past middle age are considered incompetent and behind the times and have a difficult time gaining employment if they find themselves in need of a job. For example, women who are divorced or widowed in middle age as well as middle-aged men and women who were laid off during the recession of the past few years often face serious age discrimination when they seek a new job. All of these cultural factors contribute to psychological abuse of the elderly. For example, in the 2009 film *Up in the Air*, the director included several real people—not actors—who had been recently laid off. The majority of those featured are middle-aged. One woman, in her forties or fifties, notes, "There will be people more qualified than me now," in recognition of the fact that young people just coming out of college will have the up-to-date skills that employers are looking for, whereas she views herself as more or less "past due."

Who Are the Perpetrators?

Perpetrators may be family members, caregivers, or even acquaintances—basically, anyone with whom the elderly person has any regular or ongoing contact.

Who Is at Risk?

Persons who are isolated and lack social or emotional support are particularly vulnerable. Additionally, because psychological abuse is built on cultural ideologies of age and because these ideologies are gendered, racialized, and shaped by factors such as disability, women, racial and ethnic minorities, and elderly individuals with physical disabilities will be at greater risk for suffering psychological abuse because they "fit" the stereotypes invoked by **ageism**—a set of beliefs that construct the elderly as less competent, dumb, behind the times, forgetful, lacking in physical abilities, and even asexual.

What Are the Indicators?

As with other types of abuse, there can be both physical and behavioral indicators. Physical indicators may include somatic changes or decline, while behavioral indicators are ways victims and abusers act or interact. As always, some of the indicators listed below can be explained by other causes, and no single indicator can be taken as conclusive proof; patterns or clusters of behaviors are more likely to be present when psychological abuse is taking place. As always, because any indicator, regardless of its origin, may be a symptom of a problem, the presence of any indicator should be examined so that its cause can be determined and solutions identified.

INDICATIONS OF PSYCHOLOGICAL ABUSE

Physical Indicators

- significant weight loss or gain that is not attributed to other causes
- stress-related conditions, including elevated blood pressure, irritable bowl syndrome, unexplained and frequent headaches, or the onset of any other somatoform disorders

Behavioral Indicators Exhibited by the Perpetrator

- isolates the senior emotionally by not speaking to, touching, or comforting him or her

Behavioral Indicators Exhibited by the Elder

- has problems sleeping
- exhibits depression and confusion
- cowers in the presence of abuser
- is emotionally upset, agitated, withdrawn, and nonresponsive
- exhibits unusual behavior usually attributed to dementia (e.g., sucking, biting, rocking)

As with other forms of family abuse, psychological abuse is often "undervalued." People often assume that if there are no bruises or cuts or broken bones that the abuse is not as harmful. Yet the impact of psychological abuse is often as significant if not more significant than physical abuse. As noted, there can be physical outcomes and stress-related diseases as well as psychological trauma that can cause severe damage to the elderly victim. In surveys, elderly women reported that not only was psychological abuse the most common form of abuse they experienced, but when several types of abuse were present, they ranked it as the most devastating (Mouton et al. 2004).

Sexual Abuse

Sexual abuse is any form of nonconsensual sexual contact, including rape, molestation, or any unwanted or coerced touching. Sexual abuse also includes *any* sexual conduct with a person who lacks the *mental capacity* to exercise consent or the physical capacity to exercise refusal; for example, an elderly person who has suffered a stroke may be unable to speak despite their cognitive capacity to understand the situation.

Who Are the Perpetrators?

Perpetrators of sexual abuse include attendants, employees of care facilities, family members (including spouses), and others who have the opportunity to have unsupervised contact with an elderly victim. Facility residents sometimes assault fellow residents.

Who Is at Risk?

- the majority of identified victims are women, but older men have been sexually abused in both domestic and institutional settings
- persons with physical or cognitive disabilities
- persons who lack social support and are isolated
- persons who the abuser believes will not be able to reveal that the abuse is taking place because they either lack the physical capacity to do so—perhaps they have had a stroke and cannot speak—or are afraid to report the abuse or lack the cognitive capacity to understand what is happening to them or report it

This last risk factor is important because it is similar to that which puts children at risk for sexual abuse, especially by family members. Family members who sexually abuse children or the elderly often rely on the fact that the victim is too vulnerable and scared to reveal that the abuse is taking place. This vulnerability is a critical quality that the abuser uses as he or she selects a victim. Thus, very careful attention must be paid to elderly individuals and children who carry this "risk factor."

What Are the Indicators?

As with the other forms of abuse, there can be both physical and behavioral indicators. Physical indicators may include injuries or bruises, while behavioral indicators are ways victims and abusers act or interact with each other. Some of the indicators listed below can be explained by other causes (e.g., inappropriate or unusual behavior may signal dementia or drug interactions), and no single indicator can be taken as conclusive proof. Rather, one should look for patterns or clusters of indicators that suggest a problem. For example, one of the more recent controversies in retirement communities and assisted living centers is the rise of senior residents having sex and with it a rise in the rate of sexually transmitted diseases (STDs). That said, in the case of sexual abuse there are very few physical or behavioral indicators that could be attributed to any other cause and thus should be investigated immediately. For example, though one might suffer a hip fracture by falling—as opposed to being pushed—a woman is unlikely to develop vaginal tearing from anything other than aggressive sexual contact.

BOX 5.4   SENIOR STDS

STDs Spread Among Boomers, Seniors
You're Never Too Old for HIV, Activist Says

Darlene Dunn, Staff Writer

Updated 3:54 p.m. CDT September 23, 2008

Jane Fowler found herself back on the dating scene after being married 23 years. Then, she found out she had HIV.

"I was not promiscuous at all," Fowler said. "I went out with men who were known to me. They had been married and had divorced. They were acquaintances."

After dating a few years and having unprotected sex, the mother and grandmother got her diagnosis when she was 56.

"I thought they mixed my blood up with someone else's," Fowler, now 73, said.

She hadn't felt it necessary to use condoms.

"Women who had gone through menopause or a procedure to not get pregnant didn't use rubbers. That's what we called them," she said. "They were strictly used for contraception, so if you didn't need contraception, why did you need a condom?"

No matter what their ages, Fowler cautioned everyone about the dangers of having unprotected sex. She said protection is a must for everyone who isn't in a mutually monogamous relationship where both people are sure they are disease-free.

"If your partner refuses to use protection, you better find a new partner," she said.

Fowler's warning comes at a time when more vigilance is needed.

According to research in the journal of Sexually Transmitted Infections, the rates of sexually transmitted infections have doubled among the over 45 population in less than a decade.

The most commonly diagnosed infection among the over 45s was genital warts, accounting for almost half of the episodes. Herpes was the next most common, accounting for almost one in five.

Cases of Chlamydia, herpes, warts, gonorrhea and syphilis all rose sharply.

Christopher Scipio, a holistic herpes and human papillomavirus specialist, agrees with Fowler that people should discuss practicing safe sex. He added that baby boomers should also talk about what they have and have not been tested for.

Scipio, 43, was diagnosed with herpes at 24 years old. He wanted to turn a negative into a positive with his practice, which provides an individualized approach to treating the virus.

He said that women typically have more symptoms than men, and women 35 to 50 have hormonal imbalances and this may trigger outbreaks.

He added that it is important for Baby Boomers to get tested and then be honest with prospective partners.

Dr. Dorree Lynn, a psychologist, author and founder of *50 and Furthermore* said the problem can be attributed to seniors being left out of the conversation involving safe sex.

BOX 5.4   **SENIOR STDS** *continued*

"Sex in nursing homes is more common than ever," Lynn writes. "The perception among seniors is that having unprotected sex doesn't matter. They don't need birth control, so they don't use condoms. Wrong. Assisted living residences, retirement homes and families are in denial. Behind closed doors or curtains, elder couples are in fact doing it. I'd like senior facilities to work out plans that allow their residents to have intimacy, including sex, in safe, inviting and protected environments."

Lynn added that experts believe HIV infection rates among older Americans are likely higher than statistics show.

"Many of the symptoms of AIDS are often falsely diagnosed because they mimic the natural aging process," Lynn writes. "Sometimes, it's difficult for physicians to determine if a person has the flu or is infected with the virus. Symptoms of both may include night sweats, chronic fatigue, weight loss, dementia and swollen lymph nodes."

"So many seniors are returning to the dating scene after being divorced or widowed, and many aren't aware of the prevalence of sexually transmitted diseases and therefore fail to take the proper precautions," Lynn writes. "Testing and educating seniors of all ages is a must. We want them happy, healthy and alive."

SOURCE: http://www.lifewhile.com/health/17506370/detail.html.

INDICATIONS OF SEXUAL ABUSE

Physical Indicators

- genital or anal pain, irritation, or bleeding
- bruises on external genitalia or inner thighs
- difficulty walking or sitting
- torn, stained, or bloody underclothing
- sexually transmitted diseases

Behavioral Indicators

- inappropriate sex-role relationship between victim and suspect
- inappropriate, unusual, or aggressive sexual behavior

THEORETICAL EXPLANATIONS

Several theoretical models have been developed or adapted in an attempt to explain elder abuse. Here we will briefly review each and provide a discussion of the strengths and weaknesses of each.

Psychological Models: Psychologists and public health researchers have investigated the support for a **psychological model** for explaining elder abuse. This model focuses primarily on individual factors in predicting perpetrators of elder abuse. The most common psychological factors that emerge from these studies are a history of violent behavior, mental illness, and substance abuse (Wang et al. 2009). Pillemer and Finkelhor (2010) found that when surveyed, care providers for the elderly identified their own psychological problems as a greater cause of elder abuse than the qualities of the person being cared for. The data and case studies that we have provided in this chapter suggest that psychological models have many strengths in explaining elder abuse. The reader will recall, for example, that financial abuse often occurs when a care provider who suffers from substance abuse is looking for money to either pay for the abused substance or handle debts that have accrued as a result of the substance abuse. Psychological models fail to explain cases of abuse when the care provider is not suffering from either mental health issues or substance abuse, nor do they explain other patterns of elder abuse, such as the fact that in family settings, it is often perpetrated by women, while it appears to be an "equal opportunity" crime when it occurs either in institutions or as part of a scam.

Social Learning Theory: **Social learning theory** could be applied to understanding elder abuse, though it is not commonly done. Social learning theory argues that socialization creates patterns of behavior: children learn by watching their parents and other important adults—teachers, religious leaders, coaches—behave, and they pattern their own behavior on what they observe. According to social learning theorists, an adult caregiver who engages in elder abuse would have likely grown up in a situation where they were exposed to abuse. One of the strengths of this theoretical perspective is that it explains the intergenerational transmission of violence: in particular, boys who grow up in violent homes are far more likely to be abusive as adults, especially with their female partners (Ehrensaft and Cohen 2003). There are several weaknesses of social learning theory as it would be applied to the case of elder abuse. First, the majority of elder abuse is not physical, but rather it is neglect, emotional, and financial. It is unlikely that these forms of abuse would be learned. Second, the evidence for intergenerational transmission of violence focuses on the experience of boys; men and women perpetrate elder abuse at about the same rates (Cooper, Selwood, and Livingston 2008). Last, in general, social learning theory is not widely used by family violence scholars because it fails to address patterns of abuse and fails to hold abusers accountable.

Symbolic Interaction Theory: Though **symbolic interaction theory** is not applied to the study of family violence in general or elder abuse in particular, one of its components, role theory, is useful in explaining family violence. Role theory postulates that there are prescribed roles for the elder and the care provider. When individuals behave in ways that are aligned with our expectations for these roles, then interactions go smoothly; when behaviors are contradictory to our expectations, then conflict will arise. In the case of elder care, abuse is more likely to occur when the expectations the caregiver has for the elder's behavior are not met—for example, if the elder is demanding or difficult to deal with. Indeed, in their meta-analysis, Cooper and colleagues argue that paid care providers are less likely to abuse their charges because paid caregivers work fewer hours and have more realistic expectations for care providing (Cooper, Selwood, and Livingston 2008).

Social Exchange Theory: Pioneers of family violence research Richard Gelles and Murray Straus developed a specific form of **social exchange theory** in order to explain family violence. The reader will recall a lengthy discussion of family violence theory in Chapter 3. In sum, social exchange theory purports that abuse and neglect are more likely to occur when the balance of power in the relationship shifts. This theoretical perspective is quite useful in explaining neglect and abuse that is perpetrated by adult children caring for their aging parents: the long-standing flow of resources from parents to children is reversed, and resources must now flow from child to parent. This theoretical perspective is not as useful for explaining abuse and neglect perpetrated by paid care providers and domestic violence that has been ongoing and continues into the later years in life.

Situational Theory: One of the theories most commonly used to understand and explain family violence, and elder abuse and child abuse in particular, is situational theory. **Situational theory** suggests that the strains, stresses, and burdens that are typically part of long-term caregiving to needy individuals—the elderly and young children—can lead to abuse. Thus, elderly persons who have many of the risk factors that we presented earlier in this chapter (e.g., having dementia and other cognitive diseases, suffering with incontinence, and requiring extensive care for daily needs) present a higher risk for being abused. Similarly, care providers who are ill-equipped to provide care, who lack the resources necessary to provide appropriate care, and those with other life stressors, including being part of the sandwich generation, are predicted by situational theory to experience higher risks for abuse. Again, like social exchange theory, the primary weakness of situational theory is its limited ability to explain long-term intimate partner violence that continues into old age.

Ecological Theory: Similar to situational theory, **ecological theory** focuses attention on the other contexts in which the victim and the abuser "reside"—for example, their other relationships, including marriages and friendships, their involvement in work or church, and any other institution that might provide social support. Again, though seldom used to explain the causes of family violence, ecological theory is useful in that it elucidates the role that social support networks can play in *reducing* the likelihood of abuse or neglect occurring. When paired with situational theory—which best explains the risks for abuse—it is useful for explaining the *protective qualities* that researchers have identified and we have discussed in this chapter, including the reduced likelihood for abuse when victims are ambulatory and cognitively intact. As with the other theories, its major weakness is that it cannot explain long-term intimate partner violence.

Feminist Theory: **Feminist theory**, as discussed at length in Chapter 3, is based on the assumption that patriarchy creates a gender-based hierarchy that structures all of social life. Feminist theory is the only theory that adequately explains elder abuse when it is the continuation of intimate partner violence. Given that this remains the most common form of violence experienced by the elderly (Pillemer and Finkelhor 2010), it is critical to include a feminist perspective in analyzing, understanding, and predicting violent elder abuse. Feminist theory is also the most appropriate model for understanding and explaining sexual abuse, which is primarily perpetrated by men regardless of the gender of the victim. That said, the primary weakness of feminist theory is its inability to adequately explain all other forms of abuse and neglect that are experienced by the elderly, including abuse by paid care providers, abuse by children who are caring for aging parents, and abuse that is perpetrated by a spouse—male or female—who is caring for the other and does not onset until later life.

While the field of elder abuse lacks a unifying theoretical framework to guide research, analysis, intervention, and prevention (Bonnie and Wallace 2003), drawing on the strengths of each of the different theoretical frameworks and incorporating the contributions each can make can improve our understanding of elder abuse.

CONCLUSIONS

Elder abuse is a relatively new social problem that was first recognized by scholars and practitioners only during the last half of the twentieth century. As noted, this is partly because, like so many forms of family abuse, elder abuse tends to occur behind closed doors in the privacy of an elderly person's home and partly due to the changing demographics of the United States. The past century has seen a dramatic rise in the life expectancy for all Americans, and thus the percentage of the population that reaches "old age" has also risen dramatically. Quite simply, there is now a population of older Americans who can be abused.

Along with the rise in life expectancy comes the likelihood that we will experience both chronic and terminal illnesses that cause us to require significant assistance and may make us dependent upon others not only for our health matters but for our daily care as well. The stresses associated with caring for an aging and often ill parent or grandparent are believed to be part of the cause of certain forms of elder abuse, specifically physical abuse, neglect, and financial abuse. This is exacerbated by the fact that many caregivers are part of the sandwich generation and thus caring for their own children and families as well.

In addition, because not all adult sons and daughters are in a position to care for aging parents—in part because they may live in different parts of the country as a result of job requirements or because they cannot afford to retire themselves and devote themselves to the care of their aging parents—and because some of the chronic and terminal diseases that afflict the elderly require some sort of institutional care, the number of elderly living in an institutional setting has risen dramatically over the past half century and with it the probability for abuse by nonrelative caregivers. Elder abuse, like child abuse, is tragic in part because it involves abusing or taking advantage of the most vulnerable persons in our society.

There are reasons to be hopeful. First and foremost is the fact that elder abuse is now recognized by researchers and practitioners, and as a result research is being done and policies are being developed to prevent elder abuse and intervene in it when it occurs. For example, we are seeing modifications of Adult Protective Services—the elderly version of Child Protective Services—as a social service option for intervening in elder abuse. Second, as a result of some cases of financial abuse as well as the growing attention that dementia garners—spurred largely by the impact on former National Football League players who have some notoriety and celebrity and who tragically develop dementia very early in life, in their forties and fifties, as a direct result of concussions and head trauma—more and more people are aware of the challenges of aging and the importance of appropriate care. Third, as baby boomers have experienced the sandwich generation and soon will begin to be considered "elderly," this large demographic group that holds more resources than any other in the United States is beginning to bring its own resources and attention to the issues of aging generally, and this impacts the movement around elder abuse as well. Thus, we have every reason to be hopeful that the next decade will result in improvements in the lives of our elderly. We turn now to a discussion of abuse at the other end of the age spectrum: child abuse.

RESOURCES

National Committee for the Prevention of Elder Abuse: http://www.preventelder abuse.org/
Journal of the American Medical Association Fact Sheet on Elder Abuse: http://jama .ama-assn.org/cgi/reprint/302/5/588.pdf

BIBLIOGRAPHY

Arias, Elizabeth. 2010. *United States Life Tables, 2006.* Washington, DC: US Department of Health and Human Services, National Center for Health Statistics.

Bonnie, Richard J., and Robert B. Wallace. 2003. *Elder Mistreatment: Abuse, Neglect, and Exploitation in an Aging America.* Washington, DC: National Academies Press.

Cooper, Claudia, Amber Selwood, and Gill Livingston. 2008. "The Prevalence of Elder Abuse and Neglect: A Systematic Review." *Age and Ageing* 37: 151–160.

Ehrensaft, Miriam, and Patricia Cohen. 2003. "Intergenerational Transmission of Partner Violence: A 20-Year Prospective Study." *Journal of Consulting and Clinical Psychology* 7: 741–753.

Hattery, Angela J., and Earl Smith. 2007. *African American Families.* Thousand Oaks, CA: Sage.

Lachs, Mark S., and Karl Pillemer. 2004. "Elder Abuse." *Lancet* 364: 1192–1263.

Mouton, Charles P., Rebecca J. Rodabough, Susan L. D. Rovi, Julie L. Hunt, Melissa A. Talamantes, Robert G. Brzyski, and Sandra K. Burge. 2004. "Prevalence and 3-Year Incidence of Abuse Among Postmenopausal Women." *American Public Health Association* 94: 605–612.

National Center for Health Statistics. 2004. *Health, United States, with Chartbook on Trends in the Health of Americans.* Atlanta: Centers for Disease Control.

Pillemer, Karl, and David Finkelhor. 2010. "Causes of Elder Abuse." *Journal of Orthopsychiatry* 59: 179–187.

Reis, Harry T., and Peter Franks. 1994. "The Role of Intimacy and Social Support in Health Outcomes: Two Processes or One?" *Personal Relationships* 1: 185–197.

Shapiro, Thomas. 2003. *The Hidden Cost of Being African American: How Wealth Perpetuates Inequality.* New York: Oxford University Press.

Sneed, Michael. 2001. "Ordeal Exposed Many Problems." *Chicago Sun Times*, December 17.

Wang, J. J., M. F. Lin, H. F. Tseng, and W. Y. Chang. 2009. "Caregiver Factors Contributing to Psychological Elder Abuse Behavior in Long-Term Care Facilities: A Structural Equation Model Approach." *International Psychogeriatrics* 2: 314–320.

6 Abuse Across the Life Course

Child Abuse

A trial began in Dallas Wednesday (July 2010) for a man accused of locking his girlfriend's children in a hotel bathroom and starving them for up to nine months.

The man charged in the case, Alfred Santiago, had lived in the hotel room with the children's mother, Abneris Santiago. The two share a last name, but were not married. A fourth child, a 1-year-old girl who was Alfred Santiago's biological daughter, was found healthy and unharmed. . . . A doctor has said the children appeared to have been starved and that their condition was life-threatening. The 11-year-old said she had been sexually assaulted, and the eldest son was covered in bruises from a beating authorities said was delivered by his mother's boyfriend.

—"Trial Begins for Dallas Father Accused of Starving Kids," July 27, 2010

This chapter will focus on various aspects of child abuse. We will include discussions of parental abuse of children, sibling abuse, sexual abuse, as well as abuse by nonrelatives that impacts family life—for example, abuse by caregivers, clergy, coaches, and other mentors. In addition to reviewing trends and data on various forms of child abuse, we will review the theories that have been developed to explain it. Finally, we will include a discussion of the legal response to child abuse and the controversies that surround the often highly charged claims of child abuse. This chapter will provide a framework for understanding highly publicized instances of child abuse as well.

OBJECTIVES

- To provide an overview of the prevalence of various forms of child abuse as they occur in the contemporary United States
- To explore the different types of child abuse, including physical abuse, sexual abuse, and neglect
- To provide an overview of physical child abuse by nonfamily members, typically in institutional settings, including juvenile prisons

- To examine the disturbing nature of sexual abuse by mentors—coaches, the Catholic Church, and others—as well as the rise in sexual predatory abuse that is enhanced by the Internet and social networking sites like Facebook
- To familiarize the reader with the legal responses to child abuse of all forms
- To summarize the recent changes in prevention and intervention strategies that move beyond the criminal justice system and include health care and social services

KEY TERMS

emotional abuse	parent and caregiver risk factors
witnessing violence	cycle of abuse
physical abuse	family structure risk factors
neglect	noncoresidential parents
sexual abuse	child risk factors
mandatory reporters	shaken baby syndrome
child protective services (CPS)	ephebophilia
Guardian Ad Litem (GAL)	environmental risk factors
foster care	protective factors

INTRODUCTION

In the last chapter we examined the phenomenon of elder abuse, and we argued that part of the tragedy of elder abuse beyond the devastation for individuals who are victims or the loved ones of victims is the fact that elder abuse is a stain on a culture and society that is built on the principles of equal rights, including the right to pursue happiness. In the cases of both elder abuse and child abuse, the most vulnerable of our citizens are denied the rights on which our society is built, and this makes their experiences, when taken as a whole, that much more tragic. In this chapter we explore the phenomenon of another vulnerable group of Americans: children.

A BRIEF OVERVIEW

As discussed at length in Chapter 2, historians and other scholars reasonably argue that child abuse and neglect have occurred throughout most of human history. As we moved into the latter half of the twentieth century and the beginning of the twenty-first century in the United States, our understanding of child abuse has shifted significantly in ways that can be described as "prochild." For example, standards regarding corporal punishment have changed not only in the family but also in institutions such as public schools (*Journal of Blacks in Higher Education* 2001), and the right of a child to an education has been recognized and affirmed by Supreme Court decisions. Thus, the era in which we live represents many changes in our collective beliefs about child abuse as well as significant advancements in our laws regarding the rights and protections for children. Yet despite these advances in broadening the definitions of child abuse and revising the laws to protect children, child abuse rates continue to rise.

PREVALENCE OF CHILD ABUSE

According to the CDC, which gathers statistics on child abuse monthly and annually and reports them in easy-to-access "fact sheets," in 2009 more than 5.8 million children in the United States were involved in 3.2 million acts of abuse.* More than 5 children die *every day*, or 1,800 children per year, as a direct result of child abuse, yet abuse and maltreatment are listed on death certificates in perhaps only 15 percent to 35 percent of the cases in which abuse is the cause or a contributing factor. Sadly, 75 percent of the children who die each day of child abuse are under the age of four (http://www.cdc.gov/violenceprevention/pdf/CM-DataSheet-a.pdf).

As the data in Figure 6.1 demonstrate, the number of children who die each day has risen steadily over the past decade, which reflects both an increase in the size of the US population, which topped 300 million in 2008, as well as our failure as a society to keep our children safe.

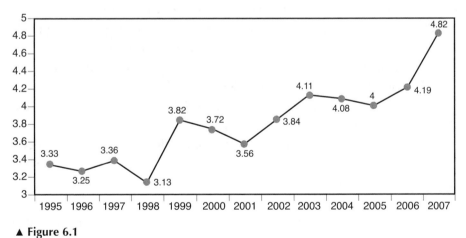

▲ **Figure 6.1**
Number of Child Deaths per Day Due to Child Abuse and Neglect

Source: ChildHelp (http://www.childhelp.org/)

---

* Reports of an abusive event can involve more than one child, which is what accounts for the discrepancy between the number of cases and the number of children.

TYPES OF CHILD ABUSE

As was the case with elder abuse, there are many different forms that child abuse can take, including physical abuse, sexual abuse, emotional abuse, and neglect. In this section we discuss each type of abuse by providing definitions, warning signs, and illustrations.

The core element that ties all forms of child abuse together is the emotional effect on the child. According to the think tank and resource center ChildHelp: "Children need predictability, structure, clear boundaries, and the knowledge that their parents are looking out for their safety. Abused children cannot predict how their parents will act. Their world is an unpredictable, frightening place with no rules. Whether the abuse is a slap, a harsh comment, stony silence, or not knowing if there will be dinner on the table tonight, the end result is a child that feels unsafe, uncared for, and alone" (http://www.childhelp.org/).

Emotional Abuse

Emotional abuse involves talking to a child in a manner that makes him or her feel inferior and inadequate. Distinct from discipline, which might involve explaining to a child how his or her behavior is unacceptable or hurtful, emotional abuse often involves telling children that they are "dumb" or "stupid" or in severe cases blaming them for the parent's problems—for example, by telling a child that the parent would not have lost his or her job or would not have trouble paying the bills if it were not for the child. Emotional abuse often involves humiliating the child in public—for example, calling a child a "crybaby" or pointing out in public that a child is still wetting the bed or having "accidents." These kinds of comments are humiliating and often leave deep and long-term emotional and psychological scars. Emotional abuse can also involve ignoring a child as part of "punishment," withholding affection, and exposing children to violence in the household, such as the beating of a sibling or the torture of a pet.

ChildHelp (http://www.childhelp.org/), a nonprofit foundation that was developed to act as a clearinghouse for statistics on child abuse, to develop educational materials and programming designed to prevent child abuse, and to provide intervention programs for victims of child abuse, is an excellent source of data on the rates of various forms of child abuse as well as for practical information regarding child abuse. In addition to being a clearinghouse for statistics and prevention programming, ChildHelp is also a reporting agency with direct links to county Child Protective Services in each of the fifty states. ChildHelp provides the following list of warning signs of emotional abuse in children:

- excessively withdrawn, fearful, or anxious about doing something wrong

- shows extremes in behavior (extremely compliant or extremely demanding; extremely passive or extremely aggressive)
- does not seem to be attached to the parent or caregiver
- acts either inappropriately "adult" (taking care of other children) or inappropriately infantile (rocking, thumb-sucking, throwing toddlerlike tantrums)

Witnessing Violence

Relatively recently, scholars of child abuse and practitioners have begun to recognize the role that **witnessing violence**, especially domestic violence, has on young children. In particular, when boys witness domestic violence, their risk for growing up to beat their own wives and girlfriends *triples* (Ehrensaft and Cohen 2003). As a result of this significant outcome—a topic to which we will devote the entire next chapter—scholars and practitioners have begun to formally identify children who witness domestic violence as child abuse victims. This label is important for many reasons, first and foremost because labeling the witnesses of domestic violence *as victims* entitles them to the types of social services that are generally restricted to victims. For example, children who witness domestic violence and live in counties where this is labeled as child abuse are entitled to counseling, intervention programs, and the development of family safety plans. Additionally, this identification as victims of child abuse renders them eligible for court interventions. For example, the repeated witnessing of domestic violence by a child may result in a hearing to determine whether the child should stay in the home or be removed temporarily or permanently. Though jurisdictions vary greatly in terms of their support for defining the witnessing of domestic violence as child abuse, one good example comes from the state of Minnesota, where any child determined by the police to have been "in sight or sound" of domestic violence is thereby considered a victim of child abuse and is referred to all of the relevant responders, including Child Protective Services.

A child who is witnessing domestic violence in the home may exhibit many of the same symptoms of children who are experiencing emotional abuse, including low self-esteem, being withdrawn, and so forth. Unfortunately, the most significant indicator may not be visible for years, and that is the likelihood, especially for male victims, of becoming batterers. As we will discuss at length in the next chapter, attention to child witnesses of domestic violence is critical to interrupt the cycle of violence.

Physical Abuse

As the name implies, **physical abuse** entails causing physical injury to a child. Note that the intent of the harmful action does not determine whether it is abusive, only the outcome. But understanding the intent—a common cause of injury, referred to as shaken baby syndrome, which is unintended but can cause severe injury—may help social workers and agents of the court determine appropriate intervention strategies for the adult who is engaging in child abuse. We will return to a lengthy discussion of shaken baby syndrome later in the chapter.

As was the case with elder abuse, certainly injuries can and are sustained by children every day in the normal context of their lives; children fall down the stairs, they fall off bikes, and so forth, which can result in the same kinds of injuries that are typical of child abuse: common injuries include bruises, lacerations, broken bones, and burns. Thus, any discrete incident is not necessarily an indicator of child abuse. That said, physicians, teachers, coaches, and other adults who interact with children should investigate any injury, and they should pay particular attention to a pattern of injuries that seems to defy explanation. For example, sustaining multiple broken bones across a school year might indicate that abuse is taking place. Similarly, with radiological technologies, physicians can identify patterns of abuse based on recently healed or unhealed injuries that were never treated but appear on an X-ray.

ChildHelp provides the following list of warning signs of physical abuse in children:

- frequent injuries or unexplained bruises, welts, or cuts
- being watchful and "on alert," as if waiting for something bad to happen
- having injuries with a distinctive pattern such as marks from a hand or belt
- shies away from touch, flinches at sudden movements, or seems afraid to go home
- wearing inappropriate clothing to cover up injuries, such as long-sleeved shirts on hot days

Neglect

As noted in Figure 6.2, child neglect is the most common type of child abuse, accounting for approximately 60 percent of all abuse cases. Similar to neglect as a form of elder abuse, **neglect** that constitutes child abuse appears as a pattern of failing to provide for a child's basic needs, whether it be adequate food, clothing, hygiene, or supervision. Child neglect is not always easy to spot. For example, unless a child becomes seriously ill from malnourishment, it may be difficult to spot a child who is not getting an adequate diet. Perhaps the most difficult form of neglect to identify is a lack of supervision. It is not uncommon among low-income, single mothers to leave their children unattended at night while they sleep so that the mother can work a better-paying third-shift job. These instances are difficult to spot unless tragedy strikes. For example, every year children die in home fires that began while their mothers were at work and the children were left unattended. Quite often these mothers were not being intentionally neglectful but were doing their best to provide a steady income for the family in a market where child care costs often consume an *entire* minimum-wage paycheck. Similarly, there are many children in extremely low-income families who meet the technical definition of neglect in terms of adequate food and housing, yet the only real "crime" is that their caregivers—often single mothers or grandmothers—are very poor and do not receive adequate support from the government to provide for the children in their care (Edin and Lein 1997). This situation does not negate the impact of the neglect on the child, but rather indicates the need to understand the source of the neglect in order to design appropriate interventions. Poor mothers may not need classes in parenting or the proper care of their children, but what they often need is income support, housing support, and child care support so that they can work to earn a living and be sure their children are adequately taken care of while they labor. Thinking about child abuse in this way is part of what distinguishes a sociological approach from some other approaches. Though we acknowledge, and will discuss in the subsequent section, individual explanations for child neglect—being a young parent, not having an adequate understanding of what children need, or simply being a neglectful person—as sociologists we believe it is important to keep our focus on structural explanations as well because these are often ignored by the general public. One rarely hears, for example, from newscasters telling a tragic story or politicians' discussion of the state of the American family the role that poverty plays in a parent's ability to provide adequately for his or her children. It is far "easier" to blame "bad" parents than to point out that inequalities are very real in the United States, and these inequalities produce child victims of neglect.

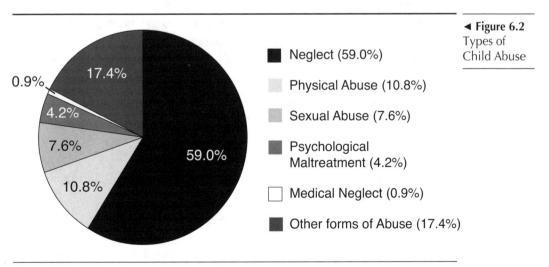

◄ Figure 6.2
Types of
Child Abuse

Source: ChildHelp (http://www.childhelp.org/)

It is also important to note some of the individual causes of child abuse. In many cases, child neglect occurs when a parent becomes physically or mentally unable to care for a child, such as with a serious injury, untreated depression, or anxiety. Other times, alcohol or drug abuse may seriously impair judgment and the ability to keep a child safe. In interviews we conducted with men and women who had recently been released from prison, we heard countless stories of neglect that were related to untreated drug addiction. Because many drugs suppress an addict's appetite for food, children of drug addicts often live every day with empty refrigerators and cupboards (Hattery and Smith 2010).

Depression and other mental illnesses may have this effect as well. Thus, the neglect experienced by children of drug addicts or untreated mentally ill parents may run the gamut from lack of food to soiled clothing, from infrequent bathing to a lack of supervision. In extreme cases, we heard about children growing up without functioning indoor plumbing and being forced to Dumpster-dive for food. Again, as with poverty, understanding the source of the neglect does not negate the impact of it on the child victims. However, failing to understand the source of the neglect limits our ability to propose appropriate interventions.

One final complicating factor in child neglect cases is that older children might not show outward signs of neglect, especially if they have been experiencing it for a long period of time. They may have become used to presenting a competent face to the outside world and figured out how to get access to the things they need, like food and clothing, in order to do so. In many cases, older children adopt the role of the parent—especially in cases of untreated addiction or mental illness—and do their best to prevent or interrupt the neglect of their younger siblings. Though having to take on the role of a parent is a form of abuse or neglect that is difficult to substantiate, according to ChildHelp, it may be an indicator of emotional abuse. Either way, the reader can imagine that having to take on the role of "parent" to younger siblings can take a terrible toll on older children.

ChildHelp provides the following list of warning signs of child neglect:

- clothes are ill-fitting, filthy, or inappropriate for the weather
- hygiene is consistently bad (visibly soiled, matted and unwashed hair, noticeable body odor)
- untreated illnesses and physical injuries
- is frequently unsupervised or left alone or allowed to play in unsafe situations and environments
- is frequently late to or missing from school

In sum, neglected children are not getting their physical and emotional needs met, and they suffer consequences that range from mild to very serious as a result, and include physical consequences, emotional or psychological consequences, and behavioral consequences.

Physical consequences of neglect may be immediate—such as a "failure to thrive" among infants—but they can also be long-term, such as poor brain development, delayed speech, and inhibited growth that results from long-term malnourishment. Emotional or psychological consequences include depression, anxiety, and an inability to bond with a parent and can include an obsession with food, which can lead to behavioral consequences, including hoarding or stealing. Other behavioral consequences include a higher rate of teen pregnancy and a higher rate of contracting a sexually transmitted disease while a teen—both of which may be a result of seeking affection through sex, sexual abuse, and even selling sex in order to get access to money to buy food and clothes. Child victims of neglect and all forms of abuse also have higher rates of drug and alcohol abuse, and they are more likely to be involved in the juvenile justice system.

Sexual Abuse

Unlike adults, children are legally unable to consent to sexual contact, and therefore *any sexual act—consensual or not—with a child under the age of sixteen (or eighteen, in some states) is considered sexual abuse.* **Sexual abuse** may involve sexual intercourse, but is more likely to be sexual touching or molestation. In addition, it is important to recognize that sexual abuse does not always involve body contact. Exposing a child to sexual situations or sexual material also constitutes sexual abuse, whether touching is involved or not. In one case in which one of the authors was involved as an advocate, the victim was a young teenage girl whose father was taking sexually explicit pictures of her and selling them as part of a child pornography ring. He was prosecuted for both child pornography—which involves possessing nude or sexually explicit images of a child under the age of consent—as well as sexual abuse, based on the fact that the simple act of taking the pictures constituted a sex crime.

The sexual abuse of children is most likely to take place between the child and an adult the child knows. Often, but not always, this adult is a family member, with the most likely perpetrator to be the child's stepfather or mother's boyfriend. However, as we have become increasingly aware due to stories in the news media, children are also at a reasonable risk for sexual abuse from adults who work with children, including Catholic priests, coaches, Scout leaders, and other adult mentors. Every year stories are reported in the media about the sexual abuse of young athletes by their coaches. In the winter of 2011 a scandal broke in USA Swimming, in which, much like the Catholic Church sex scandal (which we will discuss at length in Chapter 10), not only were coaches molesting and assaulting athletes, but the administrators for USA Swimming were aware of the allegations and did nothing, other than suggest that a coach about whom rumors were circulating leave his current pool and relocate. We present a snippet of one case here.

BOX 6.1   SWIMMER'S MOLESTATION

Swimmer Shares Story of Molestation
Updated: May 9, 2010, 6:39 a.m. ET

Editor's note: Julia is a 15-year-old girl from San Jose, Calif. For 10 months, beginning just after her 14th birthday, she was molested by her swim coach, Andy King, until she came forward and her parents called the police. Julia's cooperation with law enforcement led to King's conviction, ending what prosecutors said was 31 years of sexual abuse against a number of his young swimmers. King, 62, pleaded no contest to 20 counts of molestation and is serving a 40-year sentence at Mule Creek State Prison in California.

Source: http://sports.espn.go.com/espn/otl/news/story?id=5174757.

In a forthcoming book by Sugar Ray Leonard, Olympic gold medalist in boxing, he alleges that he, too, was sexually molested by a coach at the age of fifteen. It is clear that this type of abuse knows no bounds with regards to gender, race, or the type of sport. All that is necessary for the abuse to occur is for a coach who has the intention to molest to have the opportunity to be alone with an athlete who is vulnerable. And given the relationship that most coaches have with athletes—they control their playing time, they control their practice regimen, they may be references for college coaches who are recruiting the athlete—*athletes are almost always in a vulnerable position* in their relationships to coaches.

The least-common type of sexual abuse but the one that receives the most attention is the abuse that typically accompanies abductions and murders of young boys and girls. We will provide illustrations of these types of sexual abuse cases later in the chapter, as they are critical to the development of the legal response to child abuse and child sexual abuse in particular.

Finally, we note that contrary to what many people believe, it is not just girls who are at risk. Boys and girls both suffer from sexual abuse. The shame of sexual abuse makes it very difficult for children to come forward. They may worry that others will not believe them or will be angry with them or that it will split their family apart. Because of these difficulties, false accusations of sexual abuse are not common, so if a child makes an accusation or confides in someone, it should be taken very seriously. In fact, because boys may feel higher levels of shame, due to our culturally dominant beliefs about male sexuality—males are supposed to have a higher sex drive, they are supposed to want more sex partners, adolescent males are supposed to desire initiation into sex with an older and more experienced woman like a teacher or babysitter, and so on—the sexual abuse of boys is likely to be even more underreported than that of girls. To illustrate, think about the media coverage that male sexual abuse victims often receive, as was the case of child molester and teacher Mary Kay Letourneau.

BOX 6.2   MARY KAY LETOURNEAU

Mary Kay Letourneau Marries Former Victim

May 20: On this day in 2005, ex-teacher and convicted pedophile Mary Kay Letourneau, 43, marries her former victim and the father of two of her children, Vili Fualaau, 22. Just nine months earlier, Letourneau had been released from prison after serving a seven-and-a-half year sentence for raping Fualaau.

Letourneau first met Fualaau when she was a teacher at Shorewood Elementary School, in the Seattle suburb of Burien, Washington, and he was a second-grader. During the summer of 1996, Letourneau, then 34 and a married mother of four, began a sexual relationship with her former sixth-grade student, then 12.

The relationship was eventually discovered and in February 1997, Letourneau was arrested for rape. In May, the former teacher, who was born Mary Katherine Schmitz in California in 1962, gave birth to the couple's first child, a daughter named Audrey. That August, Letourneau pled guilty to two counts of second-degree child rape. Judge Linda Lau of King County Superior Court showed Letourneau leniency by suspending her 89-month sentence and the former teacher was ordered to serve six months in jail, attend a treatment program and have no contact with Fualaau. Her case sparked a tabloid frenzy as well as a national debate over whether female sex offenders are treated differently than men who commit similar crimes.

On February 3, 1998, after being released from jail in six months, Letourneau was discovered in a parked car with Fualaau and arrested for violating the conditions of her suspended sentence. Investigators found a large amount of cash in the vehicle, along with a passport and some baby clothes, indicating that the couple might have been planning to flee the area with their young daughter. Three days later, on February 6, Judge Lau reinstated Letourneau's original sentence and sent her back to prison. In October, Letourneau gave birth to her second child with Fualaau, a daughter named Alexis. The children were raised by Fualaau's mother while Letourneau remained in prison. Fualaau and his mother, Soona, later sued the Highline School District and the city of Des Moines, Washington, for over $2 million, claiming police and school officials didn't do enough to protect Vili. In May 2002, a jury ruled the Fualaaus were not entitled to any money.

In August 2004, Letourneau was released from prison, and a judge lifted a ban prohibiting her from contacting Fualaau, by then an adult. On this day in 2005, Letourneau

continues

BOX 6.2   MARY KAY LETOURNEAU *continued*

and Fualaau wed, amid tight security, in a ceremony at the Columbia Winery in Wood-inville, Washington, outside Seattle. The couple's two daughters served as flower girls and Letourneau's daughter from her first marriage, which lasted from 1984 to 1999, was the maid of honor. The television show *Entertainment Tonight* negotiated exclusive rights to film the ceremony.

SOURCE: http://www.history.com/this-day-in-history/mary-kay-letourneau-marries-former -victim.

ChildHelp provides the following list of warning signs of child sexual abuse:

- trouble walking or sitting
- displays knowledge or interest in sexual acts inappropriate to his or her age, or even seductive behavior
- makes strong efforts to avoid a specific person, without an obvious reason
- does not want to change clothes in front of others or participate in physical activities
- an STD or pregnancy, especially under the age of fourteen
- runs away from home

Child Sexual Abuse and the Internet

The Internet has created a whole host of new ways in which to engage in child sexual abuse. For example, sexual predators often initiate contact with prospective victims using social networking sites like Facebook. Once they establish trust, they arrange to meet their potential victim, often luring her or him with alcohol or drugs, and then proceeding to sexually abuse them. Child trafficking and child pornography, often engaged in by adult relatives of child victims, is also greatly facilitated by the Internet. A parent wishing to "sell" a son or daughter into prostitution can utilize the Internet to find prospective "pimps" or "johns"; similarly, a stepfather seeking to circulate images of his stepson or -daughter will likely circulate these using the Internet.

Additionally, almost daily there is a news report of a case of child sexual abuse or of an adolescent having committed suicide based on information that was circulated over the Internet.

Perhaps most disturbing is the way in which the Internet and social media have been used to engage in child sexual abuse. Again, almost daily, a news outlet re-

---

TYLER CLEMENTI

In the fall of 2010 there was a rash of suicides that involved young men and women who were "outed" as gay or lesbian. In one particularly well-covered case, social media led to the "outing" that eventually led to the suicide. Tyler Clementi, a Rutgers University first-year student, was exploring his sexuality. Suspecting that he might be gay, Clementi's roommate, Dhuran Ravi, set up a webcam in their room to capture and broadcast from their room one evening when Clementi had indicated he was bringing a friend over. Ravi then invited others to watch while Clementi engaged in sexual behavior with another man. The next day, when Clementi learned of the broadcast and his "outing," he jumped from the George Washington Bridge in an act of suicide.

---

ports on a "sting" operation in which undercover police and FBI agents, posing as preadolescent girls, receive solicitations for sex. In a typical scenario of actual abuse, a sexual predator "friends" a young girl on Facebook. They begin chatting using Facebook, text messages, instant messaging, and email. After "grooming" the victim, the sexual predator arranges for a meeting. When the girl arrives, he often plies her with alcohol or drugs and then proceeds to sexually molest or assault her. Thousands of these cases occur every year, and the sting operations often capture predators who have assaulted dozens of girls by the time they are caught.

The Internet has also allowed for the perpetuation of controversial organizations of men who advocate sex between adult men and preadolescent and adolescent boys. These groups are considered by the majority of the public as well as all scholars and practitioners to be engaging in child sexual abuse. And we agree. We include some material on this movement so that the reader is made aware of its existence and perspective. In short, these men argue that sexuality is not and should not be limited by age; humans are sexual at birth until death, and thus it is unnatural to impose any limitations on children's sexuality. Though scholars of sexuality confirm some sexual function in babies and toddlers—for example, often by the age of two boys will regularly have erections (Mayo Clinic Health, http://www .mayoclinic.com)—it is also widely understood that this natural function is not *sexual behavior*. Children lack the cognitive ability to understand sexuality, and thus, as a culture, we in the United States prohibit sexual behavior between adults—who have the cognitive ability to understand sexual behavior—and children. The man-boy love movement is an example of a group of men who believe that children should be allowed to engage in sexual behavior of all types, including with adults.

BOX 6.3	**MAN-BOY LOVE MOVEMENT**

FEEDBACK
Letters From Our Readers

Dear NAMBLA, I will be out of this jail in nine months for good and will lend my services as needed to further the fight for freedom to chose whom a man, as well as a boy, can be with and LOVE. We both know that sex is not the main thing. It's the love and care that is shared between the two.

I myself have been involved in a relationship with a boy since he was eight years old. He is 16 years old now and we still have the same love, care, and joy. Foolish people may think he is "too young to make up his mind" or that "I made up his mind for him." To that I say BULLSHIT! Everything has been consensual, plus we did not even have any sexual contact until the year of his sweet sixteenth birthday (and boy was it sweet). As life isn't fair, we are apart for the first time in eight years, but only for nine months. He comes to see me every weekend and we talk and laugh, then a sad time comes when he has to leave. This kid is very normal. He does things all boys his age do. He has a girl friend and a boy friend (me). I respect him and he respects me. Maybe one day he'll get married and have "not to fret." He'll always love me for the things I've taught him, the love I've given him so freely, and the happiness we've shared with each other. So in closing, I say keep sending the Bulletins. After I read them I send them to my friend and love. If loving Robbie is wrong, I don't want to be right! Courage to all the other boys, men, girls, and women that want to just love each other. You're not alone! One day these fools will see that LOVE IS GOOD in whatever form it comes in.

Source: From the NAMBLA Bulletin, Vol. 13, No. 10, Pg. 6, Dec 1992.

The BLOGO was designed . . . to celebrate man/boy love. This symbol is also used by adult men who seek to engage in sex with under-age boys as a symbol that is easily recognizable to other men who "love" boys.

We wanted to create an image that was not too "in your face" so as to permit the user to acknowledge it's true meaning or . . . be as non-commital as the situation demands.

MANDATORY REPORTERS

One of the aspects of child abuse that makes it distinct from other forms of abuse is the designation of a class of people referred to as "mandatory reporters." The Child Abuse Prevention and Treatment Act (CAPTA), which was renewed in 2003, requires that all fifty states have requirements and processes for the mandatory reporting of the physical or sexual abuse of children or child neglect. **Mandatory**

reporters include "health care providers and facilities of all types, mental health care providers of all types, teachers and other school personnel [including coaches], social workers, day care providers and law enforcement personnel. Many states require film developers to report" (Child Abuse and Prevention and Treatment Act 2003). We note that the requirement for film developers to report suspected child abuse arose from the fact that amateur child pornographers were often taking pictures of their own children or of neighborhood children and having these images developed by local companies like Walgreens, before circulating the images via mail or on the Internet. Thus, film developers played a critical role in detecting child pornography rings. Today, because most images are taken electronically and uploaded directly to the Internet or printed on home printers, the role of film developers in detecting child pornography has likely decreased.

In the majority of situations, cases reported by mandatory reporters are referred to the state's Child Protective Services.

> **Child Protective Services** is the local agency in each county that is legally charged with investigating allegations of child abuse or neglect.

It is important to note that children are not necessarily removed from the home in all cases, but CPS officials have the legal right to remove children and place them in foster care if the investigation reveals that this is the most appropriate intervention. In addition to criminal charges that may be brought by CPS, child abuse is frequently part of child custody cases—which are civil court matters—as well. Because children, especially those who are abused by their parents or parent figures, may be reluctant to speak on their own behalf—for fear of losing their parent(s), being removed from the household, or even just angering a parent who has been abusive to them—many states have established a legal advocate whose sole concern is the best interest of the child.

> **Guardian Ad Litems (GALs)** are individual volunteers who are trained to serve as an advocate for the child. The legal interest of the GAL is only the child, not his or her parent or anyone else. GALs are typically asked to assist with the investigation of child abuse and child custody cases, and because their sole interest is the best interest of the child, judges often take their recommendations very seriously.

We encourage anyone who is interested in working toward the safety of children to consider being trained to volunteer as a GAL; we have taught numerous students who have volunteered as GALs. It is a wonderful experience and can be a great way to determine if one should pursue some career path in a variety of fields that serve child victims, including social work and the law.

| BOX 6.4 | GUARDIAN AD LITEM (GAL) PROGRAMS |

In 1983, the N.C. General Assembly established the Office of Guardian ad Litem (GAL) Services as a division of the N.C. Administrative Office of the Courts. N.C. General Statute 7B-601 specifies the appointment and duties of the Program. As outlined, when a petition alleging abuse or neglect of a juvenile is filed in district court, the judge appoints a volunteer Guardian ad Litem advocate and an attorney advocate to provide team representation to the child, who has full party status in trial and appellate proceedings. All Guardian ad Litem advocates are supervised, supported and trained by program staff in each county of the state. Through this collaborative model involving Guardian ad Litem attorney advocates, volunteers and staff, all North Carolina children who are alleged by the Department of Social Services to have been abused or neglected receive Guardian ad Litem legal advocacy services.

The role of Guardian ad Litem advocates is to:

- Fulfill state and federal statutory mandates to protect and promote the best interests of juveniles in abuse and neglect court proceedings
- Help move children out of the court system in a timely manner and into a safe permanent home
- Conduct independent investigations to determine the facts, needs of the child and the resources appropriate to meet those needs
- Determine the wishes or expressed preferences of the child and report those to the court
- Provide a voice for abused and neglected children in every county of the state

Source: North Carolina Administrative Office of the Courts, October 2010, www.ncgal.org.

Foster care refers to the temporary housing of children under the age of eighteen with an adult care provider.

Foster "parents" may be relatives, or they may be individuals with whom the child has no relationship. Foster parents receive a small stipend from the government to cover the additional costs of caring for the child. They must also go through a training and certification process to ensure that they are capable of caring for a child. Though "temporary"—and most children spend less than two years in foster care—many children live in foster care for the majority of their childhoods; some stay with the same family for so long that they are eventually legally adopted by them. Other children may cycle among different foster care providers, which is very disruptive and less than ideal. Foster care may be invoked when children are removed from their homes, when their custodial parent goes to prison, or in other cases in which their home is determined by a court as less than suitable.

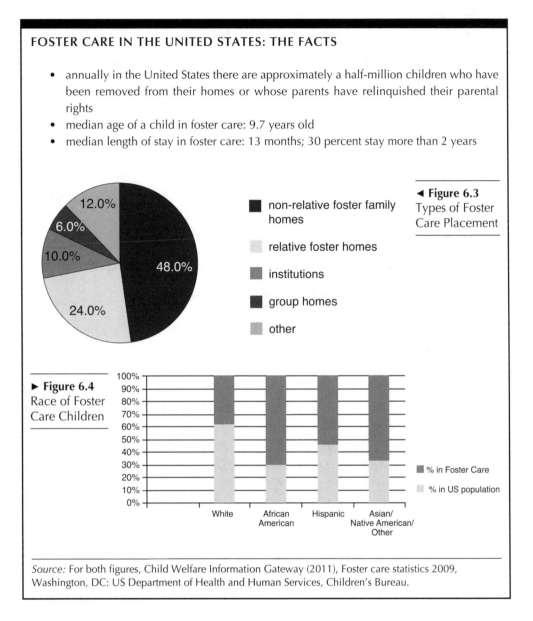

FOSTER CARE IN THE UNITED STATES: THE FACTS

- annually in the United States there are approximately a half-million children who have been removed from their homes or whose parents have relinquished their parental rights
- median age of a child in foster care: 9.7 years old
- median length of stay in foster care: 13 months; 30 percent stay more than 2 years

◄ **Figure 6.3**
Types of Foster Care Placement

non-relative foster family homes

relative foster homes

institutions

group homes

other

► **Figure 6.4**
Race of Foster Care Children

% in Foster Care

% in US population

Source: For both figures, Child Welfare Information Gateway (2011), Foster care statistics 2009, Washington, DC: US Department of Health and Human Services, Children's Bureau.

Failure to report suspected child abuse can result in both a criminal charge—typically a misdemeanor—as well as civil liability. In contrast, those who report have immunity in the case—they cannot be charged with child abuse or neglect—and they are protected from liability if there is no finding of abuse in the case. This is particularly interesting when we consider the sex abuse scandal plaguing the Catholic Church. Legally, priests or bishops who suspected abuse could have reported it without any legal penalty. That they did not in hundreds of cases speaks volumes about the hierarchy of church law over state law. We will feature the case of the Catholic Church in Chapter 10.

RISK FACTORS

Research conducted by the Office of Child Abuse and Neglect, part of the Department of Health and Human Services, identifies four domains of risk factors for child abuse and neglect (Goldman et al. 2003): parent or caregiver factors, family factors, child factors, and environmental factors.

Parent or Caregiver Risk Factors

There is no research to suggest that there is any prototype of an abusive parent.

Parent or caregiver risk factors refer to a set of risk factors for becoming abusive or neglectful of their children.

One of the primary risk factors for engaging in abusive or neglectful behavior is having been the victim of abuse or neglect as a child or having been exposed to abuse in one's household while growing up. We will explore this link at much greater length in the following chapter, but there are three key factors to address here. First, though the risk for perpetrating abuse or neglect is greater for those who were child victims—as many as one-third of all victims of child abuse grow up to perpetrate it—the majority of child victims do *not* grow up to be abusive parents.

Cycle of abuse: refers to the fact that rates of perpetrating child abuse are significantly higher among parents who were abused or who witnessed abuse as children.

The seemingly intergenerational transmission of abuse or what is often called the "cycle of abuse" has little to do with genetics or biology and much to do with socialization and learned behavior. Parents who grew up without good role models for how to parent lack the information and modeling to be good parents themselves; parents who grew up watching adults "solve" problems through violence, for example, may grow up without the appropriate tools for conflict resolution and may engage in violence to address their own problems. Thus, there is no question that one's childhood impacts the "tool kit" one takes into parenthood. We will explore this in much more depth in the next chapter.

A second risk factor that can affect child neglect is substance abuse and mental illness. Parents or primary caregivers who are substance abusers or addicts are at increased risk for engaging in physical abuse and neglect. One study reports that 40 percent of confirmed child abuse cases involved a parent with substance abuse or addiction problems (Children of Alcoholics Foundation 1996). The same is true for parents with mental illness. In both cases, the parent may have compromised judgment and impaired decision-making skills that may lead to abuse or neglect.

A third risk factor for engaging in child abuse or neglect is age. Younger parents, especially teenagers, are at a greater risk for engaging in physical child abuse and neglect than older parents. There are a multitude of reasons for this, including the developmental age of most teenagers, their limited ability to handle stress, their lack of realistic expectations for children's behavior—especially infants and toddlers—and their lack of knowledge about appropriate discipline. Additionally, teenage parents are far more likely to hold other risk statuses for abuse: the likelihood that they are single parents, that they are less likely to be employed, that they are more likely to be on welfare, and that they are less likely to have graduated from high school contributes to the relationship between age and risk for perpetrating physical child abuse and neglect (Goldman et al. 2003).

Family Structure

> **Family structure risk** refers to the fact that certain family forms or structures create situations in which child abuse is more likely to occur.

Children growing up in single-parent households are at a higher risk for all forms of child abuse and neglect. Indeed, the rate of child abuse for children growing up in single-parent households is double that of children living in two-parent households (Goldman et al. 2003). As with children of teenage parents, the sources of increased risk for physical abuse and neglect in single-parent households are similar: they are more likely to live in poverty, there is stress associated with being the sole care provider, and so forth (Goldman et al. 2003). In addition, children in female-headed single-parent households are at an increased risk for sexual abuse; stepfathers and mother's boyfriends are the single biggest demographic group perpetrating child sexual abuse. The general understanding is that the incest taboo that prohibits sexual contact between blood relatives, which we discussed at length in Chapter 2, is the strongest factor in reducing or limiting father-daughter incest. In contrast, the lack of a biological connection between stepfathers and stepdaughters appears to be less powerful than social norms against incest, and thus rates of incest are higher in stepfamilies.

Regardless of the marital status of the parents, the presence of a strong relationship between child and father reduces the risks of all forms of child abuse and neglect (Goldman et al. 2003). This finding confirms the argument that it is the stresses of single parenting that increase a child's risk for being a victim of abuse or neglect, not the individual qualities of the single parent herself. When those stresses are reduced by coparenting, even by noncoresidential parents, the risk for abuse is diminished.

> **Noncoresidential parents** are parents who do not live together, but they cooperate or share in the caring for and rearing of their children.

Another pathway by which single parenting may be linked to greater rates of child abuse and neglect is the instability in the housing of single mothers (Edin and Lein 1997; Seccombe 1998). Children whose mothers have chaotic or constantly shifting housing—often characterized by "doubling up" or living in single-family dwellings with other family members—are at a higher risk for neglect simply because of the instability and the overcrowding of the household (Goldman et al. 2003). In addition, because these arrangements may also involve living temporarily with the mother's or grandmother's boyfriend, the risk for sexual abuse is increased as well.

It is important to point out that children living with single fathers may also face somewhat higher risks for abuse and neglect, but some important differences exist. First, father-headed households are *no more likely* to be poor than two-parent households; thus the risk for abuse and neglect that is associated with poverty is not greater in single-father-headed households as it is in mother-headed households. Second, there are simply too few father-headed households—according to the US Census only 2 percent of children live in father-headed households—to conduct reliable research; because the rate of father-headed households is so low, most researchers lump all single-parent families together. Last, it is important to point out that there is no reason to assume that the risk for abuse and neglect that is associated with the stress of being a single parent would be any less in father-headed households than in mother-headed households. Thus, we can expect that the rate of child abuse and neglect would be somewhat higher in father-headed households, but it would not approach the level of mother-headed households because father-headed households are far less likely to be poor. Furthermore, because there is no evidence that stepmothers or fathers' girlfriends are likely to sexually abuse sons (or daughters), the rate of sexual abuse in father-headed households would likely not be higher than in two-parent households.

Based on a national study by the Department of Health and Human Services, Administration for Children and Families (ACF), compared to children in two-parent households, children being raised by single parents had:

- a 77 percent greater risk of being physically abused
- an 87 percent greater risk of being harmed by physical neglect
- a 165 percent greater risk of experiencing notable physical neglect
- a 74 percent greater risk of suffering from emotional neglect
- an 80 percent greater risk of suffering serious injury as a result of abuse
- a 120 percent greater risk of experiencing some type of maltreatment overall.

The entire report may be accessed at http://www.acf.hhs.gov/programs/opre /abuse_neglect/natl_incid/nis4_report_exec_summ_pdf_jan2010.pdf.

Given the fact that at the beginning of the twenty-first century there are increases in both the divorce rate and the skyrocketing rate of nonmarital childbirths, especially to African American mothers (Hattery and Smith 2007), we need to pay special attention to children living in single-parent households to be sure that they are safe and that their parent has adequate resources to provide for the needs of the child.

That said, staying married "for the children" does not ensure their safety. One of the highest risk factors for child abuse is the presence of domestic violence. As we will discuss at much greater length in the following chapter, progressive advocates of child safety have begun to argue that exposure to domestic violence in and of itself constitutes abuse, and in some states, as noted above, including Minnesota where we did research on intimate partner violence, when police officers responding to a domestic violence event discover children who are "in sight or sound of" the domestic violence, the children are automatically referred to CPS.

Child Factors

> **Child risk factors:** qualities of children that put them at increased likelihood for being abused.

It is with caution that we write about "child factors," as this can easily be misinterpreted to suggest that certain children are to blame for being abused. Under no circumstances is a child responsible for being abused. Ever. That said, there are "qualities" of children that increase their risk for being victims of abuse: age and disability.

Age: Though the relationship between age and the risk for abuse is not entirely clear-cut, there are several trends that are worthy of exploration. First, the risk for serious physical abuse is highest for children between the ages of one and three and then begins to decline. In contrast, the risk for child neglect increases with the age of the child. These trends are best explained by considering the different needs of children. Infants and young children require the most intense and constant care, and thus the increased risk for physical abuse may be driven by the stresses associated with parenting infants and toddlers. Infants between the ages of three and six months are at increased risk for injury for two reasons. First, because very young children are so small and fragile, it is "easier" for a parent or caregiver to significantly injure a child by simply shaking her or him.

SHAKEN BABY SYNDROME

A controversial medical term, **shaken baby syndrome**, is used to describe brain trauma that is not accompanied by dramatic exterior symptoms and often leads to death. According to Dr. Nakagawa, associate professor of neurology at Wake Forest University School of Medicine, what makes the diagnosis "shaken baby syndrome" problematic is not the resultant injuries, but rather linking the direct behavior to the direct outcome. For example, it is not always possible to determine that a particular incident of shaking caused the brain injury that resulted. That said, Dr. Nakagawa confirms that there is no controversy surrounding the neurological understanding of the impact of various body movements that result in brain trauma.

▶ **Figure 6.5**
Shaken Baby
Syndrome

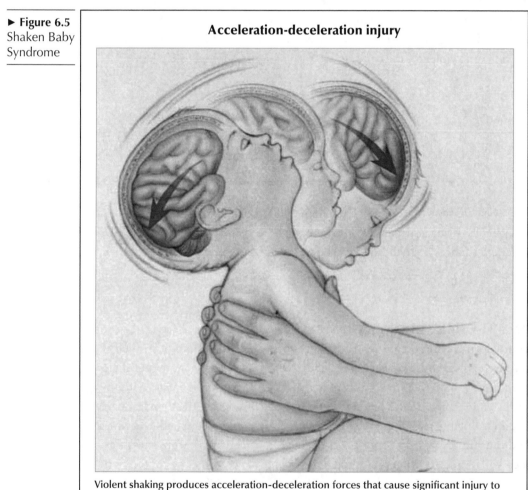

Acceleration-deceleration injury

Violent shaking produces acceleration-deceleration forces that cause significant injury to the brain. Rotational forces exerted on the brain result in shear injury.

Source: Dr. Nakagawa

Thus, the medical data are clear. As shown in Figure 6.5, the acceleration and deceleration that are associated with shaking a baby can result in brain trauma, brain injury, and even death. In exchanges with Dr. Nakagawa and his colleague Dr. Stizel—a specialist in concussions at Wake Forest University School of Medicine—they confirm that much like the concussion controversy in the National Football League, though it is difficult to determine which "hits" result in specific brain trauma, it is well understood that repeated "hits" will eventually result in brain trauma and even injury.

BOX 6.5 KEY FACTS ABOUT SHAKEN BABY SYNDROME

- Shaken baby syndrome (SBS) results from violent acceleration-deceleration forces that cause brain injury in children

- SBS is not caused by playful bouncing

- SBS is not accidental trauma

- Short falls, from less than four feet, do not result in the type of injury seen in SBS

- No period of lucidity follows injury caused by violently shaking an infant. Injured infants and children show signs of head trauma almost immediately

- SBS is not caused by vaccinations

- Posterior rib fractures are a marker for child abuse

- Diffuse hemorrhagic retinopathy is a sign of abusive head trauma

SOURCE: Dr. Nakagawa

Second, infants at this age are at risk for being shaken because of a phenomenon termed "the period of purple crying." The period of purple crying refers to the fact that at this developmental stage, infants cry more than at any other time in their lives. During this phase infants not only cry more but often seem inconsolable, there is often no apparent reason for the crying, they may appear to be in pain, and the crying may last for hours and tends to commonly occur at an already stressful time of day: late afternoon and early evening. For more information on the period of purple crying, we recommend the website http://www.purplecrying.info/sections/index.php?sct=1&.

Though the risk for being neglected increases with age, infants are far more likely to die from neglect—a phenomenon termed *nonorganic failure to thrive*—than older children. Presumably, this is because older children are more capable of obtaining food from other sources, whereas infants are entirely dependent upon their parents or caregivers for their entire nutritional input (Goldman et al. 2003).

Some research suggests that there is a much less significant relationship between emotional abuse and sexual abuse and age, though preadolescence seems to be the highest-risk age for sexual abuse, especially of girls (Goldman et al. 2003). The lack of a correlation between age and emotional abuse is not surprising; yelling at a child or calling him or her a derogatory name—the hallmarks of emotional abuse—can happen with children of any age, and thus the age of the child may not be related to his or her risk for emotional abuse. With regards to sexual abuse, the primary factor influencing the high risk that preadolescent girls face for abuse by a male family member—father, uncle, stepfather—is directly related to their sexual development. In order to avoid the complications of pregnancy, much of the child sexual abuse young girls experience—especially by family members and friends—ceases by the time they reach menarche. Of course, there is also a body of scientific research on men who are sexually attracted to preadolescent bodies—both male and female. This condition is termed *ephebophilia*.

Ephebophilia is the sexual attraction by men to preadolescent bodies. Though most people diagnosed with ephebophilia are men, their attractions are to both preadolescent boys and girls.

Yet it is also important to note that the teenage years are the greatest risk years for both boys and girls for sexual abuse by people outside the household. This is attributable to the fact that it is at this age when parents begin to give their children more freedom from parental supervision, this is when overnight trips for sports or youth groups begin, and thus the opportunity for abuse opens up in ways that make this age group particularly vulnerable to sexual abuse.

Disabilities: According to Goldman and colleagues (2003), children with disabilities experience "higher rates of maltreatment than do other children. A national study, completed in 1993, found that children with disabilities were 1.7 times more likely to be maltreated than children without disabilities" (US Department of Health and Human Services Child Welfare Information Gateway, http://www.childwelfare.gov/pubs/usermanuals/foundation/foundatione.cfm).

As with age, one of the explanations for this relationship seems to be the additional stress that raising a child with disabilities may place on a parent. Additional sources of stress may come "from the child him- or herself" in the sense that many physical and cognitive disabilities result in significantly greater caregiving needs, similar to the case with infants and toddlers as well as elders, as we explored in the previous chapter. Additionally, sources of stress may be compounded with certain communicative disorders such as autism in which the child may have such difficulty communicating that the parent or caregiver feels isolated and unsupported. Another source of stress that is rarely discussed is the economic stress associated with certain physical and cognitive or developmental disabilities. In cases of a child's severe physical disability, parents may face a host of financial burdens, including operations to correct abnormalities, health aids—expensive wheelchairs, for example—and even modifications to the home. Rarely do people realize that the majority of these needs are not covered by any insurance, and thus the financial strain may produce stress that is released in abusive or neglectful ways.

Similarly, having a child with a disability often puts tremendous strain on marital relationships, especially if the disability is the result of genetics, in which case one parent may feel guilt associated with passing on a defective gene and the other may feel anger and resentment. For a variety of reasons—including disagreements over treatment and care—parents of children with disabilities are more likely to divorce, and the strain of being a single parent raising a disabled child may lead to abusive or neglectful behavior (Marshak and Prezant 2007). For a fictionalized account of a family struggling with raising a differently abled child, we recommend Jodi Picoult's novel *Handle with Care* (2009), which is the story of a family raising a child with osteogenesis imperfecta—a genetic bone disorder.

It is also important to note that children with disabilities are far more likely to be placed for adoption or put into foster care, and any time in foster care increases the likelihood of experiencing abuse or maltreatment. Additionally, the National Council on Disability reports that once inside the foster care system, children with disabilities are 1.5 to 3.5 times more likely to be abused or neglected than their able-bodied counterparts. Furthermore, they suggest that foster care children with disabilities are one of the most vulnerable populations in the United States, yet their needs are grossly understudied and underfunded (http://www.ncd.gov/newsroom/publications /2008/FosterCareSystem_Report.html).

Last, the National Council on Disability and scholars including Goldman and colleagues (2003) suggest that an additional problem that disabled children face occurs after the abuse has begun; in cases of development or cognitive delay, children who are being abused may be less able to recognize the abuse as inappropriate, name it, or report it than their similarly aged counterparts. Children with physical disabilities may be less able to protect themselves. For example, in the novel *Handle with Care*, the mother character faces inquisitions about child abuse because her daughter, who suffers from "brittle bone" disease, sustains many fractures across her childhood. In cases such as this, one can imagine that an abusive parent would be able to easily explain away concerns of abuse by pointing to the characteristics of the child's disease. But in the majority of cases where there is no easily acceptable explanation, it seems probable that interventions come later for abused or neglected children with disabilities, and thus the abuse goes on longer and the possibility for injury and other long-term outcomes increases.

Environmental Factors

Goldman and colleagues (2003) identify three **environmental risk factors**—qualities of the physical environment under which children and their families live—that contribute to an increased risk for child abuse and neglect: poverty and unemployment, social isolation and lack of social support, and living in a violent community.

Poverty and Unemployment

We have talked at length about the role that poverty and unemployment play in child abuse and neglect. Statistics compiled by Goldman and colleagues (2003) and presented on the Child Welfare website (http://www.childwelfare.gov/pubs/user manuals/foundation/foundatione.cfm) demonstrate the relationship: "Children from families with annual incomes below $15,000 in 1993 were more than 22 times more likely to be harmed by child abuse and neglect as compared to children from families with annual incomes above $30,000" (US Department of Health and Human Services Child Welfare Information Gateway).

Scholars suggest four "theories" for explaining the relationship between poverty and an increased risk for child abuse and neglect (Plotnik 2000).

- As noted above, poverty leads to parental and familial stress that increases the chances and rate of abuse and especially neglect.
- Poverty itself compromises the ability of a parent to provide adequate care and meet all of the needs of the child.
- There may be a relationship between parental poverty and the likelihood of parental substance abuse.
- Finally, some scholars suggest that the risk for child abuse and neglect is not necessarily higher among low-income families, but rather abuse and neglect are more likely to be detected in low-income families and ultimately referred to CPS. This may occur for a variety of reasons, including the stereotypes that professionals such as teachers and health care providers may hold about the poor as well as a fear of reporting an affluent or well-known family in the community. We note that this explanation has been offered by many feminist scholars of poverty (Chasnoff, Landress, and Barrett 1990; Edin and Lein 1997; Hattery and Smith 2007; Neuspiel 1996).

Social Isolation and Social Support

Goldman and colleagues (2003) review a series of studies that suggest that parents who abuse or neglect their children report experiencing "greater isolation, more loneliness and less social support" (as presented on the website Child Welfare Information Gateway, maintained by the US Department of Health and Human Services, http://www.childwelfare.gov/pubs/usermanuals/foundation/foundatione.cfm, based on Goldman et al. 2003). Though more research needs to be done to determine whether isolation is a cause or result of abuse, the relationship between social isolation and child abuse is widely accepted by practitioners, and thus programs to alleviate isolation, such as Welcome Baby, were created.

Violent Communities

One of the greatest contributions sociologists make to understanding phenomena such as child abuse is their focus on structural and institutional, rather than individual, factors. Beginning at the very end of the twentieth century, criminologists and sociologists focusing on poverty and race or ethnicity began to focus their attention on the role that the environment of a community may play in individual and family life. For example, noted sociologist William Julius Wilson (1996) asked, what role does a high level of unemployment in a neighborhood play in shaping individuals' attitudes toward work? Following this approach, scholars interested in child welfare began to wonder about the role that violence in neighborhoods plays in shaping abuse in individual families. Scholars who focus on the ecology of child abuse and neglect note, "Children living in dangerous neighborhoods have been found to be at higher risk than children from safer neighborhoods for severe neglect and physical abuse, as well as child sexual victimization. Some risk may be associated with the poverty found in dangerous neighborhoods, however, concerns remain that violence may seem an acceptable response or behavior to individuals who witness it more frequently" (Cicchetti, Lynch, and Manly 1997; see also US Department of Health and Human Services Child Welfare Information Gateway, http://www .childwelfare.gov/pubs/usermanuals/foundation/foundatione.cfm).

Role of the Economy

Given the fact that poverty and unemployment are related to higher rates of child abuse and neglect, as noted specifically by ecological theories, such as Cicchetti and colleagues purport (1997), we conclude this section by asking, will the recession that began in 2007 lead to higher rates of child abuse and neglect driven by stress and poverty? We suggest that the financial crisis—accompanied or even driven by high rates of unemployment and housing foreclosures—will likely cause a temporary spike in the physical and emotional abuse of children as well as child neglect. In Chapter 8 we will explore the role that the economy plays in intimate partner violence. And though our argument in that chapter will be far more complex and specific, we suggest here that the recession may have deep and long-lasting consequences for children, as we expect child abuse and neglect to be both more prevalent and more severe.

Protective Factors:
Reducing the Risk for Child Abuse and Neglect

Goldman and colleagues (2003) suggest that just as there are factors that increase the likelihood of child abuse, there are protective factors as well.

> **Protective factors:** any quality of the child, the parent, the family, or the environment that reduces the likelihood that a parent will be abusive or neglectful and that a child will be victimized.

Obviously, eliminating certain risk factors will be protective, such as living in a two-parent family, having adequate financial resources, becoming a parent after age twenty-five, having fewer children, and so forth. Of more interest, however, is the ability to reduce the risk for child abuse or neglect by targeting "at-risk families" and changing their risk factors into protective factors. Goldman and colleagues (2003) suggest that social support and a network of resources can serve as a protective factor even for a family that is otherwise at high risk. For example, a parent who was abused as a child will be less likely to become an abusive parent if he or she has access to appropriate counseling and therapy, parenting classes, and social support. This is the entire premise behind the Welcome Baby program, which, though it reaches out to the majority of new parents, targets those with risk factors including poverty; previous abuse; mothers who delivered drug-addicted, underweight, or premature babies; and so forth. This feature comes from the Welcome Baby program in Durham, NC, but many counties around the United States have Welcome Baby programs.

BOX 6.6	WELCOME BABY

Welcome Baby is a nation-wide program funded in large part by the local Exchange Clubs. Welcome Baby is present in the majority of counties across the United States. Welcome Baby provides parenting education and support to families with young children. Our services are available for free to all county residents with newborns and children to age 5.

PARENTING EDUCATION AND SUPPORT: Welcome Baby strives to answer the many child development and infant care questions parents have during their children's first years. We offer weekly classes on a variety of parenting topics. We also distribute developmental guides, offer telephone support to parents of newborns, have a discussion group for parents of newborns, maintain a lending library of books and videos, and our staff is available to discuss your individual parenting concerns.

BOX 6.6	**WELCOME BABY** *continued*

NOW & LATER: Informal discussion group where parents of newborns gather NOW and discuss topics relevant to their new lifestyle and responsibilities, such as, Infant care, feeding, crying, sleeping, and returning to work. Additional topics covered are parent adjustment, emotional ups and downs, body changes, relationship changes, etc. So that LATER, parents will have an established support network to share and grow with as their children grow. Now & Later meets for 8 weeks. Refreshments are provided.

CAR SEAT SAFETY PROGRAM: Free classes on the correct use and installation of infant/toddler and booster car seats are offered several times each month. Families who complete the class are eligible to purchase seats on a sliding fee scale.

CRIBS FOR KIDS: Welcome Baby is the local affiliate of the national Cribs for Kids© program. Through donations, we are able to distribute cribs to families referred through agencies providing in-home services and nurse home visit programs. Families receiving cribs also receive safe sleep educational information. The goal of the program is decreasing SIDS (Sudden Infant Death Syndrome).

DEVELOPMENTAL GUIDES: Welcome Baby's newsletter, *Welcome Words*, discusses the milestones and challenges of each age. *Welcome Words* covers the changes in children and the concerns of parents at each age. The newsletters are available bi-monthly until your child is age 1 and then twice/year until age 5.

SPANISH SERVICES: All Welcome Baby services are available in Spanish.

THE GIVING CLOSET: Families can visit our free clothing closet four times during the program year (July 1 thru June 30th) to select children's clothing, maternity wear and infant equipment when available. Donations of clean infant and toddler clothing are accepted as well as baby furniture.

COMMUNITY RESOURCES: Welcome Baby can serve as a link for families to other community resources. This listing describes some of the services available in Durham County. Families can call the Welcome Baby office for additional assistance and professionals can access the confidential referral system.

VOLUNTEER OPPORTUNITIES: Welcome Baby's programs are only possible through the work of many volunteers. Opportunities are flexible from visiting families at the hospital and offering support to parents of newborns to assisting at the clothing closet and providing childcare during Welcome Baby's parenting classes. Together our volunteers help care for the children of our community.

LENDING LIBRARIES: Welcome Baby offers a lending library of books and videos on topics pertaining to newborns, their care and development and many other child rearing and parenting topics. The library is located at the Welcome Baby office.

Source: Exchange Scan: http://www.exchangescan.org/welcomebaby.html

What is missing in this approach is a national-level campaign that focuses on child welfare. For example, given the huge role that poverty plays in both abuse and neglect, if the welfare laws were reworked to focus on the needs of poor children, rather than as a penalty to their parents who are stereotyped as being lazy and poor decision makers (Seccombe 1998), more resources would be made available to children living in poverty, and this would most likely reduce their risk for abuse and neglect. We will expand this discussion at the end of the chapter and will revisit it again in the final chapter of the book, which is devoted to solutions. We turn now to a discussion of the outcomes of child abuse on the victims.

OUTCOMES OF CHILD ABUSE

As we have noted throughout this chapter, one of the saddest outcomes of child abuse is the likelihood that it will be repeated intergenerationally. Because this will be the major focus of the following chapter, here we focus on some of the more immediate outcomes for children who experience abuse and neglect. We focus on three key areas: substance abuse, high-risk sexual behavior, and interactions with the criminal justice system.

Substance Abuse and Mental Health Issues

Mary Pipher, in her book based on working with adolescent girls in therapy, noted a very strong relationship between abuse, especially sexual abuse, and both substance abuse and mental health issues (1994). Quantitative data reviewed and reported by Lalor and McElvaney (2010) noting the relationship between being a victim of child abuse and both substance abuse and mental health issues thus confirm Pipher's qualitative findings:

- more than 60 percent of people in drug rehabilitation centers report being abused or neglected as a child
- about 80 percent of twenty-one-year-olds that were abused as children met criteria for at least one psychological disorder; the two most common are anxiety disorder and depression

In fact, in one of your author's hometowns the local Boy Scout leader was convicted of sexually abusing the Scouts. The accusation arose from a Scout who in the seventh grade was being treated for drug addiction. During his therapy he revealed the abuse, and his counselor—a mandatory reporter—brought the tragic accusation to light. This is unfortunately an all-too-common scenario.

High-Risk Sexual Behavior

Victims of child abuse, especially sexual abuse, are also at high risk for engaging in risky sexual behavior. We will spend a great deal of time disentangling this very disturbing phenomenon in the next chapter when we examine a phenomenon we term *premature sex engagement* and its relationship to intimate partner violence. But for our purposes here we provide the following statistics provided by ChildHelp (http://www.childhelp.org/):

- abused teens are three times more likely to practice unsafe sex, putting them at greater risk for STDs
- abused children are 25 percent more likely to experience teen pregnancy

Crime

Victims of child abuse are also prone to engage in activities that land them inside the criminal justice system as perpetrators. The statistics provided above contribute to our insight regarding this relationship. As noted, victims of child abuse are far more likely than their peers to use and abuse alcohol and drugs, which is often a pathway into the criminal justice system. For example, among the most common juvenile misdemeanors are citations for underage drinking or possession offenses—both alcohol and marijuana. National statistics on child abuse reveal the following (http://www.childhelp.org/):

- children who have been sexually abused are 2.5 times more likely to abuse alcohol
- children who have been sexually abused are 3.8 times more likely to develop drug addictions

Additionally, as we will discuss at length in the following chapter, female victims of child sexual abuse are twice as likely as their peers to become battered women. Experiences with sexual abuse—for both boys and girls—as well as battering often lead victims to seek an escape from the abuse. It is not at all uncommon for the escape to involve behaviors that can also be a pathway to the criminal justice system, including running away or truancy, which can require juveniles to be put into detention centers; passing bad checks or stealing in order to generate the money needed to run away; and prostitution—which is especially common among victims of sexual abuse, both boys and girls—as a strategy to facilitate living on the street once a victim has run away. All of these activities expose the victims to the criminal justice system, and these seem the most likely pathways for victims of child abuse into the criminal justice system (Hattery 2008, 2009; Odem 1995; Pipher 1994). According to Goldman and colleagues (2003),

- while fewer than 5 percent of all boys were abused as children, 14 percent of all men in US prison were abused as children
- while fewer than 20 percent of women experience any type of abuse, 36 percent of all women in prison were abused as children
- children who experience child abuse and neglect are 59 percent more likely to be arrested as a juvenile, 28 percent more likely to be arrested as an adult, and 30 percent more likely to commit a violent crime

Entering the criminal justice system as a juvenile is problematic for many different reasons, including the stigma and the fact that children who enter the system are three times more likely to be incarcerated as adults than those who were never detained as juveniles. Additionally, however, juvenile detention centers can also be a site of further abuse: physical, emotional, and sexual. And though we are not advocating for a dismantling of the juvenile justice system, as the stories of abuse emerge, they illuminate not only the horrors of the abuse but also the role the system plays in further abusing young boys, adding to the already increased risk these boys face for being abusive in adulthood. Thus, we are forced to question the system of juvenile detention and recommend that it be overhauled with a rehabilitative goal in mind rather than a punitive and abuse mission that only makes the likelihood of transforming a young boy into a productive citizen unlikely at best. We illustrate from an investigative report on the juvenile system in Florida, one that has faced scrutiny over the past decade because of boys who died while in custody.

BOX 6.7   FLORIDA SCHOOL FOR BOYS

"For Their Own Good": A St. Petersburg Times
Special Report on Child Abuse at the Florida School for Boys
By Ben Montgomery and Waveney Ann Moore, Times *Staff Writers, April 17, 2009*

MARIANNA—The men remember the same things: blood on the walls, bits of lip or tongue on the pillow, the smell of urine and whiskey, the way the bed springs sang with each blow. The way they cried out for Jesus or mama. The grinding of the old fan that muffled their cries. The one-armed man who swung the strap.

They remember walking into the dark little building on the campus of the Florida School for Boys, in bare feet and white pajamas, afraid they'd never walk out.

For 109 years, this is where Florida has sent bad boys. Boys have been sent here for rape or assault, yes, but also for skipping school or smoking cigarettes or running hard continues

---

BOX 6.7   FLORIDA SCHOOL FOR BOYS *continued*

from broken homes. Some were tough, some confused and afraid; all were treading through their formative years in the custody of the state. They were as young as 5, as old as 20, and they needed to be reformed.

It was for their own good.

Now come the men with nightmares and scars on their backsides, carrying 50 years of wreckage-ruined marriages and prison time and meanness and smoldering anger. Now comes a state investigation into unmarked graves, a lawsuit against a dying old man. Now come the questions: How could this happen? What should be done?

Those questions have been asked again and again about the reform school at Marianna, where, for more than a century, boys went in damaged and came out destroyed. You can read the entire Pulitzer Prize–winning series on our course website.

SOURCE: http://www.tampabay.com/specials/2009/reports/marianna/

Child abuse can also be systemic in other institutions, including those designed to help children. In June 2011, CNN broke a story about a "therapy" program run at UCLA in the 1960s that encouraged or even required parents to engage in physically abusing their children as part of a program designed to cure their homosexuality.

BOX 6.8   KIRK MURPHY

Therapy to Change "Feminine" Boy Created a Troubled Man, Family Says
By Scott Bronstein and Jessi Joseph, CNN, June 7, 2011

Kirk Murphy liked to play with "girls' toys" when he was 5 years old. His mother thought a psychologist could change this.

"Well, I was becoming a little concerned, I guess, when he was playing with dolls and stuff," Kaytee Murphy told Anderson Cooper on *CNN*. "It just bothered me that maybe he was picking up maybe too many feminine traits."

Murphy's mother enrolled him in a government-funded experiment at UCLA in the 1970s, where he was treated by doctoral student George A. Rekers. After 10 months of formal treatment, which included physical punishment, Rekers said Murphy no longer exhibited feminine behavior and had been successfully treated.

But in a special report on "Anderson Cooper 360," Murphy's family claimed this treatment led to his suicide at age 38.

Murphy's mother, brother and sister described the treatment as "severe." Murphy, who was called "Kraig" in the case study, was monitored and rewarded for playing with masculine toys. If he played with feminine toys, his father was instructed to "spank" him,

BOX 6.8   KIRK MURPHY *continued*

sometimes with a belt. Murphy's mother said that what happened to her son "would be abuse" by today's standards.

In Rekers' study documenting his experimental therapy (PDF), he writes about a boy he calls "Kraig." Another UCLA gender researcher confirmed that "Kraig" was a pseudonym for Kirk.

"Kraig, I think, certainly was Rekers' poster boy for what Rekers was espousing for young children," said Jim Burroway, a writer and researcher who has studied Rekers' work.

The Experiments

The therapy at UCLA involved a special room with two tables where "Kraig's" behavior was monitored, according to the study.

"There was a one-way mirror or one-way window—and some days they would let him choose which table he would go to," said Maris, who has read about the experiments.

At one table Kirk could choose between what were considered masculine toys like plastic guns and handcuffs, and what were meant to be feminine toys like dolls and a play crib. At the other table, Kirk could choose between boys' clothing and a toy electric razor or items like dress-up jewelry and a wig.

According to the case study, Kaytee Murphy was told to ignore her son when he played with feminine toys and compliment him when he played with masculine toys.

Harsh Beatings

At home, the punishment for feminine behavior would become more severe. The therapists instructed Kirk's parents to use poker chips as a system of rewards and punishments.

According to Rekers' case study, blue chips were given for masculine behavior and would bring rewards, such as candy. But the red chips, given for effeminate behavior, resulted in "physical punishment by spanking from the father."

Mark said he was told to participate in the chip reward-and-punishment system as a way to make Kirk feel like the system was OK.

The family said the spankings were severe. Maris remembers "lots of belt incidents." She escaped the screaming by going to her bed to "lay in the room with my pillow on my head." Later, she would go to Kirk's bedroom and "lay down and hug him and we would just lay there, and the thing that I remember is that he never even showed anger. He was just numb."

During one particularly harsh punishment, their mother recalls, her husband "spanked" Kirk "so hard that he had welts up and down his back and on his buttocks."

She remembers her son Mark saying, "Cry harder, and he won't hit so hard." She says, "Today, it would be abuse."

BOX 6.8   **KIRK MURPHY** *continued*

Sometimes Mark would try to protect his brother, to make his beatings less severe.

"I took some of the red chips and I put them on my side," said Mark, as tears came to his eyes. But he said the beatings were still frequent.

Kirk's formal clinical treatment lasted 10 months, but the family said some of the treatment techniques and practices lasted longer at home.

SOURCE: http://articles.cnn.com/2011-06-07/us/sissy.boy.experiment_1_kraig-experimental -therapy-feminine-traits?_s=PM:US.

CONCLUSIONS

If you have been lucky enough to have been spared experiencing child abuse or neglect, then you should count your blessings. But whether or not you have, this problem affects you. Child abuse leads to problems that impact all members of society, including increasing the rates of drug and alcohol abuse and addiction and "deviant" behavior that leads to juvenile detention and incarceration. "The annual cost of child abuse and neglect in the United States for 2007 would be $104 billion" (Wang and Holton 2007, 2). Thus, it is clear that in order to create a society in which we are all safe and functioning and contributing at our highest levels, it is paramount that we prevent, intervene in, and ultimately reduce the prevalence of all forms of child abuse. Additionally, as noted throughout this chapter, experiencing abuse as a child puts one at significantly higher risk for being in an abusive relationship in adulthood—either as a perpetrator or as a victim, involved in intimate partner violence, child abuse, or elder abuse. Thus, if we are interested in breaking the cycle of violence, then we have an interest in interrupting child abuse when it occurs and seeking better strategies for preventing it.

We conclude this chapter with a discussion of intervention and prevention strategies.

Intervention

Unfortunately, child abuse occurs. Annually, there are more than 5 million cases of child abuse reported in the United States. Perhaps even more tragic is the fact that many children are "repeat" victims; even after a complaint is filed, it is not uncommon for the abuse to continue. Thus, we must develop more successful intervention strategies. As we have noted throughout this book, and especially in Chapter 2, family violence has long been considered a private problem, and law enforcement and even social service agencies have been reluctant to intervene unless the abuse reaches a certain level. However, this approach leaves millions of children living with neglect and abuse. Tragic as this is, it also puts them at higher risk for substance abuse, sexually risky behavior, and abuse in adulthood. Thus, we advocate a more proactive approach to intervention. Of course, it is difficult to suggest that in all cases of suspected abuse children should be removed from their homes and put into a foster care system that ultimately puts them at an even greater risk for abuse. In fact, this may always be a last resort. That said, we need to develop intervention strategies that protect children and allow them to stay in their homes, teach parents better parenting skills, and have some measure of accountability. This will not be easy, as these services are expensive to provide, the agencies that currently provide them are understaffed and underfunded, and with the current economic climate, it will be difficult to develop and implement these programs in the near future.

Ideally, based on the research of practitioners and scholars who focus on child abuse, we would recommend the following:

- investigate *all* reports of child abuse
- create sanctions for mandatory reporters who fail to report suspected abuse
- increase training for all mandatory reporters
- increase accountability among professional organizations, such as churches and athletic programs, where adults come in regular contact with children and where rates of abuse are unusually high
- require parents in any case of suspected abuse to attend mandatory parenting classes and tie the completion of these classes to being released from probation in cases where abuse is substantiated
- better supervise the system of foster care, where rates of abuse are higher than in nonfoster families
- overhaul the system of juvenile detention so that juvenile offenders are rehabilitated and treated, not subjected to further abuse
- most important, take child abuse seriously, as the damage we are doing to our future generation is nothing less than tragic

Prevention

As with all forms of family violence, the real difference can be made by developing successful prevention programs. If we can prevent abuse and neglect from occurring to begin with, we save not only the tragedy of the abuse, but millions of dollars—in medical costs, court costs, custody costs, and subsequent costly behavior by the child, including substance abuse and deviance—in dealing with it once it has occurred. We highlight two areas for prevention: prevention programs and structural changes in the United States.

Prevention Programs: As many people note, one has to get a license to drive a car, but one does not need a license to become a parent. We are not advocating that this become the case. We are acknowledging that parenting is difficult and that resources should be provided to all new parents. The Welcome Baby program in Durham, North Carolina, one of many iterations in counties around the United States, is an example of a type of program that needs to be available to all new parents nationally. Second, there are risk factors associated with the child, the parents, and the family structure that increase the likelihood of abuse and neglect. Thus, parenting classes and other resources should be readily available and targeted toward these at-risk groups, including teenage parents, single parents, low-income parents, parents on welfare, parents who are struggling with substance abuse, as well as parents of children with disabilities. Again, these types of programs will cost money, but because models with proven track records, based on best practices, already exist, fully funding these existing programs and expanding them nationally would be steps in the right direction. We will detail more of these programs in Chapter 14.

Structural Changes: As we discussed at length in the section on child neglect, which accounts for more than half of all reported cases of child abuse, there is a strong link between neglect and poverty. Though some parents simply do not know how to care for their children or choose not to, many other parents know how to care for their children and desperately want to, but find themselves in a position where they are unable to meet their child's basic needs. Poverty leaves many families unable to provide for the nutritional needs of their children. In fact, a recent study in our hometown of Winston-Salem, North Carolina, revealed that more than a quarter of all families reported food insecurity—that is, they skipped meals each week because they could not afford to buy food. These problems have only been exacerbated by the recession that began in 2007 and the limiting of food stamps and other poverty-related benefits for the long-term unemployed. Housing projects create another challenge. Walking through any public housing project in urban or rural America will expose one to a set of circumstances that by their very definition can be considered neglect or abuse. Living without adequate heating or cooling, living without adequate plumbing, living with rodent infestations, and living with lead paint are all part of the reality of low-income existence for many people in America; children living in such conditions are suffering from neglect. Additionally, housing projects are notoriously violent places to live, and this exposure to violence constitutes an environmental cause of child abuse. Low wages not only impact a parent's ability to provide adequate nutrition, clothing, and shelter for one's children, but coupled with the high costs of child care may adversely affect one's ability to provide adequate supervision as well. Inadequate supervision can constitute neglect and can lead to abuse, as unsupervised children are more likely to be targets of sexual abuse by babysitters and nonfamily members and drug exposure.

Thus, we advocate many changes to the US economy and the system of social welfare that would alleviate multiple problems, including high rates of neglect and abuse among low-income and poor people living in the United States. First and foremost, we advocate that employers be required to pay a living wage. While CEOs make millions of dollars per year in compensation alone, the people working for them often make just minimum wage, $7.50 an hour. If wages were raised to a living, rather than minimum, wage, this would provide many parents the resources to provide for the basic needs of their children. Additionally, the current system of social welfare needs to be substantially overhauled so that it is not a punitive system for parents who make bad choices, but a safety net for the children of those parents. If we were to structure public housing, food stamps, and child care subsidies with the best interests of children in mind, these programs could significantly change the experiences of many low-income and poor children regardless of the choices their parents made or did not make.

Jimmy Carter is quoted as saying that a measure of a society is how it treats its most vulnerable citizens. Children are, without a doubt, among the most vulnerable of all citizens. And our treatment of them, as a society, by failing to protect them and provide for them when their parents cannot or will not, is a disgrace. If we expect to maintain a position of leadership in the global economy of the twenty-first century, we must address issues of child abuse and neglect, take them seriously, and invoke both interventions and preventive measure that reduce the impact of abuse on our most vulnerable yet richest resource: our children.

Afterword: At the time this book was going to press the child sex abuse scandal at Penn State broke. Former Penn State assistant coach Jerry Sandusky was indicted on forty counts of child sexual abuse. Legendary head coach Joe Paterno was fired, as was the Penn State president Graham Spanier; other top officials were fired or resigned, and two were arrested for failing to appropriately report the abuse. Although we don't yet know the outcome of the case, we point the interested reader to our course website for a series of articles as well as the full text of the grand jury indictment. This case has the potential to shape not only our understanding of child sexual abuse but also to suggest the kinds of consequences associated with the failure of institutional leaders to report it.

RESOURCES

ChildHelp: http://www.childhelp.org/
Department of Health and Human Services: http://www.acf.hhs.gov/programs/cb/stats_research/

LaLee's Kin (2001, HBO) (we highly recommend this film that illustrates the ways in which poverty can produce child neglect)

Picoult, Jodi. 2009. *Handle with Care.* New York: Washington Square Press.

Welcome Baby Program: http://www.exchangescan.org/

BIBLIOGRAPHY

Chasnoff, I. J., H. J. Landress, and M. E. Barrett. 1990. "The Prevalence of Illicit-Drug or Alcohol Use During Pregnancy and Discrepancies in Mandatory Reporting in Pinellas County, Florida." *New England Journal of Medicine* 322: 1202–1206.

Child Abuse and Prevention and Treatment Act. 2003. Washington, DC: US Department of Health and Human Services.

Children of Alcoholics Foundation. 1996. *Collaboration, Coordination, and Cooperation: Helping Children Affected by Parental Addiction and Family Violence.* New York: Children of Alcoholics Foundation.

Cicchetti, D., M. Lynch, and J. T. Manly. 1997. *An Ecological Developmental Perspective on the Consequences of Child Maltreatment.* Washington, DC: US Department of Health and Human Services, National Center on Child Abuse and Neglect.

Edin, K., and L. Lein. 1997. *Making Ends Meet: How Single Mothers Survive Welfare and Low-Wage Work.* New York: Russell Sage Foundation.

Ehrensaft, M., and P. Cohen. 2003. "Intergenerational Transmission of Partner Violence: A 20-Year Prospective Study." *Journal of Consulting and Clinical Psychology* 7: 741–753.

Goldman, J., M. K. Salus, D. Wolcott, and K. Y. Kennedy. 2003. *A Coordinated Response to Child Abuse and Neglect: The Foundation for Practice.* Washington, DC: Office of Child Abuse and Neglect, US Department of Health and Human Services.

Hattery, A. J. 2008. *Intimate Partner Violence.* Lanham, MD: Rowman and Littlefield.

———. 2009. "Sexual Abuse in Childhood and Adolescence and Intimate Partner Violence in Adulthood Among African American and White Women." *Race, Gender, and Class* 15, no. 2: 79–97.

Hattery, A. J., and E. Smith. 2007. *African American Families.* Thousand Oaks, CA: Sage.

———. 2010. *Prisoner Reentry and Social Capital: The Long Road to Reintegration.* Lanham, MD: Lexington Books.

Journal of Blacks in Higher Education. 2001. "The University of Alabama: Where Racial Segregation Remains a Way of Life." Vol. 32.

Lalor, K., and R. McElvaney. 2010. "Child Sexual Abuse, Links to Later Sexual Exploitation/High-Risk Sexual Behavior, and Prevention/Treatment Programs." *Trauma, Violence, and Abuse* 11: 159–177.

Marshak, L. E., and F. P. Prezant. 2007. *Married with Special-Needs Children: A Couple's Guide to Keeping Connected.* Bethesda, MD: Woodbine House.

Neuspiel, D. R. 1996. "Racism and Perinatal Addiction, Ethnicity, and Disease." *New England Journal of Medicine* 6: 47–55.

Odem, M. E. 1995. *Delinquent Daughters: Protecting and Policing Adolescent Female Sexuality in the United States, 1885–1920.* Chapel Hill: University of North Carolina Press.

Pipher, M. B. 1994. *Reviving Ophelia: Saving the Selves of Adolescent Girls.* New York: Putnam Press.

Plotnik, R. 2000. "Economic Security for Families with Children." In *The Child Welfare Challenge: Policy, Practice, and Research,* edited by P. J. Pecora, J. K. Whittaker, A. N. Maluccio, and R. P. Barth, 2: 95–127. New York: Aldine de Gruyter.

Seccombe, K. 1998. *So You Think I Drive a Cadillac? Welfare Recipients' Perspectives on the System and Its Reform.* New York: Allyn and Bacon.

"Trial Begins for Dallas Father Accused of Starving Kids." 2010. Associated Press, July 27. http://www.beaumontenterprise.com/news/local/Trial_begins_for_father _accused_of_starving_kids.html.

Wang, C.-T., and J. Holton. 2007. *The Estimated Cost of Child Abuse and Neglect in the United States.* New York: Pew Charitable Trust.

Wilson, W. J. 1996. *When Work Disappears: The World of the New Urban Poor.* New York: Alfred A. Knopf.

7 Outcomes of Child Abuse

Increased Risk for Experiencing Violence in Adulthood

She would go downtown and take out warrants out on him and restraining orders and he'll go back and one night she took and killed him, you know they got into a fight, and one night she took and got it, they got into a fight, and she grabbed a pistol and shot him in the head.

—EDDIE, fortysomething African American man, North Carolina

Following the previous chapter on child abuse, this chapter will focus on the impact that experiences with and exposure to violence in childhood have on experiences with family violence, and intimate partner violence in particular, in adulthood. The chapter will be broken into two sections: the impact on girls who experience physical or sexual abuse (or both) in childhood and their probability for experiencing family violence in adulthood and the impact on boys who witness violence growing up and their likelihood of battering their partners in adulthood. This chapter will include both statistical and ethnographic data that illustrate the power of this relationship.

OBJECTIVES

- To educate the reader about the three forms that childhood sexual abuse takes: premature sex engagement, incest, and child prostitution
- To provide illustrations demonstrating the long-term impact of CSA on young women
- To provide illustrations demonstrating the long-term impact that witnessing intimate partner violence has on young boys
- To note the statistical relationship between CSA among girls and the likelihood of being a battered woman in adulthood
- To note the statistical relationship between witnessing IPV in one's home for boys and the likelihood of battering in adulthood

KEY TERMS

physical child abuse	situational prostitution
intimate partner violence (IPV)	liquor house
childhood sexual abuse (CSA)	order of protection
sexual scripts	intergenerational transmission of violence
premature sex engagement	theory
childhood adultification	parental violence

INTRODUCTION

This chapter serves as a transition chapter between our discussions of child abuse and intimate partner violence; in this chapter we explore the specific role that experiences with and exposure to violence in childhood play in significantly increasing the risk childhood victims and witnesses face for revictimization and becoming perpetrators of violence in adulthood. At the beginning of the 2000s, we conducted face-to-face, in-depth interviews with nearly one hundred adult men and women who were living with intimate partner violence. Though we had read the literature that demonstrated that girls who grew up experiencing child sexual abuse were at risk for revictimization in adulthood (rape) (Lalor and McElvaney 2010 provides an excellent summary of this research), and though we were well aware that boys who witness violence in their households are at significantly higher risk for growing up to batter their future wives and girlfriends, it was in talking with real men and women who had these experiences in childhood that we learned just how profoundly child abuse—as victims and witnesses—shapes victims' lives well into adulthood. The tragedy of their experiences puts a "face" on the child abuse statistics that we reviewed in the previous chapter. In this chapter we will explore the experiences of both boys and girls; we begin with a discussion of the ways in which child sexual abuse experienced by girls makes them vulnerable to intimate partner violence in adulthood.

OUTCOMES OF CHILD ABUSE ON WOMEN

In the interviews we conducted with women, we focused on their experiences growing up, dating, and in their adult intimate relationships. Inside of these discussions we were surprised and troubled by the frequency with which experiences with sexual abuse tumbled out of them while we talked. The analysis in this chapter highlights the ways in which these experiences with sexual abuse that occurred in childhood and the teen years affect women's ability to cope with battering in their intimate relationships in adulthood. Specifically, abuse in childhood lowered young women's self-esteem, it put them at risk for other behaviors—drug and alcohol abuse and multiple sex partners (Lalor and McElvaney 2010)—that are also risk factors for being a victim of IPV (Browne 1989), and childhood sexual abuse in particular seems to erode young women's personal boundaries so that they are less able to protect themselves from exploitation and interpersonal assaults in general, including intimate partner violence (Raphael 2004). We begin with a discussion of the statistical data that examine the outcomes of childhood abuse—both physical and sexual—that girls experienced and their probability for revictimization in adulthood and then move to illustrations provided by the women we interviewed. These interviews allow us to better understand the *process* by which child abuse leads to revictimization in adulthood.

Abuse in Childhood and Abuse in Adulthood

In national studies, at least half of all women report at least one incident of *physical abuse* by a parent or caretaker before age eighteen (Tjaden and Thoennes 2000).

> **Physical child abuse:** As the reader will recall from the previous chapter, physical abuse can include beating a child with one's hand or with an instrument, pushing a child, throwing things at a child, burning a child with hot instruments including cigarette lighters, scalding a child with hot water, tying a child up, or any other sort of action that causes physical injury to a child.

Though women who were victims of child abuse are not significantly more likely to grow up to be battered in adulthood (46 percent are, but 53.3 percent are not), women who *were victims* of child abuse are *twice as likely* to experience intimate partner violence as women who were not physically assaulted in childhood (46.7 percent compared to 19.8 percent) (Tjaden and Thoennes 2000).

> **Intimate partner violence (IPV):** abuse that occurs between adults—and teenagers—who are in a relationship with each other; they may be dating, living together, married, or even "exes." IPV can include physical, emotional, or sexual abuse. We will have a lengthy discussion of IPV in the next chapter.

In other words, slightly more than half of women who were physically abused in childhood *do not* grow up to be battered in adulthood (53 percent), but the *risk* for IPV is *twice as high—46.7 percent as compared to 19.8 percent*—for female victims of child abuse than for those women who were not abused as children.

The relationship between being sexually abused in childhood and being raped in adulthood follows a similar path.

Child sexual abuse involves any sort of sexual contact between a child and an adult (or significantly older teenager). Most often CSA involves sexual touching or sexual manipulation or both, but it can and does include sexual intercourse—vaginal, oral, and anal—as well. CSA can also involve exposing children to adult sexual images or forcing them to watch pornography or even witness adult sexual acts.

Women raped as minors are *twice as likely* to be raped in adulthood (18.3 percent compared to a rate of 8.7 percent for women who were not raped in childhood). However, as was the case with physical child abuse, most women who are raped in childhood are *not* raped in adulthood—tragically 18.3 percent of those raped in childhood are raped as adults, but 81.2 percent of those raped in childhood are *not* raped as adults.

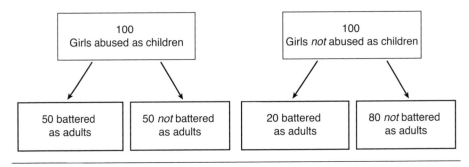

▲ **Figure 7.1**
Relationship Between Abuse in Childhood and Being Battered in Adulthood

The increased probability for revictimization is confirmed by Lalor and McElvaney's extensive review of empirical studies. They note, "Numerous studies have noted that child sexual abuse victims are vulnerable to later sexual revictimization, as well as the link between child sexual abuse and later engagement in high-risk sexual behaviour. Survivors of child sexual abuse are more likely to have multiple sex partners, become pregnant as teenagers, and experience sexual assault as adults" (2010, 159). In short, though most girls who experience sexual abuse or physical violence *are not* victimized in adulthood, victims of childhood sexual or physical abuse *are twice as likely* to experience the *same type of abuse in adulthood as their non-childhood victim counterparts*.

The question becomes how abuse in childhood creates a *pathway* to abuse in adulthood. In her study of stripping and prostitution, Raphael explicates the ways in which sexual abuse and exploitation diminish self-esteem and can create a pathway to intimate partner violence. She notes that prostitution and violence destroy the body's boundaries. "If your body does not present limits to other people, you begin to feel that you do not have a right to exist, to take up space" (2004, 164). In other words, once a girl's personal boundaries have been violated by a sexual abuser, it is as if she loses her ability to enforce the boundaries of her body when other people attempt to violate her. Tragically, as Raphael so eloquently articulates, child sexual abuse teaches girls and young women that they have *no right* to control their own bodies or limit other people's access to their sexuality.

Beyond Raphael's *qualitative* research, there is little statistical research on the relationship between *sexual abuse* in childhood or adolescence and *physical abuse* in adulthood that allows us to consider the probability that female victims of CSA are disproportionately likely to experience IPV in their adult relationships. Based on our interviews with battered women who reported experiencing sexual abuse as children, we identify the *processes* by which early childhood sexual abuse led to revictimization, through both poor partnering decisions made in an attempt to escape the sexual abuse they were experiencing and their limited agency in ending IPV when it did occur.

INTERVIEWING VICTIMS OF VIOLENCE

People who have never conducted in-depth interviews with victims of violence are often very surprised by the level of intimate details that subjects are willing to share with complete strangers. Even for the seasoned researcher, there is often concern that with each new project, one will not be able to elicit the information that is most interesting and most pertinent to the project. Across several different projects, we have learned that there are several keys to successful interviewing. First, when one conducts research on a painful topic, it is critically important to establish trust and rapport with the subject. Second, much like therapeutic relationships, sometimes people are more willing to disclose painful and even shameful experiences with a stranger, someone they will never see again, than their family members or close friends. Thus, it is not unusual to learn that our conversation is the first time an individual has talked about her or his experiences. Third, we have found that victims of gender oppression (rape, IPV) are often ashamed of their experiences, and they have encountered people who are literally shocked by their stories. Therefore, they tend to start out mildly and slowly reveal the real tragedy of their experiences. It is critical that the researcher express sympathy but not shock at these revelations. By accepting the extraordinary experiences of these women, the researcher develops the trust necessary for the revelation of increasingly intimate and increasingly shocking events.

Though not all girls who are sexually abused in childhood and adolescence grow up to be battered women, there does seem to be a significant relationship between being a battered woman and early experiences with rape and incest (Lawless 2001; Wesley 2006).

Among the women in this study, CSA fell into three distinct categories:

- premature sex engagement (our term)
- incest
- childhood prostitution

We begin with some descriptive data on the forms of childhood and adolescent sexual abuse and then examine the two "survival" strategies that put victims of CSA at risk for IPV:

1. marrying as teenagers to escape incest and prostitution
2. choosing intimate partners who could protect them from outside violence but who ended up abusing them

Childhood Sexual Abuse: Premature Sex Engagement

One of the first things that struck us in interviewing battered women was their sexual "initiations"—their first sexual experiences. The majority of women we interviewed overall and *all* of the African American women we interviewed experienced sexual initiation at very young ages and with significantly older boys or men, rather than their peers.

There is ample research to suggest that preteens and young teenagers often engage in sexual experimentation with each other. In a common scenario in the United States, preteen and early-teenage boys and girls engage in sexual experimentation—kissing, "petting," and so forth—in which neither party knows what to expect. In this type of scenario, when neither party has more knowledge or experience, the experimentation is as balanced as possible in a patriarchal culture in which expectations on boys and girls are different and can shape their behaviors. For example, boys may push for more sexual experiences, and girls may resist based on the sexual scripts that dominate our beliefs about sexuality.

Sexual scripts: the set of cultural norms that govern sexual behavior, including who should or can initiate sex and which role each participant will play in the encounter. The dominant sexual scripts in the United States are gendered: boys and men are supposed to desire sex anytime, anyplace, and any way, whereas women are supposed to have less interest in sex overall, less interest in multiple sex partners, more conservative beliefs about sex practices (for example, regarding anal sex), never initiate sex, and resist men's advances. We note that there are other sexual scripts that are specific to sexual orientation, but for our purposes here, we discuss the heterosexual sexual scripts that dominate teenage sexual experiences in particular.

In contrast, in some cultures sexual initiation is believed to be the responsibility of the older members of the community. Older women and especially older men will "initiate" teenagers in order to "teach" them how to be sexual. This is believed to be an ideal circumstance because then when they marry, the partners are guaranteed that each will "know what to do" and be a satisfying lover.

What we learned about in our interviews was distinct from this type of "culturally institutionalized" sexual initiation. In contrast, the experience difference led to the older participant (always the man) being able to exploit a young woman who did not know what to expect, who did not perhaps understand what was happening, and who could be convinced to engage in activities she might not want to. Think about the ways in which this is illustrated by the urban myths that emerge when we teach courses in human sexuality. When we ask students what myths they have heard about sex, the *women* will admit to having been told by boys:

1. you cannot get pregnant if you have sex while standing up
2. douching with Coke will prevent pregnancy
3. "blue balling" is dangerous for me (boys or men)

There are other examples as well. The ability to manipulate and exploit in the context of sexual initiation is significantly increased when one partner has significantly more personal experience with sex—and frequently more partners—than the other.

In order to capture the uniqueness of these sexual initiations, we coined the term *premature sex engagement*. **Premature sex engagement** refers to experiencing one's first sexual intercourse at a very young age with an older man. The most typical pattern that was presented in our research involved women who recalled that their first sexual experiences occurred when they were thirteen or fourteen years old with men ten years older, that is, men in their midtwenties. However, in some cases the first sexual experiences of these young teenage girls involved much older men—those in their thirties or forties.[1] Though this fits the definition of statutory rape, these women primarily defined these experiences as "consensual." The issue of consent in these cases is a tricky and complex one, as Odem (1995) points out in her historical study of sexuality; the "age of consent" laws effectively remove the possibility that girls under the age of eighteen can legally consent to *any* sexual activity. Recently, some states have modified their statutory rape laws to require age differences of at least a year—for example, sex between two seventeen-year-olds no longer meets the legal requirements of statutory rape.

This issue is further complicated by the blurring of the term *consent*. Diana Scully (1990) points out that convicted rapists' definitions of rape hinge on *their* perceptions of a woman's consent rather than the woman's own perceptions. Research on incest and CSA also notes that in many cases, victims do report "consenting." We argue that

---

BOX 7.1   GENARLOW WILSON AND STATUTORY RAPE

Outrage After Teen Gets 10 Years for Oral Sex with Girl
ABC News Primetime, February 7, 2006

A wild New Year's Eve two years ago has landed a Georgia teen in prison for 10 years on charges of child molestation in a case that has state legislators reworking the strict law that put him behind bars.

Genarlow Wilson faces 10 years in prison for what he says was consensual oral sex with a 15-year-old girl when he was 17.

Genarlow Wilson and a group of friends had the kind of bash no parent would want their teenager to attend. Crime scene investigators combing the room in a Days Inn in the small town of Douglasville, Ga., found evidence of drinking, as well as condoms and wrappers littered all over. Plus, there was a video camera.

In a portion of a tape obtained by "Primetime," Wilson, then 17 and an honor student and star athlete who was homecoming king, is seen having intercourse with a 17-year-old girl, who was seen earlier on the bathroom floor. During the sex act, she appears to be sleepy or intoxicated but never asks Wilson to stop. Later on in the tape, she is seen being pulled off the bed.

Other portions of the tape show a second girl, who was 15 and later said she did not drink that night. She was recorded having oral sex with several boys in succession, including Wilson.

The following morning, Wilson got a phone call that would change his life. He learned from a friend that the 17-year-old had gone to the police to report that she'd been raped.

"I was, like, 'What? When was this happening? Did this happen at the same party I was at?'" Wilson said. "It was shocking to me."

Source: http://abcnews.go.com/Primetime/LegalCenter/story?id=1693362&page=1. You can read more about the Genarlow Wilson case on our course website.

---

the women whom we classify as experiencing premature sex engagement fall into the same category as victims of CSA and not into the category of those cases now excluded from statutory rape. In all cases, the age difference between the girls and the men they had sex with was at least ten years. Furthermore, this age gap results in both a power differential and an "experience differential" that often left these girls feeling exploited, even when they consented.

Veta, for example, told of her first sexual experience when she was sixteen. Her "partner" was a forty-two-year-old married man by whom she would eventually become pregnant. In discussing the awkwardness of the age difference, Veta recalled telling her parents she was pregnant, and when they insisted that she bring the father of her child to their home to meet them, she realized she was bringing home to her mother and father a man who was not only married to someone else but *older than her parents*!

Of the twenty African American women we interviewed, nearly all, eighteen (90 percent) experienced premature sex engagement (several via incest or childhood prostitution). Though incredibly common among white women as well, somewhat fewer (ten of fifteen, or 67 percent) experienced premature sex engagement. Furthermore, of the white women we interviewed, only one experienced incest and none experienced prostitution. These patterns reinforce those that are reported by national studies that reveal that African American teenage girls are 1.5 times more likely to have had sexual intercourse than their white peers (Dye 2005).

Not only was early teenage sexual activity common, but it almost *always* involved older, and presumably more experienced, first sex partners. For African American women, these sexual experiences at fourteen or fifteen almost invariably led to pregnancy and a birth before the mother turned sixteen. Half of the white women who experienced premature sex engagement also became teen mothers, and they too struggled to complete high school and find jobs that paid enough so they could take care of themselves and their children. With rare exceptions, *girls* who had their first child by age sixteen dropped out of high school and failed to earn a general equivalency diploma. Race differences exacerbate this problem. Because African Americans have higher levels of *unintended unemployment* (Hattery and Smith 2007; Padavic and Reskin 2002) and because African Americans and women require more education to make the same wages as white men (Padavic and Reskin 2002), the long-term consequences of these experiences significantly shape the life chances of African American girls and their children (Hattery and Smith 2007; Maynard 1997). The failure to complete high school left these women even more vulnerable to IPV—as we will explore extensively in the next chapter—because they have little earning power in a changing economy where low-skilled employment continues to disappear (Browne 1989; Brush 2001).

Clearly, race shaped both the likelihood of experiencing premature sex engagement as well as its consequences. The fact that *nearly all* of the African American women we interviewed experienced premature sex engagement suggests that as scholars and practitioners (teachers, social workers, and health care providers), we need to adjust our understanding of the "typical" experiences of African American teenage girls to include this type of experience. Second, because we know that premature sex engagement has many consequences for young women, *especially African Americans*, these race differences demand our attention.

Without knowing it at the time when we were conducting these interviews with battered women and learning about their experiences with what we term premature sex engagement, simultaneously our colleague Dr. Linda Burton was seeing something similar in her own research. Burton coined the term *Childhood Adultification* to describe the outcomes of premature sex engagement.

> **Childhood adultification** involves contextual, social, and developmental processes in which youth are prematurely, and often inappropriately, exposed to adult knowledge and assume extensive adult roles and responsibilities within their family networks. Gendered images of African American female children were particularly negative in that they were talked about as sexual beings, immanent mothers, girlfriends, and sexual partners (Burton 2007, 329, 338).

Consequences that are also associated with early sexual intercourse that is consensual and with a same-aged partner include (Alan Guttmacher Institute 2004):

- higher rates of unintended pregnancy
- higher rates of STDs
- more sexual partners

Consequences associated with the exploitation inherent in situations that are characterized as premature sex engagement include (Sweet and Tewksbury 2000; Wesley 2006):

- higher risk for drug and alcohol abuse
- eating disorders
- self-mutilation

Consequences associated with teen childbearing include (Hattery and Smith 2007; Maynard 1997):

- failing to complete one's education
- long-term dependency on "welfare"
- overall higher fertility

Incest and Child Molestation at Home

Incest and child molestation are reported by 15 percent to 25 percent of adult women (Tjaden and Thoennes 2000). Several women whom we interviewed, white and African American, admitted to childhood sexual abuse by fathers, stepfathers, and mothers' boyfriends. Among the thirty-five women we interviewed, five (15 percent) reported at least one experience with incest. Consistent with national-level data (Tjaden and Thoennes 2000), there were very few race differences with regards to the women's experiences with incest. Regardless of women's willingness to disclose the details, scholars and practitioners need to assume a high probability for CSA when working with young women and especially young women who are in trouble or "at risk" (Gaarder and Belknap 2002; Sweet and Tewksbury 2000; Wesley 2006).

Preadolescent Prostitution: The Liquor or Drink House

Among the women we interviewed, none of the white women but 15 percent (three of twenty) of the African American women had experiences as child prostitutes. One case involved "situational prostitution"; the other two cases involved *continuous* child prostitution in drink houses run by the fathers or stepfathers of the women. "**Situational prostitution**" refers to the circumstance when a woman (or man) engages in prostitution only when it seems the most efficient way in which to meet an immediate need. The most common example of this involves *occasionally* "trading sex" for drugs.

We must begin the discussion of liquor houses with a caveat. We do not want to imply here that childhood prostitution is a normative experience for young African American women. We do suspect, however, that Winston-Salem, North Carolina, is similar in many regards to other southern communities in which there is a single major employer; in Winston-Salem this employer is R. J. Reynolds Tobacco. (Yes, the cigarettes—Winstons and Salems—are both named for the town in which they are produced.) As in many southern communities, until very recently work was segregated (Collins 1994; Hattery and Smith 2007; Shapiro 2003), and R. J. Reynolds was no exception. Though a few African Americans were hired to sweep floors and to do the most menial labor associated with cigarette production, for the most part they were excluded from working at the town's primary company. As is typical in many southern towns, African Americans were, however, called on to "service" the white community as housekeepers, nannies,[2] gardeners, and liquor suppliers (Korstad 2003; Tursi 1994; Hattery and Smith 2010). This was an especially important function during Prohibition, and the habit of going into the housing projects to imbibe that developed then continues to exist today. When conditions like these exist, the environment is primed for many exploitative and oppressive behaviors, among them prostitution. Therefore, we believe there is much to learn from the case of Winston-Salem, North Carolina.

LIQUOR HOUSES

Liquor houses are a sort of unregulated social club. In the legitimate economy they are similar to an Elks Lodge or VFW Hall. Usually, they are an apartment in the public housing projects. In a typical liquor house, a man allows a woman (and often her children) to live rent free upstairs in exchange for her (and her children) running the liquor house on the main level of the home. So that the man can drink and gamble and enjoy the liquor house he literally lives in, the woman acts as the bartender and the short-order cook (many drink houses serve simple food such as fried fish or chicken) and generally handles all of the "sales" of the liquor

continues

LIQUOR HOUSES *continued*

house—cigarettes, food, and of course liquor. Additionally, this arrangement usually involves an exchange for sex with the woman whenever he desires it. Typically, drink houses are open nearly twenty-four hours a day. The women we interviewed told us that they were horrible places to grow up because customers, mostly men, come in all times of the day and night to get a drink and a plate of food, play cards, and buy cigars or cigarettes. A typical liquor house stocks not only liquor, wine, and beer but will often serve cold sandwiches during the after-noon and fish, pork chops, and french fries in the evening. One woman we interviewed, Evie, talked, almost with pride, about how she could make the sandwiches and even pour a shot of whiskey by the time she was ten. Her face turned dark and tears filled her eyes as she talked about the men she encountered there and what they made her do—employing the euphe-mism that she had to "sit on their laps."

When we inquired about the men who frequented the drink houses, Evie—a fiftysomething African American woman we interviewed in the battered women's shelter in North Carolina—told us that of course there were the locals, men who lived in the projects, but that the primary customers were white male executives from R. J. Reynolds Tobacco Company who lived in the more affluent parts of town. These men would come during their lunch hour and at happy-hour time (usually after four in the afternoon) to consume alcohol and cigarettes and have sex before returning to their quiet, white middle-class neighborhoods.

> *Some of the Reynolds men got paid on Wednesday. They'll come in, maybe, and buy . . . give me a five, and maybe they done bought four drinks and I would have the change. Sometimes they would sell fish in there. And a lot of times, some of the guys would get the cigarettes and change cigarettes for drinks. And it was just like, I wonder that the people that lived out by a car [meaning out in the suburbs]. There was nice section. But they would come in our neighborhood, and drink, and buy women and stuff like that.*

Both of the women we interviewed (Evie and Shakira) who worked in (and in fact grew up in) liquor houses were initially lured into this work—and ultimately into a life of forced child-hood prostitution—by their fathers or stepfathers, who told them they could earn a little money making sandwiches and pouring drinks. Evie recalls that by age twelve she was frying fish and managing the food side of the operation. In addition, she admitted that her father required her to work regularly as a child prostitute; in her words, she was required to "perform favors" for the men in the drink house.

> *You can't imagine what it's like to have to sit on the laps of men when you are a ten-year-old. I hadn't even learned to ride a bike yet.*

Thus, as important as our focus is on the international world of child sex trafficking, we need to recognize that it is happening in our own communities as well and has devastating consequences on the victims, who often go on to be victims in adulthood too.

What is perhaps most striking about these stories of preadolescent prostitution is the way that they are shaped by both race and social class. Not only were the women African American and poor, but the liquor house itself was in part a product of race and class inequalities that exist in the community. In a segregated community like Winston-Salem, there are few legitimate ways for African Americans to earn a living, and those that do exist are primarily restricted to educated, middle-class, and professional African Americans and to women who were employed as domestics (Collins 1994). Poor whites were able to find work in the R. J. Reynolds cigarette factories, but African Americans were excluded from this employment option. Thus, African Americans living in the housing projects created a "service" economy that filled a niche, one that would never have been allowed to operate in most white neighborhoods regardless of their social class composition (Korstad 2003; Tursi 1994). Thus, race, class, and gender were powerful forces in shaping both the individual experiences these women had with childhood prostitution as well as the phenomenon itself. On a related note, the burgeoning international child sex trade is similar. The vast majority of children sold into childhood prostitution not only are poor themselves but come from some of the poorest countries in the world.

In response to the CSA these women experienced, the women we interviewed employed two related survival strategies: marrying to escape the abuse and choosing dangerous partners. Both strategies put these women at risk for IPV. We turn now to a discussion of the survival strategies and incredible violence that these women endured at the hands of their abusive partners, opening with the revealing story of Debbie.

Sexual Abuse and a Drive to Escape

By age seventeen, seeking answers and help, Debbie became a disciple of James and Tammy Baker's Praise the Lord (PTL) ministry. Homeless for a time, she slept in a trailer on the grounds of the PTL club in Charlotte. There she met a young man. After a few weeks they had sex, and feeling guilty about it, they married. Debbie describes her decision to marry John.

It was after three days we met that we kissed. And we never really discussed that kiss or nothing. We just liked each other right away. So he took me to a jewelry store and bought me an engagement ring and a wedding band. Then he had this necklace around his neck that said "I love you" that somebody gave to him. So he took it off and put it around my neck. Then I put the engagement ring on, and he asked me to go with him. And I said, "Sure." I wanted to be free from my family. I thought if I get married, my name changes and I'm free from my family.

Debbie, thirtysomething African American woman, North Carolina

---

For many women like Debbie, getting pregnant or married was perhaps the only route for escape (Lawless 2001). *All* of the women we interviewed who acknowledged that they had been sexually abused or prostituted in childhood entered their first intimate, romantic sexual *relationships* before they were eighteen. Frequently, these relationships involved living together (married or not) within weeks or months of meeting each other. In their eyes, moving in with another man seemed the most obvious escape route, one that almost always led to physical, emotional, and sometimes sexual abuse at the hands of their lovers (Brandt 2006; Griffing et al. 2005; Lawless 2001). In their attempts to escape the sexual abuse they were experiencing at home, these *girls* often left with the first man who would take them away (usually by marrying them), and within months it was clear to these women that they had traded one sort of violence and abuse for another. Debbie paints a graphic picture:

I wanted to please him [sexually], because my mom never talked to me or nothing. I had to figure out what I'm supposed to do. I knew you screwed, but I wanted more than that. So I looked at the videos. And when I did something on him that I learned from the video. He was like, "Oh, where did you learn to do that? You had to do it before somewhere else." But then he got sexually abusive. He wanted to, like, use objects on me and all kinds of stuff. When he did that, that's when I started hating him. And I wouldn't let him do it, and he would get mad. And then he would tear my pictures up of my family and burned them. He tore up some of my clothes he bought me. One time he got so mad, we was going down the road, and he ran his car into an overpass bridge. We were both in it, and he was going eighty miles per hour. He totaled the car, but we both walked out of it. [AH: Was he trying to kill you?] Yeah. He wanted to kill both of us.

Debbie, thirtysomething African American woman, North Carolina

---

Many, many women we interviewed reported having sex when they did not want to, though they seldom called it rape. And many reported that sex seemed to be a tool of the violence or an attempt to make up after a battering episode. They described not only the hurt of being raped by your intimate partner, the person who claims to love you, but also the consequences, such as unintended pregnancy or possible exposure to STDs, including HIV. Cheri describes her experience:

So, you know, the park. We smoke a little blunt. And then we have sex in the car, which was ironic, 'cause we'd never done this before. Okay, my pants still on my ankles, and then he just starts beating me on my face. Yeah. I mean, his was too [pants were down]. That's how, soon as he done it, it happened. He didn't even get up off of me. He just started beating me, talking about, that's what I was doing, that's what I gave to some-

body else, and just rambling on and on and on. And I crawled out of the car and crawled under my car. Then my stubborn butt wouldn't leave 'til he gave me my two hundred dollars back. Then, he was like, he was like, well, go clean your face up. . . . I had about six bones broken over here. And to this day, I can't see out this eye. I have a dislocated retina. And, so, I went a whole day without going to the emergency room 'cause I was scared. So, when I finally went to the emergency room, 'cause the eye wouldn't open up is what made me go, and I was in so much pain, I found out I was pregnant. So, I told . . . so I told the abortion clinic, if y'all don't get this baby out of me, I am. So they got me a volunteer to help pay for it, but by the time they came through, I was five months pregnant. So then that almost killed me.

Cheri, thirtysomething African American woman, North Carolina

We argue that seeking out sexual partners as a means of escape is similar to stripping and prostitution in that they all involve trading sexual access for economic support, or, as the stories of the women here illustrate, agreeing to marry (and have sex) in exchange for a place to live and an escape from the childhood abuser. The strategies employed by Debbie, like those of so many other women we interviewed, illustrate a well-established finding by scholars who study CSA: that CSA is a major pathway to careers in stripping and prostitution (Monto and Hotaling 2001; Sweet and Tewksbury 2000; Wesley 2006) and juvenile delinquency (Gaarder and Belknap 2002; Goodkind, Ng, and Sarri 2006).

In contrast, the women we interviewed who had been battered but who had *not* experienced CSA left intimate partner relationships the *first time* they were hit. As a result, they were seldom forced into the cycle of trading sexual access for the economic support of a man who would help them flee but who would also abuse them. Additionally, our interviews confirm the research of other scholars who have studied women who experienced CSA as well as IPV as opposed to those who only experienced IPV. An important pattern is revealed: "Childhood abuse, and particularly childhood sexual abuse, is associated with a pattern in which women are less likely to be in a stable marriage or a long-term cohabiting relationship but are instead more likely to experience multiple short-term unions. Adult abuse, and particularly adult physical abuse, on the other hand, is associated with a reduction in the probability of being in either form of union" (Cherlin et al. 2004, 784).

CSA and Economic Dependency in Adulthood

With regards to social class, the strategy of trading sexual access for economic support, though used by many women, for centuries, and in all cultures, is by and large a strategy that affluent women do *not* need to rely on. The middle-class women we interviewed *did not* establish a pattern of trading sexual access for economic support to flee abusive relationships. Instead, they were able to rely on their own economic assets to leave relationships when they became abusive. It is, of course, important to realize that women's access to their own resources—either resources they earned or the ability to access joint checking accounts, hold credit cards, and so forth—is a relatively recent phenomenon. We turn next to an examination of a severe case of relying on fleeing as a strategy to escape violence, as told to us by Andi.

Andi is an African American woman we interviewed in Minnesota. Andi's is yet another case of premature sex engagement. At age thirteen Andi had her first sexual relationship, with a twenty-three-year-old man. She ultimately bore two children by this man, though they never married. Because he was also a drug dealer and violent with her and the children, she decided that she needed to escape.

I knew this guy who drove a truck, and he had to go back to Chicago—I was living in Mississippi—so he took us to Chicago. I stayed in a hotel for about a week and then went to a shelter. I met this guy one day when I was outside of the shelter. And I do not know what was going through my mind, but I liked him; he was like, "Why don't you come to Minnesota with me?" So I came to Minnesota. I'd been in Chicago for a week and a half. [AH: And how quickly did you move to Minnesota?] The next day after I met him. It was like no, I didn't it was like one of those stupid, you're-risking-your-life moves, but I was like, "Hey, what do I have to lose right now? I have absolutely nothing." Everything seemed pretty good for a minute. He got a job . . . but then one night he flipped out because he found out I had smoked a blunt and that I had been around some guys. . . . We got into this fight and everything . . . he had just grabbed me, and like, slammed me into the wall. . . . He ended up hitting my face against the wall.

Andi, twentysomething African American woman, Minnesota

Andi's story, though perhaps extreme in that it involves moving several hundred miles, is typical of the stories we heard from the women we interviewed. What Andi's story illustrates is the cycle that many of the battered women we interviewed fell into, specifically their drive to replace the financial security they forfeited when they left abusive circumstances. These women often reported that they felt that their options were limited to either living alone and poor or taking a chance to improve their economic conditions by moving in with a man, sometimes a total stranger.

Though this may seem obvious, this circumstance that most women face (save the relatively small percentage who are economically self-sufficient)—for many of the battered women we interviewed, leaving a violent or sexually abusive relationship, often involving fathers, stepfathers, or older men—had plunged them into such severe poverty that they were homeless. In addition, moving out often meant that they lost their jobs because they either failed to come to work during the transition or could not continue to go to work *and* care for their children. For example, it is common in low-income families for parents to "split shifts" so that one parent watches the children while the other works, thus eliminating or significantly reducing child-care costs (Hattery 2001a, 2001b). In such instances, leaving the abusive relationship often meant leaving behind the only child care that was available and "affordable." Therefore, the pressures these women felt to find a new relationship were significant and pressing. Most of the women we interviewed reported that after leaving an abusive relationship, they often established a new relationship within weeks, often with someone they barely knew or with someone they knew had a reputation for violence, and more often than not, this new relationship, pursued as an escape, turned violent as well. Other scholars have found similar patterns in studies of homeless women who reported high rates of violence in their relationships.

It is evident that the women entered into initial adult relationships for multiple reasons (often related to childhood issues): to escape the home environment, to prove to themselves and others that they could "do it right," to achieve what they discerned as safety, security, comfort, or love (Wesley and Wright 2005, 1089). In short, as Wesley and Wright (2005) note, women who have experienced abuse typically find that their options "shrink." And this situation is further compounded by race and social class. Women with fewer of their own economic resources were more likely to jump directly into new relationships in order to avoid what they saw as a real chance they would otherwise be homeless. Furthermore, because of the strong correlation between race and social class (Hattery and Smith 2007; Shapiro 2003), this pattern was more pronounced among African American women than their white counterparts. Explicating the links among CSA, IPV, race, and the resultant economic instability contributes to our understanding of the complexities of seemingly unrelated phenomena, including the homelessness faced by women and often their children. Additionally, our research sheds light on the process by which child abuse, and CSA in particular, has long-term consequences for its victims, including homelessness—as a result of leaving the home of the perpetrator—and, ultimately, for female victims the revictimization they experience at the hands of the men who help them to escape. Understanding these links is central to reforming our responses to child abuse and responding to adult victims whose fundamental risk for IPV was the abuse they experienced as children.

Trading Sexual Access for Protection

Women who have been raped or sexually assaulted often view men as dangerous (Brownmiller 1975; Griffin 1979; Koss 1985; Koss et al. 1994). If they are sexually assaulted by someone they know, they often report feeling as if they can no longer trust anyone. Women who are raped by a stranger may develop a generalized distrust of the world, including an increased fear of being a victim of natural disasters, accidents, and so forth, as is typical of all victims of post-traumatic stress disorder (Griffin 1979; Koss 1985; Koss et al. 1994). Living with such generalized distrust, some women may put up with sexual and physical abuse by their intimate partners in exchange for the protection these men provide from the outside world (MacKinnon 1991; Rich 1980).

Ironically, wanting a protector is, by definition, wanting someone capable of violence. To defend a woman from another man's physical violence, he must himself be capable of inflicting physical harm, or of creating the threat of physical harm. Clearly, not all protectors *use* physical violence, either against women or against men, but the paradox lingers—and it played itself out especially clearly in Candy's relationship, which we examine now.

Candy was molested at age fifteen by her mother's boyfriend. Like many of the other women's stories told here, she sought adult intimate partners who would protect her even while abusing her. Candy lives/lived with Mark, a physically dominant man who is horribly abusive. Candy's **order of protection** (a 50-B)—a civil order granted by a judge that prohibits any physical contact and often phone, text, and email contact—prohibits them from living together. However, according to Candy, when we interviewed her they were living with each other off and on and were continuing to have a sexual relationship, another violation of both the 50-B and the terms of Mark's treatment program. As we noted in the previous chapter, this was so common that many social service agencies are beginning to recommend family counseling and safety plans rather than rely on protective orders that are often ignored by the couple as well as law enforcement. We will discuss protective orders at length in Chapter 13.

Among many incidents that have taken place over many years, Mark choked Candy until she was unconscious, beat her against the stick shift of their car until her pelvis broke—causing her to miscarry their child a few days later—slapped her, pulled her hair, jumped on her and broke several ribs (almost causing an additional miscarriage and landing Candy in the hospital for two days), and bit her in the face at least ten times. At five feet nine and 120 pounds, Candy is extremely thin. At 300 pounds, even Mark's slaps are extremely dangerous. Candy also indicated that Mark had raped her "once or twice." When we met Candy, this level of battering had been going on for four or five years. However, Candy rationalized that although Mark may beat her, abuse her emotionally, and rape her, *he did not allow anyone else to treat her this way.*

Candy stays with Mark because he provides protection from the violence she fears she might otherwise experience at the hands of a stranger. The abuse she experiences with Mark is predictable, making it preferable to the unpredictable nature of sexual harassment and sexual and physical assault that women face in the workplace and outside world (MacKinnon 1991; Rich 1980).

When things were good, they were so good. Like I said, I was always secure with him. He might try to hit me and he might try to kill me, but nobody else was going to do it. Nobody else was going to talk bad to me or hurt me or talk bad about me. That just wasn't going to happen. I was secure in that sense with him. He was going to protect me from everybody else.

Candy, twentysomething white woman, North Carolina

Candy's quote not only illustrates an extreme example of the types of violence these women live with, but also demonstrates her cognizance of her situation. Many people believe that battered women have no agency or do not know how to make good choices. Candy's statement is clear: she understands very clearly the trade-off that she is making. And, though extreme, Candy's case illustrates the trade-off that many battered women make: choosing life-threatening violence that is predictable over the kind of random violence they perceive awaits them in the streets. In Candy's case, this choice also puts her at risk of becoming one of the thirteen hundred women who are murdered by their partners and ex-partners each year. And it illustrates, profoundly, the terrible mistake that is made when we teach our young women (in health classes, for example) and our daughters at home that they should fear strange men—and adjust their behavior accordingly (for example, by not walking alone after dark, by not jogging on secluded paths, or by not accepting drinks from men they do not know). Although this is all good advice, it renders invisible the reality that *their greatest risk for violence is in their own homes*. Last, it seems very clear that Candy's general distrust and fear of the violence that awaits her are a direct result of the molestation she experienced at age fifteen, by a man she had never met, a man her mother brought home from the racetrack earlier that evening.

A Life of Illegal and Illegitimate Behavior

Sexual assault and sexual abuse are significant events in any woman's (or man's) life. As noted by many scholars, including Pipher (1994), Wolf (1992), and Lalor and McElvaney (2010), many girls and women who are raped or sexually abused rely on dangerous coping strategies: they medicate the pain with alcohol or drugs or attempt to become "sexually invisible" by developing anorexia, bulimia, and overeating; some will go so far as to end the pain by committing suicide or going "crazy."

Although rape and sexual abuse are so prevalent in the lives of girls and women—one-quarter will experience sexual abuse by the time they are twenty-five years old—and under these circumstances it is impossible to prevent all rape and sexual abuse, those who deal with its victims note the importance of support and a healthy environment in which to heal. The women that we interviewed had neither a healthy environment nor the financial resources to get the support they needed. For Evie in particular, the effects of being forced to work as a child prostitute in her father's drink house, living in a violent household, and living in poverty, *all of which amount to child abuse and neglect*, had lifelong effects.

Evie was exposed to many different avenues for making money in the illegitimate economy while she was working at the drink house. As one can imagine, based on the trauma she experienced as a child prostitute, she escaped prostitution as soon as she could, and as an adult she never returned to this way of life as a long-term solution to earning money, though, as was the case with many of the other victims of childhood sexual abuse, she did, sometimes, trade sex for the financial support of a male partner: a place to live, some food on the table, or some drugs, what we term *situational prostitution*. However, for the majority of Evie's life, she supported herself in all sorts of ways. Her father was a numbers writer,[3] and she learned the numbers trade in the liquor house. As a teenager, she began running numbers for her father. She also learned to deal drugs and would also steal clothes and accessories from stores at the mall and sell them in "after"-market outlets, usually through "fences" who sold stolen property out of the trunks of their cars in the housing projects or in the parking lots of shopping centers in low-income neighborhoods. She worked for a while in a laundry, but she was always engaged in running numbers and dealing drugs, even when she was employed, and often she used her job as a distribution point, weaving legitimate work with illegitimate work.

As we talked more and more about her adult life, Evie talked about the only legitimate job she had ever had. For the past four years prior to our interview she had worked as a cook at the county hospital, a job she got when she was forty-six years old. Evie had not had a "real" job, full-time in the legitimate labor market, until she was forty-six years old! This was not because she had been out of the labor market raising children and taking care of a home, or because she was on welfare, but because she had always been able to support herself by working in the illegitimate economy. When we met Evie in the shelter, she had just lost her job at the hospital due to a single absence that resulted from battering, a phenomenon we will explore in great depth in the next chapter.

Having grown up with physical, sexual, and emotional abuse, living her entire life in the illegitimate world of liquor houses and drug dealing left Evie with very little hope for her future. Typical of many victims of child abuse, Evie had never experienced any measure of stability, and this adversely affected her decision making. As Evie was describing her foray into legitimate employment, it was, perhaps, the only moment in the interview in which she smiled. She loved to cook and was happy that she could earn a living doing something she loved. The other staff in the kitchen were impressed by her skills, and when we asked what her signature dish was, she beamed and replied, "My turkey and stuffing! Everything made from scratch."

Yet we were *shocked* when in the midst of this conversation Evie stopped, opened up her pocketbook, and pulled out a receipt. She had been living at a local flop hotel for the past *four years* and had paid them almost forty thousand dollars in rent! When we remarked that for that sum, with her good job at the hospital, she could have bought a small house or at least paid on a mortgage, her face sunk. Yes, she knew that. When we asked her why she had not invested in something more permanent, even an *apartment*, which would have cost less per month and thus allowed her to save some money, she replied that it was her fear of instability. She *assumed* that she would lose her job. And of course, in the end, Evie's predictions for her life came true. Just prior to our meeting with her, she had lost not only her job but her housing as well. In essence, she had lost nearly everything except a few possessions. To put it simply, sexual abuse in childhood, when coupled with a life of poverty and an unhealthy home life, has long-term, far-reaching, in fact lifelong effects that extend into nearly all aspects of "normal" adult life, including shaping the aspirations—or lack thereof—of the female victims of CSA.

Race and Class Variation

National-level data indicate that African American women are more likely to experience rape and sexual abuse. Among the women we interviewed, though many of the white women had experienced molestation or incest, virtually *all* of the African American women we interviewed experienced CSA in the form of incest, childhood prostitution, or premature sex engagement. Analysis of National Violence Against Women Act data—see Chapter 4 and the Appendix for a descriptions of this data set—also indicates that African American women are more likely to experience severe IPV than are their white counterparts (Hattery 2008). Though there are many reasons for this, we would argue that *one key issue is the increased exposure of African American women to CSA that ultimately increases their risk for IPV in adulthood.*

Furthermore, though rates of IPV are relatively stable across time and across racial and ethnic boundaries, our analysis of the NVAW data (Hattery 2008) demonstrates that race and ethnicity shape the *forms* of violence that women experience. Overall, African American women are disproportionately likely to experience lethal and near-lethal violence. For example, they are more likely to have a weapon (knife or gun) used against them, and they are more likely to be "beat up" (Hattery 2008). Our interviews confirmed this quantitative finding as well. White women were less likely to report injuries that required a visit to the emergency room or other forms of medical attention than were their African American counterparts. African American women reported incidents such as being hit in the head with a ball-peen hammer, being hit in the mouth so hard that one woman's teeth punctured both her top and bottom lips, being threatened with a shotgun, and being beaten beyond recognition—reported by the batterer who was also a boxer and had recently killed another boxer in the ring.

Similarly, research on the effects of child physical and sexual abuse demonstrates that African American children who are abused or neglected are more likely to be involved in criminal activity as juveniles and adults than are white children who experienced abuse or neglect in childhood (Widom and Maxfield 2001). For girls, arrests were most often reported for alcohol and drug violations (Widom and Maxfield 2001), which is consistent with the research on "self-medicating" by female victims of CSA (Browne and Finkelhor 1986; Hanson 1990; Kendall-Tackett, Williams, and Finkelhor 1993; Pipher 1994; Rind, Tromovitch, and Bauserman 1998; Sturza and Campbell 2005). Understanding clearly the likelihood of revictimization for female victims of child abuse and CSA in particular, and based on the realities that minority and low-income girls are more likely to experience CSA as well as a greater risk for IPV (regardless of their experiences with CSA), additional attention and resources must be dedicated to our most marginalized and vulnerable citizens. We turn now to a discussion of the impact of childhood violence on men.

THE IMPACT OF VIOLENCE IN CHILDHOOD ON MEN

Growing up in a violent household, especially one that involves IPV, is a significant predictor of violence in adulthood. Family scholars like Straus and Gelles talk about this as the **intergenerational transmission of violence theory**: the theory that a propensity toward committing violence is transmitted from parent to child, from father to son.

In their study of men, Ehrensaft and Cohen (2003) report that experiencing child abuse *doubles* one's risk for beating one's intimate partner in adulthood. *But witnessing violence in childhood triples one's risk for growing up to become a batterer.* Ehrensaft and Cohen also report that child abuse and witnessing parental violence put individuals (both men and women) at risk for drug abuse, mental health "diseases," and other negative behavior. Few researchers dispute the fact that child abuse or growing up witnessing intimate partner parental violence is detrimental to the healthy development of children. (We use the term **parental violence** here to stand for violence perpetrated between the intimate partners who are raising children. We fully recognize that in many cases, the batterer or the victim may not be a parent to the child. The adults may be stepparents, foster parents, even grandparents who are raising the child. The use of the term *parental* is merely a tool to reduce the cumbersome nature of the discussion for the reader.)

Discussions of the intergenerational transmission of violence theory are wrought with controversy. Critics of the intergenerational transmission of violence theory point to the fact that the *majority* of boys who grow up in violent homes do not grow up to abuse either their own children or their female partners (Kaufman and Zigler 1987). Others are critical of the term because it implies a genetic transmission. We will discuss this critique in the concluding chapter, arguing that the intergenerational transmission of violence can be understood by examining the ways that men, especially violent men, *teach* their sons to be men rather than interpreting the cycle of violence as genetic transmission.

To ignore the fact that boys who grow up experiencing violence or witnessing it often grow into men who perpetrate it would be to ignore one of the processes by which IPV becomes part of intimate relationships. It would also be dismissive to ignore the powerful impact of childhood abuse on the men we interviewed. As we noted in the previous chapter, witnessing parental violence is a form of child abuse that has long-lasting and devastating consequences on male victims. Many of the men that we interviewed grew up in households that were violent. Men like Darren grew up in households in which their fathers physically abused their mothers:

I saw the violence growing up. I can remember him standing over my mother with an iron in his hand and me drawing a .22 rifle on him to make him back up. Stuff like that. I can remember him choking my mother when I was seven, eight, nine years old. And all my friends are going to the kitchen window. There he is; he's got her over the sink. It was violent. Nobody was ever hospitalized or anything like that, but it was usually associated with his drinking.

Darren, fortysomething white man, North Carolina

In addition to the physical violence that occurred between Darren's parents, he described his father as emotionally absent; in fact, he indicated that his father was incapable of expressing emotion. After his parents divorced, he saw his father only five or six times in the next twenty years until his father's death. On one of the rare occasions that Darren did see his father, they were having an argument about his father's absence and lack of guidance, and Darren's father became physically violent with him.

He got up and he backed me up against a wall, and he was just quivering from head to toe. . . . He said, son, I love you, but I'll kill you. . . . He was just unable to handle the emotional side about losing his family.

Darren, fortysomething white man, North Carolina

Other men grew up in homes in which their fathers were physically abusive to them:

Yeah, yeah, but I don't want him [my son], you know what I mean, to grow up and go through what we been through, you know what I'm sayin', I believe in discipline, I give out spankin's, but I just don't want him to go through what me, my brother, and my sister went through with this dude [his stepfather], you know what I'm sayin', 'cause I still got scars from when he beat us. He beat me with an extension cord, hit me in the face, yeah, he left a scar down my face, you what I'm sayin', so I had to stay out of school for a while on that, you know. He used to taunt my brother all the time. You're a punk, you're a pussy, you're a pussy, you know what I'm sayin', you ain't never gonna be nothing, you're stupid, dumb, you see what I'm sayin', so me and him, he had grabbed me by my neck and broke my glasses because this one particular day he kept calling my brother a punk, you're a punk, you're a pussy, you're a punk, so he had went outside and got into some altercation with some dude [laughing], he came home, the dude kicked his ass [laughing], so when he came home I was like I guess you the punk and the pussy now, you know, so I guess that comment made him mad, and he grabbed me by my neck, so me and him start fightin', you know, but just by me making that comment I didn't care about gettin' beat up or gettin' a whippin', I just feel good that he got hit [laughing], you know what I mean, that was a great feeling, you know what I mean.

Manny, thirtysomething African American man, North Carolina

Finally, though much less common, several of the men we interviewed grew up in households in which one parent killed the other, as Eddie's mother did.

The Impact of Prostitution on Sons

Earlier in the chapter we discussed at length the impact of prostitution on girls and young women. Many of the men we interviewed also grew up with prostitution. In these cases it was their mothers who worked as prostitutes, frequently in tandem with a drug addiction. Again, the impact on these young men was severe. Boys growing up in these households were often introduced to the drug culture and began using drugs themselves at an early age. We would also argue that these boys and young men were also learning important lessons about women from the johns they "serviced": that women's primary function is to satisfy men's sexual needs, that women's own interests and desires are unimportant, and that women are not to be respected or trusted. Unfortunately, they carried these views into their own adult relationships, as noted by Eddie, whose mother killed his father:

At the course of time I even would see my mother stick needles in her arms, shooting heroin, you know, and it just became a life for me that I had developed some bad habits from the people that I was hanging around and from I seen in my past, all that I knew what I knew and during the course of years, during the course of these years, in school, I would go to school, you know, lay my head on the desk, wouldn't focus on the work, or cuss the teacher out, skip school, goin' to school, having marijuana, school just wasn't important to me. It had no benefits to me whatsoever, because I had already had made up my mind that I was going to be a drug dealer because, you know that's all I had seen, that's all I had developed. I thought that getting high and drinking was the way to go because that's all I developed throughout my years of coming to be a early teenager and uh, because all the abusive and damage I seen from my parents, all the damage of the people that I seen and hung around them. It became a habit to me, and by the time I was sixteen years old I was selling drugs and, uh, toting guns, and snorting cocaine, smoking crack at the age of sixteen years old, um, stealing cars, you know, the situation had gotten worse. I was snorting heroin, you know. The situation had just gotten bad at the age of sixteen, and therefore due to the fact that I had been in so much trouble, the judge sentenced me to go to Morganton High Rise for young men, a young prison camp in Morganton, North Carolina, and I was there and I went there, I caught ten years when I was sixteen years old. The judge gave me ten years.

Eddie, fortysomething African American man, North Carolina

Race and Class Variation

Much research documents the fact that rates of physical abuse of boys cross all race and class lines (Tjaden and Thoennes 2000). Thus, the role that race and class play in the intergenerational transmission of violence is in some ways minimal. However, the interviews that we conducted with batterers of different racial or ethnic and class backgrounds illuminate the ways in which race and class *do shape* the relationship between male child abuse or witnessing of abuse and battering in adulthood. The situation for men is similar to that for women: because minorities and the poor are significantly less likely to report abuse or have it interrupted when it occurs, the cycle of interpersonal violence is more likely to continue.

African American men also face distinct differences that shape their likelihood for seeing interpersonal violence propagated from one generation to the next. Most of these forces, such as unemployment, will be discussed in the next chapter. However, it is important to point out here that there are other individual risk factors such as drug abuse, prostitution, and homicide that young African American men are disproportionately likely to be exposed to that shape their decisions and behaviors in adulthood (Wilson 2009). African American men (and women, as noted above) are far more likely than their white counterparts to grow up in families that subsist in the illegitimate economy, a risk factor for exposure to drug abuse and prostitution. Homicide rates are substantially higher in the African American community as well. According to the Centers for Disease Control, homicide constitutes the fifth leading cause of death for African American men. In fact, in 2010, the *New York Times* explored the fact that the homicide rate in New York City has actually produced *a one-year drop in average life expectancy for African American men in New York*, so common is the homicide of young black men (Rabin 2010). As is the case with Eddie, one can only speculate on the impact that witnessing a domestic violence homicide had on his own violence in adulthood. This increased exposure to severe violence certainly impacts the likelihood that African American men will grow up to batter their intimate partners.

CONCLUSIONS

Clearly, the relationships among CSA, IPV, race and ethnicity, and social class are complex. We have argued here that African American women's disproportionate exposure to CSA puts them at increased risk for IPV in adulthood. As noted by sociologist Deborah King (1988), the impact of race, class, gender, and other social statuses is not "additive" but rather intersectional or "multiplicative." In order to truly understand the differences in the experiences of IPV for African American and white women, we need to understand the complexities of being a white woman or being an African American woman and how this status intersects with other systems such as access to shelters, health care, stable employment, and the criminal justice system that shape both the risk for IPV as well as the services available for women who find themselves faced with IPV. The same is true of social class. The fact that social class and race are so conflated exacerbates the situation for African American women. In terms of CSA and IPV (the focus of this chapter), we need to pay attention to the fact that African American women who are sexually abused as girls will, on average, have less access to treatment (mental health services, counseling) that if successful in producing healing may reduce their risk for IPV in adulthood.

For men, most boys who grow up in violent homes do not grow up to become abusive themselves. But the impact of the abuse they witness or experience is severe nonetheless. For so many of the men we interviewed, white or African American, the homes they grew up in were extremely violent. In some cases, they experienced violence themselves, but far more commonly they watched their fathers (or stepfathers) beat their mothers. This confirms the finding that Straus and Gelles and others have reported that boys who grow up watching their fathers (or stepfathers) beat their mothers *are at the greatest risk for growing up to beat their own female partners* (Ehrensaft and Cohen 2003). Because understanding the concept of the intergenerational transmission of violence theory is critical to the solutions we propose for reducing *all* forms of family violence, we will return to this discussion of intergenerational transmission in the concluding chapter.

Furthermore, it is clear that we cannot understand African American women's experiences with IPV until we understand their relation to African American men

(Hattery and Smith 2007). Because of a long history of segregation and antimisce-
genation laws coupled with the continued abhorrence by many whites of black-
white marriage—a 2011 survey conducted by Public Policy Polling reported that 60
percent of white Republicans in Mississippi believe interracial marriage should be *illegal* (http://www.publicpolicypolling.com/pdf/PPP_Release_MS_0407915.pdf)—
most African American women who are in relationships are involved with African
American men; interracial marriage rates for African American women are less than
2 percent. Thus, an additional "risk" that African American women face is linked
to their partnerships with African American men, who, like them, are situated in a
particular space in the opportunity structure that heightens the probability that they
will engage in violence against their female partners (Hattery and Smith 2007; Smith
2008).

Finally, we note that one question that is always asked with regards to these "stories" is why these women sought out relationships with men as a route to escape
sexual abuse. Part of the answer is quite simple: in most cases, these women were
poor and unable to make a living on their own. In short, they were economically
vulnerable. Of all the themes that run through the scholarly literature used in developing an effective model for understanding, preventing, and interrupting IPV, that
of "economic vulnerability" was the most frequently cited by interviewees.

Furthermore, the majority of African American women and some (about 25
percent) of the white women we interviewed were pregnant as teenagers; most
dropped out of school. Thus, they were extremely limited in their ability to provide
for themselves economically, and they sought out relationships with men who they
thought could put a roof over their heads and some food in their children's bellies
and provide some level of support for them. This is one of the most powerful ways
in which class inequality shapes exposure to IPV. Why? Because women who are
marginalized and denied access to the opportunity structure are vulnerable to and
at increased risk for violence both in the streets and at home.

Last, of course, we ask the question in reverse: what girl or young woman would
not want to escape incest or childhood prostitution? Given their resources, most relied on very dangerous ways in which to effect the escape. Their response teaches us
more about the tragedy of CSA than about their decision-making processes. Their
experiences with incest and childhood prostitution left them feeling so desperate
that they would do literally anything to escape.

Though we will make many policy recommendations in the final chapter, we
note here that it is clear that because of the strong relationship between childhood
sexual abuse (for women) and child abuse and witnessing intimate partner parental
violence (for men) and IPV in adulthood, interventions with the child victims of
abuse, including those who witness it, are critical and are likely to produce a sharp
reduction in the incidence of IPV in adulthood. In the next chapter, we will examine
the structural causes of IPV such as unemployment and incarceration.

NOTES

1. As stated, in some cases the age differences were smaller, only ten years. Yet we argue that for a teenager, this age difference still represents a huge gap in knowledge about sex and power in the "relationship."

2. For a carefully researched, award-winning novel on the subject, we recommend Katherine Stockett's book *The Help*.

3. Individuals will place "numbers" on the days of horse races with a bookie. Depending on the outcome, they can win considerable amounts of money for a small investment, sometimes as little as a quarter. When they "hit," the bookie collects a percentage of the take. See St. Clair Drake and Horace Clayton, *Black Metropolis: A Study of Negro Life in a Northern City* (1945), for a further explanation and discussion of what they refer to as the "policy station" (380–381).

BIBLIOGRAPHY

Alan Guttmacher Institute. 2004. *U.S. Teenage Pregnancy Statistics: Overall Trends, Trends by Race and Ethnicity, and State-by-State Information.* New York: Alan Guttmacher Institute.

Brandt, J. E. 2006. "Why She Left: The Psychological, Relational, and Contextual Variables That Contribute to a Woman's Decision to Leave an Abusive Relationship." PhD diss., City University of New York.

Browne, A. 1989. *When Battered Women Kill.* New York: Free Press.

Browne, A., and D. Finkelhor. 1986. "Impact of Child Sexual Abuse." *Review of the Research, Psychological Bulletin* 99: 66–77.

Brownmiller, S. 1975. *Against Our Will: Men, Women, and Rape.* New York: Simon and Schuster.

Brush, L. D. 2001. "Poverty, Battering, Race, and Welfare Reform: Black-White Differences in Women's Welfare-to-Work Transitions." *Journal of Poverty* 5: 67–89.

Burton, L. 2007. "Childhood Adultification in Economically Disadvantaged Families: A Conceptual Model." *Family Relations* 56, no. 4: 329–345.

Cherlin, A. J., L. M. Burton, T. R. Hurt, and D. M. Purvin. 2004. "The Influence of Physical and Sexual Abuse on Marriage and Cohabitation." *American Sociological Review* 69, no. 6: 768–789.

Collins, P. H. 1994. "Shifting the Center: Race, Class, and Feminist Theorizing About Motherhood." In *Mothering: Ideology, Experience, and Agency*, edited by E. Glenn, G. Chang, and L. Forcey, 45–66. New York: Routledge.

Drake, S. C., and H. Clayton. 1945. *Black Metropolis: A Study of Negro Life in a Northern City.* Chicago: University of Chicago Press.

Dye, J. L. 2005. *Fertility of American Women.* Washington, DC: US Census Bureau.

Ehrensaft, M., and P. Cohen. 2003. "Intergenerational Transmission of Partner Violence: A 20-Year Prospective Study." *Journal of Consulting and Clinical Psychology* 7: 741–753.

Gaarder, E., and J. Belknap. 2002. "Tenuous Borders: Girls Transferred to Adult Court." *Criminology* 40, no. 3: 481–517.

Goodkind, S., I. Ng, and R. C. Sarri. 2006. "The Impact of Sexual Abuse in the Lives of Young Women Involved or at Risk of Involvement with the Juvenile Justice System." *Violence Against Women* 12, no. 5: 456–477.

Griffin, S. 1979. *Rape: The Politics of Consciousness*. New York: Harper & Row.

Griffing, S., D. F. Ragin, S. M. Morrison, R. E. Sage, L. Madry, and B. J. Primm. 2005. "Reasons for Returning to Abusive Relationships: Effects of Prior Victimization." *Journal of Family Violence* 20, no. 5: 341–348.

Hanson, R. K. 1990. "The Psychological Impact of Sexual Assault on Women and Children: A Review." *Annals of Sex Research* 3: 187–232.

Hattery, A. J. 2001a. "Tag-Team Parenting: Costs and Benefits of Utilizing Non-overlapping Shift Work Patterns in Families with Young Children." *Families in Society* 82, no. 4: 419–427.

_____. 2001b. *Women, Work, and Family: Balancing and Weaving*. Thousand Oaks, CA: Sage.

_____. 2008. *Intimate Partner Violence*. Lanham, MD: Rowman and Littlefield.

Hattery, A. J., and E. Smith. 2007. *African American Families*. Thousand Oaks, CA: Sage.

_____. 2010. "Cultural Contradictions in the South." *Mississippi Quarterly* 63, no. 2.

Kaufman, J., and E. Zigler. 1987. "Do Abused Children Become Abusive Parents?" *Journal of Orthopsychiatry* 57: 186–192.

Kendall-Tackett, K., L. Williams, and D. Finkelhor. 1993. "Impact of Sexual Abuse on Children: A Review and Synthesis of Recent Empirical Studies." *Psychological Bulletin* 113: 164–180.

King, D. 1988. "Multiple Jeopardy, Multiple Consciousness: The Context of a Black Feminist Ideology." *Signs* 14, no. 1.

Korstad, R. 2003. *Civil Rights Unionism: Tobacco Workers and the Struggle for Democracy in the Mid-Twentieth-Century South*. Chapel Hill: University of North Carolina Press.

Koss, M. P. 1985. "The Hidden Rape Victim: Personality, Attitudinal, and Situational Characteristics." *Psychology of Women Quarterly* 9: 193–212.

Koss, M. P., L. A. Goodman, A. Browne, L. F. Fitzgerald, G. P. Keita, and N. F. Russo. 1994. *No Safe Haven: Male Violence Against Women at Home, at Work, and in the Community*. Washington, DC: American Psychological Association.

Lalor, K., and R. McElvaney. 2010. "Child Sexual Abuse, Links to Later Sexual Exploitation/High-Risk Sexual Behavior, and Prevention/Treatment Programs." *Trauma, Violence, and Abuse* 11: 159–177.

Lawless, E. J. 2001. *Women Escaping Violence: Empowerment Through Narrative*. Columbia: University of Missouri Press.

MacKinnon, C. 1991. *Toward a Feminist Theory of the State*. Cambridge: Harvard University Press.

Maynard, R. A. 1997. *Kids Having Kids: Economic Costs and Social Consequences of Teen Pregnancy*. Washington, DC: Urban Institute Press.

Monto, M. A., and N. Hotaling. 2001. "Predictors of Rape Myth Acceptance Among Male Clients of Female Street Prostitutes." *Violence Against Women* 7: 275–293.

Odem, M. E. 1995. *Delinquent Daughters: Protecting and Policing Adolescent Female Sexuality in the United States, 1885–1920.* Chapel Hill: University of North Carolina Press.

Padavic, I., and B. Reskin. 2002. *Women and Men at Work.* 2nd ed. Thousand Oaks, CA: Pine Forge Press.

Pipher, M. B. 1994. *Reviving Ophelia: Saving the Selves of Adolescent Girls.* New York: Putnam Press.

Rabin, R. C. 2010. "Longevity: For New York Men, a Life Expectancy Gap." *New York Times*, August 30.

Raphael, J. 2004. *Listening to Olivia: Violence, Poverty, and Prostitution.* Boston: Northeastern University Press.

Rich, A. C. 1980. "Compulsory Heterosexuality and Lesbian Existence." *Signs* 5: 631–660.

Rind, B., P. Tromovitch, and R. Bauserman. 1998. "A Meta-Analytic Examination of Assumed Properties of Child Sexual Abuse Using College Samples." *Psychological Bulletin* 124: 22–53.

Scully, D. 1990. *Understanding Sexual Violence: A Study of Convicted Rapists.* Boston: Unwin Hyman.

Shapiro, T. 2003. *The Hidden Cost of Being African American: How Wealth Perpetuates Inequality.* New York: Oxford University Press.

Smith, E. 2008. "African American Men and Intimate Partner Violence." *Journal of African American Studies* 12, no. 2: 156–179.

Stockett, K. 2009. *The Help.* New York: Amy Einhorn Books.

Sturza, M. L., and R. Campbell. 2005. "An Exploratory Study of Rape Survivors' Prescription Drug Use as a Means of Coping with Sexual Assault." *Psychology of Women Quarterly* 29: 353–363.

Sweet, N., and R. Tewksbury. 2000. "What's a Nice Girl Like You Doing in a Place Like This? Pathways to a Career in Stripping." *Sociological Spectrum* 20: 325–343.

Tjaden, P., and N. Thoennes. 2000. *Full Report of the Prevalence, Incidence, and Consequences of Violence Against Women: Findings from the National Violence Against Women Survey.* Washington, DC: US Department of Justice.

Tursi, F. 1994. *Winston-Salem: A History.* Winston-Salem, NC: John F. Blair.

Wesley, J. K. 2006. "Considering the Context of Women's Violence: Gender, Lived Experiences, and Cumulative Victimization." *Feminist Criminology* 1, no. 4: 303–328.

Wesley, J. K., and J. D. Wright. 2005. "The Pertinence of Partners Examining Intersections Between Women's Homelessness and Their Adult Relationships." *American Behavioral Scientist* 48, no. 8: 1082–1101.

Widom, C. S., and M. G. Maxfield. 2001. *An Update on the Cycle of Violence.* Washington, DC: National Institutes of Justice.

Wilson, W. J. 2009. *More than Just Race.* New York: W. W. Norton.

Wolf, N. 1992. *The Beauty Myth: How Images of Beauty Are Used Against Women.* New York: Anchor Books.

8 The Economy and Intimate Partner Violence

Violence by men against members of their own family is one of the most common yet perplexing forms of criminal behavior. One interpretation is that intrafamily violence is instrumental behavior that is used by domineering men to control their partners and children. . . . There are 2.5 to 4.5 million physical assaults inflicted on adult women by their intimate partner per year.

About one-third of female homicide victims in the United States [are] killed by their husband or partner.

—DAVID CARD AND GEORGE B. DAHL,
"Family Violence and Football: The Effect of
Unexpected Emotional Cues on Violent Behavior"

This is the first of two chapters that are devoted *entirely* to discussions of intimate partner violence in heterosexual couples. In contrast to the discussions of child abuse and elder abuse, which were organized around the types of abuse experienced, these two chapters are organized around the two dominant forces that shape intimate partner violence: structural factors, especially the economy, and cultural norms. Because this is the first chapter devoted to examining intimate partner violence, we begin by providing an overview of IPV, the forms it takes, and its prevalence in the US population. We then move our discussion to the role that structures play in shaping IPV. Perhaps the most powerful structure shaping IPV is the economy, and of particular concern to researchers and service providers in the second decade of the twenty-first century is the way in which the "great recession" that began in 2007 has impacted IPV. We will also explore the role that an individual's social class plays in shaping their experiences with IPV and how it impacts women's responses to IPV when they find themselves victims of it. Last, we will provide some suggestions for ways in which transformations in the economy would lead to reductions in IPV.

OBJECTIVES

■ To provide an overview of IPV and familiarize the reader with the forms it takes
■ To provide the reader with some basic statistics on IPV
■ To examine the predictors of IPV: individual factors, "couple" factors, and structural factors
■ To explore the ways in which the economy contributes to and shapes intimate partner violence
■ To introduce the reader to the role that economic systems play in creating inequality and shaping gender relations
■ To examine the ways in which the economic system of a particular culture contributes to (or not) the rates of intimate partner violence
■ To explore differences in rates of intimate partner violence across class groups in the United States, and specifically the role that social class plays in shaping one's risk for intimate partner violence

KEY TERMS

intimate partner violence	social structure
physical abuse	ecological fallacy
emotional or psychological abuse	social class
stalking	macro level
sexual abuse	micro-level status inconsistency
domestic violence homicide	compulsory partnering
intimate terrorism	labor market
situational couple violence	wage discrimination
economic systems	occupational sex segregation

INTRODUCTION

The first of several chapters devoted to a discussion of intimate partner violence (IPV), this chapter will begin by describing IPV as it occurs in the United States and providing statistics on its prevalence. Second, as in the previous chapters, here we will examine the factors that shape one's risk for IPV. After we have briefly discussed individual and "couple" factors, the remainder of the chapter will be devoted to the key structural factor that shapes IPV: the economy. As noted above, we will discuss the role of the economy at the individual level (one's social class) and at the societal level (the overall role of economic systems in shaping IPV).

This chapter and several of the following are unique in this text because they include data that we gathered. As we briefly discussed in Chapter 1, between 2001 and 2004 we conducted interviews with nearly one hundred men and women who live with intimate partner violence. We interviewed whites, African Americans, and some Hispanics. About half of the sample of individuals we interviewed were in relationships with each other; this allowed us a unique opportunity to see both sides of the story, so to speak. As we noted in our discussion of methods in Chapter 4, qualitative interviews allow for the exploration of a phenomenon at significantly greater depth. Our interviews allow us to explore the processes by which risk factors for engaging in intimate partner violence, for example, lead to actual battering in one's relationship. Our interviews provide the reader with a much more complex and in-depth view of the ways in which intimate partner violence takes place in the contemporary United States. That said, because our work is qualitative, we also examine the work of researchers who conduct broad, national studies in order to provide the reader with an expansive, overall view of the prevalence of intimate partner violence. One way to think about this is that our interviews provide the contours and shape to the two-dimensional "map" created by the research conducted on national samples. In several of the subsequent chapters, we will draw on the words of the men and women we interviewed in order to illustrate key concepts. This allows the reader to see the world of IPV through the people who are living it. We begin our discussion with an overview: some definitions and some statistics.

DEFINITIONS AND STATISTICS

Intimate Partner Violence: **Intimate partner violence** refers to the physical, emotional, psychological, and sexual abuse that takes place between intimate partners. These partners may be married or in a long-term committed relationship, or they may be dating. They may be living together or not living together. They may be separated or even divorced. They may be heterosexual or homosexual. What distinguishes intimate partner violence from other forms of family violence and other forms of interpersonal violence is that it occurs between two people who claim or claimed to love each other.

Physical Abuse: **Physical abuse** refers to violence that is physical. It can range from a slap or a push to kicking, biting, punching, or hitting with an object. Victims of physical abuse often sustain cuts, bruises, and lacerations; they frequently sustain broken bones; and in extreme cases they experience violence that hospitalizes them. When we first began interviewing battered women, we were stunned at the level of physical violence that was going on in our own community. We met a woman who had been hit in the head multiple times with a ball-peen hammer that required dozens of stitches; we met a woman who had been slammed so hard into the stick shift of her car that she broke her pelvis; we met a woman who was hit so hard in the mouth that her teeth punched through both her top and her lower lips. We met a woman who was bitten regularly in her face, apparently as a way of "marking" her. At the extreme, physical violence can result in permanent injury and even death. According to the Bureau of Justice Statistics, which counts only those crimes reported to the police, in 2009 a half-million acts of IPV were reported (Catalano et al. 2009). Statistics that are based on national samples of women report that approximately 25 percent of women reported an act of violence in the previous twelve months and nearly half reported at least one act of IPV in their lifetimes (Tjaden and Thoennes 2000). The reader will recall from our discussion of methods in Chapter 4 that one of the problems associated with all forms of family violence is the likelihood that they will be underreported; thus, most scholars agree that estimates generated through national probability samples are more accurate than official crime statistics.

As we discussed in Chapter 3, some scholars of family violence believe it is important to distinguish between two types of intimate partner violence, intimate terrorism and situational couple violence. We provide a brief overview of our longer discussion in Chapter 3 here.

Intimate Terrorism: Leone and her colleagues describe **intimate terrorism** as "a partner's attempt to exert control over his partner using a broad range of power and control tactics, which include physical violence" (2004, 473).

Situational Couple Violence: In contrast, **situational couple violence** "does not exist within a general pattern of controlling behavior. This form of violence is not motivated by a desire to control and over power a partner or a relationship, but rather occurs when specific conflict situations escalate to violence" (Leone et al., 473).

Emotional or Psychological Abuse: **Emotional or psychological abuse** refers to the type of abuse that is designed to belittle and humiliate the victim. It is the most common form of abuse; it coexists with all other forms of abuse. Many victims report that it is as painful as physical violence (Browne 1989; Hattery 2008). Quite often, emotional or psychological abuse is verbal and ranges from name-calling to verbal assault—berating someone for a mistake or for doing something the "wrong way." Emotional or psychological abuse often involves public humiliation—for example, women often reported that their husbands or boyfriends called them names in front of their friends. A common scenario involved the husband inviting friends over to watch a sports event and berating his wife for not providing proper food or enough beer. Public humiliation frequently involves calling one's wife names or referring to her as "dumb" or saying "she doesn't know anything" in a public setting, such as when shopping or doing business at a bank. Emotional or psychological abuse can also involve terrorizing one's partner by tapping her phone, hacking into her email, following her to work or on errands, and so forth. We explore these types of behaviors at length in Chapter 12.

Stalking: **Stalking** is a particular kind of psychological abuse that we discuss separately because it has become the focus of recent domestic violence and dating violence legislation. Stalking can involve some of the behaviors previously mentioned, including tapping phone lines, hacking into email accounts, and following the victim as she travels to work or school, on errands, and so forth. Stalking can also involve harassment, including incessant phone calls or text messages and banging on the door for hours, demanding to be let into her home. National probability studies reveal that 5 percent to 7 percent of women reported that they were stalked in the previous twelve months, with lifetime estimates likely to be much higher (Tjaden and Thoennes 2000). Stalking is particularly common among violent couples who have separated or divorced, and it is also a common part of dating violence, especially among adolescents and college students. One of the authors had a student in class who shared that her boyfriend demanded that she be on Skype with him at all hours of the day and night—except for when she was in class—and if he could not see her through the webcam he installed on her computer, he would call her cell phone and her roommate's cell phone for hours until she would respond to him. She asked the author if this was unusual; yes, the author responded. It is stalking, it will likely get worse, and she should end this relationship. Stalking came to the attention of domestic violence advocates in the 1980s, and in 1990 the first antistalking legislation was enacted. Because it is so common in certain type of intimate relationships, especially dating and among couples who have separated, and because it is relatively easy to document in the age of cell phone technology and computers, it is one of the forms of violence that is more likely to be prosecuted.

Sexual Abuse: **Sexual abuse** refers to any forced, coerced, or undesired sexual behavior. Though most commonly thought of as rape (we will discuss marital rape at length in the next chapter), sexual abuse typically involves forcing a woman to engage in sex acts that she does not desire. So, for example, a woman who might be more than willing to have sexual intercourse with her husband may find that when he is drunk and unable to sustain an erection, he will penetrate with an object; women have reported being penetrated with curling irons, beer bottles, and many other objects that result in internal injuries. Again, based on national probability samples, it is estimated that 4.8 million IPV rapes are perpetrated each year (Tjaden and Thoennes 2000). As we will discuss at length in the next chapter, sexual abuse is very common, but for a variety of reasons, including beliefs about sexuality and the lack of physical evidence, it is rarely prosecuted.

Domestic Violence Homicide: **Domestic violence homicide** simply refers to the most severe outcome of physical violence: homicide. Domestic violence homicide can be intentional or result from a severe beating that may take place in minutes or hours that leaves the victim dead. More than thirteen hundred women are murdered per year by their intimate and ex-intimate partners, and domestic violence homicide accounts for one-third (33 percent) of all female homicide (Bureau of Justice Statistics, http://bjs.ojp.usdoj.gov/content/homicide/family.cfm). It is also important to note that in cases of domestic violence homicide, when the perpetrator is male, he often kills children, and it is not uncommon for him to attempt or commit suicide. Each year between two and three hundred men are murdered by their spouses or ex-spouses (Bureau of Justice Statistics, http://bjs.ojp.usdoj.gov/content/homicide/family.cfm). As the research of Angela Browne (1989) reveals and the documentary film work on the Framhingham Seven illustrates, the majority of male victims of domestic violence homicide are killed by wives and partners whom they have been abusing.

We turn now to a discussion of the research that has revealed risk factors for experiencing IPV.

RISK FACTORS FOR EXPERIENCING IPV

Like other forms of family violence, there are factors that increase the probability that IPV will occur. There are three types of risk factors: those associated with the individual—either the perpetrator or the victim—factors associated with the couple, and structural factors. We begin by examining individual risk factors.

Individual Risk Factors for IPV

There are several factors that increase one's likelihood of perpetrating IPV:

- gender
- witnessing IPV in the household in which one grew up; boys who witness IPV are three times more likely to perpetrate IPV in adulthood than men who did not witness IPV in childhood
- substance abuse or addiction
- poverty
- unemployment
- a history of incarceration
- a history of anger management problems, including fighting and assaults

Though all of these factors increase one's probability for violence, the two most important predictors are gender and witnessing domestic violence in childhood.

When people discuss domestic violence, they often overlook the fact that simply being male significantly increases one's likelihood of becoming abusive. The greatest individual risk factor for men, as we discussed at length in Chapter 7, is their exposure to IPV in childhood. It is important to point out that none of these risk factors guarantees that someone will become abusive; in fact, most people with the greatest risk factors do not become abusive. That said, when we consider prevention strategies, intervention strategies, and dating practices, it is important to understand the differential risk individuals may have toward violence.

There are several factors that increase the probability that one will become a victim of IPV. These include:

- gender
- being a victim of child abuse and child sexual abuse in particular
- poverty
- race or ethnicity
- unemployment
- teen pregnancy
- early sexual initiation
- substance abuse or addiction

As was the case with perpetrators, it is important to point out that by far the single greatest risk factor for becoming a victim of IPV is gender. Women are the victims in 90 percent of all IPV cases, and additionally, compared to male victims, they are more likely to sustain injuries that require medical attention or be killed by intimate or ex-intimate partners. As we explored at length in the previous chapter, women who are the victims of child abuse and CSA in particular are at significantly greater risk for becoming victims of IPV in adulthood. Last, we note that women of color, and African American women in particular, experience significantly higher rates of IPV than their white counterparts (Tjaden and Thoennes 2000). As was the case with risk factors for perpetrating IPV, it is important to note that even the presence of several risk factors does not mean that an individual will eventually be battered. It is important to understand these risk factors, however, as we create intervention and prevention programs. In particular, as we noted in the previous chapter, victims of CSA need significant attention in order to prevent a lifetime of abuse.

"Couple" Risk Factors for IPV

In addition to factors that place individuals at greater risk for IPV, there are a series of factors that when present in a couple increase the likelihood that violence will become part of the relationship.

- marrying before the age of twenty-five
- having a child before the age of twenty-five
- having more than the average number of children, and especially having children close together
- poverty
- unemployment
- substance abuse or addiction

As was the case with child and elder abuse, many of the risk factors associated with couples are related to stress; when a couple has several factors that increase the likelihood that they will have conflict—they are young parents, they have many children, they are facing financial problems—the very presence of the conflict increases the risk of IPV. As always, it is important to point out that this does not mean that all poor people or all teen parents or all large families will experience IPV. Rather, it is important to recognize that these couples face a greater likelihood of violence, and we need to design prevention programs that target "at-risk" couples.

Structural Risk Factors for IPV

In addition to risk factors associated with either individuals or couples, there are also structural factors that increase the likelihood of IPV occurring in a population. As Sanday (1981) noted in her examination of gender-based violence (sexual assault, rape, battering, and sexual harassment) cross-culturally, those cultures that are characterized by high levels of hierarchy and stratification—where people are ranked by their status, especially sex, age, and social class—that prohibit women's leadership and that have a double sexual standard for men and women, especially the presence of polygyny or the ability to take several wives, all forms of gender-based violence are higher. In cultures that are relatively egalitarian—be they postindustrial cultures like Sweden or Norway or subsistence cultures like the !Kung of Botswana—rates of gender-based violence are significantly lower.

The United States is a culture based on significant stratification—dividing people by race, gender, religion, social class, age, and so forth—and a high degree of hierarchy among these competing groups, and thus people living in the United States are at higher risk for living with IPV than individuals in many other cultures. In contrast, however, women in the United States are at significantly lower risk for experiencing violence than women in parts of Africa and the Middle East (Kristoff and WuDunn 2009).

Within the United States, since that is the main focus of this discussion, the primary structural factor that impacts the risk for or rate of IPV is the economy. **Economic systems** that engender equality tend to exist in cultures that are otherwise egalitarian (e.g., Sweden), and economic systems that perpetuate inequality tend to exist in cultures that are otherwise stratified, like the United States. In addition to the overall impact of the economic system operating in a culture, which is relatively fixed across time, the state of the economy itself, whatever its form, also influences the rate of IPV present in a culture. In particular, not only are rates of IPV expected to be higher in a capitalist economy than a socialist one, but rates of IPV are also expected to be higher during periods of economic downturn and recession than during periods of relative prosperity. Because the nature of economic systems and the state of the actual economy both influence rates of IPV in a given culture, we devote the remainder of this chapter to a discussion of the relationship between the economy and IPV.

STRUCTURAL FACTORS THAT SHAPE IPV

One of the distinguishing features of sociology as a discipline is the focus on the structural and institutional aspects of society as opposed to the individual within society.

> **Social structure** refers to the way social positions, social roles, and networks of social relationships are arranged in our institutions, such as the economy, polity, education, and organization of the family. A social structure could be a labor market that offers financial incentives and threatens financial punishments to compel individuals to work, or it could be a "role," associated with a particular social position in an organization, such as a church, family, or university (e.g., pastor, head of a household, or professor), that carries certain power, privilege, and influence external to the individuals who occupy that role (Wilson 2009, 4).

Though as noted above there are individual factors and "couple" factors that shape one's risk for IPV, these lists of factors are simply useful in identifying patterns in IPV; it is not a random event. However, unlike in other disciplines such as psychology, sociologists adhere to a core principle that patterns cannot be used to assess an actual person's risk for experiencing an event; this principle is called the ecological fallacy.

> **Ecological fallacy:** Ecological fallacy refers to the fact that aggregate-level data cannot be used to predict individual-level risk for an event or experience. For example, as noted in Chapter 7, boys who witness violence in the households in which they grew up are at three times the risk for becoming batterers in adulthood than their counterparts who did not experience witnessing violence in their childhood homes (Ehrensaft and Cohen 2003). That said, if we had one hundred young men enrolled in a course on marriage, and half of them had witnessed violence in the homes in which they grew up, we could not predict with any degree of certainty *which*, if any, of these men would grow up to be batterers, only that three times more of the fifty who had witnessed abuse would abuse their own partners compared to the rate among the fifty who had not; incidentally, some of the fifty boys who had *not* witnessed abuse growing up would also grow up to be abusive partners.

Our argument, then, pertaining to the behavior of batterers is based on the distinction between what any one individual might do or say and how his or her actions are shaped by his or her circumstances. It is, of course, the classic problem that sociologists pose when trying to make sense of unclear or irrational human actions: the tension between individual agency and structural constraints (Connidis and McMullin 2002; Lin 2000).

THE ECONOMY AND IPV

The economy and intimate partner violence are interconnected in many different ways, at both the macro and the micro levels.

> **Macro and micro:** Sociologists distinguish between, on the one hand, individual experiences ("**micro level**") and structural or institutional experiences ("**macro level**"). Being poor is a micro-level factor related to IPV. Living during the recession that began in 2007 is a macro-level factor related to IPV.

The Micro Level: Social Class and Money

At the micro or individual level, finances and money are strongly linked to IPV. A common belief about couples is that they fight about two things: money and children. There is no doubt that money is an important part of family life. Generally, couples argue about how to obtain money, how to spend money, how to manage money, who should be earning the money, and by what means it should be earned. As we will discuss at length in Chapter 9, dominant beliefs about masculinity prescribe that "real" men must be successful breadwinners, and all the men we interviewed and the analysis from others indicate that money was something they argued about often and specifically. For white men, their female partners' critique of them as breadwinners was a significant trigger for IPV (Dunleavey 2009).

Control of the family economic resources is important for many different reasons. But in families that involve abuse and violence, the degree to which women have access to these resources is critical to their ability to exit or escape these relationships (Hattery 2008). In addition, access to financial resources is directly linked to the mode of leaving; poor women are forced to seek assistance at shelters, whereas more affluent women may take a hotel room or even rent a separate apartment. However, access to financial resources is by no means a guarantee of exit, as many affluent battered women do not leave their abusive partners for the same reasons middle-class or poor women do not: because they love their partners and because they believe they will change.

Affluence is a complex part of the IPV puzzle because battered women in affluent households often have the resources to leave, but frequently they also have a great deal to lose. There are many examples of this in the world of sport, business, entertainment, and politics (Hattery 2008, 20). These stories are difficult to unearth. From Anna Quinlen, former op-ed writer for the *New York Times*, to Farrah Fawcett, the actress and sex symbol, women in the upper classes have been the victims of IPV, but their stories are rarely heard outside a tight-knit "community" of close friends and therapists. Why? They, like all battered women, are mostly afraid and ashamed to go public with their pain (Weitzman 2001). For example, Susan Weitzman's unique study of upper-class women who are battered is possible only because of a particular niche that she occupies: that of therapist. As part of her practice, upper-class women who are having "trouble" in their marriages come to her for therapy, and during the course of this therapy, stories of violence tumble out.

BOX 8.1   WARREN AND FELICIA MOON

Personal Foul
Arrested for Attacking His Wife, Pro Football Star
Warren Moon Vows There Will Be No More Violence
By Patrick Rogers

As in so many cases of family violence, the reasons remain hidden. But when 7-year-old Jeffrey Moon called 911 in Missouri City, Texas, on July 18, one thing was terribly clear: his father, Warren Moon, 38, widely regarded as one of pro football's most wholesome role models, and his mother, Felicia, 38, an advocate for battered women, were having a furious confrontation. Felicia later told police Moon had struck her in the head with his open hand, choked her, then pursued her in his car as she fled in another automobile.

After refusing to talk to police for three days, Moon solemnly apologized to his wife of 14 years during a July 21 press conference. . . . Later, in an interview with *People*, he was less circumspect. "Yes, this was a case of domestic violence," he says. "[It] did not happen because I hate my wife or I decided to come home and beat my wife one day. It was about things happening inside myself."

As vexing as the charges of womanizing may have been, Moon says they weren't the cause of his problems at home. "My wife understands that I am out a lot . . . and I have female friends," he says. "Other women have never been a problem to her, because she knows where I sleep every night."

Instead, Moon blames his high-profile career, which he describes as a source of constant pressure. His off-the-field work—as vice president of a Texas real estate firm, as a

continues

BOX 8.1   WARREN AND FELICIA MOON *continued*

pitchman for companies like Northwest Airlines and Burger King and as a correspondent for the TNT cable network—left little time, he says, for his wife and their children, Joshua, 14, Chelsea, 12, Blair, 10, and Jeffrey. "It really kind of overloaded me as far as my schedule. [But] it wasn't like I was out having a good time. I was working and making money."

For now, Felicia Moon seems to have accepted her husband's apologies. "Warren and I have been having marital problems lately, but none as serious as that which occurred on [July 18]," she said at the press conference. "Since then my top priority has become to seek professional support."

Source: http://www.people.com/people/archive/article/0,,20101266,00.html.

Charges were never officially filed in the Moon case because Mrs. Moon refused to press charges. Why would a self-proclaimed advocate of battered woman and a victim herself refuse to press charges? We would argue that because in the balance, Mrs. Moon, like many wives of powerful, influential, affluent men, had a lot to lose, mainly money and thus her standard of living. Though Mrs. Moon most likely had the assets to exit, she chose not to. It is important to point out that this is true in most, if not all, battering relationships. There are always push-and-pull factors that make staying or exiting complex decisions. Furthermore, at the time of the writing of this book, the news is filled with accounts of women who stay with powerful men despite their infidelities (Maria Kennedy Shriver and Arnold Schwarzenegger) and even charges of rape (the chief of the International Monetary Fund, Dominique Strauss-Kahn, and Anne Sinclair). In both of these cases, the women had their own vast wealth, but they chose, at least temporarily, to stand by and stay with their husbands.

Though social class may have only a limited effect on *whether* battered women leave, it most certainly affects the *ways* in which they do. Affluent women rarely wind up in shelters, for example, because they frequently have access to resources that will facilitate temporary housing arrangements. That is, they can afford to stay in a hotel, rent an apartment, or even live with family or friends who are also more likely to have the resources necessary to accommodate a long-term guest. In contrast, most of the poor women we interviewed were from poor families who were not in a financial position to help them. If they were to move in with family, as some of them did, this often resulted in two or three whole families living in two- or three-bedroom apartments.

SOCIAL CLASS

Social class: When the average person thinks of the term *social class*, they are generally thinking about how much money somebody makes. Sociologists generally define social class as a combination of three variables:

1. income
2. education
3. occupation

In general, though not always, individuals who are members of the "upper" class make a lot of money (income); they have attained a high level of education, perhaps a professional degree (medical degree or law degree); and they work in prestigious occupations such as medicine or law or as college professors or investment bankers. In contrast, people who are of a lower class typically earn low wages, have less education—perhaps they have graduated from high school or maybe not—and they work in less prestigious occupations, as construction workers or secretaries or even in service jobs such as in fast food or retail at the local mall. Sociologists also recognize something we refer to as "**status inconsistency**." Status inconsistency refers to the fact that sometimes one or more of the variables that make up "social class" are inconsistent with the others. For example, teachers have a high level of education, they work in a relatively prestigious occupation, but they make relatively low salaries. For example, the average high school teacher, even with a master's degree, will likely make less than fifty thousand dollars per year. Even college professors with a PhD will typically earn less than one hundred thousand dollars per year. In contrast, professional athletes, who often have only a high school degree, earn tens of millions of dollars per year.

Fact: the median household income for the United States is approximately fifty thousand dollars annually. This means that half of all American households earn *less than* fifty thousand dollars per year, and half earn more. Thus, the typical high school teacher is earning only what the average American household earns, despite his or her educational achievements and commitment to the important task of teaching.

Though class privilege can provide alternatives to staying in an abusive relationship or fleeing to a shelter, affluence does not protect women from experiencing IPV. When we analyzed data from the National Violence Against Women Survey (Tjaden and Thoennes 2000) specifically to examine the relationship between types of violence experienced and social class, we found that rates of violence remained high among middle-class, upper-middle-class, and affluent women. The data in Table 8.1 are limited to middle- and upper-income households, those who are affluent. In the analysis, the rates of violence reported by middle-class and upper-class women were compared to the rates reported by working-class and poor women. In the VAWA data, upper-class women were those designated as living in households earning at least eighty thousand dollars per year, or approximately 1.5 times the median household income. On only a few types of violence (as denoted by the asterisks) were rates of violence *less common* among affluent than working-class and poor women. Thus, it is safe to say that affluence is *not* a buffer from IPV.

Table 8.1. Intimate Partner Violence and Social Class: Percentage of Affluent Women Reporting Physical Violence

| | HOUSEHOLD INCOME | |
Types of Physical Violence	Upper-middle 50–80 K	Upper >80K
Partner throw something at woman that could hurt her*	9.4%	7.2%
Partner pulls woman's hair*	9.1%	8.3%
Partner slaps woman	20.2%	18.8%
Partner kicks or bites woman	6.0%	4.3%
Partner chokes or drowns woman*	5.4%	4.9%
Partner hits woman with an object	6.8%	5.4%
Partner beats woman up*	8.7%	8.6%
Partner threatens woman with a gun*	5.1%	2.9%
Partner threatens woman with a knife	3.4%	4.3%
Partner uses a gun on woman	2.0%	1.8%
Partner uses a knife on woman	1.7%	2.4%

* indicate physical violence that is significantly LOWER among affluent women than middle class and poor women. All other forms of physical violence are *not* significantly different by household income (social class).

Significance based on Chi-Square analysis with p-values <.10

Analysis were performed using the data collected as part of the Violence and Threats of Violence Against Women survey, a national probability sample of men and women. Descriptions and data can be found at: http://www.icpsr.umich.edu/cgi-bin/SDA

We turn now to an exploration of the complex relationship between IPV and economics. This relationship can be best described as a "chicken and egg" relationship. In some cases, the batterer prevents the woman from working or gaining access to economic resources as a way of keeping her in the relationship, and in other cases the battering results in lost wages and even the loss of a job: women are fired for missing work due to injury, and women are fired because their batterers show up at work and harass them. In violent couples, preventing women from working is a tool of control; they are rendered completely economically dependent upon their male partners, and they have few if any options for leaving. Stalking women at work is another form of control utilized by batterers; an intended consequence of stalking is to control women's behavior, and an unintended consequence of stalking at work is that it can lead to the victim being fired and thus rendering her economically dependent upon her male partner. Additionally, both control strategies increase the difficulty for women to leave abusive relationships; they not only lack the financial resources, but also lack the ability to make the types of friendships and connections that can also create the kind of help needed to facilitate leaving an abusive relationship. In the following section, we explore the strategies utilized by batterers and the outcomes of these behaviors.

"You Can't Work": A Tool of Control

Because IPV has its roots in anger and control, as noted in our discussion of intimate terrorism, many batterers seek to control every movement of their partners. Often this includes a prohibition on labor-force participation (Atkinson, Greenstein, and Lang 2005). Among the women we interviewed, this was slightly more common in white households, but it was prevalent in African American households as well.

In some violent families, female employment is threatening to a batterer for several practical reasons: it provides income that would allow a battered woman to successfully leave by breaking the economic dependency the batterer can extort from his partner, it is often the source of friends in whom the victim could potentially confide about the violence, and it often provides interactions with men of whom the batterer is extremely jealous (this will be explored in more depth in Chapter 12). Thus, many battered women find that they are prohibited from working outside the home (Browne 1989). The story of Josie, a woman we interviewed, illustrates this concept.

Josie's Story

Now in her early fifties, Josie had worked as a nurse her entire adult life. Josie liked the independence that being employed offered. She also enjoyed the friendships she made at work. But John, her boyfriend, was extremely jealous of these friendships, especially the working relationships she had with men. Many times he showed up unexpectedly at the nurses' station at the hospital where Josie worked. One day, after showing up at her station to find that she was out to lunch with a group of her coworkers, including an older man who she acknowledged was no sort of romantic threat ("Not even Viagra would help him!"), John beat her for the first time. Following this, John forced her to quit her job. He justified this request by saying that he had always wanted to take care of Josie and that he did not want her to have to work so hard.

The rage John expressed at Josie's imagined infidelity was completely consistent with other stories we heard. One young woman, Amy, told us that her partner regarded everyone she worked with as an erotic threat:

He told me—he gave me a certain day I had to quit my job because he didn't trust me with anybody I worked with. Any guy whatsoever, if I talked to them, I was screwing them. It didn't matter. He accused me of stuff all the time.

Amy, twentysomething white woman, North Carolina

John's attempt to prohibit Josie from working, which was typical of many of the men and women we interviewed, was not really about wanting to "take care of her"; in fact, it was one of the many ways in which he was attempting to control Josie's life. After she disclosed the first beating to a friend at work, this friend, whose husband was a police officer, encouraged Josie to search their house.

Josie's search revealed significant evidence that John was in fact monitoring all of her phone calls and comings and goings. Josie received her second and final beating the night that John found job applications she was sending out in the mailbox. Desiring to return to work for both the self-fulfillment and the economic reward, Josie had prepared and mailed several job applications. When John found these, he beat her severely, and when she left John she never returned. Ironically, Josie had prepared the job applications with the intention of finding a new place for both herself and John, including a move to a new community. His temporary job was about to end, and she was planning for their future together, not attempting to desert him, though that was his perception.

Josie's story illustrates many of the threats batterers feel from their female partners' employment, but it also highlights the power that resources, access, and opportunity create for women who are ready to leave. And it was precisely these "resources" at work that allowed Josie to leave. Josie had made friends at work on whom she could rely for help. After the second and final beating, Josie's friend took her to the emergency room and helped her to arrange for her escape, even sneaking into Josie's house to retrieve the cash Josie had in her pocketbook—saved from her latest paycheck—in order to purchase a bus ticket and flee the state.

Coworkers provide other forms of support for battered women as well. Though the following case is unusual in its *outcome*, in terms of the experience it is actually quite common. Many battered women we interviewed or read about recalled having to go to work the day after a beating, when bruises were still blooming and lacerations still covered with bandages. They knew that their coworkers noticed, and sometimes they reported that their coworkers expressed concern. What makes the story presented below unusual is the role that a coworker played in the successful prosecution of the batterer.

Because employment represents women's freedom from economic dependency on men and is thus threatening to a batterer, he will frequently restrict her employment opportunities (Browne 1989). Many women we interviewed reported that

BATTERED WOMAN SAVED BY COWORKER

Diane Sawyer interviewed a battered woman whose coworker saved her life. The coworker began noticing that her friend was showing up to work periodically with bruises or black eyes. She was afraid to say anything about what she was seeing, but began recording the events on her desk calendar. When the battered woman went to court and argued that the abuse was constant and had been occurring for years, the coworker's calendar, which was entered into evidence, was the linchpin that led to the batterer being sentenced to a decade in prison—quite a lengthy sentence for IPV. The entire *20/20* episode can be viewed at http://www.youtube.com/verify_age?next_url=http%3A//www.youtube.com/watch%3Fv%3DiJfIZ ZqOnMM.

their male partners controlled the logistics of work: where she worked, who she was allowed to befriend at work, and demanding her paycheck be turned over entirely to him. Stella notes that often the abuse that Will perpetrated on her was triggered when she would not hand over her paycheck to him.

He didn't become abusive to me until I quit [using crack]. And then, I wouldn't give him any more money. And when he was coming down [from a high], he'd get violent and I'd go to work and have choke marks on my throat. He fractured my shoulder blade once 'cause he threw me in the bathroom and I hit the towel bar. Hitting my head against the wall. His favorite one was the choking, though.

Stella, twentysomething African American woman, Minnesota

In addition to these restrictions, in a beating or repeated beatings, the batterer essentially destroys his victim's freedom by ruining her career and her physical health in one blow. Symbolically, this is consistent with a variety of the accounts we heard from the women we interviewed. Many of them changed jobs, either to accommodate their partner's wishes or to get away from their abuser. Most of the women also reported having to call in sick on the days following a beating. Josie recalled that after the first beating, her jaw was so swollen that she called in sick and missed a couple of days of work. In some cases, the women were just too physically injured to work. More frequently, however, they were too embarrassed to show up at work with bruises and cuts that they had sustained at the hands of a man who claimed to love them.

Many battered women are beaten so frequently that they cannot afford to miss work every time they are beaten. Several with whom we talked shared their secret techniques for covering up the cuts and bruises, techniques that allowed them to go to work following a beating. In fact, on the day we interviewed Candy she was bruised and battered from a beating a few days before and showed us, almost with pride, how skillfully she had masked the bruises with makeup. Over a long period of time, however, the loss of wages and the potential loss of one's job due to truancy leave many battered women, even those who remain employed, economically dependent on their male partners.

"He Showed Up at Work Brandishing a Gun": Fired Because of IPV

Though injuries account for most absences from work, the action of men showing up unexpectedly at work, as Josie's partner, John, did, is also a problem. Browne (1989) argues that this type of intrusion is yet another form of control and emotional abuse in which batterers engage. This type of intrusion allows batterers to monitor the actions and interactions of their partners, and because it is random and unannounced, it allows them to create a situation in which battered women are in a constant state of alert or fear, never knowing when or where their abusive partners might show up unexpectedly. The random nature of this activity makes it a successful strategy for batterers to indirectly control their partners, who must be always on their "best behavior" so as to avoid being "caught" doing something "wrong"—defined as anything the batterer disapproves of—and then being beaten for it later. Josie describes a day when John showed up unexpectedly at her nurses' station during one of her evening shifts:

I asked him what he was thinking. That was my job. I told him that if he went in there and showed his ass, people were going to think that I get off work and this is what I go home to and this is the way she probably really is. And I told him that I'm a professional at my job. I'm still funny and I'm still mouthy, but I'm professional. I do my job and I do it damn well. And I told him he couldn't go up there and show his behind. I told him I wouldn't put up with it. He would say, "I'm sorry, baby, I'm so sorry." Then three weeks later, everything started coming to a head.

Josie, fiftysomething white woman, North Carolina

Gus, an African American man who was arrested for beating his wife, told of the day he was arrested. Gus believed that his wife was having an affair. They had an argument, and she admitted that she was in love with another man. In addition, she told Gus that she wanted a divorce and that she was moving in with her new boyfriend, which she did soon after. Gus could not believe the relationship was over, he could not believe that she had cheated on him, and he continued to believe that he was the best person for her. He wanted her back. Unable to convince her with words, he showed up at her office—she was a receptionist in a local pediatrician's office—with a gun and insisted that she leave with him. She was unwilling, so he kidnapped her at gunpoint and drove her across state lines to her mother's house, hoping that her mother would talk some "sense" into his estranged wife.

This showing up at working unexpectedly, in and of itself, can be understood as emotional abuse. In addition, it is embarrassing when one's angry and loud partner shows up at your job demanding to know where you are, as this behavior is disruptive to the workplace. Brush (2011) refers to this as "domestic violence spilling over into work."

Even if the partner is not angry or armed, such erratic behavior is highly unprofessional. Even if you are not a battered woman, try to imagine for yourself your own partner showing up unexpectedly at your job, demanding to know what you are doing and who you are talking to. It would be absurd, just as it is for battered women.

This behavior often leaves a battered woman even more vulnerable to her batterer, for without a job—Gus's wife *was fired* after he showed up at her office and kidnapped her at gunpoint!—and an independent income, she is that much more economically dependent upon an already controlling and abusive man. We turn now to a discussion of macro-level economic factors that shape IPV.

The Macro Level: Economic Systems and the Economy

In this section we will explore the structural aspects of the economy that contribute to intimate partner violence. Specifically, we will examine the ways in which capitalism creates a labor market based on wage discrimination, which produces economic dependency at the individual level and **compulsory partnering** at the societal level. We will conclude this discussion by discussing the recent changes in the economy and how we can expect these to shape the prevalence of IPV.

Wage Discrimination and Economic Dependency

One of the central features of the **labor market** in the United States is stratification by race and gender. This stratification arose from a variety of forces and has several important outcomes, which we will briefly review.

From the initial settlement by Europeans of what would become the United States up through the middle of the nineteenth century, the United States was primarily an agricultural economy. There were two key defining features of this agricultural economy: small family farms and the plantation economy of the Southeast. Both played a role in shaping the segregated labor market that emerged during the Industrial Revolution. On the small family farm, women were an important part of agricultural production. That said, they were often relegated to certain tasks, and among the most important was the care of the house—cooking and cleaning—and the children. On the plantation, people of African descent were held as chattel slaves, and it was on their backs that the huge plantations were not only run but turned huge profits for the planters. With the dawn of the Industrial Revolution in the middle of the nineteenth century, several key transformations occurred that built on existing patterns, shaping the labor market in ways that continue to persist today.

Specifically, as factories were being built and mines were being established—two of the hallmarks of industrialization—the owners of these factories and mines believed that women were entirely unsuitable for this work (they were too frail and too important to the running of the home), and African American men, though strong enough for the work, were considered too dumb and too lazy for the "new" work that was emerging. Additionally, the planters relied too heavily on their male slaves to do the work of the plantation that they would not have favored leasing out their labor force to factories or mines. Thus, from the very beginning of the Industrial Revolution, work, which had previously not been segregated by gender, became highly segregated by both race and gender; white men were the exclusive beneficiaries of this new, difficult, but highly lucrative work. It would not be until World War II that women or minorities would be able to penetrate the workplaces created by industrialization.

In response to the need for men to fight in World War II, both women and African American men were hired to work in factories and other industries as "replacement" workers. Because both groups were still viewed as inferior, as well as to protect the white men who remained or had returned from war, women and African American men (African American women were by and large denied access to these jobs and continued to work primarily as domestics [P. Collins 1994; for a novelized version we recommend Kathryn Stockett's *The Help*]) were relegated to the lowest-level jobs, and they were paid inferior wages—which was legal (Hattery 2001; Padavic and Reskin 2002). This set the stage for a labor market that continues to be segregated.

> **Occupational sex segregation:** the fact that the majority of jobs are dominated by one sex or the other; men and women do different jobs or work in entirely different industries.

Today, in the top-ten occupations that employ men—construction, plumbing and other trades, truck driving—fewer than 5 percent of the employees are female. Similarly, in the top-ten occupations that employ women—teaching, home health care, nursing, administrative assistant work—more than 98 percent of the employees are women. Similarly, many occupations, especially in certain regions of the country such as the South, are highly racially segregated as well (Padavic and Reskin 2002).

One of the most significant consequences of occupational sex segregation is wage discrimination. In fact, when every other explanation—differences in education, differences in the number of hours worked, differences in taking time out to raise children, and so forth—is controlled for, the strongest predictor of wages is occupational sex segregation (Padavic and Reskin 2002). Essentially, men work in occupations that pay more than women. As noted above, the majority of American men work in industries with relatively high wages, including occupations that are far more likely to be unionized—such as construction or plumbing or electrical work—which produce higher wages and benefits. In contrast, the majority of women work in occupations that are among the lowest paid, including as teachers, day-care providers, home health workers, and administrative assistants. Thus, by virtue of working in different industries, women and African Americans suffer from severe **wage discrimination**. In 2011 women still earned, on average, only 77 percent of what their male counterparts earned. And, unfortunately, when controlling for men and women doing the same job, men still outearn women by 20 percent.

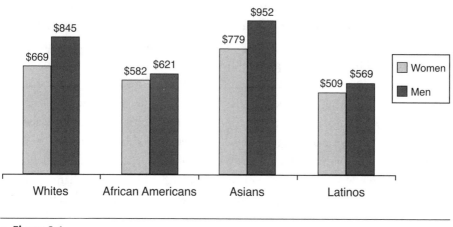

▲ **Figure 8.1**
Women's and Men's Median Weekly Earnings, by Sex and Race/Ethnicity

Source: http://www.catalyst.org/publication/217/womens-earnings-and-income

One of the clearest and most problematic outcomes of wage discrimination is that because women earn less than men, they are often *economically dependent* upon them (Browne 1989; Engels with an introduction by Leacock 1884; Hattery 2001, 2008; Rich 1980). Economic dependency leaves women vulnerable to IPV for two key reasons: they may feel that they have to put up with the abuse in order to continue having access to the resources the batterer provides—recall the text box of an affluent woman, Felicia Moon, who made the decision to stay despite the abuse in her marriage—and their economic dependency makes it very difficult for them to amass the economic resources that are critical to leaving abusive relationships. This situation increases a woman's dependency on her male partner because she may feel she has no other choice but to return home to her abuser because she has no other way to keep a roof over her head and food in the refrigerator.

Anyone who has talked with or interviewed women in a battered women's shelter knows that in many cases, they flee with only the clothes on their backs and any possessions they can fit in a duffel bag. Many women who flee violence find themselves homeless, living in a shelter, faced with the challenge of setting up a new life, finding a job in a new city or state, saving up the money for a rent deposit, and all within sixty to ninety days of arriving at the shelter, depending on the policies of that particular shelter. We turn now to a discussion of the way in which wage discrimination and the accompanying economic dependency heighten the incentive for women to stay with abusive men or seek out new relationships in order to meet their economic needs.

Wage Discrimination and Compulsory Partnering

For one hundred or more years, feminists have been debating the costs and benefits of marriage for women. Among the first marriage "resistors" was Charlotte Perkins Gilman. She argued that marriage required that women give up their identity and their power and become nothing more than cooks and maids for their husbands.

A hundred years later, Adrienne Rich (1980) argued that beliefs about femininity—women are "designed" to marry and raise children—and wage discrimination *required* women to seek partnerships with men. Think for a minute about a thirty-five- or forty-year-old single man who, depending on his social status, may be defined as an "eligible bachelor." Yet a woman of similar status is an "old maid." Conventional wisdom holds that a woman is better off with *any* man than *no man at all*. Second, Rich (1980) argues, because of the severe wage discrimination women face in the labor market, it is virtually impossible for them to achieve middle-class status, or better, unless they have the benefit of a man's wages (for an update, see Richardson 1996). Thus, marriage—or long-term partnering—is a virtual economic necessity except for the small percentage of women who either inherit wealth or achieve in the well-paying professions.

Often at the end of an interview with a woman who had spent an hour or two or more telling of her experiences with IPV, frequently at the hands of more than one man, we would ask her, "So, what's next? Are you going back to him? Have you had enough of men for a while?" So often the answer she gave was that she was going back or already had or had moved on to yet another male partner.

Economic dependency can trap women with abusive men, but it can also be a strong pull into relationships. Many of the women we interviewed indicated that the thing that initially attracted them to their boyfriend or husband was his ability to "pay the rent" or feed her children. Connie recounted meeting a boyfriend, who would later abuse her, this way: She was out in the front yard with several children, some of them hers. It was her birthday. This man drove by and told her she was pretty. He asked if he could get her anything, and she smiled and said lunch for the children. He returned a few minutes later with *two buckets* of Kentucky fried chicken, enough to feed all the children. That night they went out on a date, and within weeks they were living together.

When we asked battered women what qualities they hoped or planned to look for in the next man in their lives, the most common response was: that he be employed. Clearly, they recognize their own need for the economic support of a male partner.

Many of the women we interviewed talked of moving out of the shelter (in North Carolina) and into an apartment with men they had met at the mall only a few days or weeks before. Andi's story is typical and differs from others we heard only in that it involves moving several hundred miles (as opposed to down the street or to the next town):

Yeah, I got my older son, I got all my stuff, and we went to Chicago. Um, with me working for the moving company, I knew this guy who drove a truck, and so he was up there and he had to go back to Chicago, so he took us to Chicago. I stayed in a hotel for about a week and then went to a shelter. I stayed in the shelter, but, mind you, I'm a hot girl, so, I don't know, but I stayed in the shelter for, like, three days and then met this guy. One day when I was outside of the shelter. And I do not know what was going through my mind, but I liked him; he was like, "Why don't you come to Minnesota with me?" So I came to Minnesota. I'd been in Chicago for a week and a half. [AH: And how quickly did you move to Minnesota?] The next day after I met him. It was like no, I didn't it was like one of those stupid you're-risking-your-life moves, but I was like, "Hey, what do I have to lose right now? I have absolutely nothing."

Andi, twentysomething African American woman, Minnesota

Andi took a big risk by moving away from her family and friends with a man she barely knew. And, unfortunately for Andi, that risk was realized not long after she moved with "this guy" to Minnesota. Isolated from family and friends, living with his family because they could not afford a place of their own, Andi was in a situation of extreme dependence. She depended on "this guy" for the roof over her head and the food in the refrigerator, and consistent with Engels's notion of economic exchange (Engels and Leacock 1972), "this guy" demanded that Andi have sex with him, that she be faithful to him, and that he follow her rules. When she did not, he beat her up.

One night he flipped out because he found out I had smoked a blunt and that I had been around some guys. Well, first he had just grabbed me, and like, slammed me into the wall, and me, I'm not gonna just stand there so, like, I try to shove him off me. And I grabbed his shirt up, like, roped it up like that, and then I kept telling him "get off me," and stuff and, no, he steady slinging me around and stuff, and he ended up hitting my face against the wall.

Andi, twentysomething African American woman, Minnesota

This form of economic dependency is brutal and sometimes lethal for women, and especially African American women, because they have less education and lower wages, and hence are particularly vulnerable to this type of economic dependency. What this type of dependency really means is the selling or trading of one's sexuality in exchange for having one's basic needs met. It is *a trade-off no one should ever have to make.*

RACE AND CLASS ANALYSIS

Women's economic dependence on men, which leads to the demand for compulsory heterosexuality, does vary by one's membership in various social categories. Women with little education, few job skills, and few resources in their extended families, and poor women of all racial and ethnic groups, are more likely to remain with men or move in with them soon into the relationship than are middle-class women. Because African American women are more likely to have less education, fewer labor market skills, and fewer resources like bank accounts or family members with extra resources that could be borrowed than their white counterparts, they are more vulnerable to IPV than are white women (Hattery 2008; Tjaden and Thoennes 2000).

In contrast, because white women have lower overall rates of being employed—25 percent are stay-at-home mothers—they experience a different vulnerability to IPV. Young white women—who have high rates of employment—may be less likely to seek out a man for economic support initially, but once they are involved in the relationship and have begun childbearing, they are more likely to be out of the labor force as stay-at-home mothers, and thus may be forced to stay with an abusive partner longer. In contrast, African American women, who are more likely to be employed, but earning low wages, may seek male partners in order to meet their basic financial needs. But because African American women have always had and continue to have overall higher rates of employment (P. Collins 1994)—despite the fact that these jobs are most likely to be low wage—by virtue of being employed, African American women have more access to opportunities such as contacts, friends who will intervene or help, and even their own wages, all of which are necessary to leave abusive relationships. Thus, African American women may be more likely to *leave* abusive relationships, but they will frequently bounce from one abusive relationship quickly into another—as Andi did—for economic reasons. In other words, just as threats to the breadwinner role exist for all men even while being shaped by race and class, economic vulnerability and the need for compulsory partnering are experienced by all women, though the form this vulnerability and the response to this compulsion they take are highly shaped by race and social class. We conclude the chapter with a brief discussion of the recent recession.

THE RECESSION

Scholarly research often takes many years to move from data collection to publication—where it can be accessed by others. Thus, there is very little research yet available that examines the role of the recession that began in late 2007 on changes and trends in IPV. That said, other measures of changes in the trend—such as calls to domestic violence hotlines and data on the number of women and their children utilizing shelters, which are reported by local and state domestic violence service providers—give us some idea about the role that the recent recession is playing in domestic violence. Based on our discussion throughout this chapter, we would expect that rates of domestic violence would be increasing as a result of unemployment, higher rates of poverty, and declining earnings even among middle-class Americans. All of these factors are risk factors for IPV as well as situations that lead to high conflict in relationships. For example, one of the most common fights that we heard about in our interviews involved men losing their jobs. For a woman whose husband or partner has lost his job, she is likely to be concerned in a practical way about the money that will no longer be coming into the household, and she may also question her husband's or partner's manhood or masculinity, which is often perceived as a threat to him. Finally, the recession has added additional stresses to families who may be worried about other things as well, such as losing a job, financing a college education, or having to open their home up to relatives who are even worse off than they are. Thus, at both the micro and the macro levels, we can anticipate that the recession will have contributed to a climate in which IPV is even more common. A report from MSNBC provides data that illustrate this point:

> Some hospitals report seeing more than twice as many shaken babies as a year ago. Deaths from domestic violence have increased sharply in some areas.
>
> Calls to domestic-violence hotlines have risen too, and more than half the callers said their families' financial situation has changed recently.
>
> Across the country, these and other signs point to another troubling effect of the recession: The American home is becoming more violent, and the ailing economy could be at least partially to blame. (2009)

Based on our discussion in this chapter, we can anticipate that over the next few years, as data are collected by scholars but also by agencies, we will see that the recession that began in 2007 has contributed significantly to a rise in intimate partner violence and other forms of family violence as well.

CONCLUSIONS

The stories presented in this chapter suggest that at both the micro and the macro levels, the economy is a major structural force that shapes IPV. At the structural level, battering reinforces men's advantage in the labor market. Batterers restrict or prohibit women's labor-force participation. Battered women often struggle to advance or even remain employed because in many cases they must miss work due to the physical, psychological, and emotional injuries they experience at the hands of their male partners. Another way of seeing this is that battering reduces the threat of female competition in the labor force. In this way, all men, even those who do not batter, benefit from the ways in which battering eliminates women as competitors in a tight labor market.

The effects of IPV on individual women are well documented (Browne 1989; Dobash and Dobash 1979; Hattery 2008; Walker 1979). Although some research has focused on men who batter, most of the attention has been directed toward predicting which men will batter and which intervention programs are most successful at treating those who do. There have been even fewer attempts at examining the ways in which IPV operates at both the individual and the structural levels to produce a model for family and the workplace that rewards male privilege (even for men who do not batter) and limits women's access to the opportunity structure (even for women who are never battered).

This chapter moves us beyond individual explanations for IPV and analyzes these data with attention to the role that social structures, specifically the economy, play in shaping IPV as it occurs in the United States. As a result, a clearer picture of both the individual and the structural causes and effects of IPV emerges herein. These findings suggest that to reduce or eliminate IPV in the United States will mean more than simply teaching individual men not to hit or instructing individual women on how to escape. Rather, the economy of the United States must be transformed such that wage discrimination disappears and women—either in relationships or single—are no longer economically dependent on men. Reducing economic dependency will reduce women's vulnerability for violence. We acknowledge that this is a hefty recommendation, and we will devote far more time to discussing it in Chapter 14.

In the next chapter we will examine the cultural supports for IPV, namely, the ways in which constructions of masculinity and femininity create rigid gender roles that almost inevitably lead to IPV.

RECOMMENDED FILMS

Sleeping with the Enemy (1991), starring Julia Roberts, details the experiences and flight of an affluent woman

RESOURCES

Centers for Disease Control and Prevention, "Costs of Intimate Partner Violence Against Women in the United States," April 2003: http://www.dvrc-or.org/domestic /violence/resources/C61/

BIBLIOGRAPHY

Atkinson, Maxine P., Theodore N. Greenstein, and Molly Monahan Lang. 2005. "For Women, Breadwinning Can Be Dangerous: Gendered Resource Theory and Wife Abuse." *Journal of Marriage and Family* 67: 1137–1148.

Browne, Angela. 1989. *When Battered Women Kill*. New York: Free Press.

Brush, Lisa. 2011. *Poverty, Battered Women, and Work in US Public Policy*. New York: Oxford University Press.

Card, David, and George B. Dahl. 2011. "Family Violence and Football: The Effect of Unexpected Emotional Cues on Violent Behavior." *Quarterly Journal of Economics*.

Catalano, Shannan, Erica Smith, Howard Snyder, and Michael Rand. 2009. *Female Victims of Violence*. Washington, DC: US Department of Justice.

Collins, Patricia Hill. 1994. "Shifting the Center: Race, Class, and Feminist Theorizing About Motherhood." In *Mothering: Ideology, Experience, and Agency*, edited by E. Glenn, G. Chang, and L. Forcey, 45–66. New York: Routledge.

Collins, Randall. 1992. *Love and Property from Sociological Insight: An Introduction to Non-obvious Sociology*. London: Oxford University Press.

Connidis, Ingrid, and Julie McMullin. 2002. "Social Ambivalence and Family Ties." *Journal of Marriage and Family* 64: 558–567.

Dobash, R. E., and R. Dobash. 1979. *Violence Against Wives: A Case Against Patriarchy*. New York: Free Press.

Dunleavey, M. P. 2009. "The 12 Biggest Reasons Couples Fight over Finances." December 4. http://articles.moneycentral.msn.com/CollegeAndFamily/LoveAnd Money/The12BiggestReasonsWeFightOverFinances.aspx.

Ehrensaft, Miriam, and Patricia Cohen. 2003. "Intergenerational Transmission of Partner Violence: A 20-Year Prospective Study." *Journal of Consulting and Clinical Psychology* 7: 741–753.

Engels, Friedrich. 1884. *The Origin of the Family, Private Property, and the State*. Introduction by Eleanor Leacock. New York: International Publishers.

Engels, Friedrich, and Eleanor Leacock. 1972. *The Origin of the Family, Private Property, and the State*. New York: International Publishers.

Hattery, Angela. 2001. *Women, Work, and Family: Balancing and Weaving*. Thousand Oaks, CA: Sage.

_____. 2008. *Intimate Partner Violence.* Lanham, MD: Rowman and Littlefield.

Kristoff, Nicholas, and Sheryl WuDunn. 2009. *Half the Sky: Turning Oppression into Opportunity for Women Worldwide.* New York: Alfred A. Knopf.

Leone, Janel M., Michael P. Johnson, Catherine L. Cohan, and Susan E. Lloyd. 2004. "Consequences of Male Partner Violence for Low-Income Minority Women." *Journal of Marriage and Family* 66, no. 2: 472–490.

Lin, Nan. 2000. "Inequality in Social Capital." *Contemporary Sociology* 29: 785–795.

MSNBC. 2009. "Domestic Abuse on Rise as Economy Sinks: Hotline Calls Up from Last Year as Are Cases of Shaken Baby Syndrome." April 10. http://www.msnbc.msn.com/id/30156918/ns/health-health_care/#.

Padavic, Irene, and Barbara Reskin. 2002. *Women and Men at Work.* Thousand Oaks, CA: Pine Forge Press.

Rich, Adrienne. 1980. "Compulsory Heterosexuality and Lesbian Existence." *Signs* 5: 631–660.

Richardson, Diane (ed.). 1996. *Theorising Heterosexuality.* Buckingham: Open University Press.

Sanday, P. R. 1981. "The Socio-cultural Context of Rape." *Journal of Social Issues* 37: 5–27.

Tjaden, Patricia, and Nancy Thoennes. 2000. *Full Report of the Prevalence, Incidence, and Consequences of Violence Against Women: Findings from the National Violence Against Women Survey.* Washington, DC: US Department of Justice.

Walker, Lenore E. 1979. *The Battered Woman.* New York: Harper & Row.

Weitzman, Susan. 2001. *Not to People Like Us: Hidden Abuse in Upscale Marriages.* New York: Basic Books.

Wilson, William J. 2009. *More than Just Race.* New York: W. W. Norton.

Cultural Factors and Intimate Partner Violence

When I'm old and getting gray, I'll only gang-bang once a day.
—Fraternity ditty

A good wife always knows her place.
—From the 1955 *Housekeeping Monthly* guide to being a good wife

This chapter examines the ways in which beliefs about what it means to be a man (masculinity) and what it means to be a woman (femininity) create an environment ripe for intimate partner violence. In addition, this chapter will explore the ways in which there is racial and ethnic variation in beliefs about masculinity and femininity and how this variation shapes the violence that is perpetrated and experienced. This chapter will conclude with insights into the ways in which prevention and intervention programs need to address cultural differences if partner violence is to be reduced in all communities.

OBJECTIVES

- To explicate the dominant constructions of femininity that are often invisible because of their widespread acceptance and pervasiveness
- To explicate the dominant constructions of masculinity that are often invisible because of their widespread acceptance and pervasiveness
- To examine the ways in which cultural constructions of femininity can lead to the acceptance of submissive gender roles for women that often leave them vulnerable to IPV
- To examine the ways in which cultural constructions of masculinity can lead to the acceptance of male dominance in relationships that can lead to tolerance for and even expectations of expressions of male violence
- To provide a set of recommendations for transforming and expanding cultural expectations for men and women so as to broaden gender roles and reduce IPV

KEY TERMS

masculinity	breadwinning
femininity	sexual double standard
culture	sexual prowess
gender roles	marital rape exemption
Cool Pose	cult of domesticity and cult of true womanhood
patriarchy	public-private split

INTRODUCTION

In the first chapter of our book, we argued that all of the statistics indicate that above and beyond all else, IPV is a gendered crime: women are *by and large* the victims, and men are *by and large* the perpetrators. In this chapter we examine the ways in which American **culture**, and particularly definitions of **masculinity** and **femininity**, contributes to a culture of violence, especially violence against women. We begin with some definitions.

Culture ". . . refers to the sharing of outlooks and modes of behavior among individuals who face similar place-based circumstances . . . or have the same social networks. Therefore, when individuals act according to their culture, they are following inclinations developed from their exposure to the particular traditions, practices, and beliefs among those who live and interact in the same physical and social environment" (Wilson 2009, 4).

Masculinity: What it means to be a man in a given culture; the qualities that we attribute to manliness and the roles we associate with men. Chafetz identified seven areas of traditional masculinity: physical, functional, sexual, emotional, intellectual, and interpersonal (1974, 34–35).

Femininity: What it means to be a woman in a given culture; the qualities that we attribute to womanliness and the roles we associate with women. Traditional areas of femininity include verbal, relational, deferential, and submissive roles.

Gender Roles: Gender roles refer to the concept that certain behavioral patterns are associated exclusively or almost exclusively with a particular gender. For example, men are believed to be workers, breadwinners; they take out the garbage and wash the cars; at work, they are the boss. Women are believed to be suited to taking care of the home and the family, to being less interested in work, to rarely being the boss, and to being the emotional center of the family.

Femininity and masculinity and their associated gender roles can be conceptualized as mutually exclusive and binary and oppositional. In other words, they are two sides of the same coin. Any quality generally attributed to men (masculinity) will have its opposite attributed to women (femininity). That is to suggest that men are aggressive; women are passive. Men are dominant; women are submissive. Men work, and women stay at home. Men discipline children, and women nurture. Men serve in the military and play sports, and women shop and create scrapbooks.

BOX 9.1   MASCULINITY AND FEMININITY

Hofstede: Masculinity/Femininity

This dimension focuses on how, and the extent to which, a society stresses achievement or nurture. Masculinity is seen to be the trait which emphasizes ambition, acquisition of wealth, and differentiated gender roles. Feminism is seen to be the trait which stress caring and nurturing behaviors, sexuality equality, environmental awareness, and more fluid gender roles.

Hofstede's definitions:

"Masculinity stands for a society in which social gender roles are clearly distinct: Men are supposed to be assertive, tough, and focused on material success; women are supposed to be more modest, tender, and concerned with the quality of life."

"Femininity stands for a society in which social gender roles overlap: Both men and women are supposed to be modest, tender, and concerned with the quality of life."

From Hofstede (2001), *Culture's Consequences,* 2nd ed. p. 297.

Traits of Masculinity/Femininity

	High Masculine	*Low Masculine (Feminine)*
social norms	• ego oriented	• relationship oriented
	• money and things are important	• quality of life and people are important
	• live in order to work	• work in order to live
politics and economics	• economic growth high priority	• environment protection high priority
	• conflict solved through force	• conflict solved through negotiation
religion	• most important in life	• less important in life
	• only men can be priests	• both men and women as priests
work	• larger gender wage gap	• smaller gender wage gap
	• fewer women in management	• more women in management
	• preference for higher pay	• preference for fewer working hours
family and school	• traditional family structure	• flexible family structure
	• girls cry, boy don't; boys fight, girls don't	• both boys and girls cry; neither fight
	• failing is a disaster	• failing a minor accident

It is important to note that we do not necessarily endorse these constructions of masculinity and femininity, but note that they are extremely widely adhered to. It is also important to note that stereotypes do not apply to everyone; rather, they are reflective of both dominant patterns but, more important, beliefs about what men or women *should do*. We know many women who play sports and do not like to shop and many men who enjoying cooking and do not hunt. But what we also know is that when we measure who is doing what, our behaviors and preferences fall along decidedly gendered lines. In fact, when we do an exercise in our classes asking students to identify traits that are associated with men and women, a list very similar to that in the accompanying text box is generated. What is important is not that we endorse these rigid and oppositional constructions of gender roles, but that when we understand not only the social constructions of masculinity and femininity but the way in which they are pitted as binary and oppositional, we can begin to see more clearly, as we argue, that IPV is an *almost* inevitable outcome of masculinity and femininity as they are defined in the contemporary United States. We begin with a discussion of masculinity.

BOYS WILL BE BOYS: CONSTRUCTIONS OF MASCULINITY AND INTERPERSONAL VIOLENCE

What do you envision when you think of a man who beats up his woman?[1] Is he a factory worker who comes home, puts on a white "wife beater," drinks a "working-class" beer like Old Milwaukee (as opposed to sipping a pinot grigio), and socks his wife in the mouth when the meat loaf she cooked for dinner is not ready on time or, worse yet, is burned? The truth is there is no explicit description of a batterer. Men who batter are of all races and ethnicities, all ages, all levels of education, and all different occupations, and they live in all different regions of the country. We argue here that if anything distinguishes batterers from men who do not batter, it is two things, men who batter are well socialized into hypermasculinity, and battering can be best understood as a response to perceived threats to a batterer's masculinity (Franchina, Eisler, and Moore 2001). The question for us in this chapter is: to what degree do beliefs about what it means to be a man both tolerate if not require physical dominance over one's female partner and demand a violent reaction when one feels one's masculine identity is threatened?

Masculinity

What does it mean to be a man in our society? Masculinity is a set of characteristics that we often associate with men (Mansley 2007). From an early age, most children raised in the United States will ascribe qualities such as strength, power, height, and financial power to boys and men (Connell and Messerschmdt 2005; Connell 1990). What is more, not only do we associate these traits with men, but men are "essentialized" by these traits. In other words, men in general are reduced to the qualities and traits that are the core definition of masculinity: physical strength, aggression, economic power, and sexuality. Despite differences by race, ethnicity, sexual orientation, and social class, as well as individual differences— many men are monogamous, many men settle their conflicts through dialog rather than physical fights—the image by which most men judge themselves and are judged can be boiled down to a few qualities or statuses: "In an important sense there is only one complete unblushing male in America: a young, married, *white*, urban, northern, heterosexual, Protestant, father, of college education, fully employed, of good complexion, weight, and height, and a recent record in sports. . . . Any male who fails to qualify in any one of these ways is likely to view himself— during moments at least—as unworthy, incomplete, and inferior" (cited in Kimmel 2005, 5). Kimmel is arguing that despite individual and population differences, the qualities associated with being a man are relatively universal.

We ask: are these characteristics found among men of other races and ethnicities, or are there alternative constructions of masculinity for men of other racial and ethnic backgrounds? Some say yes.

African American Masculinity: The Cool Pose

For example, the most cited attempt at understanding African American male masculinity is attributable to the work of Majors and Bilson (1992, 44) who make the argument that "**Cool Pose**" is an attempt to make the African American male more visible; "Cool Pose" is a way to counteract the requirements in the list above—white, college educated—that many African American will never achieve and replace them with other qualities that describe a different type of masculinity. They go on to argue: "Cool Pose is a ritualized form of masculinity that entails behaviors, scripts physical posturing, impression management, and carefully crafted performances that deliver a single, critical message: pride, strength, and control. . . . It eases the worry and pain of blocked opportunities. Being cool is an ego booster for black males comparable to the kind white males more easily find through attending good schools, landing prestigious jobs and bringing home decent wages" (1992, 4–5).

Majors and Bilson (1992) argue further that African American men are on a disturbing roller-coaster ride through African American male pathology. It is here that one finds not only failure in school but also extreme violence and criminality, hyper drug use and abuse, and an illogical connection to parenting that preferences procreation (making babies) to parenting (raising children) (Sampson 1987). They conclude that African American men construct their masculinity behind masks, worn to survive not only their second-class status but also their environment (Majors and Bilson 1992). This does not mean, however, that African American men, or any other group, construct their masculine identities only in alternative ways, but do so in response to the dominant constructions of masculinity that are widely available in the culture.

Discourses of Masculinity

Certain well-known men in our culture would be readily identifiable as "men's men" or "manly men." Most of the exemplars, or "ideal types," as sociologist Max Weber would call them, come from the realms of sports, entertainment, politics, and occasionally big business. What do these men have in common? They are successful, affluent, "strong," good-looking, and mostly white, and according to popular discourse, they have multiple female sex partners. Regular men, masculine men, have access to images of these *quintessential* men by watching mainstream television and movies.

Think for a moment about the images that are transmitted into our homes and that influence our beliefs about masculinity. Arnold Schwarzenegger as "the Terminator," Sylvester Stallone as "Rocky," Denzel Washington the "entrepreneur" and womanizer in "American Gangster," and James Bond the assassin and womanizer (his image has been a source for the discourse on masculinity for four decades). College and professional sports provide yet another genre in which these images are generated, be it LeBron James dunking over his competitors and running down the court pumping his chest, Bret Favre playing through every conceivable injury with the hopes of carrying his team to victory, or Sidney Crosby delivering a debilitating check that leaves his opponent unconscious on the ice. All of these images transmit the belief that real men, masculine men, are powerful, strong, dominating, and rich. Consider the advertisements that run, especially during sporting events. The time is filled with ads for trucks "built Ford tough" and "home makeovers" that feature cases of Bud Light. The Marines are looking for "the few, the proud." Either central to the ads or in the background there are always beautiful women who admire the men for their strength, success, and beer-guzzling ability.

These images bombard us from the 24/7 broadcasts on CNN and ESPN as well as in the images that are created for music videos, shows, and broadcast on MTV, VH-1, and BET, just to name a few networks. The important point here is that a *specific construction of masculinity* is being transmitted to the young men (and women) who are watching. Not only are boys and men learning how to be "men," but women are learning what they should not only expect but desire in men.

The construction of masculinity that dominates in US culture is not random, but is built around the principles of **patriarchy**.

PATRIARCHY

Patriarchy is a social system in which men (and boys) have greater access to opportunities, resources, and power.

Cultural indicators of patriarchy include:

- the belief that men are smarter than women, especially in science and math. Recall former Harvard University president Larry Summers, who argued that the reason men dominated faculty positions in science and math was due to their intellectual superiority (Summers 2005). This assumption reduces the number of women competing for the top-paying, more prestigious positions in science, engineering, and math.
- the belief that women are more suited to taking care of the home and family, and thus they should focus less on their occupations. This assumption reduces the number of women competing for jobs and thus gives men greater access to those jobs.
- the belief that women should defer to their husbands on financial matters. This assumption results in men having more access to and more decision-making power when it comes to spending from the family bank account.
- the belief that men are better logical thinkers. This belief results in men having greater access to political and social power as politicians and leaders of all the major industries.

The Roots of Masculinity

Structural-functionalists such as Parsons and Bales (1955) argue that men and women have evolved both biologically and socially toward distinct spheres of specialization. Based on this perspective, men and women are believed to be *biologically* suited for different tasks. As a result, men have come to dominate the *instrumental* sphere, whereas women have been relegated to the *expressive* sphere (Hattery 2001). The instrumental role, according to Parsons and Bales (1955), refers to the activities associated with providing for the basic needs of the family. In contrast, the expressive role refers to meeting the emotional needs of family members. Parsons and Bales (1955) argue that the contemporary division of household labor can be traced back to our earliest roots as humans. For example, they suggest that a man's greater ease at being away from his children for forty-plus hours per week, and even traveling away from home as part of his job, has evolved out of the time in human history when men went on long, extended hunting trips in search of meat. These hunting excursions encouraged a more detached masculine character (Hattery 2001).

With regard to the contemporary American family, the perspective of Parsons and Bales has been used to conceptualize appropriate **gender roles** for men and for women.

For example, we argue that when masculinity (and femininity) is constructed in such a way as to generate these rigid and narrow gender roles, it contributes to a culture of violence against women. Furthermore, when we carry Parsons and Bales's argument that gender roles arise out of biological necessity to its logical conclusion,

---

GENDER ROLES

Gender roles: a set of behaviors that indicates one's gender, specifically the image projected by a person that identifies their femaleness or maleness; an overt public presentation of gender identity.

- men are supposed to be the breadwinners in their families
- men are supposed to be the decision makers in their families
- men are supposed to be the disciplinarians of their children
- women are supposed to care for the household—cooking, cleaning, and laundry
- women are supposed to be the caregivers and nurturers of their children
- women are supposed to "take care" of their husbands

IPV can be (mis)understood as a "natural" outgrowth of the biology of men and women rather than a "natural" outgrowth of a system of patriarchy. Parsons and Bales's belief that gender roles are based in biology is the underpinning for beliefs among biological as well as social scientists in genetic sex differences. This general belief that men and women are *biologically different* and thus suited to different tasks is both dominant and pervasive today. It is a part of the dominant ideology that is derived directly from patriarchy (Epstein 2007).

We illustrate the point with a well-publicized example. In the spring of 2005, then Harvard president Larry Summers, addressing a gathering of science, technology, engineering, and math scientists from the most prestigious institutions—including Harvard, MIT, and Yale—argued that women were underrepresented as tenured and promoted faculty in departments such as math, physics, and engineering because they were *biologically inferior* in math (Bombardieri 2005; Summers 2005).

Biological and genetic explanations for gender differences perpetuate the belief that men beat up women because they are biologically programmed toward violence and that women need to be disciplined for the same reasons, because they are biologically inferior and like children need to be trained and "corrected." For example, as we will discuss at length in Chapter 10, much of the support for IPV comes from an interpretation of the Bible that charges men as being, like Jesus, the head of the household and women and children as being, like all Christians, inferior beings who are in need of guidance and sometimes punishment. The reader will also recall from our discussion in Chapter 2 that undergirding the history of our domestic violence laws was the belief that men were superior, and thus they were instructed to guide and, if necessary, discipline physically their wives (and children) who were believed to be inferior. This becomes a convenient and popular explanation for IPV that treats it as immutable, inevitable, and individual rather than structural. In other words, as long as battering is a result of individual men getting "out of control," then one never has to examine the role that male superiority, power, and patriarchy play in IPV. This is akin to Summers's explanation for the underrepresentation of women in the sciences—women's lack of innate ability at math remains an individual problem—rather than focusing attention on the structural barriers women in the sciences face, including the well-documented inequities in funding, salary, and lab space in studies of gender equity at technology universities including MIT, which in the 1990s was forced to conduct a gender-equity study as a result of potential law-suits by women faculty, who were able, in fact, to prove they were victims of gender-based discrimination (Massachusetts Institute of Technology 1999).

MASCULINITY AND IPV

When scholars analyze the images that transmit beliefs about masculinity and the rigid construction of gender roles, they note that several traits have come to *signify manhood* in contemporary America, including physical strength and power, aggression, financial success, and sexual prowess (Kimmel 2005; Messner 2002). With remarkable consistency, the key issues that both batterers and battered women identified as the "triggers" to *violence* are both men's successes in **breadwinning** and their performance in the bedroom, what we term *the two Bs*.

Breadwinning in the Current Economic Climate

The first *B* is breadwinning. Breadwinning has long been defined by both popular discourse and sociological theory as one of the key roles that men in our society must play. This belief has persisted despite the fact that beginning in the 1980s, married women's labor force participation and contribution to their overall household incomes have steadily increased (Hattery 2001; Padavic and Reskin 2002).

Kimmel argues that one outcome of the contemporary political, economic, and social climate, replete with declining real wages for men (Padavic and Reskin 2002) and soaring unemployment, is that men's ability to establish a masculine identity vis-à-vis their success in the labor market is tenuous at best and leaves men feeling threatened by the possibility that they are not masculine enough. "At the grandest social level and the most intimate realms of personal life, for individuals and institutions, American men have been haunted by fears that they are not powerful, strong, rich, or successful enough" (Kimmel 2005, 8). The reader will recall from our lengthy discussion in the previous chapter that all of Kimmel's concerns are likely to be magnified by the recession that began in late 2007. As a result, "American men try to *control themselves*; they project their fears on to *others*; and when feeling too pressured, they attempt to *escape*" (9).

Kimmel (2005) calls into question a dilemma for men in the United States. As they are struggling in order to define themselves as "real" men through economic success, they see the rules changing; suddenly, they are competing *against* women for jobs they once monopolized. Given Kimmel's argument that in this economic, political, and social landscape masculinity is already at risk, it seems that threats to masculinity—especially those related to the two *B*s (breadwinning and the bedroom), the organizing principles of intimate partner relations—and especially those threats coming directly from men's intimate partners, will be particularly powerful. According to Kimmel's argument, men would be left feeling particularly vulnerable.

If this is true, and a man's reaction to feeling humiliated is "invariably violent," or if—in a less extreme interpretation—as Michael Kimmel notes, men's reaction to vulnerability is to *control*, then it seems that battering is a logical and probable outcome of threats to men's masculinity and power inside of the context of patriarchy. And, as we discussed in the previous chapter, all available indicators suggest that IPV as well as other forms of family violence have been on the rise as the economy has been on the decline.

We turn now to the men's own explanations for their violent episodes. *These are not justifications for battering and should not be seen as such.* What they do provide is an opportunity to examine battering through the lens and words used by men who batter. These are *their explanations for their behavior.* We argue that though men who batter rarely offer a critical perspective, nor do they often recognize the position of privilege they occupy in a patriarchy, listening to the voices of men who batter offers insights that are important to incorporate into broader proposals for radical social transformation.

Threats to the Breadwinner Role

Threats to the provider or breadwinner role come in several different forms: men's own failure as providers, not being able to keep up with the demands of their wives or girlfriends, and frustration with wives and girlfriends who wanted to be "kept" when this was really an unrealistic expectation.

Women as "Nags"

The majority of men we interviewed indicated that their wives and girlfriends failed to recognize *their efforts* as providers. Put in their terms, these men felt "nagged." These men reported that their wives or girlfriends nagged them about not earning enough money, not being able to provide the standard of living they believed they deserved, and not providing them with the means necessary to keep up with their girlfriends and coworkers.

Eddie is an African American man in his late thirties who lives in North Carolina. In addition to owning his own painting company, he is a professional boxer. He has been involved in several *violent relationships* with ex-girlfriends as well as with his wife. When we asked Eddie to talk about conflict in his marriage, he indicated that he and his wife frequently argued about money:

Small stuff, you know. She's always complaining about that I don't treat her like a wife, because I don't buy her what she wants, things like I can't afford, she always throw up in my face like what her friend's husband, what kind of car he bought her and what kind of gifts he bought her. Of course he can buy her a brand-new car when he the assistant chief executive at Wachovia. And uh, she a RN, got a master's degree at Wake Forest, you know, and she complain about, oh and he just bought this $160,000 house and you know you married me and you supposed to do this for me and my children, well what you, what you gonna do for yourself, and she always just nick-nagging at me.

Eddie, thirtysomething African American man, North Carolina

From Eddie's perspective, not only is this nagging unwarranted—he sees himself as a good provider who is doing the best he can—but his wife is not contributing financially to the household:

My wife hasn't worked, man, right now she don't even work. She, we don't get no kind of assistance, we don't get no kind of assistance, I make the money. She just get a little small child support check from their father, that's it.

Failure as a Provider

Many of the men and women we interviewed identified unemployment or underemployment as significant sources of conflict in their relationships.

Darren is a white man in his midforties who resides in North Carolina. When we asked Darren to describe the incident in which he hit his wife and was subsequently arrested, he described an argument about money. He and his wife had a particularly heated debate over a vacation and his perception that his wife had foolishly paid too much for what turned out to be a disastrous airline flight. The argument lasted for a week during which time Darren attempted to discuss the issue with his wife, and she refused to even speak to him. This eventually erupted into a heated debate. While he was yelling at her, his wife ran into the kitchen.

I went into the kitchen. I grabbed my wife around the neck. I laid her on the kitchen floor. She rose up. I slapped her. She rose up again; I slapped her again. And then I made some threats. . . . And I told her, listen, let's go sit down in the living room and we're going to talk about this and you're going to listen to me. Okay? I'm taking control of the situation, is how I felt. I'm going to take over. You're going to listen to me, regardless of whether you want to or not. You're not going to turn your back on me, you're not going to give me a sneer, you're not going to make a snide remark, you're going to listen to what I have to say.

Darren, fortysomething white man, North Carolina

Darren puts his reaction into context; rationalizing their violence was an extremely common reaction and tactic among batterers:

I was making a lot less money than I was in Washington State. And I was contributing a lot less to the household. I didn't have all the great benefits that I had in Washington. I didn't feel like I was the man of the house, you know. I was kind of hurting here. She had made a couple of cracks, you know, about the way things are different. And about if I was single, I could barely get by [laughing] on what I make, and all this stuff. In the past, she had said these things, and it stuck. We lived in a nice neighborhood—a really nice neighborhood. There was a president of a company next door, a psychiatrist across the street, a business owner down the street. It was a really nice neighborhood. And here I was; I'm a pipe fitter, a pipe welder. I came home dirty and I worked with my hands. I started . . . [laughing] the neighbors were really clean when they got home . . . and I started having these, gee . . . self-esteem issues. So, when my wife would reject me and when she would resent me, showed resentment, I'm thinking, well, gee, you know, maybe the money thing is a problem because she inherited a million dollars, more or less. She bought a $625,000 house with it, and furniture and all that stuff. And here I am working at the mill in Concord. And she's making all the major purchases. Things were out of balance financially.

Darren, fortysomething white man, North Carolina

This imbalance of economic power provided Darren with a justification, in his mind, for beating his wife. He interpreted his wife's economic power as a threat to his self-esteem. In short, Darren beat his wife when he felt his masculine identity vis-à-vis his economic power in the household was threatened. We turn now to a discussion of the second measure of masculinity: sexual prowess, otherwise known as the second *B*, the bedroom.

The Bedroom

Sexual prowess encompasses several issues, including men's ability to satisfy their partners and men's ability be a "player" by gaining access to multiple sexual partners, often through sexual conquest. Each year these issues erupt on college campuses when young men—often members of fraternities (see Sanday 2007) or football and basketball players—are accused of the sexual conquest of young women on campus. The Duke lacrosse case, though it was never prosecuted, brought national attention to the relationship between sexual conquest and masculinity (Hattery and Smith 2007b).

As old as America, perhaps most of the world, is the **sexual double standard** for men and for women. This double standard prescribes that men should or can have more sexual experiences and more sexual partners than women. The evidence for this is overwhelming and far-reaching (see Epstein 2007 for a historical overview). Consider, for example, the fact that polygyny (having more than one wife) was the dominant marriage form throughout history and across the globe (see the Human Relations Area Files, housed at Yale University, http://www.yale.edu/hraf/) and continues to exist in parts of Asia, Africa, and the Middle East (Sanday 1981). Typically, the only prohibition against multiple wives in these cultures is the ability to provide economically for them. Furthermore, in the United States, despite a thirty-year trend of declining age at first intercourse and a decline in the percentage of newlyweds who are virgins at the time of marriage, American boys become sexually active a year or more earlier than their female peers, who are more than twice as likely to be virgins on their wedding day (Alan Guttmacher Institute 2004). Finally, compare the language we use to describe men who have multiple sex partners to the language we use to describe women who do. We do not have to make a list here to demonstrate that virtually all the words for men are positive (*player, stud*), and all of the terms for women are negative (*loose, whore, slut*).

When taken together, the sexual double standard, the history of polygyny, and the acceptance and praise awarded men who engage in sexual conquest, it is clear that sexual prowess is an important part of masculinity in the contemporary United States—if not in the world more broadly. Given the importance of sexual prowess in constructions of masculinity, men were reluctant to discuss their failures in this area—though they were happy to share their successes in the bedroom with us. However, wives and girlfriends were not so closed-lipped on this issue.

In some cases, wives and girlfriends admitted to us that they were dissatisfied with their sex lives, and they talked about how they expressed this dissatisfaction to their male partners. Charlotte is a woman in her early fifties who is married to Perry, also in his fifties. This is Charlotte's second marriage and Perry's first. They married each other when they were well into their forties. Charlotte and Perry are both white Americans who live in North Carolina.

In discussing their relationship Charlotte talked openly about her dissatisfaction with Perry as a "lover." From Charlotte's perspective, their sexual relationship, the second measure of a masculine man, was unsatisfying. Charlotte indicated that she had to beg Perry to have sex with her and that his lack of attention to their sex life contributed to her feeling badly about herself:

A lot of times I would say, why? Please. What is your problem? It would be like two weeks, three weeks. I'm thinking, you know, I'm going to go get sewed up. I told him I was going to go have it sewed up. I did. I would actually tell him that. I said, I might as well just go to the doctor and have it completely . . . And he looked at me like, well, can you do that? (laughing).

Charlotte, fiftysomething white woman, North Carolina

Both Charlotte and Perry admitted that after this accusation, their fight turned violent. Perry not only hit Charlotte but also threw numerous household items at her, including dishes and a lamp. Charlotte sustained facial lacerations and bruising, and Perry was arrested for domestic violence.

Chris and Wanda also have had physical fights that erupted around her dissatisfaction with their sex life:

[Chris] don't appreciate nothing. So now you know, you're slacking up on everything, even the sex too now. Like sex, like it's a reward or something. NO way. And you know I'm a scuppy. I'm a freak, you know, I like my groove on when I want it. And you're going to tell me no? Oh, hell no. It's time for you to go 'cause I don't need you. 'Cause I got, I can go over here to Lovin' Fun [a lingerie store], I can buy anything, any toy I need and make love to myself 'cause I don't need you. And suck my own titty and everything. I'm just going to be frank. And so, all hell breaking . . . I am so serious! Y'all laugh, but I'm so serious.

Wanda, fiftysomething African American woman, Minnesota

Because we interviewed both of them, we are able to confirm that they both see Wanda's accusation that Chris lacks sexual prowess by failing to satisfy her as *triggering* his violent explosion; he must "put her in her place":

We was in the basement and she wanted more sex or whatever . . . that's when I had to throw the jabs at her and stuff.

Chris, fiftysomething African American man, Minnesota

Taken together, the sexual double standard and the prevalence of male sexual privilege are evidence of a pervasive sexual ideology that locates sexual prowess at the core of masculinity. Essentializing men as sexual conquistadores results in many problems in relationships, including sexual abuse and marital rape. To recapitulate, it works this way: men grow up learning that conquest is part of the way that men obtain sex. The more women a man can "conquest," the more of a "man" he is. Furthermore, men (and women) are taught that men have a right to seek sex, and they will, and that it is up to women to act as gatekeepers, to decide when to "give it up." This set of antagonistic relationships results in men believing they have a right to sex whenever and with whomever they desire it. When women attempt to act as gatekeepers, saying no, men believe they are being denied what they have a right to have. This is especially the case when the woman saying no is one's wife or long-term partner (Hattery and Kane 1995).

Marital Rape: Sexual abuse of one's spouse or partner is one of the most difficult aspects of IPV for a variety of reasons; it is difficult for the victim, it is difficult to prosecute, and it is the form of IPV that is the least understood in the general public. In her study of battered women who kill their abusive partners, Angela Browne found that one of the key factors that differentiated women who left abusive relationships by either divorce or by homicide from those who did not was the presence of marital rape. Browne describes the rape that one of the women she interviewed, Molly, experienced regularly: "And sometimes he raped her. Molly didn't think you could call it rape, when it was your husband, but he was very rough during lovemaking—pinching and biting and treating her with anger. At these times he was like another person; he didn't seem to know her or realize what he was doing. Molly began to have constant bruises and bite marks" (Browne 1989, 39).

In addition, despite changes in the laws around wife abuse across the twentieth century that transformed marital rape into a crime, the marital rape exemption existed in many states well into the 1980s.

> The **marital rape exemption** refers to exemptions in the state domestic violence statutes that *precluded* marital rape as a form of battering. Wives, even if they were separated from their husbands, were not legally allowed to bring a charge of rape against them, regardless of the severity of the sexual assault.

Even after the lifting of the marital rape exemption in all fifty states, nearly thirty years ago, it remains extremely difficult for a woman to charge her legal husband with rape and even more difficult to find a prosecutor who will argue her case. Despite the fact that sexual abuse is common among victims of IPV—one in four women, or 25 percent, report being raped or having sex with their husbands when they did not want to (Russell 1990; Tjaden and Thoennes 2000; Warshaw

1988)—it is violent, it is a tool of power and control, and it is devastating to the victim, Americans' attitudes about sex and sexual abuse in relationships are extremely conservative. In a study performed by one of the authors in the mid-1990s, even among college students, only 25 percent of men and 45 percent of women considered a scenario describing marital rape to be "unacceptable," and far fewer indicated that it constituted "rape" or a crime (Hattery and Kane 1995).

Sexual abuse is a common tool for batterers because, as most scholars of rape point out, it is one of the most humiliating experiences for a woman (or a man) (Brownmiller 1975). Indeed, the purpose of sexual assault—whether it be perpetrated by a stranger or a relative—is to humiliate the victim and remind her (or him) of the power the perpetrator has over the victim. This makes it an incredibly powerful tool of domestic violence but also as terrorism of marginalized groups—gay men, transgender individuals—and a tool of war (Kristoff and WuDunn 2009). Thus, why is there so much resistance in the attitudes of Americans for understanding marital rape as a type of domestic violence and for supporting its prosecution? We argue, as many others do, that much of this lies in the marital transaction we described in the previous chapter. Marriage has long been based on the understanding that a woman trades access to her sexuality for the economic support and companionship of her husband. Based on tradition, which continues today, this transaction was considered to be permanent—for life—and to hold in any circumstance. This belief was the basis for the marital rape exemption; quite simply, if a woman had agreed to offer free access to her sexuality and without the possibility of refusal to her husband, then he was permitted by tradition and law to have sex with her whenever and however he chose, even if she did not want to and even if they were separated. It was quite simply not possible to rape one's wife. Though this is no longer the case legally, as we discussed at length in Chapter 2 there is very often a long lag between changes in the law and changes in attitudes and beliefs. We, as a society, have a long way to go before we will have reached a point in which we understand the reality of marital rape and offer victims the protection and intervention they deserve.

Sexual Conquest, Jealousy, and IPV

Aside from the obvious—marital rape—how does the sexual double standard contribute to IPV? Perhaps the single most common theme in the interviews with both men and women was the issue of jealousy on the part of the men. All or most of the men worried about or believed that their female partners were sleeping ("talking") with other men. This constituted a significant threat to their masculinity, simply because an integral part of sexual prowess is the ability to keep your woman satisfied and thus not straying.[2] As a result, many men engaged regularly in hypercontrolling behavior meant to prevent their female partners from having contact with other men. This, of course, is in addition to the violent outbursts and beatings that were dramatic but occurred less frequently.

Eddie recounts the night that he caught his former girlfriend with another man and probably engaging in prostitution. That night he admitted to beating her to the point that she was unrecognizable. If the description is not powerful enough, remember that Eddie is a boxer and had once beaten a man in a boxing match so badly that he killed him. Eddie's fists are, indeed, lethal weapons.

So what had happened was, come to find out she had got a hotel room at the Innkeeper on Broad Street. I would call her and she would keep going in the car. Later on that Saturday night she was coming up Fourteenth Street and I seen her and her cousin was out there and you know, so I told him I would pay him if he would stop her when he saw her coming, when he catch her coming up the street. So he agreed, for a fee. He took and stopped her, and when she stopped, I snuck up behind the car and jumped in and I was like if you don't pull off I will break your face, you know, I told her that. So she got scared and she pulled off. . . . I smacked her when I got into the car, and she said well I been at the hotel with another guy. . . . When we got back to the room, you see, I knew that he used to smoke those rocks inside the cigars, so we, she took me to her room she had cigar butts in the ashtray, and I know she didn't smoke them like that, but I know he did, the one that she had just dropped off. Then I seen her underwear by the shower and her bra, as if she had took a shower and just slipped on something to come out to drop him back off, so when I got in there and seen that I lost my mind, man, and I beat her so badly, man. I beat her so bad until, they couldn't hardly recognize her, man. Her eyes were swollen, her mouth was busted, I had chipped her teeth.

Eddie, thirtysomething African American man, North Carolina

Because masculinity is defined by such a narrow range of behaviors, the two *B*s, with the greatest weight resting on these two aspects, breadwinning and "the bedroom," many men construct most or all of their gendered identity—as masculine men—around their success (or failure) at these two roles.

At an individual level, this may not seem so extraordinary. Men must simply get a job, work hard, make money, and satisfy their female partner. However, examining this from a structural or sociological perspective, we see that success or failure in this arena is not entirely up to individual effort. As was detailed at length in Chapter 8, especially with regards to successful breadwinning, individual performance is heavily structured by external forces such as the economy, returns on human capital, and race and class discrimination (see especially Hattery and Smith 2007a).

RACE, CLASS, AND GENDER: INTERPRETING DIFFERENCES ACROSS GROUPS

The precise mechanism by which failure in the breadwinner role triggers violence among men is mitigated or shaped by race and ethnicity. As noted by Kimmel (2005) and others, white men feel especially threatened when they cannot meet the role of sole provider. This is illustrated best by Darren, whose story is above.

In contrast, as a result of a long history of unemployment for African American men and ready employment (as domestics) for African American women coupled with a long history of sharing the provider role that dates back to slavery (Collins 1994; Hattery 2001; Hattery and Smith 2007a), most African American men *expected* their wives and girlfriends to work outside of the home and contribute financially to the household, as noted by Eddie. For African American men, then, the frustration or "trigger" to violence arose from a situation in which their female partners *refused to work* yet desired a standard of living that the men could not deliver on their own. What is interesting to note is that breadwinning is a significant "trigger" for both white and African American men, but the "trigger" is set off differently; that is, the "trigger" is structured and shaped by race and ethnicity, social history, and the contemporary sociopolitical climate (Smith 2008).

Similarly, sexual prowess is experienced differently for men of different racial and ethnic groups. Coming out of a stronger tradition of Protestantism and conservative Christianity, white men are less likely to assess their sexual worth by multiple sex partners but instead focus on their sexual behavior within the context of relationships that demand absolute monogamy. They are particularly threatened when they suspect that their female partners are being unfaithful.

In contrast, African American men, as many scholars, including Patterson (1999), note, have the lowest marriage rates of all men in the contemporary United States (see also Hattery and Smith 2007a for a long discussion of marriage in the African American community). Popular culture paints a picture of African American men as "players" on a sexual conquest for multiple female partners (Smith and Hattery 2006; Hattery and Smith 2007b; Smith 2009). Yet they too are especially threatened when they believe that their wives or girlfriends are being unfaithful. Ironically, in the case of African American men, the majority admitted freely that they had another woman on the side—as evidenced by the lyrics of the most popular rap music songs, including those by artists such as R. Kelly ("Double Up") and Fabulous ("Baby Girl")—but they expected absolute devotion and faithfulness from their female partners, whom they admitted they suspected of cheating.

This suspicion was the primary cause of a great deal of violence in their relationships. As with so many things, interviews with women confirmed this high level of jealousy that African American women were subjected to by their male partners, yet the vast majority of African American women confirmed that they were not having affairs, but all reported that they were aware that their jealous male partners were.

We turn now to a discussion of a case that is particularly illustrative: the US military.

THE MILITARY

The military creates an environment that is ripe for intimate partner violence for a variety of reasons. In this section we will explore the special environment created by the military and offer examples of cases in which the culture of the military and the stresses of the current wars led to tragedy in military families. The military is a unique institution in American life for a variety of reasons, several of which create a culture ripe for IPV. First and foremost, the military is a culture unto itself, and this culture is one of hypermasculinity. Simply watching a small number of television advertisements pitched at recruiting young men into one branch of the military or another reveals this: the Marines advertise—while showing athletic men scaling mountains and brandishing weapons—"The Few, the Proud, the Marines!" Films such as *A Few Good Men* and *GI Jane* along with the *Rambo* series and many others reinforce the pivotal role that hypermasculinity plays in the military and the identity construction of soldiers.

The military is one of the most sex-segregated institutions in American life. At its peak, which it is currently, the military is approximately 6 percent female. But perhaps more important is the history of segregation—both gender based and racial—and the continued ban on women serving in combat roles. Though women have been involved in military operations for decades—for example, during World War II women pilots were contracted to fly planes from the factories where they were constructed to the military bases where they would be put into missions—they have not always been official members of the military, which means they could not access military benefits. Until very recently, they were limited to a small number of roles—as nurses and administrative assistants in Korea and Vietnam. Even today, the vast majority of military space is space that is virtually completely dominated by men. With only 6 percent of the US military being composed of women, it is not impossible to imagine that there are whole units that have no female personnel. And given the restrictions on their exposure to combat situations, especially in the war theaters, this segregation is a "normal" way of life. Much like other segregated institutions—the Catholic Church and the world of most professional sports—the military can be characterized as being a site of high levels of violence against women. Moreover, though it is not our focus here, we note that regularly female cadets in the prestigious military academies, as well as female military personnel—both enlisted staff and officers—make claims of sexual harassment and rape. The military's own estimates are that as many as half of all women serving in the military report confidentially that they have experienced either one or both; most disturbing in this statistic is the fact that the harassment and abuse are perpetrated not by the enemy as part of a capture or torture but by their own colleagues, the servicemen with whom they serve.

When complaints are made, be they of harassment or rape by a fellow service person or claims of domestic violence either on or off base, the military is unlike any other US institution in that it has its own system of justice. Though a military wife who is being beaten by her husband might call 911, it is far more likely the case that she will call the military police. As a result, the vast majority of violence that military women and wives face is handled from within. It is not difficult to understand then that the response to the reports is not always in the best interest of the victims. As we will discuss at length in Chapter 13, the response of the civilian legal system—be it to allegations of domestic violence or child or elder abuse—is fraught with problems for the victims, and these problems are further exaggerated in the military because of its unique nature as a sex-segregated institution and because of its desire to keep its problems out of the purview of the more critical public. Much like the Catholic Church sex scandal, which we will discuss in Chapter 10, when a sex-segregated institution is faced with policing its membership for violence against women, the outcome almost always favors the men involved, rarely addresses the needs of the victim, and engages in tremendous antics designed to keep the incident from ever becoming public. The following case illustrates this point.

BOX 9.2   WILLIAM AND ERIN EDWARDS

When Strains on Military Families Turn Deadly
By Lizette Alvarez and Deborah Sontag, February 15, 2008

A few months after Sgt. William Edwards and his wife, Sgt. Erin Edwards, returned to a Texas Army base from separate missions in Iraq, he assaulted her mercilessly. He struck her, choked her, dragged her over a fence and slammed her into the sidewalk.

As far as Erin Edwards was concerned, that would be the last time he beat her.

Unlike many military wives, she knew how to work the system to protect herself. She was an insider, even more so than her husband, since she served as an aide to a brigadier general at Fort Hood.

With the general's help, she quickly arranged for a future transfer to a base in New York. She pressed charges against her husband and secured an order of protection. She sent her two children to stay with her mother. And she received assurance from her husband's commanders that he would be barred from leaving the base unless accompanied by an officer.

Yet on the morning of July 22, 2004, William Edwards easily slipped off base, skipping his anger-management class, and drove to his wife's house in the Texas town of Killeen. He waited for her to step outside and then, after a struggle, shot her point-blank in the head before turning the gun on himself.

SOURCE: Alvarez and Sontag 2008.

The military is also uniquely situated because it is an institution dependent on weapons. Although this seems simplistic and straightforward, it is worth noting that the very presence of and easy access to weapons is a likely contributor to the high rates of domestic violence homicide that we see on US military bases. When coupled with the fact that many soldiers returning from active duty are struggling with mental health issues and trying to reintegrate into family life, the transition can be tragic. For example, the military estimates that at least half of all soldiers returning from a war theater are suffering from some mental health issues, including post-traumatic stress disorder (Hoge et al. 2004). This type of stress can understandably lead to strains on intimate partner relationships and, without proper attention, may result in episodes of IPV. "'I don't think there is any question about that,' said Peter C. McDonald, a retired district court judge in Kentucky and a member of the Pentagon's now disbanded domestic violence task force. 'The war could only make things much worse than even before, and here we had a system that was not too good to begin with'" (Alvarez and Sontag 2008).

Additionally, men coming home from serving abroad face struggles with regards to family reintegration and especially concerns about jealousy. If their wives have established or strengthened relationships while their husbands were absent, the husbands may be resentful of these relationships and certainly jealous if these friendships are with men, and this jealousy, especially when accompanied by mental health issues, may lead to violence. Though we will never know the exact cause of the domestic violence homicide epidemic at Fort Hood, we can speculate that all of the factors here contributed to this tragedy.

BOX 9.3   RICHARD AND MICHELE CORCORAN

Base Crimes
The Military Has a Domestic Violence Problem
By Karen Houppert, July–August 2005 Issue

At North Carolina's Fort Bragg this February, Army Special Forces trainee Richard Corcoran got mad at his estranged wife, Michele. He'd gotten mad before, but this would mark the sixth and final time the Cumberland County Sheriffs Department would be called to break up a "domestic disturbance" between Corcoran and his wife. At 8:30 p.m. Corcoran arrived at his wife's house and went after 30-year-old Michele with a gun, firing at her as she fled to a neighbor's. (She was wounded but survived.) He shot and wounded another Fort Bragg soldier who was in the house and then shot and killed himself—all while his seven-month-old daughter lay in another room.

continues

BOX 9.3   RICHARD AND MICHELE CORCORAN *continued*

He joins a band of brothers. Corcoran's is the 10th fatality in a slew of domestic violence homicides involving Fort Bragg soldiers since 2002; in one six-week spree four Army wives were murdered by their husbands or ex-husbands. Including nonfatal incidents, there were 832 victims of domestic violence between 2002 and 2004 at Fort Bragg alone, according to Army figures.

And yet Corcoran's attack stands out. Not only had he just attended a mandated anger-management class on-post that same afternoon—calling into question the efficacy of these sessions that the Army considers the cornerstone of its domestic violence treatment program—but Corcoran had a past that should have kept him out of the Army in the first place: He had been indicted for rape at the age of 19.

SOURCE: http://motherjones.com/politics/2005/07/base-crimes.

We've been discussing how beliefs about masculinity contribute to a culture that is ripe for intimate partner violence. It is also important to understand that the very nature of masculinity requires a particular, specific, compatible construction of **femininity**. We turn now to a discussion of beliefs about femininity.

HOW TO BE A "GOOD" WIFE: CONSTRUCTIONS OF FEMININITY AND INTERPERSONAL VIOLENCE

Femininity: what it means to be a woman in this culture. It is widely believed that women should take care that they are beautiful, well mannered, capable of creating an appropriate home and cooking good meals, and that although they may be employed, their priority is on their families.

A Brief History of Women's Roles

Across the relatively brief history of the United States, the gender role expectations of wives have been relatively stable. This is not to say that the norm of the stay at home mother, so aptly illustrated in 1960s television shows such as *Leave It to Beaver* and the *Brady Bunch*, was always dominant. However, one of the authors has argued elsewhere (Hattery 2001) that despite the lack of dominance of this family form, many Americans talk with nostalgia about "the good old days" when men were the breadwinners and women were homemakers, both occupying completely separate and nonoverlapping spheres of social life. Part of the lure of this nostalgia is the widespread belief that "the good old days" were really the way things "always were" until this *preferable* way of life came to an abrupt halt thanks primarily to the sexual revolution of the 1960s and 1970s, when women began, in greater numbers, to be educated, to enter the labor market in numbers greater than during the World War II period, and to gain some measure of control over their reproductive lives as a result of the birth control pill and legalized abortion (Luker 1985).

Despite the valiant efforts of historians such as Stephanie Coontz (1992, 1997), who uses empirical evidence to debunk many myths about family life, especially the myth of the dominance of the traditional family replete with the breadwinner father and the stay-at-home mother, this nostalgia for the 1950s has seen a powerful resurgence among politicians, the Christian Right, and groups with wide appeal such as the Promise Keepers. The "Family Values" rhetoric advanced by groups such as the Promise Keepers is appealing because it is focused on social problems, such as teen pregnancy, drug abuse, and school violence, which trouble many (if not most) Americans. The solutions proposed by groups touting "Family Values" rhetoric is also appealing because the strategies focus on increasing rates of marriage, decreasing single-parent households, and urging traditional gender roles that allow women to return to a focus on caring for the children and the home. But this is rhetoric not based in empirical realities; simply willing the divorce rate to be lower or the rate of marriage to be higher does not address the structural impediments to long-term marriage, including the economy, the strains of the recession, and the rate of violence in many homes. Additionally, there has never been a time when families relied more on women's wages, and thus a return to traditional gender roles, even in married couple households, is not only unlikely but impossible for the majority of American families. Yet the *norm* of the stay-at-home mother survives and is preferred by many despite its lack of reality (Hattery 2001; Hays 1996).

The Cult of Domesticity

Across all of US history, the home has been women's domain. Padavic and Reskin (2002) identify the home as the "private" sphere and the workplace as the "public" sphere. Though the **public-private split** was indeed real, the assumption that economic production was relegated entirely to the public sphere is in fact false. During the agricultural era that dominated American history, many women *were also involved* in the economic production of the farm. On the typical "family farms" that dominated the Midwest, women were responsible for small animals (chickens), milking (on dairy farms), large vegetable gardens, and farm processes such as milk and egg production. Yet historical accounts (Coontz 1992, 1997; Wolf 1992) reveal that in addition to this "economic" work, women were relegated to the home and to all of the tasks associated with it. Of course, African American women were also highly involved in agricultural work, though under slavery and the system of share-cropping that later replaced it, their involvement for centuries brought no economic advantage to their families (Hattery and Smith 2007a).

Earlier in the chapter we outlined the functionalist perspective on gender roles as proposed by Parsons and Bales (1955). Women, they argued, are the *expressive* leaders in the household, and with that position comes the work of the home, including the care of the children, but of equal importance the care and nurturing of the husband. Thus, women were to cook each evening a warm meal. They were to design and decorate a home that was relaxing, and they were to limit the chaos in the home by teaching their young children to be quiet and calm when the man of the house arrived home each day. This ideology was later termed the *cult of domesticity*. As part of the exchange, the worker, the instrumental leader of the family using Parsons and Bales's model, earned a wage. The requirement of the husband then was to provide for the economic needs of the family by turning over at least some of his earnings to the wife so that she could purchase the necessary goods in order to run the household and rejuvenate her husband through food and a comfortable home.

The **cult of domesticity**, or the "**cult of true womanhood**" as it is sometimes called, is an ideology built around the idea that a woman's place is in the home. Not only did women belong in the home, but successful homemaking was critical in moving from the status of "girl" to that of "woman." Though women had always been assigned the role of keeping up the home and the family, the rise of the cult of domesticity really began in the early 1900s and reached its peak in the 1950s and 1960s. Despite a modest decline in importance, which began in the 1970s, it remains at the core of constructions of our beliefs about femininity today (Hattery 2001; Wolf 1992). This is evidenced by both the empirical data that indicate that women who are married or in relationships with men continue, regardless of their employment status, to do the lion's share of the housework—twenty-five hours on average per week compared to men's seven hours (Bianchi, Robinson, and Milkie 2007)—and the fact that many women report continuing to feel the pressures associated with the work of the home, including home-cooked meals (despite working forty hours per week), the responsibilities for caring for their children, or arranging child care (Hattery 2001). Consider the media, for example, and television shows with titles like *Desperate Housewives* or *The Real Housewives* as well as advertisements. The vast majority of cooking and cleaning products continue to be advertised toward women: using female actors who are thrilled with the scent of laundry detergent and broadcast during the "soap" hours, noon to four o'clock, weekdays.

In the early 1900s, the Industrial Revolution was in full force in the United States, and this led to the public-private split Padavic and Reskin (2002) so aptly describe. Along with the Industrial Revolution came the urbanization of US society, and increasingly women's work "at home" no longer included working in a garden or tending to small animals. Instead, women had more time to engage in child rearing and in caring for the home. Especially for upper-class white women, the care of the home—decorating, maintaining, even cooking—became an art rather than a simple task. With the completion of the national rail system, for example, access to a greater variety of foods, especially fruits and vegetables, as well as products to decorate the home was opened up to the middle class, whereas these "luxuries" had initially been available only to the affluent (Veblen 2008). With access to more and more foods and goods—often items that were not "native" to a woman's area of residence, and thus not familiar—more and more training was required to teach young women how to make a proper home. Thus, we see the rise of "finishing" schools. It is also important to note that the exclusion of women from education and the professions meant that finishing schools and "professionalizing" the care of the home were the only options available for women who had intellectual or professional goals.

For a variety of reasons, the cult of domesticity, which had become an important part of the construction of femininity in the United States, reached a peak and ultimate ideological dominance by the 1950s, following two historical periods when women's involvement in the paid labor force was relatively high: the Great Depression, when women sought work to offset the lost wages of their husbands, and during World War II, when women took over factory jobs left vacant by men who were sent off to war. Especially during the World War II period of women's employment, along with earning a wage, working provided women with skills and the independence they had previously been denied (Hattery 2001; Padavic and Reskin 2002; Wolf 1992).

When men returned from the war, women were displaced from the labor market (Kossoudji and Dresser 1992). A series of laws made it legal to dismiss women from any job and replace them with veterans who had returned from war. Although some women happily left the labor force to return home, many did so reluctantly. In order to ease the pain of this dismissal as well as to meet the needs of this new woman, one who was more likely to have a college degree, who had learned a trade, or who perhaps even built cars or bombs, several forces coalesced to *professionalize* and *glamorize* the work and the life of the housewife (Wolf 1992). The work of the home was defined as essential to the role of being not just a good wife, but also a good *woman*. Women were warned in television ads, magazine reports, and political rhetoric that their primary responsibility was to their home and the care of their family and that to fail at such would be to doom their entire family to certain failure. Women began to be taught about the dangers of dust in their homes, for example. And one always worried that the white-glove testers might appear on your doorstep to assess not just your skills in dusting but also your success as a true woman. Television and print ads for home appliances showed beautiful women vacuuming with a Hoover or doing laundry with a Maytag or cooking with a new GE oven in ways that were highly sexualized. The positive outcomes of doing housework and using these appliances were not limited to the women themselves, for these actions translated into happy husbands and successful children, or so the ads said.

Women had demonstrated that they were intelligent and capable. They had managed every conceivable industry from factories to health care in the absence of men created by the demands of World War II. But the country was not ready for women to enter these professions permanently. Therefore, entire curricula were designed to educate women on the virtues of the cult of domesticity. It was believed that women were being educated and prepared for lives as housewives. We've seen a resurgence of this ideology recently. In 2005 a series of articles in the *New York Times* featured female graduates of the prestigious Ivy League colleges like Harvard and Yale who allegedly gave it all up in order to stay at home and realize their true calling. Critics wonder about the efficiency of paying upwards of a quarter of a million dollars for an education that one will use primarily at home, and others worry that women waited too long and fought too hard for admission to these prestigious institutions—many of which did not integrate the sexes until the 1970s—to "throw it all away" (Story 2005).

BOX 9.4   CYNTHIA LIU

Many Women at Elite Colleges Set Career Path to Motherhood
By Louise Story, New York Times, September 20, 2005

Cynthia Liu is precisely the kind of high achiever Yale wants: smart (1510 SAT), disciplined (4.0 grade point average), competitive (finalist in Texas oratory competition), musical (pianist), athletic (runner) and altruistic (hospital volunteer). And at the start of her sophomore year at Yale, Ms. Liu is full of ambition, planning to go to law school.

So will she join the long tradition of famous Ivy League graduates? Not likely. By the time she is 30, this accomplished 19-year-old expects to be a stay-at-home mom.

"My mother's always told me you can't be the best career woman and the best mother at the same time," Ms. Liu said matter-of-factly. "You always have to choose one over the other."

At Yale and other top colleges, women are being groomed to take their place in an ever more diverse professional elite. It is almost taken for granted that, just as they make up half the students at these institutions, they will move into leadership roles on an equal basis with their male classmates.

There is just one problem with this scenario: many of these women say that is not what they want.

Many women at the nation's most elite colleges say they have already decided that they will put aside their careers in favor of raising children. Though some of these stu-

BOX 9.4   CYNTHIA LIU *continued*

dents are not planning to have children and some hope to have a family and work full time, many others, like Ms. Liu, say they will happily play a traditional female role, with motherhood their main commitment.

What seems new is that while many of their mothers expected to have hard-charging careers, then scaled back their professional plans only after having children, the women of this generation expect their careers to take second place to child rearing.

For many feminists, it may come as a shock to hear how unbothered many young women at the nation's top schools are by the strictures of traditional roles.

"They are still thinking of this as a private issue; they're accepting it," said Laura Wexler, a professor of American studies and women's and gender studies at Yale. "Women have been given full-time working career opportunities and encouragement with no social changes to support it.

"I really believed 25 years ago," Dr. Wexler added, "that this would be solved by now."

SOURCE: http://www.nytimes.com/2005/09/20/national/20women.html?pagewanted=all.

Many dispute this claim that women were being prepared for a life at home; rather, they argue that women were committing themselves to the difficult and important work of mothering. As many women one of the authors interviewed as part of another study would remark, "What could be more important than caring for my children?" (Hattery 2001). Yet by the 1960s, the age of marriage was young—around twenty-one for women—as was the age of first childbirth. Fertility rates had fallen to 2.5 children per woman, and life expectancy was longer—around seventy-two years for women. The typical woman in the United States could expect to have "launched" her children by her early forties and have another twenty-five to thirty years to live. If women were staying home just for the important work of child rearing, then we would expect to see these women enter or return to the labor force in their forties when their children were "launched." However, this did not happen. Why? *Because the cult of domesticity glorified not just child rearing, but housework.* Women were being educated to be good wives, not just good mothers, both of which were essential qualities of good women. The socialization girls were receiving for their future roles as wives was simultaneously constructed as formal education for this "career."

While the boys in high school were taking "shop" class and gaining skills that would serve them in the labor market, specifically in entering the highly paid, unionized trades, women were taking "home ec," learning skills that would serve them as they strove toward the ultimate goal: being a good wife, as defined by the cult of domesticity. We include here, in its entirety, an illustration of what young women in the 1950s were learning about what it meant to be a good wife. This kind of course is also depicted in the film *Mona Lisa Smile.*

► **Figure 9.1**
The Good
Housewife

The Good Wife's Guide

From *Housekeeping Monthly,* May 13, 1955.

- Have dinner ready. Plan ahead, even the night before, to have a delicious meal ready on time for his return. This is a way of letting him know that you have been thinking about him and are concerned about his needs. Most men are hungry when they get home and the prospect of a good meal is part of the warm welcome needed.

- Prepare yourself. Take 15 minutes to rest so you'll be refreshed when he arrives. Touch up your make-up, put a ribbon in your hair and be fresh-looking. He has just been with a lot of work-weary people.

- Be a little gay and a little more interesting for him. His boring day may need a lift and one of your duties is to provide it.

- Clear away the clutter. Make one last trip through the main part of the house just before your husband arrives. Run a dustcloth over the tables.

- During the cooler months of the year you should prepare and light a fire for him to unwind by. Your husband will feel he has reached a haven of rest and order, and it will give you a lift too. After all, catering to his comfort will provide you with immense personal satisfaction.

- Minimize all noise. At the time of his arrival, eliminate all noise of the washer, dryer or vacuum. Encourage the children to be quiet.

- Be happy to see him.

- Greet him with a warm smile and show sincerity in your desire to please him.

- Listen to him. You may have a dozen important things to tell him, but the moment of his arrival is not the time. Let him talk first - remember, his topics of conversation are more important than yours.

- Don't greet him with complaints and problems.

- Don't complain if he's late for dinner or even if he stays out all night. Count this as minor compared to what he might have gone through at work.

- Make him comfortable. Have him lean back in a comfortable chair or lie him down in the bedroom. Have a cool or warm drink ready for him.

- Arrange his pillow and offer to take off his shoes. Speak in a low, soothing and pleasant voice.

- Don't ask him questions about his actions or question his judgment or integrity. Remember, he is the master of the house and as such will always exercise his will with fairness and truthfulness. You have no right to question him.

- A good wife always knows her place.

Note: There is some debate about the authenticity of this particular "guide," but many women we spoke with who were in high school in the 1950s, including the mother of one author, verified that these guides did exist and were part of the high school curriculum many girls received.

Setting aside for a minute one's like or dislike of this sort of "advice," let's consider the impact of this prescription on status, power, and ultimately violence. First, we argue that this is not simply "advice," which implies that one can either take it or leave it. This message was not up for debate. Young women were being instructed by their teachers in the academic setting (not clubs or voluntary activities) in how to be a good wife. A young woman could read a magazine such as *Ladies' Home Journal* or watch the television and be bombarded with images of women's success—as wives—being inextricably linked to their use of appliances. Relaxing in front of popular television shows of the time, which would have included *Leave It to Beaver* and *Peyton Place*, women (and men) were bombarded with a clear message that *essentialized housework as central to being a successful woman* as well as being a good wife. Being instructed in such a message in the landscape of the 1950s would have cemented the importance of adopting the "wife" role in the marriage. *This was not optional.*

Furthermore, it is important to realize the power of defining masculinity, as was discussed in the earlier part of this chapter, in relation to work, while defining femininity in relation to the relationship. One definition leads to independence and the other to dependence. A man's ability to have a roof over his head and food in his stomach was tied to his ability to work and earn a living. A woman's ability to have a roof over her head and food in her stomach was tied to finding a man and keeping him and, more important, relied on his generosity toward her.

Young women today may no longer be indoctrinated into lives of second-class citizenship through such glaring messages as this, but the cult of domesticity remains dominant. As noted, especially on particular cable channels (TLC, A&E), advertisements run from morning until late afternoon showing attractive women engaged in the labors of the home. One particular ad features Kelly Ripa, the daytime talk show host, demonstrating the thrill she receives from using her LG washer and dryer and being able to shower her children with clean and neatly folded clothing that she deposits in their drawers and closets.

Further evidence for this perpetuation of the cult of domesticity comes through examining "self-help" books targeted at women. A tour of Amazon.com or a stroll through Barnes and Noble reveals a plethora of books instructing women on the benefits of giving over power to their husbands or, these days, "partners." And lest you believe these ideas are simply relics from a time gone by, Laura Doyle authored several books in the late 1990s and early 2000s that offer women advice on how to become submissive to their husbands. For example, her book *The Surrendered Wife: A Practical Guide to Finding Intimacy, Passion, and Peace with Your Man*, published in 1999 and released in paperback in 2001, offers just this advice. A careful examination of the chapter titles is revealing: "Give Up Control to Have More Power," "Abandon the Myth of Equality," and "Relinquish the Chore of Managing the Finances." We offer an excerpt to illustrate our point: "Respect means that when he takes the wrong freeway exit you don't correct him by telling him where to turn. It means that if he keeps going in the wrong direction you will go past the state line and still not correct what he's doing. In fact, no matter what your husband does, you will not try to teach, improve, or correct him. That is the essence of a surrendered wife" (2001, 35). Perhaps more troubling than the advice that you should allow your husband to behave stupidly, as this excerpt seems to advise, is the advice to give up management of the finances. As noted in the previous chapter, one of the critical barriers to leaving that battered women face is lack of access to financial resources (Browne 1989; Gelles 1997; Hattery 2008; Koss et al. 1994).

It is precisely this power imbalance that creates a situation ripe for IPV. "How to Be a Good Wife" and *The Surrendered Wife* are not simply guides to pampering your husband. If you read them carefully, it means putting his needs above your own, it means your problems are less important than his, and it means that he can behave however he chooses, even staying out all night, a right he has earned by working so hard. In fact, these guides to being a good or surrendered wife are guides to accepting your status as a second-class citizen and accepting male domination: the man, we are reminded, is the master of the house, and the woman is not to question his decisions.

The Surrendered Wife and IPV

When one reads books like *The Surrendered Wife*, one quickly finds that the rhetoric is justified by a caveat about the "good husband." Women's concerns about giving up power are dismissed by suggesting that a good man will not take advantage of this structured power differential codified in the institution of marriage. And perhaps this is true. But there are several troubling problems with this approach.

The Surrendered Wife and the Master of the Bs

When men and women in America enter partnerships, they do so in the social landscape outlined in this chapter. Men are socialized to believe that masculinity means earning a good wage and being the master in the bedroom. As both the batterers and the partners of violent men confirm, when some men experience threats to their masculine identity, they engage in IPV. They slap, kick, punch, blacken eyes, break bones, bite, berate their partners with horrible names, and sometimes even rape their partners. When women enter these partnerships believing they are second-class citizens and believing that men should have total sexual freedom, that women should serve their man's every need, that they should put his needs above their own, then they remain vulnerable to these slaps, kicks, and blows that render them injured and sometimes kill them.

Accepting even a *portion* of this inequality leaves women at risk for abuse. Structured inequality, and the acceptance of it, creates a set of social arrangements that results in 4 million acts of IPV *reported* per year. Perhaps the most troubling part of this is the pattern—which has increased in the past decade or so, as evidenced by books like Laura Doyle's—of women encouraging other women to accept this form of oppression and second-class citizenship. Unfortunately, the statistics on IPV and the stories of battered women tell us that millions of women in the United States live as second-class citizens not only in the public sphere where they experience sexual harassment (MacKinnon 1991) and wage discrimination (Padavic and Reskin 2002) but also in the private sphere where they are subjected to millions of acts of violence, emotional abuse, and rape per year. In fact, Candy's story illustrates the dilemma that many women face: they fear harassment and violence in the public sphere—sexual harassment at work, men cat-calling them on the streets, men trying to pick them up in bars—and in some cases they accept oppression and abuse in the private sphere in order to avoid it in public:

When things were good, they were so good. Like I said, I was always secure with him. He might try to hit me and he might try to kill me, but nobody else was going to do it. Nobody else was going to talk bad to me or hurt me or talk bad about me. That just wasn't going to happen. I was secure in that sense with him. He was going to protect me from everybody else.

Candy, twentysomething white woman, North Carolina

Race, Class, and Gender Analysis

As we have argued elsewhere (Hattery 2001; Smith 2008), dominant ideologies, by definition, pervade the ideological landscape for all living in the United States, yet many individual actors, especially racial and ethnic minorities and the poor, may resist the dominant ideology or develop nonconforming ideologies (see Hattery 2001; Smith 2008; and Therborn 1980).

We would argue that acceptance of and resistance to dominant constructions of femininity vary across race and ethnicity and class groups. For example, the degree to which women adopt the culture of domesticity has varied. In fact, historically, white middle-class women have enlisted the labor of African American women and Latinas they have employed as domestics (Romero 1992; see Stockett 2009 for a fictionalized example) as "partners" in their quest for domestic success. For these women, who were working long hours for low wages, they had very little time or energy left to focus on their own homes or children. Furthermore, as many scholars have noted (Collins 1994; Hattery 2001; Romero 1992; Segura 1994), the opportunity to be a stay-at-home mother has eluded most women of color and poor whites, even during the 1950s and 1960s when this traditional family form dominated in the white middle-class community.

Some might look at the gap in marriage rates, especially between African American and white women, as further evidence for a belief that African American women are more likely to resist the cult of domesticity than are their white counterparts. However, based on interviews with both African American and white women, we argue that although marriage rates differ, and there are many explanations for this (see Burton 1990; Hattery and Smith 2007a; and Patterson 1995), *heterosexual partnering* did not vary. In other words, despite the fact that very few of the African American women we interviewed were legally married (only 10 percent were married) and almost all of the white women we interviewed were, there was no difference in the likelihood of being in a partnership or committed relationship; African American women were simply less likely to *marry* their intimate partners (Passel, Wang, and Taylor 2010). Additionally, Passel and colleagues note that there is only a small difference in the marriage rates of whites and Latinas, and that which does exist is primarily among undocumented Latinas who fear that a marriage might lead to deportation.

CONCLUSIONS

Intimate partner violence is a cause of great injury to many women and even becomes fatal for some. It is easy to argue that "bad" men batter and that "weak" women submit to it or will not leave. These explanations are compelling because they focus on individual explanations and because they suggest that as long as you marry a "good" man, you will be fine.

Synthesizing the arguments regarding dominant beliefs about masculinity with those regarding dominant beliefs about femininity leads to the conclusion that elements of ideologies of masculinity and elements of ideologies of femininity are mutually reinforcing, and together they work to maintain a system of gender oppression—an inequality regime (Acker 2006)—that leaves women vulnerable to IPV and lets men off the hook when it occurs. Thus, both systems will have to be unseated before we can expect to see a reduction in IPV. We will return to a much more in-depth discussion of this as well as a discussion of recommendations in the concluding chapter. We note here, however, that a more clear and precise understanding of these constructions of masculinity and their racial and ethnic variations will, if employed, lead to more culturally specific and effective prevention and intervention programs for men at risk for battering and for girls at risk for growing up and being forced to make choices that leave them vulnerable to IPV, and these will be articulated in the final chapter. In the next chapter, we turn to a discussion of the specific role that religion—which can be considered a generator of ideology—plays in IPV and child abuse; specifically, we examine the ways in which religious leaders often fail to intervene in IPV and child abuse cases and thus contribute to its perpetuation.

RECOMMENDED FILMS

Mona Lisa Smile (2003): This film, set in the 1950s, is an excellent example of the ways in which the cult of domesticity was taught deliberately to young women as a way to "keep them in their place."

NOTES

1. Although it is now a part of our colloquial speech, the original citation for "Boys will be boys" is from Sir Anthony Hope Hopkins. See, especially, "Boys will be boys. And even that wouldn't matter if only we could prevent girls from being girls." Anthony Hope (1863–1933), *Dolly Dialogues*, no. 16 (1894).

2. A recent article in the *New York Times* on "genital cutting" summarizes nicely the motive behind this practice, one that remains widespread in Africa and the Middle East: to keep women faithful. Celia W. Dugger, "Senegal Curbs a Bloody Rite for Girls and Women," *New York Times*, October 15, 2011.

BIBLIOGRAPHY

Acker, Joan. 2006. *Class Questions, Feminist Answers*. New York: Routledge.

Alan Guttmacher Institute. 2004. *U.S. Teenage Pregnancy Statistics: Overall Trends, Trends by Race and Ethnicity, and State-by-State Information*. New York: Alan Guttmacher Institute.

Alvarez, Lizette, and Deborah Sontag. 2008. "When Strains on Military Families Turn Deadly." *New York Times*, February 15.

Bianchi, Suzanne, John P. Robinson, and Melissa A. Milkie. 2007. *Changing Rhythms of American Family Life*. New York: Russell Sage Foundation.

Bombardieri, Marcella. 2005. "Summer's Remarks on Women Draws Fire." *Boston Globe*, January 19.

Browne, Angela. 1989. *When Battered Women Kill*. New York: Free Press.

Brownmiller, Susan. 1975. *Against Our Will: Men, Women, and Rape*. New York: Simon and Schuster.

Burton, Linda. 1990. "Teenage Childbearing as an Alternative Life-Course Strategy in Multi-generational Black Families." *Human Nature* 1: 58–81.

Chafetz, Janet Saltzman. 1974. *Masculine/Feminine or Human? An Overview of the Sociology of Sex Roles*. Itasca, IL: F. E. Peacock.

Collins, Patricia Hill. 1994. "Shifting the Center: Race, Class, and Feminist Theorizing About Motherhood." In *Mothering: Ideology, Experience, and Agency*, edited by E. Glenn, G. Chang, and L. Forcey, 45–66. New York: Routledge.

Connell, R. W. 1990. "An Iron Man: The Body and Some Contradictions of Hegemonic Masculinity." In *Sport, Men, and the Gender Order: Critical Feminist Perspectives*, edited by M. Messner and D. Sabo. Champaign, IL: Human Kinetics Books.

Connell, R. W., and James Messerschmdt. 2005. "Hegemonic Masculinity: Rethinking the Concept." *Gender and Society* 19: 829–859.

Coontz, Stephanie. 1992. *The Way We Never Were: American Families and the Nostalgia Trap*. New York: Basic Books.

_____. 1997. *The Way We Really Are: Coming to Terms with America's Changing Families*. New York: Basic Books.

Doyle, Laura. 2001. *The Surrendered Wife*. New York City: Fireside.

Engels, Friedrich. 1884. *The Origin of the Family, Private Property, and the State*. Introduction by Eleanor Leacock. New York: International Publishers.

Epstein, Cynthia. 2007. "Great Divides: The Cultural, Cognitive, and Social Bases of the Global Subordination of Women." *American Sociological Review* 72: 1–22.

Franchina, Joseph J., Richard M. Eisler, and Todd M. Moore. 2001. "Masculine Gender Role Stress and Intimate Abuse: Effects of Masculine Gender Relevance of Dating Situations and Female Threat on Men's Attributions and Affective Responses." *Psychology of Men and Masculinity* 2: 34–41.

Gelles, R. J. 1997. *Intimate Violence in Families*. Thousand Oaks, CA: Sage.

Hattery, Angela. 2001. *Women, Work, and Family: Balancing and Weaving*. Thousand Oaks, CA: Sage.

_____. 2008. *Intimate Partner Violence*. Lanham, MD: Rowman and Littlefield.

Hattery, Angela J., and Emily W. Kane. 1995. "Men's and Women's Perceptions of Non-consensual Sexual Intercourse." *Sex Roles* 33: 785–802.

Hattery, Angela J., and Earl Smith. 2007a. *African American Families*. Thousand Oaks, CA: Sage.

_____. 2007b. "Duke Lacrosse: An Exploration of Race, Class, Power, and Privilege." In vol. 2 of *Learning Culture Through Sports*. New York: Rowman and Littlefield.

Hays, Sharon. 1996. *The Cultural Contradictions of Motherhood*. New Haven: Yale University Press.

Hoge, C. W., C. A. Castro, S. C. Messer, D. McGurk, D. I. Cotting, and R. L. Koffman. 2004. "Combat Duty in Iraq and Afghanistan, Mental Health Problems, and Barriers to Care." *New England Journal of Medicine* 351: 13–22.

Kimmel, Michael. 2005. *Manhood in America*. New York: Oxford University Press.

Koss, M. P., L. A. Goodman, A. Browne, L. F. Fitzgerald, G. P. Keita, and N. F. Russo. 1994. *No Safe Haven: Male Violence Against Women at Home, at Work, and in the Community*. Washington, DC: American Psychological Association.

Kossoudji, Sherrie, and Laura J. Dresser. 1992. "Working Class Rosies: Women Industrial Workers During World War II." *Journal of Economic History* 51: 431–446.

Kristoff, Nicholas, and Sheryl WuDunn. 2009. *Half the Sky: Turning Oppression into Opportunity for Women Worldwide*. New York: Alfred A. Knopf.

Luker, Kristin. 1985. *Abortion and the Politics of Motherhood*. Berkeley and Los Angeles: University of California Press.

MacKinnon, Catharine. 1991. *Toward a Feminist Theory of the State*. Cambridge: Harvard University Press.

Majors, Richard, and Janet Bilson. 1992. *Cool Pose: The Dilemmas of African American Manhood in America*. New York: Lexington Books.

Mansley, Elizabeth. 2007. "Man Up: Exploring the Relationships Between Race, Social Class, Intimate Partner Violence, and the Construction of Masculinity." PhD diss., University of Delaware.

Massachusetts Institute of Technology. 1999. *A Study on the Status of Women Faculty in Science at MIT*. Boston: Massachusetts Institute of Technology.

Messner, Michael A. 2002. "Playing Center: The Triad of Violence in Men's Sports." In *Taking the Field: Women, Men, and Sports*, edited by M. A. Messner, 27–62. Minneapolis: University of Minnesota Press.

Padavic, Irene, and Barbara Reskin. 2002. *Women and Men at Work*. Thousand Oaks, CA: Pine Forge Press.

Parsons, Talcott. 1956. *Family, Socialization, and Interaction Process*. London: Routledge and Kegan Paul.

Parsons, Talcott, and Robert Bales. 1955. *Family, Socialization, and the Interaction Process*. Glencoe, IL: Free Press.

Passel, Jeffrey, Wendy Wang, and Paul Taylor. 2010. "Marrying Out: One-in-Seven New U.S. Marriages Is Interracial or Interethnic." PEW Research Center, June 4. http://pewsocialtrends.org.

Patterson, Orlando. 1995. Review of *The Bell Curve Wars*, edited by Steven Fraser. *USA Today* 124: 96.

———. 1999. *Rituals in Blood: Consequences of Slavery in Two American Centuries*. New York: Basic Civitas.

Rich, A. 1980. "Compulsory Heterosexuality and Lesbian Existence." *Signs* 5: 631–660.

Romero, Mary. 1992. *Maid in the U.S.A.* New York: Routledge.

Russell, D. 1990. *Rape in Marriage*. Bloomington: University of Indiana Press.

Sampson, Robert J. 1987. "Urban Black Violence: The Effect of Male Joblessness and Family Disruption." *American Journal of Sociology* 93: 348–382.

Sanday, Peggy Reeves. 1981. "The Socio-cultural Context of Rape: A Cross-cultural Study." *Journal of Social Issues* 37: 5–27.

———. 2007. *Fraternity Gang Rape*. 1990. Reprint, New York: New York University Press.

Segura, Denise A. 1994. "Working at Motherhood: Chicana and Mexican Immigrant Mothers and Employment." In *Mothering: Ideology, Experience, and Agency*, edited by E. Glenn, G. Chang, and L. Forcey, 45–66. New York: Routledge.

Smith, Earl. 2008. "African American Men and Intimate Partner Violence." *Journal of African American Studies* 12: 156–179.

———. 2009. *Race, Sport and the American Dream*. 2007. Reprint, Durham, NC: Carolina Academic Press.

Smith, Earl, and Angela Hattery. 2006. "Hey Stud: Race, Sex, and Sports." *Journal of Sexuality and Culture* 10.

Stockett, Kathryn. 2009. *The Help*. New York: Amy Einhorn Books.

Story, Louise. 2005. "Many Women at Elite Colleges Set Career Path to Motherhood." *New York Times*, September 20.

Summers, Lawrence. 2005. "Remarks at National Bureau of Economic Research Conference on Diversifying the Science and Engineering Workforce." Office of the President, Harvard University, Cambridge, MA.

Therborn, Göran. 1980. *The Ideology of Power and the Power of Ideology*. London: Verso.

Tjaden, Patricia, and Nancy Thoennes. 2000. *Full Report of the Prevalence, Incidence, and Consequences of Violence Against Women: Findings from the National Violence Against Women Survey*. Washington, DC: US Department of Justice

Veblen, Thorstein. 2008. *Theory of the Leisure Class*. New York: Oxford University Press.

Warshaw, R. 1988. *I Never Called It Rape: The MS Report on Recognizing, Fighting, and Surviving Date and Acquaintance Rape*. New York: Harper & Row.

Wilson, William J. 2009. *More than Just Race*. New York: W. W. Norton.

Wolf, N. 1992. *The Beauty Myth: How Images of Beauty Are Used Against Women*. New York: Anchor Books.

10 Religion and Family Violence

What is a good enough reason for divorce? Well, according to Rick Warren's Saddleback Church, divorce is permitted only in cases of adultery or abandonment—as these are the only cases permitted in the Bible—and never for abuse. As teaching pastor Tom Holladay explains, spousal abuse should be dealt with by temporary separation and church marriage counseling designed to bring about reconciliation between the couple. But to qualify for that separation, your spouse must be in the "habit of beating you regularly," and not be simply someone who "grabbed you once" (Joyce 2009).

OBJECTIVES

- To provide the reader with an overview of the role that religion has played in shaping family violence—especially child abuse and domestic violence
- To acquaint the reader with the specific texts and passages that institutionalized religions rely on for shaping appropriate gender roles and parent-child roles
- To explore the ways in which institutionalized religions have responded to family violence vis-à-vis texts and passages
- To examine the response that individual spiritual leaders have to victims that seek assistance
- To provide recommendations for transforming religion from an institution that directly and indirectly supports family violence to one that participates effectively in its eradication and prevention

KEY TERMS

religiosity
theory of secularization

INTRODUCTION

There has long been tension between religious institutions and the public, as well as public institutions including law enforcement, regarding matters of the family. Whereas we argued, in Chapter 2, that one of the barriers to intervening in family violence was the notion that it was "private," this is not so much the case for religious institutions, which have a long history and tradition of commenting on and otherwise being involved in the private matters of the family. One reason for this is the tensions that have always existed between religious institutions and the secular world. For example, one area of high tension is reproductive rights and technologies. In response to the ever-increasing ability of people to control their reproductive lives through scientific technologies that run the gamut from restricting pregnancy (birth control pills, IUDs) to increasing fertility (in vitro fertilization, egg donation), fundamentalist religions are organized around an ideology that prohibits the control of reproduction based on a belief that it is akin to "playing God," and religious leaders often preach on these issues, write pamphlets on these topics—Rick Warren's quote above is illustrative—and presumably incorporate these notions into couples' counseling. In this chapter we explore these tensions and the ways in which religious doctrine and practice have shaped all aspects of family violence, including prescriptions for gender roles and parent-child relationships that set the stage for family violence. We also examine the institutional responses to the phenomenon of family violence that arise when individuals seek help from priests, ministers, rabbis, and other religious leaders. We begin with a brief overview of the history of the tension between religious institutions and the secular world.

TENSIONS BETWEEN RELIGION AND THE SECULAR WORLD

A brief overview of the relationship between religion and the secular world is an important starting point for laying the groundwork for understanding one of the ways in which religion shapes family violence and especially the religious response to it.

For sociologists of religion, there is a great interest in the rate to which people in a given society are affiliated with particular religions. Sociological research on religion has revealed that both the content of religious beliefs (fundamentalism as compared to more liberal ideologies) as well as the importance of religion in an individual's life (religiosity) shape a variety of attitudes and behaviors, ranging from beliefs about interracial marriage to voting patterns. The Pew Forum on Religious Life gathers statistics—primarily from the census but also from other national surveys—and compiles these data as well as an analysis in convenient reports (http://religions.pew forum.org/reports). According to these data, in the United States nearly 80 percent of Americans report being affiliated with an institutionalized religion. As Figure 10.1 demonstrates, approximately half of all Americans identify as Protestant and nearly 25 percent as Catholic. This is not surprising given that the majority of Americans trace their origin back to Protestant and Catholic countries—including western Europe and Latin America.

▼ **Figure 10.1**
Major Religious Traditions in the United States

	Among all adults . . . %
Christian	78.4
Protestant.................................51.3	
Evangelical churches 26.3	
Mainline churches..............................18.1	
Historically black churches...................6.9	
Catholic....................................23.9	
Mormon.....................................1.7	
Jehovah's Witness 0.7	
Orthodox...................................0.6	
Greek Orthodox...............................<0.3	
Russian Orthodox.............................<0.3	
Other.......................................<0.3	
Other Christian 0.3	
Other Religions	4.7
Jewish 1.7	
Reform.....................................0.7	
Conservative................................0.5	
Orthodox...................................<0.3	
Other.......................................0.3	
Buddhist....................................0.7	
Zen Buddhist................................<0.3	
Theravada Buddhist ....<0.3	
Tibetan Buddhist..............................<0.3	
Other.......................................0.3	
Muslim*....................................0.6	
Sunni......................................0.3	
Shia.......................................<0.3	
Other.......................................<0.3	
Hindu 0.4	
Other world religions.........................<0.3	
Other faiths 1.2	
Unitarians and other liberal faiths 0.7	
New Age....................................0.4	
Native American religions...................<0.3	
Unaffiliated	16.1
Atheist.....................................1.6	
Agnostic....................................2.4	
Nothing in particular 12.1	
Secular unaffiliated..............................6.3	
Religious unaffiliated............................5.8	
Don't Know/Refused	0.8
	100

Due to rounding, figures may not add to 100 and nested figures may not add to the subtotal indicated.

Source: From "Muslim Americans: Middle Class and Mostly Mainstream," Pew Research Center, 2007.

The second question that sociologists of religion are interested in is the overall religiosity of people in different societies. **Religiosity** is a way of measuring both the frequency with which people attend church as well as the level of their belief in certain core religious principles. According to Brian Anderson:

> America boasts countless houses of worship. *U.S. News & World Report* recently noted that there are "more churches, synagogues, temples, and mosques per capita in the United States than in any other nation on Earth: one for about every 865 people." And those houses overflow with worshipers. A full 22 percent of America's 159 million Christians say they attend religious services more than once a week, and almost three quarters of Christians attend at least once or twice a month. "More people in the United States attend religious services on any given weekend than watch football—in all the stadiums, on high school football fields, college campuses, and all the television sets of the nation put together," says Catholic theologian Michael Novak. (2004, n.p.)

With regards to beliefs in core principles, Anderson, citing from the Pew Report, notes the following:

> America also appears in some ways to be getting more religious, not less. The Pew Research Center found that the number of Americans who "agree strongly" with three fundamental tenets of faith—belief in God, in Judgment Day, and in the importance of prayer—has risen by as much as ten points over the last four decades. Fifteen years ago, the Economist points out, two-fifths of American Protestants described themselves as "born again"—signaling a strong embrace of Christ as personal savior. The percentage has climbed to more than half. Born-again Christians now make up 39 percent of America's adult population. Further, four out of five Americans say they have "experienced God's presence or a spiritual force," and 46 percent maintain it happens to them often. "People are reaching out in all directions in their attempt to escape from the seen world to the unseen world," pollster George Gallup, Jr., tells U.S. News. "There is a deep desire for spiritual moorings—a hunger for God." (2004, n.p.)

Thus, as the rate of Americans who report no affiliation (just over 20 percent) has been steadily rising over the past two decades, simultaneously those who are affiliated appear to be more religious—attending church more frequently and a higher percentage expressing beliefs in core religious principles. This is a perplexing question for sociologists of religion and social commentators studying the trend toward secularization or the phenomenon that has been termed the *secularization thesis*.

Peter Berger (1999), one of the leading sociologists of religion who specializes in the question of secularization, summarizes the **theory of secularization** as the prediction among scholars that modernity and religion are inversely related. This inverse relationship between modernization and religion is created in large part by the rise in the acceptance of and even prioritizing of science. The creationism-evolution debate is an illustration of this process. As Americans began to accept the tenets of evolution, they simultaneously began to discard their belief in creationism, which for many fundamentalist Christians led to a liberalizing in their views, and the impact on already liberal Christians was a trend toward lower levels of religiosity and at the extreme the rejection of religion entirely. Thus, as a culture or society or nation becomes increasingly modern, the people in that culture or society or nation will become less religious. This theory was developed largely by observing the changing role of religion and the relationship between religion and secularity in Europe. In short, Berger argues that in Europe the theory of secularization paints an accurate portrayal of the pathways of both religion and secular life. Europe has demonstrated a critical and severe shift toward secularization in two key ways: the declining importance of religion to individual Europeans as well as the dismantling of state religions—which were common throughout all of western Europe across the entire second millennia (roughly 500–1900). For example, Anderson notes:

> Numbers drawn from the long-term European Values Study (EVS) and other research underscore the degree to which Europe has abandoned its Christian heritage. For one thing, the pews of Europe's churches are often empty. In France, only one in twenty people now attends a religious service every week, and the demographic skews to the aged. Only 15 percent of Italians attend weekly while roughly 30 percent of Germans still go to church at least once a month. Indifference is widespread. A mere 21 percent of Europeans hold religion to be "very important." In France, arguably the most secular of Europe's nations outside of the formerly Lutheran countries of northern Europe, the percentage is lower still, at slightly over 10 percent. As Cardinal Dionigi Tettamanzi, archbishop of Milan, lamented in the New York Times in October, "The parishes tell me that there are children who don't know how to make the sign of the cross." Only Europe's growing Muslim population seems to exhibit any religious fervor. True, few Europeans proclaim outright atheism, and a majority still call themselves Christians. But how many are Christian in anything but a nominal sense? Not only do Europeans not go to church very often; only about 40 percent believe in heaven and only half that percentage in hell. The concept of sin is vanishing from the European mind. Just 57 percent of Spaniards, 55 percent of Germans, 40 percent of French people, and approximately 30 percent of Swedes now believe in the existence of sin. (2004, n.p.)

While Europe is becoming increasingly secular, as noted above, the opposite appears to be happening in the United States. This is vexing for two reasons: the fact that the United States leads the world in terms of modernizing as well as the fact that the majority of Americans—at least for the short haul—continue to trace their ancestry to these same countries in western Europe. Thus, Berger (1999) argues that the secularization theory applies only to Europe and must be revised with regards to the rest of the world.

Berger (1999) argues further that the tension between religion and secularization has existed from the beginnings of the United States, and for centuries across Europe. Most recently, this tension is evident in Middle Eastern countries like Saudi Arabia and Iran that are facing struggles between secular governments and Islamic governments. Indeed, in several of these countries there are two rules of law in place, the more liberal secular law and the highly conservative sharia law. Although perhaps the cases presented in the Middle East are the most obvious, secularizing forces do exist in the United States. America's highly educated, often left-leaning elites are every bit as secular as the most disenchanted Europeans (Anderson 2004). Berger says of these elites:

> Its members are relatively thin on the ground, but they control the institutions that provide the "official" definitions of reality, notably the education system, the media of mass communication, and the higher reaches of the legal system. These elites have wrought secularizing changes in law and culture over the last several decades—using the courts to drive creche displays from public property and to end prayer or religious instruction of any kind in public schools, for example. However, they have yet to persuade the majority of Americans to embrace a secular worldview themselves. (1999, 10)

Though this "control" may be disputable at least in some contexts—recall how often President George W. Bush invoked religious language and principles in his formal speeches as well as in his more informal remarks—it is important because it may lead to tensions in family violence prevention and intervention. Specifically, if church leaders perceive that they are "losing ground" in the public sphere, they may also interpret attempts by law enforcement and the criminal justice to interfere in family violence—which occurs very clearly at the core of what we consider the "private" sphere—as further threats. As a result, they may be increasingly resistant to accepting advice or help when family violence erupts among their "flock."

TEXTS THAT ARE USED TO SUPPORT FAMILY VIOLENCE

As noted by noted sociologist of religion Peter Berger (1999) and in the social commentary of Brian Anderson (2004), it is not only the increase in religiosity that they observe in the United States but the rise in *evangelical Christianity* in the United States and conservative sects of the other major religions—especially Islam and Judaism—in other parts of the world that are the most perplexing. This rise in conservative religions is of paramount importance to our discussion here, as it is these traditions that also resist the modernizing of gender roles—which often is a key point of tension from which intimate partner violence arises (see Chapter 9). Here we examine the specific texts from each of the major holy books and specific religious principles from each of the major institutionalized religions that are used to endorse and reinforce both *traditional family roles* as well as violence against women and children.

Torah

According to the National Resource Center on Domestic Violence (2007), one of the major tenets of Jewish marriage is peace in the household, or *Shalom Bayit*. Accordingly, one of the common misperceptions is that intimate partner violence and child abuse do not occur in Jewish households. Yet there is no statistical evidence to suggest that Jewish women and children are any less likely to experience violence or that Jewish men are any less likely to perpetrate it (Tjaden and Thoennes 2000). Additionally, the National Resource Center on Domestic Violence suggests that the construction of *Shalom Bayit* as primarily the responsibility of wives may prevent or inhibit Jewish women from leaving battering relationships:

> Shalom Bayit may be a reason why many Jewish women stay in abusive relationships, in that a victim of domestic violence may be reluctant to seek help because she may feel she failed at her role to maintain the peace in her home; she may be fearful of bringing shanda, or shame, on her family and the community (Jewish Women International, 1996). Many people falsely believe that domestic violence does not exist in Jewish homes, and this myth reinforces the silence that allows domestic violence to continue. By bringing attention to the abusive relationship, the victim has not only exposed her imperfect marriage, but she has also exposed the vulnerabilities of her community and may be ostracized or resented for doing so. (2007, 1)

We can speculate that a similar process inhibits the disclosure of child abuse and the reluctance of families as well as rabbis from involving law enforcement and Child Protective Services in child abuse cases; to make child abuse "public" would be to expose a household that has failed to uphold *Shalom Bayit*.

Qur'an

According to the information compiled by the National Resource Center on Domestic Violence, there are passages in the Qur'an as well that have been used by husbands and spiritual advisers to justify domestic violence.

For Muslim men and women, the Qur'an is the primary source of their faith and practice. In Islam, the focus of marriage is encapsulated in the following verse of the Qur'an: " . . . they are a sort of garment for you and you are a sort of garment for them . . . " (2:188). Qur'anic verse 4:34 is often used to justify physical abuse against a wife if she does not submit to her partner's authority. It states: Men shall take full care of women with the bounties Allah has bestowed upon them, and what they may spend out of their possession; as Allah has eschewed each with certain qualities in relation to the other. And the righteous women are the truly devout ones, who guard the intimacy, which Allah has ordained to be guarded. As for those women whose ill-will you have reason to fear, admonish them [first]; then distance yourself in bed, and then tap them; but if they pay you heed, do not seek to harm them. Surely, Allah is indeed the Most High, the Greatest. (2007)

This verse may be interpreted by batterers not only to justify physical abuse against their wives, but also to support the belief that the role of men as maintainers and protectors of their wives implies unquestionable obedience to men. Many scholars, including Laleh Bakhtiar, who is the first Muslim woman to translate the Qur'an, however, have interpreted this translation as charging men with the responsibility of financially and physically protecting and caring for their wives and families. Others have noted that the role of "protector" is synonymous with someone who has the responsibility of safeguarding the interests of another, and not the imposition of authority. If a wife is deliberately unfaithful (short of adultery) to her husband, instructions are given on how to attempt to resolve this situation. It is the husband's responsibility to first talk to her and then refuse to share her bed. If this fails to resolve the issue, then, only as a last resort before seeking a divorce, a husband may "'tap' his wife in a symbolic effort to demonstrate his seriousness in the matter. . . . Many scholars of the Qur'an have debated over the appropriate translation of the word 'tap' as the original Arabic word carries several different meanings. . . . In some texts, it is translated as 'hit' or 'strike'; however, many scholars believe that this is an incorrect translation of the original Arabic word, based on the Prophet's lifelong abhorrence of hitting women" (National Resource Center on Domestic Violence 2007, 1–2).

Bible

Turning to Christianity, the dominant religion in the United States, we also see many passages that have been used to justify abusive behavior, of both women and children. Again, quoting in its entirety from the National Resource Center on Domestic Violence:

FAMILY VIOLENCE IN *A THOUSAND SPLENDID SUNS*

Afghani novelist Khalid Hosseini published *A Thousand Splendid Suns* in 2007. This novel, the sequel to his award-winning novel *The Kite Runner*, tells the harrowing story of Mariam and Laila, the two wives of the terribly abusive Rasheed. Set in Kabul, the novel spans the period of the Soviet invasion of Afghanistan, through the reclamation of the country by the Taliban. Mariam is Rasheed's first wife, and Laila is his second, significantly younger, wife. Both women become wives to Rasheed because they are orphaned and have no means to take care of themselves. In the scene that follows, Mariam and Laila are attempting to flee both their abusive husband, Rasheed, and indeed the oppressive Taliban regime. They are arrested after being caught outdoors without the chaperone of a male relative.

"What does it matter to you to let a mere two women go? What's the harm in releasing us? We are not criminals."

"I can't" [says the officer who sends them back].

"I beg you, please."

"It's a matter of qanoon, hamshira, a matter of law. . . . It is my responsibility, you see, to maintain order."

In spite of her distraught state, Laila almost laughed. She was stunned that he'd used that word in the face of all that the Mujahideen factions had done—the murders, the lootings, the rapes, the tortures, the executions, the bombings. . . .

"If you send us back," she said instead, "there is no saying what he will do to us."

She could see the effort it took him to keep his eyes from shifting. "What a man does in his own home is his business."

"What about the law then, Officer Rahman?" Tears of rage stung her eyes. "Will you be there to maintain order?"

"As a matter of policy, we do not interfere with private family matters, hamshira."

"Of course you don't. When it benefits the man. And isn't this a 'private family matter,' as you say? Isn't it?"

Similar interpretations have been given to Biblical texts that also focus on *gender roles within heterosexual marriages*. Traditionally, Christian teaching about the roles of husbands and wives within a marriage rely heavily on Ephesians 5:21–33 (Fortune, 1991). Nine of the twelve verses discuss the responsibility of a husband to his wife. The remaining three verses, when taken in isolation, may be interpreted to imply that the husband has absolute authority over the family and this authority cannot be questioned, and that wives, in turn, must demonstrate absolute obedience and summarily submit to abuse from their husbands:

Wives submit to your husbands as to the Lord. For the husband is the head of the wife as Christ is the head of the Church, his body, of which he is the Savior. Now as the Church submits to Christ, so also the wives should submit to their husbands in everything. (Ephesians 5:22–24 in Fortune, 1991). (National Resource Center on Domestic Violence, 2007, 3 [emphasis added])

We note here that, as with interpretations made by Judaic scholars as well as by Islamic scholars, there is widespread agreement that all of the texts and passages we have identified (based on their identification by the National Resource Center on Domestic Violence) are subject to interpretation and that there are key words, such as *tap* in the Qur'an, that may be interpreted by some scholars as "strike or hit" and others as something even less than a "tap." Although it is important that we recognized these distinctions in terms of the actual justification (or not) by the three most influential institutionalized religions, we must also note that the average Christian, Jew, or Muslim is not educated in these distinctions. Furthermore, based on anecdotal evidence—our own experiences in a variety of church settings, the beliefs many of our students hold, and the experiences a dozen female seminary students shared with us as part of another project—we suggest that many of the spiritual leaders (pastors, rabbis, or imans) serving "on the ground" in literally millions of local churches and temples are not trained in the ancient languages and semantics necessary to make these distinctions as well, but many preach these verses in ways that reinforce traditional gender roles for their congregants. Thus, it seems clear that the likelihood that individuals who are abusive themselves or who in their capacity as spiritual advisers are counseling members of an abusive family may apply these passages "as is" and thus reinforce the notion that religious beliefs support and even dictate inequality in marital and parenting roles is high. Furthermore, these passages may all be extended and interpreted such as to suggest that one of the burdens and responsibilities of husbands is to discipline their wives and children—occasionally with physical abuse—in order to "train" them to be morally upstanding.

DIVORCE

Finally, the issue of divorce is an important barrier to leaving abusive homes for highly religious women. In all three of the major world religions we have been discussing, marriage is a lifelong, sacred commitment among husband, wife, and God or Allah. Some women may feel intense pressure, and they may be pressured by spiritual advisers, to remain in marriages despite the presence of abuse. In addition to the pressure that women may feel or self-impose, their husbands may also use religious ideologies of divorce and the sin of breaking the marriage bond to force their victims to stay in violent marriages. It is also important to realize that for many religious women, especially those who belong to marginalized religions—Jews in the South, Muslims in most of America—and for Christian women who live in the "Bible Belt," the congregation or temple to which they belong may provide their primary community of friends and support. Thus, a battered woman considering the possibility of divorce as a mechanism to end the violence[1] may realize that to separate from her husband will likely sever her relationship with her entire faith community. For example, in a recent study of violence among Muslim American women, participants indicated a reluctance to divorce—and many women lived with violence for years before seeking a divorce—precisely because they feared losing their spiritual community or being assigned a maligned status within a community that defines marriage as central to the spiritual life of both the individual and the community (Hassouneh-Phillips 2001).

INDIVIDUAL RESPONSES TO
FAMILY VIOLENCE BY SPIRITUAL ADVISERS

As stated above, there is a great deal of variability in the amount of formal training that individual religious "professionals"—ministers, priests, pastors, rabbis, and imans—receive. For example, though all Catholic priests must attend seminary, and though many Christian ministers do as well, there is no requirement that ministers in many of the Protestant denominations attend formal seminary before they "hang out their shingle" and open up a church. This is particularly the case in denominations that are less centralized. For example, perusing the job listings posted by the Southern Baptist Convention revealed that the formal requirements for the position of "pastor" varied and were not necessarily linked to education, though ordination as a minister was required. For example, in most Protestant churches, ordination to the pastoral office is the rite by which their various churches:

- recognize and confirm that an individual has been called by God to ministry
- acknowledge that the individual has gone through a period of discernment and training related to this call
- authorize that individual to take on the office of ministry

Additionally, the degree to which spiritual leaders receive any training with regards to family violence is even more variable. Thus, though the "official" position of all institutionalized religions forbids violence in families, the vast majority who are ministering to their religious communities are not necessarily educated about issues of family violence, and thus when family violence is exposed to a spiritual leader, his response is likely to be shaped by his own personal experiences and not as a representative of his institutionalized religion. We remind the reader that although some religious organizations have recently allowed the ordination of women, the vast majority—including *all* of the Catholic priests and Muslim imans—are men. Additionally, some denominations, most notably Roman Catholicism, require priests to be celibate and never marry. Thus, one critique of the Catholic Church resides in the fact that priests are often called to engage in counseling for engaged couples, married couples, and parents struggling with raising children, yet they have absolutely no personal experience with these relationships on which to draw.

Unfortunately, the majority of spiritual advisers are not well trained to deal with family violence, and in some cases the religious leader is himself the perpetrator of violence.

BOX 10.1   MARLEEN

Domestic Violence Within the Church: The Ugly Truth
By Chuck Colson, BreakPoint, *April 20, 2009*

A woman I'll call "Marleen" went to her pastor for help. "My husband is abusing me," she told him. "Last week he knocked me down and kicked me. He broke one of my ribs."

Marleen's pastor was sympathetic. He prayed with Marleen—and then he sent her home. "Try to be more submissive," he advised. "After all, your husband is your spiritual head."

Two weeks later, Marleen was dead—killed by an abusive husband. Her church could not believe it. Marleen's husband was a Sunday school teacher and a deacon. How could he have done such a thing?

Tragically, studies reveal that spousal abuse is just as common within the evangelical churches as anywhere else. This means that about 25 percent of Christian homes witness abuse of some kind. These numbers may shock you—and they certainly shocked me—so you may be wondering if the studies were done by secular researchers hostile to the church. I can assure you, sadly, they were not.

Denise George, a gifted writer and the wife of theologian Timothy George, has published a new book called *What Women Wish Pastors Knew*. "Spouse abuse shocks us," George writes. "We just cannot believe that a church deacon or member goes home after worship . . . and beats his wife." Tragically, however, George notes, some of these men justify their violence "by citing biblical passages."

Well, obviously they're misinterpreting Scripture. In Ephesians 5:22, husbands are told to love their wives as Christ loved the church; beating wives black-and-blue hardly constitutes Christian love. First Peter tells husbands to live with their wives considerately. And the Bible makes it clear that the church has no business closing its eyes to violent men. In 1 Timothy 3:3, the church is told that when it comes to choosing leaders, they must find men who are "not violent but gentle," sober, and temperate.

The amount of domestic abuse in Christian homes is horrifying, and the church ought to be doing something about it—not leaving the problem to secular agencies. But this is one mission field where the church is largely missing in action. And sometimes pastors, albeit with good intentions, do more harm than good.

George sites a survey in which nearly 6,000 pastors were asked how they would counsel women who came to them for help with domestic violence. Twenty-six percent would

---

BOX 10.1   MARLEEN *continued*

---

counsel them the same way Marleen's pastor did: to continue to "submit" to her husband, no matter what. Twenty-five percent told wives the abuse was their own fault—for failing to submit in the first place. Astonishingly, 50 percent said women should be willing to "tolerate some level of violence" because it is better than divorce.

The findings of this survey are shocking in and of themselves, but further raise a serious concern: that in the majority of cases when a spiritual advisor is presented with a victim of domestic violence he contributes to the abuse by sending the woman home with instructions to "be a better wife" and pray that the abuse will stop. Advice like this, George warns, often puts women "in grave danger"—and in some cases, can be a death warrant.

Pastors need to acknowledge that domestic abuse in the church is a problem, and learn how to counsel women wisely.

Stay tuned for more on this subject—one the church has not said enough about.

Obviously, Christians must uphold the sanctity of marriage. But we should never ignore the dangers of violent spouses—men who use the Bible to justify abusing, and even killing, their wives.

SOURCE: http://www.crosswalk.com/marriage/11602500/.

Responses like that of Marleen's pastor pit domestic violence advocates and religious leaders against one another. Religious leaders express the fear that secular approaches to domestic violence will result in divorce—which violates the lifelong contract that marriage is believed to be by all organized religions. Diametrically opposed are domestic violence advocates and educators who argue that no one should be subjected to abuse, no level of abuse should be tolerated, and advising a woman to "go home and be a better wife" is nothing more than victim blaming that exacerbates the problems of family violence (National Resource Center on Domestic Violence 2007).

INSTITUTIONAL RESPONSES
IN GENERAL TO FAMILY VIOLENCE

For a variety of reasons, including the tragedy illustrated above, there have been some attempts by organized religions to provide information about family violence—especially battering—and suggest some "best practices" for dealing with family violence when it is presented to an individual spiritual adviser. For example, the United States Conference of Catholic Bishops developed a website to provide advice to parish priests who are presented with victims of domestic violence (http://www.usccb.org/laity/help.shtml).

The National Resource Center on Domestic Violence makes it clear that when counseling victims of domestic violence who are deeply faithful and embedded in a faith community, the counseling will be far more effective in achieving desirable outcomes if the woman's faith is respected and utilized in the counseling. Thus, collaborations between domestic violence advocates and spiritual leaders are critical to addressing domestic violence in faith communities (National Resource Center on Domestic Violence 2007).

Unfortunately, not only have the institutionalized responses of organized religions fallen short, but in many cases the organizations themselves have chosen to turn a blind eye to violence, especially when the perpetrators are members of the faith community and even leaders in the faith community (see the previous text box). Why has the primary response of religions to family violence been so unsatisfying? Feminist theorists suggest that this is an expected outcome because at the base of it, all spiritual leaders—despite, according to various religious beliefs, being imbued with spiritual power—are men. As men, they live in a cultural landscape of patriarchy and male privilege. Even if some of these beliefs and practices diminished when they entered their spiritual vocation, they grew up and lived, usually at least for some years as adult men, in a culture that affords men the privilege to treat women and children as objects for *their use* and treats violence against women and children as unimportant and often renders the experiences of the victims invisible. In addition, as we have argued elsewhere (Hattery and Smith 2007), institutions that are sex segregated create a culture that elevates male privilege to a status that is untouchable and reduces women (and children) to the point of having no status at all. As noted, not only are all of the major world religions male dominated, but they also, to varying degrees, can be characterized as sex segregated. Catholicism and Islam are perhaps the extreme cases—Catholic priests live in sex-segregated communities, women are not allowed to hold any positions of power, and priests are believed to be extensions of Jesus himself, and in the case of Islam and conservative Jewish temples, even worship is sex segregated—while other Christian denominations and liberal Jewish temples remain highly sex segregated at least at the level of leadership and decision making. When women are excluded from having a place at the table and contributing to discussions and decisions, it is no wonder that "women's issues"—including child health and safety—are absent from the debate. And when cases of abuse are leveled against spiritual leaders, the absence of women at the table certainly shapes the response, and as we shall see in the case of the Catholic Church sex scandal, the official responses generally reinforce the privilege of men and render the allegations invisible, unsubstantiated, or unimportant.

This is exactly the motive behind a group of African American women who founded the Black Church and Domestic Violence Institute. The church has always been an important social site for African Americans, and today most African American women report belonging to a church and indicate that it is an important part of their lives (Lincoln and Mamiya 1990). But the church's response to domestic violence was minimal. Thus, the Black Church and Domestic Violence Institute fills an important niche in fighting domestic violence in the African American community. By providing training, annual conferences, and a multitude of resources that can help other spiritual leaders and congregations address the issue of domestic violence in their communities, the Black Church and Domestic Violence Institute is an example of both empowering women and transformation. We encourage the reader to visit their website, http://www.bcdvi.org/index.htm. Please see the resource section for links to other organizations pursuing similar goals.

WHAT HAPPENS WHEN THE PASTOR IS THE BATTERER?

One of the problems facing many tightly knit communities arises when men in positions of power are abusive to their wives or children or both. There are countless stories told of women abused by police officers who cannot call the police for fear they will not be believed or Native women living on Indian reservations whose abusive husbands are part of the families that govern life on the reservation (Snyder-Joy 1995).

A similar situation arises in faith communities when the pastor or any member of the church or temple leadership is the perpetrator of family violence. Obviously, when anyone in a position of power is abusive, his victims are more likely to languish in silence simply because his position is an enormous barrier to revealing the truth. Furthermore, in cases such as these, we can assume that the pastor—who is perpetrating violence—is unable to provide assistance to other victims who seek his help because of the limitations of his own experience as an abuser. This is yet another way in which religion and family violence intersect at both the individual level (the batterer and his wife) and the structural level (the inability of a victim to find assistance in her house of worship). These cases highlight the importance of groups such as the Black Church and Domestic Violence Institute, discussed above.

CHILD ABUSE:
THE SEX SCANDAL IN THE CATHOLIC CHURCH

Perhaps the most troubling case of the intersection of religion and family violence comes from the sex abuse scandal that has rocked the Catholic Church. Certainly, this case is devastating for each individual victim, but perhaps what is most troubling is the sheer enormity of the scandal—thousands of victims on at least three continents—and the *institutionalized* role of the church in covering up the abuse and thus allowing it to continue.

In short, though accusations of sexual abuse of children by priests have been around for decades, the sex abuse scandal in the Catholic Church exploded in early 2002 when hundreds of victims of Boston-area priests filed lawsuits against both the Catholic Church and Cardinal Bernard Law. Several individual priests, including Father Geoghan, were tried in criminal court and given lengthy prison sentences. In February 2002 Geoghan was sentenced to ten years in prison for molesting a ten-year-old boy.[2] More than 150 victims had come forward in his case. Additionally, these victims together filed civil lawsuits seeking monetary compensation, thus beginning the process of bankrupting the Catholic Church. Not long after the cases in Boston, several hundred victims successfully sued the Los Angeles Diocese, leading to convictions, monetary settlements, resignations, and the continued drain on the coffers of the Catholic Church. During the second half of the 2000s, the crisis erupted in Europe, with thousands of victims and hundreds of perpetrators being identified in examinations of seminaries and boarding schools throughout the British Isles. Most recently, cases have emerged in other European countries, including Portugal, and across Latin America.

Critical to understanding the sex scandal in the Catholic Church is understanding that the bishops in the United States as well as the highest-ranking papal administrators in Rome knew about sex abuse allegations that were made as early as the 1950s, 1960s, and 1970s. The official response to the allegations was to remind the victims that to make such an allegation publicly would lead to their immediate excommunication (recall that fear of separation from the faith community is a key barrier for battered women as well) and the removal of the accused to lower-profile positions. Often priests who had been accused of sexual abuse were moved from large parishes in cities and urban and suburban areas to small rural parishes. The assumption was that removing a priest to a small rural parish would limit the number of potential "whistle-blowers" and essentially render the priest's behavior "out of sight and out of mind" for his supervisors, the bishops. In fact, as occurred over and over across dioceses in the United States, Europe, and Latin America, the removal of predatory, pedophile priests simply led to more and more victims who were simply dispersed across a wider geography. In addition to putting hundreds of new children at risk for abuse, the lack of accountability sent the message to the abuser that his behavior was not of grave concern and he was free to continue abusing.

Now that these cases have begun to come to light, there have been some statements made by the pope, Benedict VI, but there has been relatively little "activity" on the matter. What does continue are hundreds of victims who are seeking monetary damages in civil law suits. The question becomes how much it will have to pay out of its coffers before the church is willing to take a *proactive* approach to abuse prevention, to investigating *all* allegations and to holding abusers accountable, rather than hiding them in less populous parishes. Curbing this type of systematic abuse would go along way toward keeping our children safe.

BOX 10.2	MARYETTA DUSSOURD

A Revered Guest; A Family Left in Shreds
By Matt Carroll, Globe Staff, January 6, 2002

Two decades later, Maryetta Dussourd remains overwhelmed by the guilt of it, how she saw the affable parish priest as such a strong role model for the seven boys she was raising that she unwittingly welcomed a sexual predator into her home.

Whatever the church knew about the Rev. John J. Geoghan in the late 1970s, Dussourd knew only that he was eager to help her with her three sons and her niece Diane's four sons who were living with her family in a small Jamaica Plain apartment.

For nearly two years, Geoghan came by to help almost nightly, always clad in his Roman collar. For the longest time, the children were terrified about the abuse, but said nothing: Geoghan fondled them in their bedrooms, sometimes as he whispered bedtime prayers. The oldest was 12, the youngest 4.

She never suspected, and the guilt at times is all-consuming.

"It was my fault, my fault," she said, as she cried on her couch. "I was responsible for my children and Diane's children. It was me who loved him, who brought him into the house, it was me."

She still struggles to come to grips with Geoghan's betrayal. She weeps as she talks about her nephews, whom she has not seen for years because she cannot bear to face them. About how it damaged her marriage, which failed, after seven children and nearly 25 years. About how one of her victimized sons is homeless, lives out of a car, and has attempted suicide.

Once a devout Catholic, she stopped attending Mass long ago because she feels the church betrayed her and the children.

It began so differently. When she met Geoghan, about 1977, she said her life revolved around family and faith. Each week, she attended prayer meetings at three churches, including St. Andrew's in Jamaica Plain, where Geoghan was assigned.

She took to Geoghan right away. "He looked like a little holy altar boy," she said. Dussourd was proud and excited as Geoghan became close to her family, a dream fulfilled for such a religious family. He visited for the next two to three years.

Dussourd worked hard to please him. Geoghan mentioned that his uncle—a monsignor—had taken away his teddy bear when he was growing up. So for his birthday, she gave him a little blue teddy bear. He was delighted.

Then the children told their aunt, Margaret Gallant, they had been abused, and Gallant told Dussourd. She was stunned. Not Father Geoghan, who had blessed the innocent heads of her children at night. It couldn't be true. But Geoghan admitted it to a pastor.

Her husband, a Baptist, was incensed. Before the couple married, he had to agree to allow the children to be raised Catholic. "He wanted to bolt up on to the altar and kill the guy," said Dussourd.

continues

BOX 10.2   MARYETTA DUSSOURD *continued*

For weeks, she wept constantly and wouldn't leave her apartment. She found little help, or solace, from friends or the church. Parishioners shunned her, accusing her of causing scandal. Church officials urged her to be quiet, for the sake of her children—and Geoghan's elderly mother. Don't sue, they warned her, because no one will believe you.

But she did sue, finally, in 1997, and the church settled under terms that remain secret. But for Dussourd, now 57, that was no victory. "Everything you have taught your child about God and safety and trust—it is all destroyed," she said.

Fr. Geoghan leaving court as a convicted sex offender. He was murdered while in protective custody in a Massachusetts prison serving a ten-year prison.

To read more and to follow the stories of other victims, the accused priests, and the diocesan response, the Boston Globe has an excellent interactive website with stories, legal documents and much more.

SOURCE: http://www.boston.com/globe/spotlight/abuse/stories/010602_dussourd_spotlight.htm.

BOX 10.3   DONALD MILLER

Sexual Abuse by Clergy in *Doubt*

It's 1964, St. Nicholas in the Bronx. A charismatic priest, Father Flynn, is trying to up-end the schools' strict customs, which have long been fiercely guarded by Sister Aloysius Beauvier, the iron-gloved Principal who believes in the power of fear and discipline. The winds of political change are sweeping through the community, and indeed, the school has just accepted its first black student, Donald Miller. But when Sister James, a hopeful innocent, shares with Sister Aloysius her guilt-inducing suspicion that Father Flynn is paying too much personal attention to Donald, Sister Aloysius sets off on a personal crusade to unearth the truth and to expunge Flynn from the school. Now, without a shard of proof besides her moral certainty, Sister Aloysius locks into a battle of wills with Father Flynn which threatens to tear apart the community with irrevocable consequences.

SOURCE: Plot summary provided by IMDb.

RECOMMENDATIONS FOR TRANSFORMATION

Much of this chapter has focused on the role that religion—religious beliefs, the attitudes of spiritual advisers, and the response by the administrators of institutionalized religion—plays in various types of family abuse. It should be clear that although there have been some good efforts at understanding and mitigating the role that religion plays in perpetuating family violence, there is much work to be done. The Catholic Church, which has suffered a serious and expansive scandal, has a long way to go to "clean up its own house" before Catholic clergy will be entrusted with caring for the victims in their parishes. There is little that can be done to force the type of systemic change that is necessary other than what is already taking place: protests and "boycotts" by Catholics, negative publicity, and expensive lawsuits. Second, clergy and religious leaders need to be trained on issues of domestic violence and child abuse so that they can offer a response and the support that helps the victims rather than revictimizes them. This is an area in which there is much room for transformation. If religious leaders at the top levels are willing to collaborate with abuse advocates to develop programs that can be used to educate and train clergy who are "on the ground" and provide them with the "best practices" for preventing and interrupting domestic violence and child abuse, then the potential to save victims from the horrors of abuse is great. The work of the United Church of Christ (UCC) provides a fine example. The UCC has researched and developed a "safe book" that can be distributed to high-level leaders as well as everyday clergy. This safe book provides information on abuse as well as the best practices for prevention and interruption. We are highly encouraged by this type of program and hope that it will be widely disseminated and utilized. The book can be downloaded at http://www.ucc.org/ministers/safe/safebook.pdf.

CONCLUSIONS

In this chapter we have set out to familiarize the reader with three important concepts:

1. the antagonistic relationship between the secular world and the religious world with special attention on how this impedes an appropriate response to family violence
2. the religious texts and ideologies for the three primary world religions that are frequently cited by batterers to justify their behavior and cited by spiritual leaders when they inappropriately counsel victims to stay in violent relationships
3. the ways in which systemic abuse by religious institutions, such as the Catholic Church sex scandal, reinforces male power and privilege and allows the abuse of women and children to be perpetuated

As we noted throughout the chapter, there is no religion that advocates violence; indeed, violence is considered to be the ultimate betrayal of trust by all of the major world religions. Although religious scholars recognize the translation problems that lead to texts that *seem* to support violence but are in fact misinterpretations of the original language, the typical priest or minister or rabbi or iman may have little access to this knowledge and information, and thus he, like the members of his congregation, is likely to absorb and perpetuate the false belief that religion dictates unequal gender roles that privilege men and require the absolute submission of wives. The power of believing in this ideology even a little bit is that it often provides a justification for battering and leaves the spiritual adviser advocating for women to "go home and be more submissive" rather than leave and even divorce an abusive husband.

Regarding the institutional level, we argued that religions are sex-segregated institutions, and this quality results in women's issues—especially child abuse and domestic violence—being rendered unimportant and even invisible. This problem is further exacerbated by the fact that among the ranks of religious leaders are men who are themselves involved in some of the worst abuse imaginable—both married clergy who batter their wives and Catholic priests who are involved in child sexual abuse. Some individual priests have molested and abused hundreds of young children. We argue, as several vocal Catholic women theologians (we note the work of Sister Elizabeth A. Johnson, professor at Fordham University, and author of *Quest for the Living God: Mapping Frontiers in the Theology of God*) have suggested, that until religions open up their leadership to women and to feminist ideals of equality, change is unlikely to occur. We applaud the victims who have had the courage to stand up and speak, for it may very well be their expensive lawsuits that eventually force transformation among institutionalized religion—especially Catholicism. We also highlighted the work of the Black Church and Domestic Violence Institute and the "safe book" developed by the United Church of Christ. The mere existence of these programs brings attention to the problems we have highlighted, and we are optimistic that they will lead to transformations at the local and regional level or within specific denominations that will improve the situation when victims—typically battered women—approach their spiritual advisers for help. We devote the next chapter to the unique case presented by homosexual families.

RESOURCES

Religion Link, "the only religion story idea and source list resource by journalists, for journalists. We're a non-partisan service of Religion Newswriters" (http://www.religionlink.com/), provides the following resources for religiously based organizations—organized by specific religions—that are working to combat issues of domestic violence and other forms of family violence.

Christian

Peace and Safety in the Christian Home is a coalition of academics, professionals, clergy, and laypeople alarmed by domestic violence in the Christian home. Its 2007 conference, "Setting the Captives Free: A Christian Theology for Domestic Violence," took place in Portland, Oregon. Read a report on its 2006 conference, "Domestic Abuse in the Church? Really!" Contact cofounder and president Catherine Clark Kroeger, an associate professor at Gordon-Conwell Theological Seminary in Massachusetts, at 508-896-3518 or catherine@peaceandsafety.com.

The Task Force to Stop Abuse Against Women was formed in 1997 by members of the international World Evangelical Fellowship to educate evangelical clergy and to reduce domestic violence. Contact chairwoman Winnie Bartel in Shafter, California, at 661-746-4748 or wit270@lightspeed.net.

The Black Church and Domestic Violence Institute trains clergy in the black church to recognize and respond to domestic violence. It is located in Atlanta. Contact the Reveren Aubra Love, founding executive director, at 770-909-0715.

Church of Jesus Christ of Latter-Day Saints

See a February 23, 2007, article about a program from the Church of Jesus Christ of Latter-day Saints to help victims of domestic violence. It is posted on the church's website.

Jewish

The Awareness Center is the Jewish Coalition Against Sexual Abuse/Assault, an international organization that addresses sexual violence in Jewish communities. It has a certification program for rabbis interested in working with victims of sexual violence. It is based in Baltimore. Contact executive director Vicki Polin at 443-857-5560 or info@theawarenesscenter.org.

Jewish Women International is an advocacy group based in Washington, DC, that promotes safe home environments for Jewish women and girls. In March 2007 the organization held its third annual international conference on domestic violence in the Jewish community. Contact Lori Weinstein, executive director, via Alix Fried, at 800-343-2823.

Muslim

The Muslim Women's League is a nonprofit organization that works to improve the status of women in the American Muslim community. Part of its mission is to create awareness about domestic violence within the American Muslim community. It is based in Los Angeles. Contact spokesperson and past president Dr. Laila Al-Marayati at 626-358-0335 or lalmara@aol.com.

The Peaceful Families Project produces workshops nationwide on domestic violence from a Muslim perspective. The organization is based in Great Falls, Virginia. Contact Farida Hakim at faridahakim@hotmail.com.

Multifaith

The FaithTrust Institute of Seattle, formerly the Center for Prevention of Sexual and Domestic Violence, is an interfaith organization that works to prevent domestic abuse in the Islamic, Buddhist, Asian and Pacific Islander, Jewish, Latino, black, Anglo, indigenous, Catholic, and Protestant communities. It is sponsoring the National Declaration by Religious and Spiritual Leaders to Address Violence Against Women, a petition that has attracted almost two thousand signatories from the spectrum of religious faiths. Contact executive director Kathryn Jans at 877-860-2255 or info@faithtrustinstitute.org.

Sakhi for South Asian Women is a community-based organization in the New York metropolitan area committed to ending violence against women of South Asian origin. Contact executive director Purvi Shah at 212-714-9153, ext.101, or purvi.shah@sakhi.org.

NOTES

1. As we note in the very first chapter of the book, the greatest risk for domestic violence homicide is when the relationship ends—through a breakup or divorce. Recall the murder of Yeardley Love, the University of Virginia lacrosse player who was murdered by her ex-boyfriend soon after she ended their relationship.

2. On August 23, 2003, only eighteen months into his prison sentence, Father Geoghan was murdered by another inmate.

BIBLIOGRAPHY

Anderson, B. C. 2004. "Secular Europe, Religious America." *CBS moneywatch.com.*

Berger, P. 1999. "The Desecularization of the World: A Global Overview." In *The Desecularization of the World: Resurgent Religion and World Politics*, edited by P. Berger, 1–18. Washington, DC: Ethics and Public Policy Center.

Hassouneh-Phillips, D. 2001. "Marriage Is Half Faith, the Rest Is Fear of Allah: Marriage and Spousal Abuse Among American Muslims." *Violence Against Women* 7, no. 8: 927–946.

Hattery, A., and E. Smith. 2007. "Duke Lacrosse: An Exploration of Race, Class, Power, and Privilege." In vol. 2 of *Learning Culture Through Sports*, ed. S. S. Prettyman and B. Lampman. New York: Rowman and Littlefield.

Johnson, E. A. 2011. *Quest for the Living God: Mapping Frontiers in the Theology of God.* New York: Continuum Press.

Joyce, K., prod. 2009. "Biblical Battered Wife Syndrome: Christian Women and Domestic Violence." Retrieved from Biblical Battered Wife Syndrome: Christian Women and Domestic Violence, http://www.religiondispatches.org/archive/1007/biblical _battered_wife_syndrome%3A_christian_women_and_domestic_violence.

Lincoln, E. C., and L. H. Mamiya. 1990. *The Black Church in the African American Experience.* Durham: Duke University Press.

National Resource Center on Domestic Violence. 2007. *Religion and Domestic Violence.* Harrisburg: Pennsylvania Coalition Against Domestic Violence.

Snyder-Joy, Z. K., ed. 1995. *Self-Determination and American Indian Justice: Tribal Versus Federal Jurisdiction on Indian Lands.* Albany: State University of New York Press.

Tjaden, P., and N. Thoennes. 2000. *Full Report of the Prevalence, Incidence, and Consequences of Violence Against Women: Findings from the National Violence Against Women Survey.* Washington, DC: US Department of Justice.

11 Violence in Same-Sex Couple Families

We began this book by making it very clear that we did not intend to write a book about family violence in which we segregated different populations by race or gender but rather incorporated discussions of racial or gender variations inside of each topic. We feel strongly that this intersectional approach to the study of family violence—and most other social phenomenon—is appropriate for a variety of reasons. The intersectional approach focuses on the fundamental "sameness" rather than the "differences" among us, the intersectional approach allows us to see the commonalities yet not render variations invisible, and last, as we have argued elsewhere, the intersectional theory on which this perspective is derived has proven to be quite powerful in explaining the ways in which experiences with family violence, societal responses to family violence, and patterns of family violence vary by race and ethnicity, gender, sexuality, and other social statuses.

In addition to presenting data on the prevalence of violence in same-sex couples, the focus in this chapter will be on exploring the ways in which models for predicting partner violence do and do not work for same-sex couples. Of primary consideration will be a discussion of the intersection of gender, sexuality, race and ethnicity, and partner violence. We will also explore the ways in which institutional discrimination shapes both experiences with same-sex partner violence and also responses to it.

OBJECTIVES

- To examine the prevalence of intimate partner violence among homosexual couples, both lesbian and gay couples
- To examine the prevalence of intimate partner violence among transgender people
- To explore the ways in which sexuality shapes intimate partner violence and to explicate the similarities and differences across sexualities
- To explore the special case that the "closet" creates for intimate partner violence in homosexual families
- To examine the criminal justice response to intimate partner violence in homosexual families
- To explore the response of other agencies (e.g., social services, shelters) to intimate partner violence and the challenges these present to homosexual victims and perpetrators

■ To suggest policies and practices that would improve the ways in which agencies and institutions respond to intimate partner violence in the homosexual community

KEY TERMS

sexual orientation	gender
lesbian continuum	intersexuality
compulsory heterosexuality	true hermaphrodite
sex	androgen insensitivity syndrome

INTRODUCTION

We have chosen deliberately to dedicate a chapter to violence in homosexual relationships because they are unique on the exact dimensions that characterize intimate partner violence: gender. As noted throughout the book, the majority of family violence is perpetrated by men against women; in short, family violence and intimate partner violence in particular are gendered phenomena. Gender is the single most powerful factor in shaping the risk for becoming a victim of violence and even more so the risk of perpetrating violence. In fact, gender shapes perpetration even more powerfully than it shapes victimhood; in cases of child abuse—and child sexual abuse in particular—men make up the overwhelming percentage of abusers. While these patterns hold across race and ethnicity, age, type of violence, and so forth, they are significantly disrupted in homosexual relationships, namely, because both the victims and the perpetrators share their gender in common. Violence in homosexual couples is *structurally different*, and thus it is important to dedicate a chapter to this phenomenon alone and explore the ways in which intimate partner violence is shaped by sexual orientation and the gender composition of the couple.

Before we begin our discussion of violence in homosexual couples, we must define some terms.

DEFINITIONS

Sexuality, or **sexual orientation**, is a concept that captures both an individual's tendencies in terms of sexual and romantic attraction as well as sexual behavior. Sexuality is highly controversial, and there are serious debates on the degree to which sexual orientation is fixed, biologically determined, a product of socialization, or an unstable concept that exists on a continuum. Here we will not go into each of these debates, but we will summarize the scholarly literature on sexuality in order to lay the foundation for our discussion of violence in homosexual families.

For most of the twentieth century sexuality was believed to exist in a set of fixed locations: homosexual, heterosexual, and more recently bisexual. Beginning with the work of Kinsey et al. (1948, 1953), scholars and researchers began to argue that sexuality exists on a continuum such that someone can be almost exclusively heterosexual, exclusively homosexual (the anchors of the continuum), thoroughly bisexual (the midpoint), or anywhere in between these fixed points. This notion of sexuality on a continuum reinforced the notion that sexuality is about attraction more than actual behavior. In other words, all people have a fundamental attraction (which varies along the continuum). This is distinct from their behavior, which may be based on circumstances or structural constraints other than attraction.

For example, D'Emilio (1983) argued that homosexuality has always existed, but the degree to which it is present as a family choice is dictated by the economic system of a society. D'Emilio illustrates this point by considering the situation in colonial America. Though there is evidence of homosexual relationships, especially among literary writers of the time who exchanged love letters even if they never engaged in sexual intercourse, there are few if any examples of homosexual families. D'Emilio suggests that this is primarily a product of the ways in which an agricultural economy constrains family choices. Under an agricultural economy in which the family farm is the primary economic unit, heterosexual couples who could "produce" a labor force by having several children would be the most successful. Families who could not produce children would be seriously disadvantaged and might even find it impossible to survive. In fact, adult children who never married—either by choice or by necessity—often stayed with their parents or other relatives who needed additional help on the family farm. Thus, individuals with homosexual attractions would have been unable to form families during the colonial period in the United States. D'Emilio notes that both the changing social climate of the second half of the twentieth century—particularly the civil rights and women's rights movements—as well as the shifting economy and the increasing acceptability of women in the labor force opened the door for the possibility of homosexual families for the first time in the history of the United States. Finally, it is worth noting that the *New York Times* (Belkin 2010) reported on a USDA report that said in 2010 the cost for a middle-class family to raise one child from birth to age eighteen was $222,360 (http://parenting.blogs.nytimes.com/2010/06/25/the-cost-of-raising-a-child/). Thus, children can now be defined as a financial drain rather than a financial asset!

Taking the "Kinsey scale" as a starting point, Adrienne Rich (1980) argues that sexual orientation should not necessarily be limited to *sexual* attraction but based on one's basic orientation toward relationships. Coining the term "**lesbian continuum**," she argued that many women—including a majority of those who identify as heterosexual—establish their primary emotive relationships with other women. Rich also described the concept "**compulsory heterosexuality**," the fact that in a patriarchal culture—where male partners can provide income and a sense of protection from the outside world—it is often necessary for women to develop romantic relationships with men even when they are attracted sexually and emotionally to women.

The vast majority of scholars of sexuality argue that homosexuality and bisexuality have always been part of human culture (see Fausto-Sterling 2000 for a particularly detailed historical account) and exist in the animal kingdom as well. These data have been used primarily to argue that sexuality is biologically determined rather than socialized. Many scholars, including Fausto-Sterling, Rich, and D'Emilio, would argue that despite the fact that sexuality is biologically determined—we are born the way we are—socialization and the social climate shape the degree to which homosexuality and bisexuality can be expressed.

More recently, scholars of sexual orientation have also explored the notion that though sexuality is biologically determined and then shaped by the social, political, and economic climate in which individuals live, it may also be "unstable." In other words, one's orientation may shift across one's lifetime. Some scholars even argue that bisexuality is not so much a fixed sexual orientation as it is a way of describing most people's sexuality; in short, most individuals may inherently have attractions— sexual, emotive, or both—to both men and women, and the expressions of sexuality and the development of relationships are shaped by an individual's needs at a particular point in time as well as the social, political, and economic context in which they find themselves. All of that said, there are two important points to keep in mind as we discuss intimate partner violence in homosexual families: First, despite all of the potential variation in sexuality, our discussion here will be limited to individuals who are actually living in homosexual relationships. Second, all of the people who respond to violence—law enforcement personnel, prosecutors, judges, social workers, and so on—generally bring with them their own understanding of sexuality when they respond to violence in a homosexual couple. Thus, all of the controversies that exist about the origins of homosexuality, our stereotypes about homosexual men and women, and our notions of bisexuality influence the ways in which we respond to violence in a homosexual couple.

STEREOTYPES OF HOMOSEXUAL MEN AND WOMEN

Because stereotypes of homosexual men and women are so common and because they shape our responses to violence in homosexual families, it is worthwhile to discuss some of the most common stereotypes. The majority of stereotypes about gay men and lesbians are derived from a lack of understanding and a tendency to conflate sexuality and gender. The assumption is that gay men are more feminine than heterosexual men and that lesbians are more masculine than heterosexual women and that these differences in femininity and masculinity are both biological and directly related to "being gay."

HOW DO STEREOTYPES IMPACT
REACTIONS BY LAW ENFORCEMENT?

When law enforcement and other "responders" to intimate partner violence invoke stereotypes they hold about homosexual men and lesbians, this may negatively or adversely impact the ways that they respond to these incidents of violence. For example, the perception that men are the stereotypical perpetrators of intimate partner violence and women are the stereotypical victims may inhibit a responding officer from recognizing male victims or female perpetrators in same-sex relationships.

In addition to the problems associated with stereotypes is the issue of the gender-based conceptualization of intimate partner violence. As we have argued throughout the book, intimate partner violence is a gender-based phenomenon that developed out of and is inextricably linked to patriarchy and inequalities of power. That said, our reason for treating same-sex intimate partner violence in a separate chapter is that same-sex violence violates our very conceptualization—at least on the surface—and thus must be considered separately. We must address this apparent contradiction head-on. It is critical that all individuals who work with victims and perpetrators of intimate partner violence have their stereotypes surrounding homosexual men and lesbians and same-sex violence debunked.

PREVALENCE

Research on the prevalence of intimate partner violence in same-sex couples reveals that the rates are similar to those in the heterosexual community, with between 15 percent and 25 percent of all gay men and lesbians reporting at least one incident of violence in their intimate relationships (Tjaden 2003). Although we will discuss some key differences in the ways in which same-sex couple violence is experienced, there is no evidence to suggest that the types of physical or sexual violence that occur in same-sex couples is any different from that experienced by heterosexual couples: victims of same-sex violence report being hit, kicked, punched, and having things thrown at them, and they report sexual abuse, with 15 percent of gay men reporting that they were raped by their intimate partners (Tjaden 2003).

Gay men and lesbians also face significantly higher rates of violence by strangers and acquaintances. One study reports that nearly half (41 percent) of young gay men and lesbians reported violence at the hands of family members, peers, or strangers (Hunter 1990). This is important to note because, as the case of Matthew Shepherd illustrates,[1] homophobia that breeds the type of violence propagated against Shepherd is the same homophobia that when internalized by a gay man or a lesbian may lead to a form of self-hatred, which, when reflected in his or her partner, may lead to violence. The following tragic case that involved one partner murdering her lover illustrates many of the nuances of violence in a homosexual partnership; the reader will note that many of the elements in this case are exactly the same in many cases of heterosexual domestic violence homicide as well.

Another challenge facing gay and lesbian victims of intimate partner violence may be their reluctance to submit a member of their community to the police and

---

BOX 11.1   SAMANTHA GUTIERREZ

"Getting Help Is Hard for Gay Domestic Violence Victims"

A year ago, Samantha Gutierrez met Tammy Starlette Miller West and fell in love. On Labor Day, that love ended in death.

The relationship showed the classic signs of domestic violence, relatives said. Gutierrez tried to leave, and filed charges against West in January.

A week before she died, Gutierrez told her sister she was planning to leave for good.

For victims of domestic violence who are in same-sex relationships, seeking and getting help is doubly hard, advocates of domestic violence say.

"They have to continually 'out' themselves in the process of trying to get help," said April Burgess-Johnson, the director of outreach and prevention for the N.C. Coalition Against Domestic Violence.

Victims of domestic violence can file for a restraining order under Chapter 50B in the general statutes. The law provides for protection for such groups as spouses, "persons of the opposite sex who live together or have lived together" and "persons of the opposite sex who are in a dating relationship or have been in a dating relationship."

It does not say anything specifically about same-sex couples, but gays and lesbians who live together can apply for restraining orders under the section of the law that covers current or former household members.

The law does not provide any protection for same-sex couples who are dating but not living together. The N.C. Coalition Against Domestic Violence has been lobbying to change the law for years but the General Assembly has resisted, Burgess-Johnson said.

The biggest challenge is getting people to take domestic violence in same-sex relationships as seriously as it is taken in opposite-sex relationships, experts say.

And because of the stigma sometimes associated with same-sex relationships, gays and lesbians are even less likely to report abuse.

"We know domestic violence statistics are overwhelmingly underreported," he said. "We just suspect that there is a greater underreporting in the gay and lesbian community because of the stigma of announcing sexual orientation."

Gay people worry about how law-enforcement and other agencies will respond to their sexual orientation, Gilreath said.

Some abusers may also intimidate their partners by threatening to expose their sexual orientation, said Christine Murray, a professor of counseling at UNC Greensboro and a

---

BOX 11.1   SAMANTHA GUTIERREZ *continued*

---

co-director of Project Safe Love, which provides resources for victims and abusers in same-sex relationships.

And if a person hasn't come out to their family, they might not be able to turn to their relatives for help, Murray said.

Some domestic-violence programs may not be suited for victims in same-sex relationships, she said. For example, a man in a same-sex relationship wouldn't be able to stay at a shelter, which in many cases is for women and children, Murray said.

The good thing is that the law is neutral, said Samuel Johnson, a Greensboro attorney who is a member of the N.C. Gay Advocacy Legal Alliance.

"You don't have to say there is a sexual relationship," he said. "If you're under the same roof, the law is not going to ask what the nature of the relationship is."

Burgess-Johnson said she has heard anecdotally that some judges misinterpret the law. She couldn't provide any concrete examples but said judges and prosecutors are much more aware of the issue. The N.C. Coalition Against Domestic Violence started an initiative called Project Rainbow Net after the death of a gay man in Davie County. Corey Hawkins had filed a restraining order against his estranged boyfriend, Rayford Clyde Hendrix, but in June 2003, Hawkins' body was found buried in Hendrix's backyard. He had been shot in the head. Hendrix was convicted of second-degree murder in the case and is now serving up to 30 years in prison.

Carol Manion, Hawkins' aunt, said her nephew had a hard time getting a restraining order because of his sexual orientation. His friends were eventually able to help him, and a restraining order was granted in September 2002.

Norma Gill is just beginning to deal with the death of her daughter, Samantha Gutierrez. "I never thought it would come to the point of a gun," she said. "You never know what goes on behind closed doors."

SOURCE: Michael Hewlett, "Getting Help Is Hard for Gay Domestic Violence Victims," *Winston-Salem Journal,* September 17, 2008.

---

the criminal justice system. Similar to the experiences of African American women who fear the treatment of their male partners by potentially racist police, prosecutors, or corrections officers (Hattery and Smith 2010), gay men and lesbians may fear the treatment their partners will be likely to receive if they are reported and arrested. This reluctance may be exacerbated for lesbians who also identify as feminists; they may worry, as Ruth's story will reveal, that they will be seen as "traitors" to their gender and their sexuality for reporting violence at the hand of a woman. Ruth's story was posted on a blog, the Experience Project, which is an online catalog of resources for lesbian victims of IPV.

BOX 11.2	RUTH

Feminist Loyalty

Ruth (48), Posted September 18th, 2010 at 2:51 PM

My story begins in 1983, I was 27 years old, and this was my third "serious" relationship with a woman. I met her through a friend and she was a real charmer. I was chronically depressed and suffered very poor self-esteem but I didn't realize that at the time—I just blamed myself for "being so useless."

I had enrolled at University, which was a huge step for me. I felt like I had messed up my life and was now struggling to "do something" with it.

I think the first signs that something wasn't right with our relationship was that my partner really resented me going to University. She was from a working class background, with an abusive father and abusive brothers. She continuously came into the little room I had set up as a study and interrupted me, mocked my attempts to study and would put the University and me down.

Her manner became more aggressive and there were lots of angry words exchanged between us. Then one day she hit me. That was the first black eye.

There were the apologies and the "making up." We both explained it away as a speed induced come-down drama and left it at that. I remember a friend remarked on the black eye and that she wasn't happy about it. I got defensive and brushed off her comments.

I didn't go and see any support services because I didn't think of what was happening as "domestic violence." I explained it away as drugs and her abusive childhood. Part of me wanted to rescue her and it seemed very anti-feminist and wrong to blame someone for their behavior when they had come from an abusive background.

The relationship soured and she took to partying without me and to bringing women home. One morning after she had brought another woman home I "lost it." I threatened her and she lashed out and gave me my second (and last) black eye.

I think it was only the physical abuse that woke me up to the subtle control and domination that had been going on in the relationship. I tolerated the put-downs, the mocking and the emotional manipulation. When someone has poor self-esteem to start with it's so easy to erode what little confidence she has down to zero. After that I decided that I really needed to salvage what dignity I had left. So I left. I did keep paying rent on the house for months as I felt guilty, coerced and bullied. She used to come around to collect the rent from me every week like clockwork and I dutifully handed it over. It wasn't until months later that I found out that the rent never got paid. She stole my money!

About eight or nine years later I did have another very short term (three months), rebound relationship with a woman (another charmer) who I didn't realise was an alcoholic. With the help of a friend I identified the **warning signs more quickly**. She pressured me to do everything with her and to spend all my money on going out with her. She was jealous, coercive, manipulative, aggressive and threatening. One night, when she was extremely drunk she aggressively tried to force me to have sex with her. It was very scary. I

BOX 11.2	RUTH *continued*

felt really, really stupid but didn't seek any help. I managed to extricate myself from the relationship but she continued to harass me with abusive letters for some time afterwards.

Even if I had thought I had a right at the time (of either situation) to access services I didn't think of myself as a victim. I just felt "it's my fault for being so stupid, so pathetic and not being able to stand up for myself." I also think that my feminist politics at the time meant that I shouldn't "blame" another woman for anything because we were all oppressed by "patriarchy" and to "blame" another lesbian would be particularly "wrong." I suspect in some ways this unsophisticated politics might still be around today—troubling some women and inhibiting them from seeking support or identifying the problem.

We need legal systems, health services and personnel that are well promoted and well equipped to deal with same sex domestic violence.

My advice to anyone else in a similar situation is, "Don't blame yourself, that is part of the cycle of abuse and control. The other person needs to take responsibility for their own behaviour, no matter what their own circumstances are or have been. Get help and get out."

Source: The Experience Project, http://www.experienceproject.com/stories/Want-To-Help -Those-Who-Experience-Domestic-Violence/1194746.

DISTINCTIONS

Though in most ways intimate partner violence in same-sex couples is no different from that of heterosexual couples, there are some critical ways in which it is. For example, when gay men and lesbians who are experiencing violence seek assistance from law enforcement, the courts, or social service agencies, the stereotypes held by those agents often influence the ways in which they respond, and indeed as Ruth's story illustrates, victims themselves may allow their beliefs about who is an appropriate victim (e.g., not lesbian women!) to cloud their own strategies for help seeking. In terms of the criminal justice system, a recent study found that when all same-sex partner incidents were considered together, there was little difference in domestic violence arrests of perpetrators in heterosexual and same-sex partner incidents. However, when male and female same-sex couples were considered separately, differences in police response became more evident. Police were more likely to make arrests in lesbian intimate partner violence cases when injuries were minor. In contrast, in gay male couples more serious injury was required for an arrest to be made (Pattavina et al. 2007). Thus, a police officer's stereotypes that women are victims and men are not may lead to his or her readiness to arrest the perpetrator when the victim is a woman, even though the perpetrator is a woman as well, and his or her reluctance to make an arrest in cases in which the victim is a male, even when the perpetrator is as well.

Other problems arise when victims of same-sex intimate partner violence seek assistance through shelters. In their book Garcia and McManimon (2010) review the history of the shelter movement, and they identify two critical problems that are specific to gay and lesbian victims, both of which develop out of heterocentric ideologies of intimate partner violence. Because men constitute the vast majority—perhaps 85 percent—of perpetrators in both heterosexual and homosexual violence and because the vast majority of victims of intimate partner violence are women, regardless of their sexual orientation, there are very few shelters that exist to serve male victims. The lack of attention to male victims is exacerbated by the fact the gendered wage gap (Padavic and Reskin 2002) produces a commonly held belief that men have the financial resources to leave threatening circumstances of any kind, and thus they are less in need of shelter services than are women. In fact, because of a substantial and well-documented "gay wage penalty" (Carpenter 2007), gay men leaving abusive relationships may not have the resources necessary to leave successfully. Second, again based on a heterocentric construction of intimate partner violence, women who are perpetrators in lesbian relationships may find that they can easily gain access to shelters by posing as victims and thus harass, threaten, and stalk their victims (Sullivan 1997). Thus, one of the additional problems that gay and lesbian victims of intimate partner violence face is the treatment they receive when they seek help.

Perhaps one of the most critical differences between violence in heterosexual relationships and same-sex intimate partner violence is the "closet." If one or both members of a same-sex couple are not "out," then the threat of "outing" can be particularly powerful. For example, a perpetrator of violence may threaten to "out" his or her partner if he or she tries to leave or calls the police. This alone can constitute a serious level of psychological abuse and can be exacerbated if the perpetrator is already "out" and thus feels no threat to his or her identity. Additionally, the knowledge that a victim will have to "out" him or herself if he or she goes to the police for help or files for a restraining order may pose a significant barrier to help-seeking behavior.

APPARENT CONTRADICTIONS: SAME-SEX VIOLENCE IS STILL ROOTED IN CONCEPTUALIZATIONS OF GENDER

Despite that fact that on the surface same-sex intimate partner violence seems to violate the most fundamental feminist premise that IPV is rooted in patriarchy and inequality in gender relations (Hattery 2008), in fact intimate partner violence in same-sex couples is built on the same premises as all forms of intimate partner violence: power, inequality, and the ability to dominate. This is not to suggest that the more "masculine" member of the couple will automatically be the perpetrator, while the more "feminine" will always be the victim. But, rather, as is the case with child abuse, elder abuse, and partner abuse, the perpetrator of violence will likely be the person with more power. This power might be physical, but is more likely to be financial, emotional, or even "out" status. For example, as noted above, if one member of the couple is "out" and the other is not, the power inherent in the ability to "out" another can be translated into all kinds of abuse in the relationship, including physical, emotional, financial, and sexual. Dennis's story illustrates a typical gay male violent relationship and also highlights the ways in which a gay or lesbian person's concerns about not being "out" to their family or not being accepted by their family can be a contributor to intimate partner violence.

BOX 11.3	DENNIS

Dennis's Story

Dennis was 22 when he got involved with Alex. In the beginning, Alex was a very fun and caring man. Four months into the relationship, Alex was supposed to join Dennis at a 4th of July barbecue. When Alex finally arrived it was after 5 o'clock, and he was very irritable. Dennis mentioned that it was too late to go to the barbecue and Alex grew angry and violent. Alex slapped Dennis and pushed him over a chair. Just as suddenly as the violence had started, it stopped. Alex apologized, fixed dinner, and served it to Dennis in bed.

Then next morning Dennis awoke with extreme discomfort in his chest. He went to the hospital, and though the doctor found that Dennis had cracked ribs, **he neglected to screen Dennis for domestic violence.** Dennis never told Alex about his ribs. He believed Alex would never hurt him again.

Over the next few months, Alex was sometimes violent when he was preparing to visit his family. He would slap Dennis, pin him down, or push him away. The violence would last for no more than a few minutes and would always conclude with an apology. Alex blamed the violence on the stress of dealing with his family.

Thinking everything would get better if they lived together, Dennis and Alex moved into an apartment on New Year's day. Dennis hoped for a new beginning. But the violence only increased.

While Dennis was at work, Alex would often borrow his car and be responsible for picking Dennis up from work at 4 p.m. He would never show up on time, often arriving one to four hours late, forcing Dennis to publicly wait for him. Eventually, there was an argument about the car. Alex pushed Dennis down the stairs, breaking his jaw in two places. Dennis had to spend two days in the hospital and his jaw was wired shut for 6 weeks. **Again, hospital personnel never inquired about the nature of Dennis' injuries.**

continues

BOX 11.3	DENNIS *continued*

When Dennis got out of the hospital, sex was the last thing on his mind. But, at any sign of hesitation, Alex would act insulted and become forceful. "We would get into bed with him raring to go and me just wanting a warm place to hide. The less interested I was in his physical desires, the more mad and more insistent he became." One night, after Dennis told Alex that he wanted to be left alone, Alex pinned him down and repeatedly punched him, rupturing his spleen. Dennis spent another two weeks in the hospital, and his spleen was removed.

Alex's violence eventually tore open Dennis' intestines. "My insides hurt so much that I could only eat one meal a day and I weighed 118 pounds. I was exhausted, having just enough energy to get through work and come home to sleep." His insides never healed and he had to return to the hospital for six more weeks, including four days in critical care after extensive intestinal surgery.

When Dennis came home from the hospital he was greeted with flowers in the bedroom and all his favorite foods in the refrigerator. For several weeks Alex was very attentive to Dennis' needs, running errands, doing the shopping, and cooking meals.

Due to continuous complications from his wounds, Dennis needed further surgery to stop some internal bleeding. His employer fired him for taking too much time off work. Dennis became financially dependant. Alex paid all the bills, and made all the decisions on what they ate and where they went.

Unable to find another job and with his disability compensation about to expire, Dennis decided to move back to New Hampshire to be with his parents. "I thought of it as a chance to take a break from the strain of everyday life and pull myself together." He left with only the clothes on his back, leaving everything with Alex.

Dennis began a new life in the Northeast, free from his batterer. Today he lives with pain and stiffness in his jaw from the break. He has had pneumonia twice as a result of having his spleen removed, and has to take daily medications to control the ulceration of the remains of his intestines. After a total of 82 days in the hospital Dennis **had never once been asked by medical personnel if he was a victim of domestic violence.**

Source: Gay Men Domestic Violence Project, http://gmdvp.org/domestic-violence/survivor -stories/ (emphasis added).

Now we turn to an examination of violence in the transgender community.

DEFINITIONS

Before we begin our discussion of intimate partner violence among intersexuals and transgender individuals, we must begin with some definitions and illustrations of these designations.

Sex Versus Gender: Beginning with the second wave of feminism, a social movement that began in the late 1960s and was largely organized around women's reproductive rights and violence against women, feminists and sociologists began to think about distinctions between sex and gender. Though we have moved beyond these distinctions, as we will explore shortly, it is important to begin with these distinctions because for nearly thirty years this conceptual model dominated the field and strongly influenced the ways in which those of us studying partner violence thought about it empirically but especially theoretically. Furthermore, at the time, this distinction was revolutionary—though not nearly as revolutionary as the current movement!

Sociologists and feminist scholars sought to distinguish between the physical body and the behaviors and practices that denote our "sex." In order to draw these distinctions, we began to talk about "**sex**" as representing the physical body that we are each born with and "**gender**" as the set of behaviors that we are socialized into and develop in order to assert our sex. Scholars argued that because of the powerful role that gender stratification plays in the United States, expressions of gender—often thought of as femininity and masculinity—were closely aligned with the two sexes: female and male. Scholars argued that this alignment was largely socialized: in other words, boys and girls were born with different body parts, but it was their socialization—which is highly gendered and distinct—that led to the development of gender. For example, boys and girls are socialized strongly to favor certain activities—sports versus nurturing games like "house" or "school"—and in some cases are punished for expressing gender-incompatible preferences. Thus, boys and girls will express distinct preferences that typically, though not always, align with their gender. But feminists and sociologists believed these preferences were developed out of socialization rather than being part of the biology of boys and girls. This distinction—that gender was a product of socialization and was therefore not "natural"—transformed our way of thinking about gender, for once one begins to think of preferences and personalities as *socialized*, we can begin to imagine the possibility that gender preferences and personalities could be changed or become variable. For example, if aggression is not inborn but trained, then boys could be socialized to be less aggressive. Though this is a widely accepted concept today, thirty years ago it was revolutionary.

West and Zimmerman (1987) argue that gender is in fact something that is performed and exists only when performed in relationship with another person. In short, West and Zimmerman suggest that when people perform traditionally "gendered" tasks—when women cook or when men take out the garbage—they are "doing gender." Acts of "doing gender" reinforce one's gender to self and others. Acts that seem to violate gender norms—gender bending—reinforce the notion that gender is not fixed or aligned exclusively with sex. Women can embrace and exhibit masculine traits and still be women and vice versa. Thus, feminist theorists and individual people began to explore the concept of gender bending as a social protest, as well as evidence that sex and gender may not be as closely aligned as was previously believed. In particular, gender bending challenged the notion that gender was a stable concept.

As the twentieth century came to a close, feminists fully embraced the notion that gender was neither stable nor rigidly aligned with sex, and they began to question the stability of biological sex. This perspective is gaining ground in scholarly communities—especially among feminists—but has been much slower to become popular among nonfeminist scholars and the "regular" world.

The argument that sex itself is not a stable or fixed concept has been largely advanced by the work of feminist biologist Anne Fausto-Sterling (2000). Based on her extensive reviews of both historical records as well as contemporary medical studies, she draws our attention to both the transgender and transsexual community as well as the relatively common medical phenomenon known as **intersexuality**.

The concept of the instability of sex itself is a more complex argument and requires that we learn a little bit about the biology of sex. Biologists had long been aware of what they term *true hermaphoditism*, which is described by Fausto-Sterling: "A **'true' hermaphrodite** bears an ovary and a testis, or a combined gonad called an ovo-testis" (2000, 37), a condition that is quite rare. However, both female and male pseudohermaphrodites, individuals with either an ovary or a testis, along with genitals from the "'opposite' sex" and other forms of what is now termed *intersexuality* (Fausto-Sterling 2000), are indeed common enough to warrant a discussion.

Based on her review of the medical literature, Fausto-Sterling argues that slightly fewer than 2 percent of all births involve some sort of ambiguous genitalia or reproductive organs. One example is **androgen insensitivity syndrome** (AIS), a congenital disorder caused by errors in gene coding that block the ability of androgen receptors to absorb androgen. Androgen is a hormone in the "male" body that facilitates the maturation of secondary sex traits, including the growth of the genitals, facial and body hair, and a leaner body type. Individuals who are born with the typical male XY chromosomal makeup but who suffer from AIS will fail to develop to sexual maturity and thus will be infertile. Despite having undescended testes, the appearance of their external sex organs will appear to be female. AIS occurs in approximately 1 in 20,000 births.

Though many transgender men and women report healthy intimate relationships, there is anecdotal evidence to suggest that they can be particularly vulnerable to intimate partner violence. One study reports that one in ten transgender and intersex men and women reported violence in their intimate relationships (Xavier 2000), whereas another study finds that half (50 percent) of transgender individuals studied reported violence—physical and sexual—in their intimate partner relationships (Courvant and Cook-Daniels 2000). One factor that may increase the probability of intimate partner violence for intersexuals, transsexuals, and transgender individuals, especially *sexual abuse*, is that they represent challenges to our binary understanding of sex, gender, or both concepts. For example, many transsexuals and transgender individuals report that their anticipation of a first sexual encounter with a new partner are anxiety filled because even if they have disclosed their "status," they can never be quite sure of the reaction of a new partner. In some cases, people seek out transsexuals and transgender individuals for sex because they are perceived to be "sex freaks." In other cases, even if they are forewarned, new partners may be "freaked out" by the appearance of the transsexual or transgender person whose very body defies our binary construction of male and female and may respond to this emotion by engaging in violence. Second, because their uniquenesses challenge our fundamental understanding of sex, in particular, intersex and trans victims are often reluctant to call the police or report the violence for fear that they will be revictimized by the very agents who are charged with their protection.

SPECIAL CHALLENGES THAT FACE TRANS AND INTERSEX VICTIMS

Trans and intersex men and women face the same challenges that gay men and lesbians face, but they also face a few additional barriers and challenges. First, although heterosexism is alive and well in the United States, support for all aspects of homosexuality—gay marriage, incorporating sexuality into nondiscrimination codes, support for hate crimes prosecution, and so forth—is on the rise, while simultaneously there is far less support for transgender issues. Thus, transgender men and women face significantly higher rates of discrimination and misunderstanding even than their homosexual counterparts. Of equal importance and significance is the fact that there is tremendous variation in the bodies of trans men and women and in their legal identity. As a result, when victims seek asylum or perpetrators are arrested, the institutions they enter are generally not adequately prepared to handle them. For example, a trans woman would not likely be admitted to a typical battered women's shelter if she has not completed genital surgery. In contrast to her self-identity, the shelter staff would consider her a man and thus a threat to the other shelter residents. Similarly, a trans man or woman who is arrested will likely be put into a cell or incarcerated based on his or her physical appearance—genitals—rather than his or her self-identity. Not only is this problematic from the perspective of the trans man or woman, but in an institutional setting like a jail or prison—where there is no privacy in showering, bathrooms, and so forth—a trans inmate will be highly vulnerable to violence and abuse by the other inmates. It is also important to note that problems often arise when dealing with hospitals, courts, and law enforcement because laws vary with regards to changing one's legal gender identity. In some states, like New York, a trans individual can petition the court to have his or her gender changed on official documents like the birth certificate and driver's license, whereas in most states the trans person has to complete sex-reassignment surgery before one's legal status can be changed. This is critical because the majority of interactions with institutions such as hospitals, schools, and the criminal justice system rely on these official legal documents to establish a person's gender identity.

CONCLUSIONS

In this chapter, we have explored the experiences of violence faced by gay men, lesbians, and trans and intersexual individuals. Overall, we argued that the experience that gay men, lesbians, trans, and intersexual individuals experience is no different from that faced by heterosexuals; the violence includes physical assault, emotional abuse, sexual abuse, and financial abuse. On the other hand, sexuality shapes the likelihood of experiencing violence and the interactions both victims and perpetrators have when they attempt to report the violence or escape it. Specifically, stereotypes and prejudices significantly inhibit the equitable treatment of both victims and perpetrators. Thus, it is critical that agents of the institutions that deal with and interact with victims and perpetrators of violence be educated about the special circumstances faced by gay, lesbian, trans, and intersex individuals in order to ensure appropriate responses that meet the needs of the victims and perpetrators.

RECOMMENDED FILMS

Boys Don't Cry (The Brandon Teena Story) (1999)
The Laramie Project (2002)
Normal (2003)
Soldier's Girl (2003)
Trans America (2005)
You Don't Know Dick (1997)

NOTES

1. For an overview of the murder of Matthew Shepherd, we refer the reader to http://www.matthewshepard.org/site/PageServer?pagename=mat_Matthews_Life.

BIBLIOGRAPHY

Belkin, L. 2010. "The Cost of Raising a Child." *New York Times,* June 25. http://parenting.blogs.nytimes.com/2010/06/25/the-cost-of-raising-a-child/.
Carpenter, C. S. 2007. "Revisiting the Income Penalty for Behaviorally Gay Men: Evidence from NHANES III." *Labour Economics* 14: 25–34.
Courvant, D., and L. Cook-Daniels. 2000. "Trans and Intersex Survivors of Domestic Violence: Defining Terms, Barriers, and Responsibilities." http://www.survivorproject.org/defbarresp.html.

D'Emilio, J. 1983. "Capitalism and Gay Identity." In *Powers of Desire: The Politics of Sexuality*, edited by A. Snitow, C. Stansell, and S. Thompson. New York: New Feminist Library Series.

Fausto-Sterling, A. 2000. *Sexing the Body: Gender Politics and the Construction of Sexuality*. 1st ed. New York: Basic Books.

Garcia, V., and P. McManimon. 2010. *Gendered Justice: Intimate Partner Violence and the Criminal Justice System*. Lanham, MD: Rowman and Littlefield.

Hattery, A. J. 2008. *Intimate Partner Violence*. Lanham, MD: Rowman and Littlefield.

Hattery, A. J., and E. Smith. 2010. *Prisoner Reentry and Social Capital: The Long Road to Reintegration*. Lanham, MD: Lexington Books.

Hunter, J. 1990. "Violence Against Lesbian and Gay Male Youths." *Journal of Interpersonal Violence* 5, no. 3: 295–300.

Kinsey, A., W. Pomeroy, C. Martin, and P. Gebhard. 1948. *Sexual Behavior in the Human Male*. Philadelphia: Saunders.

_____. 1953. *Sexual Behavior in the Human Female*. Philadelphia: Saunders.

Padavic, I., and B. F. Reskin. 2002. *Women and Men at Work*. Thousand Oaks, CA: Pine Forge Press.

Pattavina, A., D. Hirschel, E. Buzawa, D. Faggiani, and H. Bentley. 2007. "A Comparison of Police Response to Heterosexual Versus Same-Sex Intimate Partner Violence." *Violence Against Women* 13, no. 4: 374–394.

Rich, A. 1980. "Compulsory Heterosexuality and Lesbian Existence." *Signs* 5: 631–660.

Sullivan, C. M. 1997. "Societal Collusion and Culpability in Intimate Male Violence: The Impact on Community Response Toward Women with Abusive Partners." In *Violence Between Intimate Partners*, edited by A. P. Cardarelli. Boston: Allyn and Bacon.

Tjaden, P. 2003. "Symposium on Integrating Responses to Domestic Violence: Extent and Nature of Intimate Partner Violence as Measured by the National Violence Against Women Survey." *Loyola Law Review* 47: 41–54.

West, C., and D. H. Zimmerman. 1987. "Doing Gender." *Gender and Society* 1: 125–151.

Xavier, J. M. 2000. *The Washington D.C. Transgender Needs Assessment Survey: Final Report for Phase Two*. Washington, DC: District of Columbia Government.

12 Prevention and Avoidance

The Early Warning Signs

> But by the time I had found that out [that he was a crack addict], I was already madly in love with him. I mean, he was my world. . . . He was my world. He was everything.
>
> —STELLA, thirtysomething white woman, Minnesota

> I love the hell out of her. And it got to be love because we separated one time, and it just fucking hurts like hell. And like, somebody reached into my heart and just tried pulling it out. But I got over it. I moved on. I had another girl. Then all of sudden, she want to come back in my life. She's doing bad now. She can't get these kids together. You was the only one who knew how to keep my life together.
>
> —HANK, fortysomething African American man, Minnesota

This chapter will explore the ways that partner violence is often experienced by victims as a surprise because the "red flags" that point to its likelihood are so often masked by our constructions of romantic love. We will explicate the ways that common notions of romance can become pathways to abuse. For example, how does a gesture that is interpreted as romantic—like surprising a new lover by showing up at her workplace and whisking her off to lunch—turn into an abusive tactic we see in stalking? This chapter will be especially important for students who are off on their own at college exploring their sexuality and learning how to forge romantic relationships without the usual escape hatches provided by parents and family life as well as for those considering careers in social work, guidance counseling, teaching, and any other profession that involves working closely with and mentoring young adults.

OBJECTIVES

- To examine the dominant notions of romantic love in the United States
- To examine the ways in which notions of romantic love may hide early warning signs for domestic violence
- To provide examples of typical patterns of romantic relationships as well as patterns that may lead to domestic violence and note the differences and similarities
- To provide some policy recommendations so that prevention can be more effective by noting the red flags embedded in notions of romantic love

KEY TERMS

early warning signs	jealousy
intrusion	erotic property
"popping up"	prone to anger
isolation	serial abuser
possession	unknown pasts
coveture	destiny
marital rape exemption	

INTRODUCTION

One of the most frequently heard comments by scholars and practitioners who work with battered women is that they did not see the first assault coming. Yet as discussed in depth by Angela Browne (1989), many violent relationships include "early warning signs." In this chapter, we will explore the presence (or absence) of these early warning signs in the relationships that we learned about, and we will then extend this discussion beyond Browne's to an important issue that emerged in our interviews: destiny, of these two people being "made for each other," and thus their envisioning themselves together forever, despite the presence of severe physical violence and emotional abuse as well as sexual abuse.

"I DIDN'T SEE IT COMING!": THE EARLY WARNING SIGNS

In her interviews with battered women, Angela Browne (1989) notes that although the women repeatedly reported that the first assault often seemed to come out of the blue, in fact there were patterns of behavior in the relationship that were so consistent in their prediction of violence that she termed these *early warning signs*. These signs are intrusion, isolation, possession, jealousy, proneness to anger, and unknown pasts.

BOX 12.1 OPRAH WINFREY AND RIHANNA

Oprah Winfrey Has a Warning for Rihanna:
Chris Brown "Will Hit You Again"
By Helen Kennedy, Daily News Staff Writer,
Updated Sunday, March 8th 2009, 8:40 PM

Oprah Winfrey has a message for pop princess Rihanna, who prosecutors say was beaten to a pulp last month by boyfriend Chris Brown: "He will hit you again."

Former Manhattan sex-crimes prosecutor Linda Fairstein's warning is starker: He also could kill you.

Fairstein compared the fist-happy crooner to O. J. Simpson, who repeatedly beat his wife without consequence before she was slain in 1994.

Rihanna's reported reconciliation with Brown after her Feb. 8 pummeling sparked an outpouring of debate, controversy and motherly advice.

"Love doesn't hurt," Winfrey said on her show Friday, while announcing she will dedicate a program this week to discussing domestic violence.

"I want to do a show about it, dedicated to all the Rihannas of the world."

Speaking directly into the camera, Winfrey said, "If a man hits you once, he will hit you again. He will hit you again."

Sex crimes expert Fairstein warned Rihanna—as 21-year-old Barbadian singer Robyn Rihanna Fenty is known—that she risks not just another bloodying, but her very life.

"Many of the circumstances in her case were like the early warning signs in the O. J. Simpson case," Fairstein said.

She pointed to several "red flags" that suggest Rihanna could be in the same danger as Nicole Brown Simpson was 15 years ago, getting hit repeatedly but not pressing charges and then reconciling with the former running back.

The allegation that Chris Brown choked Rihanna while saying "Now I'm really going to kill you" is a particularly bad sign, Fairstein said.

"Choking behavior is a very interesting factor. It's hands on, face-to-face. It's a very intimate type of violence," she said.

New police techniques that assess an offender's potential lethality based on a list of warning factors should be used in this case, Fairstein said.

The Daily News reported this weekend that Rihanna is torn about whether to testify against Brown next month.

According to a police affidavit, the couple began squabbling after Rihanna found a text message from one of Brown's ex-girlfriends on his cell phone as they were driving through Hollywood.

Brown then allegedly punched her repeatedly, tried to push her out of the car, bashed her head against the window, bit her ear and fingers, and choked her until she nearly passed out.

continues

BOX 12.1	**OPRAH WINFREY AND RIHANNA** *continued*

Brown, 19, entered no plea last week to two felony charges of assault and making criminal threats. He is out on $50,000 bail and returns to court April 6; his celebrity lawyer, Mark Geragos, is reportedly trying to work out a plea deal.

SOURCE: http://www.nydailynews.com/gossip/2009/03/08/2009-03-08_oprah_winfrey_has _a_warning_for_rihanna_.html?print=1&page=all.

We note that O. J. Simpson was acquitted for the murder of his wife, Nicole Brown Simpson, but he was also found responsible in a civil lawsuit, and he was ordered to pay a significant settlement to her family. What is important here is that like many battered women who are murdered each year, a review of their cases demonstrates that there were "**early warning signs**" present, including, as noted, previous incidents of IPV that were either unreported or were reported but failed to elicit a satisfactory response from the criminal justice system. These failures lead to hundreds of homicides each year. We refer the reader to the film *The Burning Bed* for an accurate illustration of these failures on the part of the criminal justice system and the resultant homicide—in this real case, Francine Hughes kills her abusive partner after repeatedly seeking interventions from both the criminal justice system and the social welfare system.

Here we will briefly summarize each warning sign, and then we will provide cases from our interviews that illustrate each early warning sign.

Intrusion: "Checking In" and "Popping Up"

Browne (1989) identifies **intrusion** as the need for the batterer to monitor the comings and goings of his partner.[1] Many battered women report that they feel as if their partners "check up on them" all the time. For example, many women report that they are required to call and check in when they are not in the physical presence of their male partners. Women report being berated and often beaten when they are late or take longer than expected on an errand or a commute home from work. These outbursts of verbal venom or physical abuse (or both) can be set off by being fewer than five minutes late in arriving home. In a highly publicized case that came to our attention in the spring of 2004, a battered woman who had finally escaped after ten years of abuse reported that she was required to stay inside the house all day long. Her husband would call at all times of the day, and if she did not answer the phone on the first ring, he would come home and beat her severely. This type of control significantly restricted her movement inside the house and rendered impossible any chance that she could step out of the house, even for a breath of fresh air.[2]

Another example of this comes from Josie, whose situation we discussed at length in Chapter 8. Josie's boyfriend installed wire-tapping and recording technology in their home so that he could monitor her telephone conversations. In addition, he opened her mail, and on several occasions when she was out shopping with a girlfriend, she caught him spying on her and trailing her.

"**Popping up**" is another form of intrusion. As we detailed extensively in Chapter 8, many women and men reported this sort of behavior. Josie recounted how her partner would come by the nurses' station looking for her, and when he found she was at lunch with her colleagues, he later beat her.

Even without a physical assault, this type of control is a form of abuse. Intrusion reflects a lack of trust on the part of the batterer and engenders tremendous anxiety in the victim. It is also closely linked to jealousy; it is motivated primarily by the worry that when he cannot see his partner, she is probably with some other man.

If you have never been battered or the victim of emotional abuse and controlling behavior, then you may wonder: What woman would put up with this level of intrusion and control? How does this type of behavior become part of a long-term relationship? As will be the case with all of the other early warning signs, what is truly insidious about these early warning signs is that in a new relationship, early on, these behaviors appear to be simply expressions of love, and these acts are interpreted by the women as flirtatious or "romantic." For example, a new partner may call his or her new love during the workday just to say hello or leave messages when one or the other is out with friends or traveling. Most women would consider it romantic if their new boyfriend popped up at lunchtime for a surprise lunch or at the end of the day to whisk her off to a romantic dinner. In many new relationships, these behaviors would be considered romantic, and they would not raise any "red flags." Many women would feel swept off their feet.

Although many of us may have similar experiences, and would feel or have felt equally wooed by them, such behaviors can amount to early warning signs in violent relationships. This sort of "popping up" and calling just to say "hello" usually declines precipitously in healthy relationships. As the couple moves into a more advanced relationship, and trust is in place, there is less need for reassurance—often the real source of the constant phone calls and messages—and thus romantic behavior or gestures, including surprise visits, become less common and may be reserved for special occasions such as a birthday or anniversary.

Yet in battering relationships, these forms of intrusion increase dramatically. Calling just to say hello becomes calling to check up. Popping up as a romantic surprise turns into a way to be sure that the woman is where she said she is, it is a way of controlling her movement, and it serves to satisfy the batterer that she is not with other men. And, as noted in Chapter 8, this sort of intrusion can lead to reprimands from supervisors or even being fired from one's job. Because these abusive patterns of intrusion begin as something that seems romantic, these patterns are often overlooked by women until the level of intrusion is severe and the relationship has already become abusive.

BOX 12.2   JANET PECKINPAUGH

Former News Anchor Peckinpaugh Shares Story of Abuse, Stalking
By Janet Peckinpaugh, April 18, 2010

A year before I met him, my roommate and I saw his picture in our college yearbook.

He was the most astonishingly handsome man either of us had ever seen. He played basketball at our school, Indiana University, belonged to the best fraternity and was from an upper-middle-class family, as was I.

One year later, when he returned to school after a stint in the Marine Reserves (this was during the Vietnam War), we met. Three months later, we married. I was entering my junior year and he, who had supposedly graduated and gotten a job, was starting graduate school. At least that's what I thought.

On the second night of our marriage, he beat me.

I had discovered he hadn't graduated and there was no job. There were also no clues, no signs of his violent nature. He began stalking me. He would hide outside my classrooms or somewhere in our apartment, watching to make sure I wasn't talking to anybody.

The beatings increased. He often attacked after I made a friendly phone call to a girlfriend or had an innocent conversation with a professor on the way out of class. Rape usually followed the beating.

Then, he forbid me to see my friends and threatened me with a worse fate if I told anyone our secret. Finally, I couldn't stand it anymore. He had found a job, and I saw an opening. One day in October of that year, I dropped him at work and—with a packed overnight bag already in my car—I just kept going. I drove seven hours to my parents' house in Ohio.

They never knew why I left. I just told them that I couldn't be married anymore. I couldn't tell them the truth. Fortunately, they supported me and rebuffed him when he arrived at our house with the police in an attempt to reclaim "his property."

Even after getting away from him, I feared there would be a stigma associated with this behavior if anyone knew what I had endured. It's only been in recent years that I've been able to share my story and only with people involved in helping battered women. Domestic abuse can lead to murder. We should talk more about it and try to understand the triggers.

Several years after college, when I began working as a television reporter and anchor, I discovered that my job exposed me to potential stalkers daily. The first time was when I was working for a station in Richmond, Va. A man carrying a shotgun walked in and told

BOX 12.2   JANET PECKINPAUGH *continued*

the receptionist that I was his wife and had run away from home. Luckily, that incident was peacefully resolved.

One stalker in Richmond ran my car off the road at night and tried to pull me out of the vehicle. A passer-by called the police before he could hurt me. Yet another man hid on my bedroom balcony and watched me undress each night after I got home from work.

There were many others during my 30-year television career, but the worst was the man who tried to kidnap my precious baby. I saw someone strange on the street in front of my house as I drove away to work, then, sensing something was wrong, I circled back and arrived just as my nanny had opened the door with my child in her arms. The man, who was arrested later that afternoon, had an assault and rape rap sheet a mile long.

Stalking is a serious crime. The victim lives in constant fear, never knowing when the perpetrator will strike. Police always told me I'd be safe as long as the stalker didn't try to get close to me, close to my work, home or family.

Our laws, however, still prohibit police from interfering until they believe a crime has been committed. We must find more effective ways to protect women such as Johanna Justin-Jinich, the Wesleyan University student killed by a stalker last year, or Erin Andrews, the ESPN reporter who was shadowed and filmed undressing in her hotel room.

Stalking takes place on every college campus and in every city in the country. Abuse happens behind closed doors in every neighborhood, from the poorest to the wealthiest. Education and communication are key.

I shared my story with my son soon after he started dating. He's in college now. I hope by sharing my story publicly I will help others and they will be spared the shame, humiliation and pain that abuse and stalking bring. I hope it will prompt a healthy discussion at your dinner table tonight.

Source: http://articles.courant.com/2010-04-18/news/hc-peckinpaugh-abuse-stalking.artapr18 _1_stalking-anchor-second-night.

Isolation: Married in Thirty Days at His House

In Browne's study of battered women (1989), she found that over time, many batterers **isolated** their partners from family and friends, and this had several negative outcomes for the women. For example, many batterers prohibited their wives and girlfriends from working and required them to stay at home, usually in the house, all day long. This resulted in complete economic dependence on the batterer, it eliminated any chance for the women to amass the financial resources necessary to leave, and, perhaps most important, it severely impacted the social networks of the women (see Chapter 8 for a lengthy discussion of this point). In many cases, battered women were cut off from all family and friends. This served to keep the battering a secret, and it significantly decreased opportunities for the women to leave, as they had no friends or family who knew where they were or who could pick them up and help them to leave the relationship.

Furthermore, just as we noted in the discussion of intrusion, what woman (or man) would put up with being isolated from friends and family? Yet as with the patterns of intrusion, isolation begins slowly, it is similar to common notions of romance, and for many battered women who are leaving abusive family environments, like Debbie and Candy who were profiled in Chapter 7, this isolation from family may seem desirable at first.

Most women will remark that when a girlfriend starts dating a new man, she disappears. It is not uncommon in new relationships for the couple to isolate themselves almost 100 percent from others. Going out with friends is quickly replaced by private, intimate, one-on-one dates. In our culture, this seems "normal," just part of the "getting to know you" period in new relationships.

In healthy relationships, as the couple gets to know each other better, a pattern of mixing intimate one-on-one dates and group dates or outings with friends and family emerges. Most couples arrive at a "mix" that works for their relationship. In battering relationships, however, what begins as a preference for one-on-one, intimate dates becomes an exclusivity of the relationship such that the couple rarely, if ever, socializes with others—friends or family—and the woman is typically prohibited from any socializing on her own with friends or family. In contrast, the man often continues to have "guys' nights out" with his friends and perhaps his family.

In extreme cases, as discussed in Chapter 8 as well as in Browne's book (1989), women report that they are prohibited from working and are required—by various mechanisms such as random phone calls that must be answered on the first ring, nailing windows shut, locking doors from the outside, covering the windows with tinfoil—to stay inside the house and see no one while their partner is away from home: at work, running errands, even socializing or on outings with other women.

Furthermore, in the case of many battered women, this isolation began early and was supplemented by forced commitments. Rose, an African American woman we interviewed in North Carolina, grew up in a terribly dysfunctional family. Her father was never in her life, and her mother abandoned her and turned over custody of her to her own mother (Rose's grandmother) when she was just a young girl. When we asked her about her relationship with her mother, she indicated that she had not seen or talked to her in years and was not sure she would even recognize her.

Rose indicated that her grandmother was a good maternal figure, caring for her and nurturing her. But it is obvious that the scar of abandonment remains in Rose some forty-five years after her mother left (Rose is now in her early fifties). When she turned eighteen, she moved away to attend college. She met her husband on a blind date, and things progressed quickly, based on his wishes, not Rose's:

He was just nice. I guess I should have realized he was too possessive or something then. We hardly knew each other. He always thought I should be in my dorm. He was in the Army and he came home on weekends, and I would be gone. He would act like that's okay if I wasn't there and stuff like that. Once we got married, that changed. Then I had to be in a room or in the house all the time.

Rose, fiftysomething African American woman, North Carolina

Within a month or so of their first date, Rose was married. She skipped over this part so quickly that at one point in the interview, we asked her to return to this major event in her life. She spoke candidly, saying that her husband never asked her to marry him. In order to keep her away from other men, whom he clearly identified as potential suitors, he began telling people that they were married.

We never even talked about getting married, really. I just know he was telling people that we were getting married. But he never asked me. I was only seeing just him. His cousins and friends and people were saying that they heard we were getting married. We never had a wedding or anything. The next thing I know . . . I don't even think of it as a real marriage. I don't even know what I was thinking. It was only his mother, his grandmother, and uncle. They were the witnesses. We were at their house. She preached and signed the papers, and that was it. We were married. [AH: Would you have wanted your grandmother to be there?] Oh, my gosh. They probably wouldn't want to come. They wouldn't have let it happen. I wish I would have told somebody. I don't have any family here.

Rose, fiftysomething African American woman, North Carolina

This "marriage" seemed quite unusual to us. The more and more Rose talked about it, the more it became clear that Rose's husband used marriage as a way to both isolate Rose and possess her.[3]

We do not view Rose's experience as unique; we heard other similar stories in interviews with other women. As we noted in Chapter 8, in some cases, battered women on the run moved in with men they hardly knew in order to avoid being homeless. They understood this as an *economic* decision or exchange. And although these stories reflect more about economic dependency than isolation as the motive, the result is often isolation that is as severe as the type of isolation Rose's husband intended to create.

We return to a discussion of Andi, whose story was presented in Chapter 8. Andi moved from Chicago to Minnesota within twenty-four hours of meeting a

man outside of the homeless shelter. She and this man shared a bedroom and soon
became sexually involved. In a short time, the relationship became emotionally,
verbally, and physically abusive. Andi found herself isolated, by her choice and her
actions, from any family or friends who could come to her aid. She was literally
five hundred miles from family or friends who could help her.

Why do women make these sorts of choices, to enter into committed relationships, in some cases even marriages, so quickly? The answer lies, we believe, in two
places: living on the economic margins and fleeing abuse or neglect in their families. In the case of Rose, for example, she married her husband because she was
looking for something better, something to replace the relationship she never had
with her mother or father. In the case of Andi, she moved across state lines with a
man she did not know because she was living on the economic margins. Fleeing a
toxic environment, facing homelessness in a huge urban area, and faced with what
she perceived as very limited choices, she made a dangerous choice.

Possession: "You Belong to Me"

Another "early warning sign" is a behavior Browne terms "**possession**." For Browne
(1989), possession describes the sense of ownership that many batterers exhibit toward their female partners.

Since the beginning of time in this country, the crux of gender relations has
been men's ownership of women. This is codified in both legal and religious codes.
Violence toward women dates back centuries. "Throughout Euro-American his-
tory, wife beating enjoyed legal status as an accepted institution in western society"
(Weitzman 2001, 41).[4] When John Adams was attending the Continental Congress in 1776, his wife, Abigail, wrote to her husband, whom she addressed as
"Dearest Friend," a letter that would become famous: "In the new code of laws, I
desire you would remember the ladies and be more favorable than your ancestors.
Do not put such unlimited power into the hands of husbands" (Crompton and
Kessner 2004). But John Adams and other well-meaning men were no more able
to free women than they were their slaves. When the founders of our country
signed the Declaration of Independence, their own wives were still, in every legal
sense, *their* property. Upon marriage, a woman forfeited the few rights she had—
the legal term for this is "**coveture**," as in the man's rights "cover" his wife's—and
her husband owned her just as he owned his horse. Another example that illustrates the point: if a woman was raped, it was considered a "property" crime, not a
personal crime. A typical punishment involved the rapist being indentured to the
woman's husband, if she was married, or forced to marry her if she was single. The
rationale behind this "punishment" was that a woman's virginity was essential to
her marriageability; without her virginity intact, her father had no hope of marry-

ing her off and would be charged with providing and caring for her for the rest of his life. Thus, a marriage, even to a rapist, solved the marriageability problem that the father of a rape victim faced. Of course, today, many citizens of postindustrial societies would find this practice abhorrent, though we note here that this does continue to happen in many rural and industrializing societies in Africa and the Middle East (Kristoff and WuDunn 2009)

Men's ownership of women is ritualized in a tradition that continues into the third millennium: at a typical American wedding, the father of the bride walks the bride down the aisle and "gives her away." This ritual symbolizes the transfer of the woman from the ownership of her father to the ownership of her husband. Based on this belief that men own their female partners, if a woman engages in any interaction with another man (it need not be sexual), her husband or partner is likely to interpret this as a threat. Just as we are justified in shooting a prowler who attempts to enter our homes, men feel justified in reacting violently if they think another man is about to "steal" his woman. It is interesting to note here that most often his rage is executed against his female partner (the possession), not the other man (the intruder). This is much like someone setting their house on fire when a prowler approaches rather than shooting the prowler to prevent his entry into the home. Perhaps when seen this way, we can better appreciate the preposterous—but common—notion that men hold that beating their female partners is an acceptable and reasonable response to the fear that she will leave him for another man.

Browne's discussion of possession refers to something more, though. It also refers to the belief that when you own something, you can use it at your own discretion. This applies, according to Browne (1989), particularly to sexuality. The battered women in Browne's study recalled many experiences in which they felt that their male partners tried to "possess" them, sexually.[5] This is a polite way of saying that battered women, as noted by scholars such as Browne (1989) and Lawless (2001), reported being raped by their male partners. The reader will recall Debbie's story of marital rape and sexual abuse that we reported in Chapter 7.

The issue of marital (or partner) rape is contentious. One of the outcomes of the belief that men owned their wives that was clearly reflected in the US legal system was the "**marital rape exemption**." Essentially, this exemption made it legal for men to rape their wives; husbands were legally exempt from claims of rape made against them by their wives. These exemptions were part of the legal code well up into the 1980s, when the last remaining states finally dropped it (Garcia and McManimon 2010). Though the marital rape exemptions are now gone from the legal code in all fifty states, their sentiment often persists. In reality, rape is a very difficult crime to prosecute, especially when the victim and the offender know each other. It is nearly impossible if the victim has had consensual sex with the man she is accusing (see especially Hattery and Kane 1995). Furthermore, decades of informal observation of high-profile rape trials reveals that rape charges are generally difficult to prove if a victim has been sexually active (she is not a "virgin") and especially if she has sex with another man in the same time frame as the alleged rape, either with her husband or with someone else. For example, recall the highly publicized rape trial of Kobe Bryant. The defense argued that the victim could not have possibly been raped because another man's semen—belonging to her boyfriend at the time—was collected as evidence along with Bryant's; she was cast as a "whore" because she had sex with another man within twenty-four hours of the alleged rape. The same defense was part of the Duke lacrosse rape case. As our research and that of others documents, if a woman has consented to sex with either the perpetrator ever or anyone else recently, a rape conviction is incredibly difficult to obtain. It is clear that it will take much more time before women in our society will be able to successfully charge their intimate partners with rape (Garcia and McManimon 2010).

In addition to directly articulating rape within their partnerships, many more women reportedly had sex when they did not want to or participated in sexual acts that they did not want to in order to please their husbands and avoid further violence.

Many battered women recount instances of feeling as if they are possessions, that their male partners treat them as such. An example from the HBO film *The Burning Bed* illustrates this point well. The battered woman in the film, Fran, whose character is based on the real life story of Francine Hughes and is portrayed by Farrah Fawcett, is on the stand at her trial for murdering her abusive husband, Mickey. She is asked to describe the night of the murder. She recounts a night filled with violence, when she is beaten severely and then raped. As she is describing the rape she notes: "It was like he wanted to possess me." Browne (1989) also notes that rape in battering relationships can be experienced as attempts at possessing a woman by possessing her body. Interestingly, Browne also notes that women who are raped, possessed, in their relationships, are *more likely to leave or kill their partners than women who are not raped*. The stories we heard from battered women confirm this. Many women reported that when rape became a regular part of their experiences with their intimate partners, it was like the proverbial straw that broke the camel's back: they knew they had to leave.

Other Forms of Possession: Molding Her

Browne (1989) focuses primarily on sexual possession in battering relationships. However, we interviewed many women (and men) who talked of other kinds of possession and controlling behavior. In the context of these relationships men described shaping their female partners *to be the way that they wanted them to be*. For their part, the women acquiesced, at least temporarily, until they realized that the acquiescence was dangerous for them. Though we heard this story repeatedly, perhaps the most dramatic example came from Will and Stella, whom we interviewed in Minnesota:

When I met her, I had to mold her into the ways, into the things that I like. Okay, like with the cooking and stuff. Now she can, boy, she can put some dishes together now. I had to show her, look, this is where I like to eat, this is how I like, you know, how I like my pants folded. She used to doing laundry and would pop them out like this, instead of putting the seams together. She'd just pop them and then fold 'em like that. I'd grab them, I'm like, wait a minute. You got to fold my pants like this.

Will, fiftysomething African American man, Minnesota

JEALOUSY AND SEXUAL INFIDELITY

Jealousy, a signal of an actual or perceived violation of the sexual or erotic property exchange, was a similarly common and a particularly threatening aspect in the relationships we studied. This finding reinforces Browne's work (1989). Virtually every man interviewed suspected his female partner of infidelity, yet fewer than 20 percent of the women we interviewed admitted to having an affair. In fact, though it was the men who expressed extreme jealousy, it was often they who were actually engaged in infidelity, and most often the woman was aware of the flings with "girl-friends" or with prostitutes.

How can we understand this double standard? This is precisely the kind of question that an intersectional approach helps to explain. If for a moment we consider Kimmel's (2005) work on masculinity, Browne's (1989) work on jealousy and the need to control one's partner sexually, and Engels and Leacock's (1884) and Collins's (1992) discussion of erotic property, a clearer picture of the role of infidelity in intimate partner violence emerges. First, let us consider Kimmel (2005). A primary component of a masculine identity is sexual prowess, and one way in which to establish this is to be a "player"—to have sexual relationships with many women at the same time. Thus, we can interpret the behavior of men who are engaging in sexual infidelity as simply seeking to establish their identities as "real men." Though their female partners may not like this behavior, many women seemed to be somewhat tolerant of it, and the reality of male infidelity is absolutely taken for granted by many men. One man we interviewed, Akim, who had multiple affairs during his marriage, reflected that he had learned his attitude toward women from his older friends on the street:

And they always, influenced—you know—I used to watch them. They got girls, girls, girls, girls. So I, I basically, picked that up . . . and actually, what they were teaching me and showing me, and the, uh, examples that I was getting from them, it was not right, but it was real, you know what I mean? Yeah.

Akim, fiftysomething African American man, North Carolina

The majority of women we interviewed knew their male partners were involved with other women. In the case of Betty, Akim's wife, she knew that he was involved in a long-term relationship with another woman.

Though men do not expect their female partners to be jealous of their interactions with other women, Browne (1989) notes that jealousy was extremely common and severe among men who battered, and that it began early in the relationship. Batterers are extremely jealous of *any interaction* between their female partner and any other man. Batterers were jealous when their partners flirted, but they were also jealous when it was other men doing the flirting. As Josie's case points out (see Chapter 8), batterers were even jealous of any platonic or working relationship their female partners had with other men. This extreme jealousy, even when it was unfounded, was often the trigger of violence.[6]

MALE PERSPECTIVE ON "CHEATING"

Many batterers *define* their "outside" relationships differently than they define such relationships they suspected their wives or girlfriends of having. Typical of batterers, Hank was jealous of his girlfriend and used this unsubstantiated jealousy as a justification for emotional and physical abuse. Hank's girlfriend was in jail when we interviewed him, and when we asked Hank if he was being faithful to his girlfriend while she was serving a seven-month sentence for parole violation, he smiled and said he had some action going on the side. Here is how he put it: "I gotta get my thing thing on, you know."

When we pressed him, forcing him to deal with this apparent inconsistency, that he was admitting to cheating yet at the same time he would not tolerate any suggestion of the same by his girlfriend, he clarified things for us:

Oh, while she in prison. Nah, nah, she know about it, you see. It ain't cheating when she know about it. Hey, go ahead and do what you got to do baby, just as long as you . . . send me some money and you don't leave me.

Hank, fortysomething African American man, Minnesota

WOMEN'S EXPERIENCES WITH JEALOUSY

Most of the women we interviewed reported that they were accused by their male partners of having "outside" relationships. The frequency and severity of these accusations varied from rare to everyday. Many women reported that their male partners riffled through their pocketbooks or cell phone directories. More than one woman told of her male partner engaging in extreme behavior in order to be sure they were being faithful to them. Women we interviewed reported that their male partners conducted inspections of their bedsheets and smelled their panties in order to satisfy themselves that their women were being faithful as well as to send the message that if they detected any evidence of the presence of another sexual partner, they would respond violently.

Employing the concept of **erotic property** (Collins 1992; Engels and Leacock 1884) helps us to unlock the power of jealousy. While establishing one's sexual prowess is critical to establishing a masculine identity, this is not the case for women. In fact, women exchange access to their sexuality for the financial support and protection of the men they partner with and marry. Further, this exchange is exclusive. Thus, a woman who is unfaithful is committing perhaps the greatest violation of the sexual contract. Under this contract, men have a right to control the sexual lives of their female partners *because the women have become their erotic or sexual property*. Furthermore, when a woman commits an act of infidelity, this is perceived as an act of stealing on the part of the other man involved, aided and abetted by the woman. When women are viewed as property, they can be owned by only one man at a time. Thus, infidelity is akin to other property violations. Just as we uphold the right to defend our property, violence—at least against one's female partner—is endorsed as a "reasonable" reaction to a woman's infidelity.

Infidelity is threatening on another level as well, as it suggests that a man is unable to keep his partner satisfied. This double threat to masculinity makes infidelity a potent act and one that can, and perhaps should, be avenged by violence. The fact that in our culture we "understand" when men go into a violent rage and beat either their female partners or assault the "other" men—we term these acts "crimes of passion"—further indicates the potency of this violation: a violation of the sexual contract is a direct threat to masculine identity.

As with the other early warning signs identified by Browne (1989), jealousy is common in the early stages of intimate relationships. Before a couple makes a commitment to each other, each member often has anxiety about the level of commitment and exclusivity of the relationship. Jealousy often signals the insecurities typical of early relationships. Over time, however, in healthy relationships, as commitments are solidified and the level of trust increases, jealousy decreases. In contrast, in violent relationships, jealousy becomes more intense and more frequent as time goes on. And, as noted both here and in Chapter 9, jealously often becomes the trigger for violent outbursts. A case from the United Kingdom illustrates.

BOX 12.3   ADRIAN RAMDAT

"Obsessive and Jealous" Detective from Domestic
Violence Unit "Throttled His Policewoman Lover":
Detective Sergeant Adrian Zamdat Is on Trial for Allegedly Assaulting
His Former Girlfriend Inspector Lowe After a Series of Blazing Rows
By Andrew Levy, Last updated at 6:37 p.m. on December 3, 2008

An "obsessive and jealous" detective sergeant who worked in the City of London police's domestic violence unit throttled his lover and broke her ankle during a violent row, a court heard today.

Adrian Ramdat, 40, allegedly clamped his hands around Inspector Amanda Lowe's neck following a series of explosive arguments about her relationship with her ex, a detective chief superintendent.

The married father of two is said to have then thrown her to the floor where she heard her ankle "crack."

The court heard it was the latest in a series of rows between the couple, many caused by Ramdat's jealousy.

Prosecutor John Caudle told the court the blonde 33-year-old, who worked for the same force, had been in "hysterics" after the latest argument flared and Ramdat forced his way into the bedroom they shared.

"His face was taut with rage. He shouted at her with spittle flying out of his mouth and his eyes bulging," he said.

"He grabbed her by the throat while pushing her against the wall. He was squeezing her around the throat so she couldn't breathe.

"This went on for a period of time and Amanda realised the defendant had completely lost it and thought she was going to die."

Mr. Caudle said Ramdat let go and Miss Lowe ran to escape. But he grabbed her again and threw her onto the bed, shouting "You ****ing *****."

"Amanda made a further attempt to escape and this time the defendant shoved her against a chest of drawers and followed through with his weight so that she was winded," he added.

"He pushed her to the floor and her legs buckled under the weight. She then heard her right ankle crack and felt terrible pain."

The court was told Ramdat left the room at one point and Miss Lowe managed to call a friend, who contacted police.

BOX 12.3   ADRIAN RAMDAT *continued*

Before they arrived, he allegedly told her: "If you tell anyone, I'll come back and kill you."

Basildon Crown Court heard Ramdat, who has been suspended since an investigation was launched, met Miss Lowe met on a detective training scheme in April 2007, where he was the instructor and she a student.

They began an affair immediately and within a fortnight he left his wife and two daughters and moved into Miss Lowe's home in Chafford Hundred, Essex.

But they began rowing almost every day after she received a text message from her ex-lover, who also worked City of London police, asking if he could pick up his belongings, the court was told.

Following one argument on July 7, Ramdat allegedly shouted at her: "Right this is ****ing it."

Mr. Caudle said: "The defendant then picked her up and pushed her onto the bed with his hand over her mouth so she was unable to breathe.

"He would then relax his grip over her mouth so she could breathe again, then reapply the pressure so again she couldn't breathe.

"Then he realised she might have actually stopped breathing so he went to get her asthma inhaler and gave it to her.

"He would still not let her go, despite her begging. This went on for, on her estimation, three hours. He called her a number of names and made threats."

Ramdat eventually stormed out but returned the next morning and Miss Lowe took him back, the court heard.

The jury was told the couple argued virtually every day and Ramdat even became jealous of Miss Lowe's professional relationship with a colleague, Detective Inspector Roy West, with whom she occasionally had breakfast.

Furious at the friendship, he allegedly accused her of "being chatted up by all the men with whom she worked. He said all the people wanted to do was sleep with her."

Mr. Caudle added: "What happened was because of the defendant's jealousy about a relationship which she had had with another man before she went out with this defendant.

"That caused jealousy which caused the problems which culminated in the two counts.

"This defendant was an obsessive person, who became obsessed with Amanda's previous relationship and became preoccupied that he was a detective sergeant, whereas her previous boyfriend had been a higher ranking officer."

Source: Daily Mail, http://www.dailymail.co.uk/news/article-1091662/Obsessive-jealous
-detective-domestic-violence-unit-throttled-policewoman-lover.html#.

PRONE TO ANGER:
OTHER ASSAULTS AND PRIOR RECORDS

Many scholars who study battering report that batterers are often "**serial abusers**," moving from one relationship to another, battering each of their partners along the way.[7] As a result, battered women often report that at some point they learn about their husband's or boyfriend's previous wives and girlfriends and the violence they experienced. Browne (1989) noted that among the women she interviewed, they reported that they did not have any knowledge of the violence that plagued their male partner's past, though in many cases, the men did have previous experiences, and in some cases even criminal records, for interpersonal violence, such as fighting and assault, an early warning sign she refers to as "**prone to anger**."

Many of the men we interviewed had a history of violence, and nearly all—90 percent—of the African American men we interviewed had served time in prison, mostly for violent offenses or drugs. Certainly, this time in jail and prison added to these men's experiences with violence even if their sentences were for drugs or property crimes like breaking and entering. The reader will recall that Eddie is a professional boxer who killed someone with a punch in the ring just months before we interviewed him.

Cindy's story illustrates this particularly well. Cindy's abusive partner whose violence she had escaped by entering the shelter was the younger brother of her first love, her true love. Her first relationship, which began during her teen years, was with a man somewhat older than she, named Sam. They were involved for a few years and early on had a child together. Sam was abusive toward Cindy; he beat her several times, including hitting her with a closed fist in the face when she was a teenager and pregnant with their child.

Sam went to prison for dealing drugs, but Cindy kept in touch with him while he was locked up.[8] One day Sam called Cindy and told her that his mother had died. He asked Cindy to pick up his younger brother, Leon, and take him to the funeral. Cindy agreed. She picked up Leon and took him to the funeral, and they were "hanging out" by the end of the day. She and Leon began what would be a long-term, on-and-off, violent relationship. Soon after she and Leon moved in together, Cindy went to visit Sam in jail. She told him that she was dating one of his brothers. He asked if she was seeing this one and that one, and she repeatedly respond "no" to each inquiry. Finally, Sam said, "You're not seeing Leon, are you? He's got a lot of problems, including being violent!" She admitted that she was, in fact, involved with Leon.

In her interview, ten years after this discussion with her ex-boyfriend, Leon's brother, and six children later, she admits that she should have listened to Sam's warning. She choose to ignore it and lived a decade with this horribly abusive man.

Furthermore, knowledge of his previous violent relationships could and should have been an early warning sign for Cindy. She recalled that when she left Leon the first time and entered a shelter in another town, the social worker asked her who the man was who had beaten her so badly and cut her face with a knife. When she said it was Leon, the woman showed her a long scar on her own cheek and said that many years earlier he had done the same to her, and she was indeed one of his past partners.

I can't explain I let him do it, you know what I'm sayin' 'cause I thought he was in love with me but society ain't got shit to do wit it, you know what I'm sayin', I can't even blame it on, 'cause his mama used to beat his daddy used to beat his mama he ain't no mama's boy, he mean he too mean to be a mama's boy. I ain't the first woman that he hit. I might not be the first one that he raped, you know what I'm sayin'. . . . He ain't go rape me no more you best believe that shit 'cause I was in the counselor's and like I wrote my kids' name down this lady very educated pretty woman got a big ol' scar right there she was doing financial at one of the shelters I was at before financial care, and she looked at me, she seen my kids' name (touches the scar on her cheek), she said Leon Allen did this.

Cindy, thirtysomething African American woman, North Carolina

---

UNKNOWN PASTS:
"I MOVED IN WITH HIM THE NEXT DAY/
MARRIED IN THIRTY DAYS"

Finally, Browne (1989) notes that among the battered women she interviewed, this lack of information regarding their partner's previous experiences with violence extended to other aspects of their lives, which warning sign she refers to as "**unknown pasts**." The truth was that most battered women knew almost nothing about the past experiences of the men they partnered with.

Browne argues that this is typical of battering relationships and is difficult to detect because it is masked as romance. Battered women reported (Browne 1989; Lawless 2001) that early on in their relationships with their abusers, the men were focused on learning about them, they paid them a great deal of attention, they wanted to hear about their lives and pasts and hopes and dreams, and that at the same time they revealed very little about themselves. Many of the women interviewed by both Browne and Lawless noted that while growing up, no one had paid them this kind of attention. They were not used to being the center of attention, to being listened to. Therefore, when these men made them the center of attention and listened attentively, they did not notice that the men said very little about their own past experiences.

This sort of imbalance in information sharing has many important outcomes for the individuals involved. One outcome is that the women experience an unrealistic sense of emotional intimacy with their partners. They have shared a great deal about themselves, and they feel close to their partners, without recognizing this imbalance in emotional sharing. Thus, they make what appears to outsiders to be very unwise decisions that, in fact, feel very natural to them. The level of intimacy created in this new relationship may be greater than she has experienced in *any* relationship before, and thus she inaccurately assesses how much she can trust this new partner.

"WE WERE MADE FOR EACH OTHER"

We conclude the discussion in this chapter by focusing on one of the key factors that inhibits battered women from leaving their abusive partners: the notion that they belong together. For most people who have never been in an abusive relationship, they wonder why battered women stay. Most women will remark that if they were struck even one time, they would leave.

We have not focused on why battered women stay; rather, we have attempted to tell their stories and analyze them using a more complex framework than the simple "why doesn't she just leave?" perspective that is so common.[9] Yet throughout these chapters, we have tackled issues regarding staying and leaving and mostly come to the conclusion that battered women stay for many reasons: because in the balance they will lose more if they leave and because their personal history of abuse leaves them "handicapped" in their ability to respond to adult violence. But most often they responded that they stay because they love him. They do not like what he does or the way he behaves, but they love him.

Seldom have we read accounts of the reasons *batterers* stay. Perhaps the question seems less relevant in light of the fact that most batterers work so hard to control their female partners and literally "possess them," as noted above, that one never considers the possibility that it might be healthier for the batterer—as well as his victim-survivor—to exit the relationship. However, when one talks at length with many batterers in a nontreatment environment, as we have done, one learns that many batterers not only rationalize their violence as a reasonable response to the behavior of their wives and girlfriends, but further rationalize the violence as a way of expressing love and concern for their female partners. This is similar to the way in which some parents who physically abuse their children rationalize the abuse by indicating that "it was for their own good" or that they needed to "be taught a lesson."

Returning to Hank, whose story was presented at length earlier in this chapter, the reader will recall that Hank describes a situation in which he would return home from a long day at work—he worked as a security guard—and the house would be a mess, and there would be no dinner ready. His girlfriend would begin nagging him about something, and he would explode. He would call her a "motherfucking lazy bitch." She would attempt to run out of the house, and he would grab her and beat her to keep her from leaving.

Right, I got a fifth-degree assault with her, as far as . . . she I don't . . . I get mad at her. And then I cuss at her. I call her out a name. . . . But I, she provokes me, for me to put my hands on her. Now say, for instance, I want to walk out that door. She'll run in front of that door and tell me I ain't going nowhere. Get the hell out of the house, get away from her for a little bit 'cause I'm steamed, I'm mad. She done pissed me off. I'm mad. I want to walk out that door. She stand in front of the door and won't let me out. I try to move her. Pulling her, get away from the door. She holding the door, no, no. So I have to put hands on her to try to move her. She won't move, so I don't just hit her or anything, I try to get her out of the way. I try to . . . look, let me out. And she, that's a provocation to me. She throw things at me. She just pick up shit and she'll just throw it at me.

Hank, fortysomething African American man, Minnesota

After listening to Hank for more than an hour, we kept thinking, why would you stay with someone who annoys you so much? So, we asked Hank, "Why do you stay with her?" He responded immediately:

I love the hell out of her. And it got to be love because we separated one time, and it just fucking hurts like hell. And like, somebody reached into my heart and just tried pulling it out. But I got over it. I moved on. I had another girl. Then all of sudden, she want to come back in my life. She's doing bad now. She can't get these kids together. You was the only one who knew how to keep my life together.

Hank, fortysomething African American man, Minnesota

Many women also stay because the men they are with are "good" to their children. In many ways, what this means is that women are putting the needs of their children above their own needs.

No. I pay everything. I pay . . . and I even said that out loud in front of him. I said, I said it to one of my friends. I said, why should he leave? He doesn't contribute anything to the house. I said I pay the rent. I pay the rent. I pay the utilities. He drives my car. I put the gas in. I pay everything for the kids. I do the cooking and cleaning. Why should he leave? He's got it made. You know. And it's sad that I can realize that and I know I'm being used, but I just can't take that final step and I think it's because the kids. They love him so much, but it's even gotten to the point where they'll say, Dad's not here again. He's out with his friends. Or why can't Dad do something with us? You know.

Stella, thirtysomething white woman, Minnesota

Equally as powerful and intimately connected is the fact that in many cases, the man she is with, the man who beats her, saved her from violence in a previous relationship. But the most powerful cause of staying together, especially on the part of the batterer, seems to be the sense that "they were destined to be together."

We would argue that this sense of **destiny** is derived from the notion of possession. These men seek literally to possess their wives and girlfriends, to own them, to control them, to treat them as they wish, and they are completely unable to imagine that these women would ever leave them. Furthermore, many studies of battered women who are *killed* by their abusive partners note that the riskiest time for being murdered is at the time of separation (Browne 1989). Thus, this notion of possession woven together with the concept of "destiny" is an extraordinarily dangerous combination for battered women.

This notion of destiny is not limited, however, to batterers. Many, if not most, battered women we and others (Browne 1989) have interviewed speak in similar terms. Over and over we talked with battered women in the shelter, or in their apartments out on their own, and we always concluded the interview by asking them what would happen next. While some women reported that they were with new men because they needed a place to stay and others indicated that they were already or would soon be looking for a new man, the majority admitted that they would probably end up back with the same men they had struggled to escape. This scenario was extremely common.

CONCLUSIONS

IPV often seems to sneak up on its victims. Many battered women report that they did not see it coming. Browne's (1989) groundbreaking work on battered women who killed their abusive partners illustrates that whereas the women might not have seen it coming, there are distinct patterns in potentially violent relationships that essentially can be understood as "early warning signs." The problem is that the romantic landscape of the United States, which is heavily influenced by the media—especially romance novels and movies—serves to mask the early warning signs. A great deal of attention focused on the woman, private dates, talking about her all the time, wanting to be with her all the time, and jealousy are all within the typical range of romantic behavior in new relationships. In most healthy relation-ships, as the relationship becomes more committed and trust is built, these pat-terns decline and are replaced by other patterns. Couples spend more time apart and integrate, as a couple, into their personal social networks. In violent relation-ships, these patterns escalate, rather than diminish, and typically this escalation co-incides with the onset of violence; thus, women feel caught off-guard.

We certainly do not advocate that we remove romance from courtship. How-ever, given the importance of these early warning signs in violent relationships, women ought to be aware of these patterns and learn to take a more critical look at the behavior of new boyfriends.

We close this chapter with a discussion of obsession. Being obsessed with an-other person to the point of wanting to possess them is typical of both men who batter and the women they batter. This obsession inhibits leaving on the part of battered women and sometimes leads to murder on the part of the men. In order to reduce IPV, men must be taught that women are not their possessions to do with what they wish.

But more important—albeit more difficult to achieve—is to address the system of patriarchy that allows for men to literally "possess" or own their female partners. Any system of ownership, including slavery, capitalism, and patriarchy, that allows one class of human beings to "possess" another class of human beings will establish and reinforce inequality regimes (Acker 2006) that will inevitably lead to and de-pend upon violence as a means of keeping the inequality regime intact. In this con-text, all forms of violence against women—including sexual harassment, rape, and IPV—must be understood as being rooted in not only patriarchy, but more signifi-cantly in that aspect of patriarchy that defines women as the "possessions" of their male partners. Violence is a tool that men in a patriarchal society utilize to remind women of their status as "possessions," much like violence against slaves and later the lynching of freed African Americans was a tool whites used to remind African Americans of their status in a country ruled by a system of racial domination. When understood this way, one recommendation for reducing IPV is clearly the dismantling of all systems of domination, including patriarchy.

In Chapter 14 we will summarize the tenets and data presented in this book, and we will make policy recommendations for intervention, reduction, and pre-vention of IPV and the factors that contribute to its development and persistence. That said, here we suggest some practical prevention strategies that could be im-plemented before the system of patriarchy is fully dismantled; the wait for that to happen is a long one, and there is no reason not to develop and implement preven-tion strategies immediately.

The majority of public schools continue to require health education classes that begin in elementary school and continue through the first year or two of high school. In addition to discussing health and nutrition, these courses often involve age-appropriate discussions of controversial topics, including drug use and sex education. Our primary recommendation is that age-appropriate modules or units on healthy relationships be developed and included in the health curriculum beginning in elementary school and continuing through the first years of high school. These units could be developed around the early warning signs that Browne developed and we have expanded. As children grow older, clips from popular films, television shows, and music videos could be shown, analyzed, and discussed in order to highlight and illustrate notions of romance. Additionally, these discussions could conclude with students and teachers talking about how to interact in ways that will produce healthy rather than violent relationships. We note that the staff at the battered women's shelter in Lumberton, North Carolina, have piloted this type of programming among volunteer students in the local high school, and it has been quite successful. We should also note, however, that the parents in the local Lumberton, North Carolina, high school have been incredibly resistant to this programming—many have refused to allow their interested teenagers to participate—and therefore we acknowledge that a great deal of persuasion and education would have to be done with parents, not to mention school boards and state departments of education, before this type of programming could be implemented widely.

RECOMMENDED FILMS

The Burning Bed (HBO, 1984)
Sleeping with the Enemy (1991)

NOTES

1. Interestingly, both Brush and we explored this concept independently without being aware of each other's work. Merton refers to this as serendipity. What is important about this is the fact that we come upon this same concept without knowledge of each other's work, which suggests even more strongly the importance of this reality in the lives of battered women.

2. This woman's story of abuse that entailed being a prisoner in her own home was aired on ABC's news program *20/20* on August 13, 2004.

3. We will return to Rose's story in the section devoted to possession.

4. For an excellent review of the history of legalized violence against women, see Garcia and McManimon 2010.

5. There are other examples of men "possessing" their female partners. In many cases, women reported that they had to hand over their paychecks to men, they were treated as servants who had to do all of the household labor (cooking, cleaning, laundry, child care), and they were treated like objects whose existence was merely for the enjoyment of their male partners.

6. Evidence of the double standard is even in the language that we use to describe men who have multiple partners and women who do. Men are defined as "players," for example, whereas there are virtually no "positive" terms for women who have multiple partners. In contrast, there are virtually no "negative" terms for men who "sleep around," but the negative terms for women abound. Asking students to list these terms in class is an instructive exercise!

7. Incidentally, it is also true that many battered women move from one abusive relationship to another, never able to break the cycle.

8. Sam is still in prison serving another sentence for drugs.

9. A simple search on Amazon.com will produce, in a matter of seconds, a list of literally hundreds of books that offer women advice about how to leave abusive relationships. *Defending Our Lives: Getting Away from Domestic Violence and Staying Safe*, by Susan Murphy-Milano, is but one example.

BIBLIOGRAPHY

Acker, J. 2006. *Class Questions, Feminist Answers*. New York: Routledge.

Browne, A. 1989. *When Battered Women Kill*. New York: Free Press.

Brush, Lisa D. 2011. *Poverty, Battered Women, and Work in US Public Polilcy*. New York, NY: Oxford University Press.

Collins, R. 1992. *Love and Property from Sociological Insight: An Introduction to Non-obvious Sociology*. London: Oxford University Press.

Crompton, V., and E. Kessner. 2004. *Saving Beauty from the Beast: How to Protect Your Daughter from an Unhealthy Relationship*. 1st paperback ed. New York: Little, Brown.

Engels, F., and I. B. E. Leacock. 1884. *The Origin of the Family, Private Property, and the State*. New York: International Publishers.

Garcia, V., and P. McManimon. 2010. *Gendered Justice: Intimate Partner Violence and the Criminal Justice System*. Lanham, MD: Rowman and Littlefield.

Hattery, A. J., and E. W. Kane. 1995. "Men's and Women's Perceptions of Nonconsensual Sexual Intercourse." *Sex Roles* 33: 785–802.

Kimmel, M. 2005. *Manhood in America*. New York: Oxford University Press.

Kristoff, N., and S. WuDunn. 2009. *Half the Sky: Turning Oppression into Opportunity for Women Worldwide*. New York: Alfred A. Knopf.

Lawless, E. J. 2001. *Women Escaping Violence: Empowerment Through Narrative*. Columbia: University of Missouri Press.

Weitzman, S. 2001. *Not to People Like Us: Hidden Abuse in Upscale Marriages*. New York: Basic Books.

13 The Response to Family Violence

The Criminal Justice System and the Social Welfare System

OBJECTIVES

- To familiarize the reader with the various institutional responses to family violence
- To detail the role that health care providers—emergency rooms, pediatricians, family physicians—play in responding to family violence
- To detail the role that shelters and other social service agencies play in responding to family violence
- To detail the role that intervention programs play in responding to family violence
- To examine the ways in which the criminal justice system responds to family violence
- To examine the ways in which the criminal justice system may *increase* the probability of intimate partner violence
- To provide policy recommendations to improve our institutional response to family violence

---

KEY TERMS

health care	psychological approaches
battered women's shelters	criminal justice system
Guardian Ad Litem (GAL)	mandatory arrest laws
intervention programs	restraining order
feminist models	domestic violence courts
family systems models	restorative justice

INTRODUCTION

This chapter will be devoted to an examination of the responses to individuals and families who are experiencing family violence. We will examine responses to both the victims and the perpetrators. As we have detailed throughout the book, one of the major issues with regards to family violence is the lack of reporting and the overall lack of attention that is paid to episodes of family violence. Most research indicates that only a fraction of family violence comes to the attention of anyone outside of the family. Furthermore, when family violence does come to the attention of outsiders, most often these outsiders are treating the *symptoms* of family violence—broken bones in the emergency room, providing food stamps to a woman fleeing her batterer, providing a change of clothes for a child who comes to school disheveled—rather than the causes. Even less often is the criminal justice system involved in a way that holds the perpetrator of violence accountable. Thus, though we will of course examine the response of the criminal justice system, the chapter will focus on the response of the health care system, shelters, and intervention programs. With regards to the criminal justice system specifically, we will focus on two points of intersection between the criminal justice system and family violence: responses of the criminal justice system to family violence and the role that incarceration plays in increasing the probability for partner violence. We will conclude the chapter by providing policy recommendations for dealing more effectively with all forms of family violence, and specifically the ways that service providers who regularly interface with victims—emergency room staff, schoolteachers, social workers—can provide better referrals to victims so that the patterns of violence themselves, not just the symptoms of the violence or abuse, are addressed.

INSTITUTIONAL RESPONSES TO FAMILY VIOLENCE

As we have seen throughout this book, when family violence occurs, there are or can be a variety of institutional responses. The specific mission of the individual institution largely shapes institutional responses. It is important to recognize that institutions play very different roles in addressing family violence both because they have different missions and because their missions overlap in different ways when it comes to family violence. So, for example, medicine has as its express mission the treatment of family violence–related injury, but it may also play a significant role in detecting family violence, as we shall see below.

The Institution of Health Care

The primary mission of **health care**, as an institution, is the prevention and treatment of disease and injury. With regards to family violence, the role that health care providers play in terms of prevention and treatment varies tremendously with the *type* of violence; for example, the prevention of child abuse and neglect is more central to the mission of health care *as an institution* than the prevention of other forms of family violence. Thus, parents with newborns are not only encouraged to bring their babies in for the age-appropriate checkups and vaccinations, but often offered information on age-appropriate parenting, are asked by their pediatrician if they are having any trouble, and may be enrolled in voluntary programs run by the local hospital or by social services agencies such as ExchangeSCAN and Welcome Baby that provide monthly newsletters with information and support as they navigate the challenges of parenting newborns and infants. One national program, Exchange SCAN, the last four letters of which stand for Stop Child Abuse Now—which is present in many counties nationwide—offers a wide range of programs designed specifically to prevent child abuse and neglect. ExchangeSCAN programming is built on the assumption that a high proportion of child abuse and neglect is the result of parents and caregivers lacking accurate information regarding child development, lacking resources to meet the needs of their children, and feeling overwhelmed with the challenges of caring for young children. For example, in an attempt to prevent shaken baby syndrome, ExchangeSCAN disseminates a video to new parents on infant crying. The video, which tells the story of a baby who was shaken to death, focuses on the period that most infants go through that is characterized by higher-than-average rates of crying. The intent is to provide parents with information about these periods of crying—which typically occur between two and four months—so that if their child's crying increases during this time, they will be less likely to be overwhelmed and will simply understand this as a normal developmental stage that will pass. Locally, ExchangeSCAN targets all mothers of newborns—they are contacted first while still in the maternity ward of the local birthing center—and enrolls them in newsletter mailings, offers parenting classes and support groups, and arranges for home visits for "at-risk" families.

In some communities where rates of child abuse and neglect are of concern to local residents, nonprofit agencies have developed programs designed to prevent child abuse and neglect. Similar to ExchangeSCAN, the focus is typically on providing education to parents so that they will understand their child's developmental processes and parent in ways that reduce abuse and neglect and increase maximum development. The Arizona Children's Association (AzCA) is an example of just such a local agency.

BOX 13.1   ARIZONA CHILDREN'S ASSOCIATION

Arizona Children's Association
Description of Home Visitation with Brain Boxes®

Arizona's Children Association (AzCA) has an innovative new program designed to assist home visitation staff in ways that bring neuroscience messages to families in easy-to-understand, fun, interactive ways. The Bright Start program is a home visitation/family support service targeted toward at-risk families with children, birth to age 5, that uses learning toys and books from a unique, patented product called Brain Boxes®. The service

continues

BOX 13.1   ARIZONA CHILDREN'S ASSOCIATION *continued*

is designed to provide parents with the necessary tools to promote the optimal development of their infants and young children with a focus on early brain development using fun interactions for a parent and child that target specific areas of social-emotional and cognitive development. Services are provided by master's level clinicians and are designed to increase parenting effectiveness and to prevent children from being placed outside of their homes.

The cornerstone of AzCA's Bright Start program is the ABC's of Early Learning (Attention, Bonding, and Communication) taken from the book *Bright from the Start* written by Dr. Jill Stamm and published by Penguin Press. A training manual is provided to each home visitor that describes each of these areas in detail including how they impact a child's development along with specific activities that will stimulate optimal brain growth and development. The manual also includes sections on how the brain develops and the science of early learning. Staff have been trained on use of The Brain Box®. The Brain Box is a set of 12 aged and staged boxes with hands-on learning activities that promote healthy brain development. The Brain Boxes® are used as tools to reinforce the basics of what anyone working with a young child, whether it be a parent, caregiver, teacher or therapist, needs to know to help a child's brain develop in the healthiest way possible.

Services are provided in each participant's home, whether the infant/child's caregivers are biological, pre-adoptive, adoptive, kinship families or resource family homes. An AzCA master's level clinician trains families in the early brain curriculum and provides in-home support and follow up for families for a 3 to 12 month period, depending on the needs of individual families. In-home support focuses on helping families to implement the skills they have learned into their everyday routines.

In addition to providing this interaction opportunity, in-home staff may provide additional support services that include anger management, conflict resolution, communication and negotiation skills, stress management, parenting skills training, and problem-solving skills. Staff also provide information regarding infant and child development, home management, nutrition, job readiness training, housing search and location, and behavior management. In-home clinicians work with each family in the development of linkages with community resources to meet the family's needs, which may include a wide array of health services, child care resources, respite, domestic violence or substance abuse services. Clinicians in the program receive a minimum of one hour per week of individual supervision, as well as group supervision two to four hours per month.

Home Visitation staff in the Bright Start program receive program specific training including such topics as infant and toddler mental health, social and emotional development, engagement of families, developmental screenings, nutrition, and attachment and bonding. Specialized training is also provided on the administration of the Ages and Stages Questionnaires and the Life Skills Progression Tool, both of which are integrated into the assessment process for families involved in Bright Start services.

> **BOX 13.1   ARIZONA CHILDREN'S ASSOCIATION** *continued*
>
> Outcome measures (how measure success and how compare to bench marks, established outcome goals for perception of care surveys, peer review, outside audit compliance, etc.) are measured through several tools, including:
>
> - AzCA's perception of care survey, administered at discharge;
> - a pre-post test that measures parent/caregiver knowledge about their child's health and development, as well as understanding of successful parenting practices;
> - Ages and Stages Questionnaires, administered at specific developmental stages;
> - The Life Skills Progression Tool, administered at 6 month intervals to measure family functioning across several life domains.
>
> Prevention programs like Bright Start represent an opportunity for AzCA to impact Arizona's youngest and most vulnerable citizens in a meaningful way. Putting a focus on the healthy development of infants and young children, as well as supporting the caregivers they rely on, positions AzCA as a leader in prevention efforts across the State of Arizona.
>
> *Source:* http://arizonaschildren.blogspot.com/2010/04/brain-box-in-bag-now-available.html.

Many of the programs such as ExchangeSCAN and the Arizona Children's Association depend upon partnerships with local hospitals and clinics that provide maternity and pediatric care. Though most of the programs are developed by nonprofits, the medical community, especially pediatricians, has a vested interest in these otherwise unlikely partnerships based on both the concern that child abuse can lead to long-term and expensive health problems and the acknowledgment that parenting newborns and infants is difficult and that parents, especially new parents, need advice and help in navigating this new role. In contrast, there is very little if any attention paid to preventing either intimate partner violence or elder abuse. Certainly, there are likely to be some programs that target the prevention of elder abuse that might be disseminated when the adult child of an elderly parent attends checkups and appointments with the aging parent and in particular if the physician is involved in moving the elderly person into an institutional setting (e.g., a long-term or Alzheimer's care facility). However, in all likelihood the prevention information provided would focus on the types of elder abuse perpetrated by care providers and strangers rather than that perpetrated by family members themselves. When this attention on prevention does exist, it is distributed on an individual basis, as a response to concerns raised in an appointment, for example, rather than being disseminated systematically. Yet as we discussed in Chapter 6, caregiving for elderly parents and young children can be equally stressful, and the same types of abuse are likely to occur: physical abuse, emotional abuse, and in particular, neglect. This is no surprise given that the elderly often have needs that are similar to those of infants: they are unable to perform many self-care tasks, including toileting, bathing, and feeding. Thus, the risk for neglect is particularly high and similar to that faced by infants.

This raises the question as to why there is very little systematic attention paid to caregiving for the elderly in contrast to that which is provided for the parents of newborns. Though we are unaware of any research focusing on this question, we can speculate that there are a variety of explanations:

- as a rule the elderly are less likely to be viewed as being as overtly needy as infants
- decline in the elderly may occur slowly, whereas infants are born highly needy
- the elderly themselves may deny aspects of their decline and resist both care and thus advice for avoiding abuse and neglect
- caregiving may begin in small ways and increase over time for the elderly, whereas the reverse is true for newborns and infants, and thus the appropriate timing for information may be less clear
- those who provide care for the elderly may not be consistent: it might rotate among adult children or paid staff, and thus the physician may not see the same caregiver across visits
- though both the young and the old are devalued in our society, in this setting the elderly likely face an even greater level of being devalued than newborns and infants
- because the variation in needs of the elderly is high, relative to the needs of infants, which are more or less consistent across all healthy babies, it may be difficult or unproductive to create standard types of guides for elder care, especially if information that is not relevant in an individual situation leads to the discarding of the entire packet of information

Finally, we note that there are *no* health care programs that focus on preventing intimate partner violence. Though there is ample evidence, and we cited it in the previous chapter, that dating violence and stalking are on the increase, and that teenage girls are increasingly at risk for intimate partner violence in all forms, there is no systematic attempt to disseminate prevention information to *girls or boys* this age. We acknowledge that this is a very difficult topic to raise with a teenager, and certainly health care providers may be reluctant to scare young people, yet we strongly assert that this is a critical opportunity lost. Perhaps it is not appropriate for a health care provider to raise these issues with every patient, but we suggest several strategies for providing appropriate prevention information to teenagers and young adults:

- Put literature on dating violence in exam rooms. Curious teens as well as those who may already be experiencing violence may pick up this kind of literature.
- When teenagers and young adults seek a health care provider in order to learn about or obtain contraceptives (e.g., a prescription for the birth control pill, having an IUD inserted, or receiving Deprovera shots) or to seek help in terminating a pregnancy, the health care provider can use this opening in order to provide information, even just a pamphlet, about dating violence.

Though some of our recommendations might initiate difficult conversations, they offer an opportunity to prevent (and detect) teen dating violence. Even just making information available has the potential to prevent or interrupt violence among young people that ultimately may change their lives forever. Additionally, some states have taken a "public service announcement" approach to reaching potential victims.

BOX 13.2   VIOLENCE PREVENTION

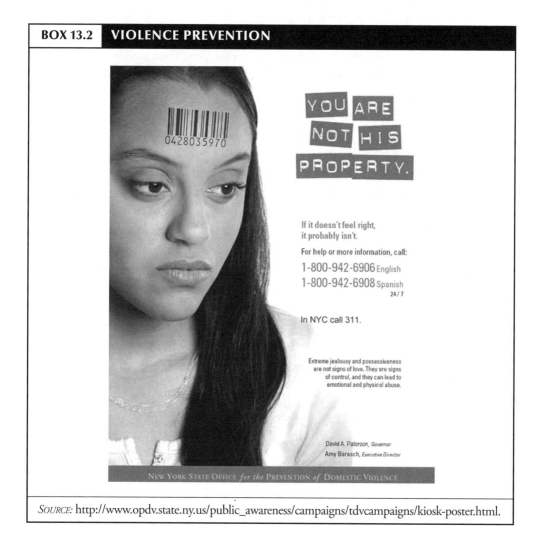

SOURCE: http://www.opdv.state.ny.us/public_awareness/campaigns/tdvcampaigns/kiosk-poster.html.

We also note that simply making information available in examination rooms has the potential to reach *adult* victims as well and to educate parents about the risks that their children face for dating violence. Proactive parents who pick up this information may have the courage they need to initiate conversations with their own children, and again this may serve to prevent (and interrupt) dating violence among their children.

Whereas health care providers have fallen far short in terms of prevention of family violence—with the powerful exception of efforts to prevent child abuse—health care providers often play a significant role in detecting family violence when it occurs, specifically in the detection of both child abuse and elder abuse, which generally, though not always, occurs in the context of regular appointments. When children and older adults are seen regularly by the same health care providers, symptoms of physical abuse and neglect may be detected; it is clearly more difficult to observe indicators of emotional, financial, or sexual abuse unless a particular complaint is made. Because neglect is often characterized by a slow decline, the key to detection is regular health care visits, and the downside is that it may take several months or even longer to detect neglect. That said, health care providers may be the best positioned of any institution to detect neglect in care and nutrition. (Many women, for example, are annoyed by the requirement of being weighed every time we go to an appointment at the clinic, but this is one of the main ways that nutritional neglect can be detected among both children and the elderly.)

Health care providers may also be the best positioned to detect all types of physical abuse—to the elderly, children, and intimate partners—when the abuse is characterized by non-life-threatening but repeated violence. For example, health care providers may detect things like burns, lashing, and their scars. The ways in which health care providers treat this information is not only subjective, but also varies by the qualities of the victim. As noted in Chapter 6, health care providers are "mandatory reporters" of child abuse. Thus, if there are significant patterns of abuse or neglect, health care providers may be the avenue to reporting the abuse to social workers. We underscore here the process of mandatory reporting. Mandatory reporting often involves first making a report to Child Protective Services, which may or may not result in criminal action being taken. In many if not most cases, CPS will identify social service and civil court solutions—for example, a child may be removed from an abusive household and put into foster care without neglect charges being filed—rather than involving the criminal justice system. There are many advantages to keeping neglect and cases of mild abuse out of the criminal justice system, including shielding children from having to testify in court, and avoiding incarcerating parents who may be, with proper education and mentoring, able to appropriately parent, and whose incarceration and their consequent removal from the family and the loss of their wages and financial support would be more detrimental to the child.

In contrast, the elderly and adults are not protected populations. Thus, when a health care provider sees indications of abuse or neglect, they are under no obligation to report their concerns. Thus, the role that routine health care providers play in detecting elder abuse and intimate partner violence is "spotty" and very much dependent on an individual provider's willingness to raise the issue with his or her patients. In fact, a recent study revealed that interventions in emergency rooms fall short more often than not: "Among abused women who were identified in the emergency departments, a social worker was provided 45 percent of the time. In only 33 percent of cases did the providers determine whether the victim had a safe place to go, and only 25 percent of the victims were referred to domestic violence services" (Rhodes et al. 2011).

One of the challenges to creating mandatory reporting laws for women and the elderly is the juxtaposition of patient privacy—the right of adults to control the access to their medical information—with the need to protect victims. It is a thorny issue; for example, we would never want to see mandatory reporting laws used to report intimate partner violence be used by unsympathetic health care providers to report a pregnancy a woman wants to keep confidential from her partner or the decline caused by AIDS used to "out" a gay patient. Thus, it is a slippery slope to recommend broader-reaching mandatory reporting laws, but we do encourage the discussion of ways in which health care providers can serve as a conduit for intervention. One compromise might be for health care providers to be required to document suspected abuse and neglect in the patient's file—for example, documenting injuries, scars, visual signs of neglect—so that if and when the patient is ready to report the abuse to the authorities, she (or he) has a medical record that documents the severity, frequency, and history of the abuse.

It is also very important to note the ways in which both prevention and detection by routine health care providers are significantly shaped by social class, race, and gender. All of these factors shape both the likelihood of prevention and detection primarily by shaping the likelihood that an individual will receive routine health care and the likelihood that this health care will be provided by the same provider, both of which are at the core of the successful delivery of prevention and detecting abuse and neglect. Obviously, the poor and those without health insurance are far less likely to receive routine health care. Simultaneously, when they do seek medical care, they are significantly more likely to seek it from urgent care clinics and emergency rooms, thus decreasing the likelihood that they will see the same health care provider more than once. Yet, as noted above, the detection of neglect and certain types of physical abuse—burns, lashes, scars—requires that the individual be seen repeatedly, over time, by the same health care provider in order to rule out the injuries being a result of an accident, which is a common explanation battered women provide. Whereas "falling down the stairs" might be accepted the first time it is presented as the explanation for bruises or broken bones, if this excuse is presented multiple times to the same health care provider, he or she is likely to be suspicious that either abuse is going on or the patient has some other condition that leads to frequent falls, such as Lou Gehrig's disease or the early stages of multiple sclerosis (MS). Thus, although social class may not shape the likelihood of being a victim of neglect or abuse, it does shape the likelihood that it will be detected by health care providers.

As with many phenomena in our culture, race and social class are highly conflated. As a result, nonwhites, especially African Americans, Hispanics, and Native Americans, are less likely to have health insurance and or access to high-quality health care (see especially Hattery and Smith 2007). The lack of health insurance generally results in individuals seeking care in emergency rooms and urgent care clinics, and this care is sought only when the individuals have a significant or severe illness or injury. Even for those who have health insurance, if they are part of an underserved population or live in areas that are considered "underserved," when they have regular visits with a health care provider, the odds that this person will be consistent are poor. As a result, nonwhite minorities, like the poor, are less likely to have access to either prevention or early detection that is potentially provided by health care providers. Thus, neglect and abuse may become more severe before they are detected, and as a result they may be elevated to the criminal justice system rather than being handled through social service agencies and other noncriminal intervention strategies. As noted above, finding social service and civil court solutions to child neglect and mild cases of abuse are almost always preferable to incarceration, especially when doing so further escalates an already overly high rate of incarceration, as is the case with African American men. As with most other things in American life, the poor and nonwhite minorities have less access to the kinds of prevention and intervention strategies that may save lives, and when intervention does occur, it is more likely to be criminal rather than civil or social, which often creates more difficulty for the entire family.

Last, we note that although girls and women are more likely to be victims of all forms of family violence, the fact that men are far less likely to have regular visits to a health care provider means that abuse and neglect among elderly men may be less likely to be detected until it has become severe. Thus, as with most aspects of life in the United States, our social location determines the role that the institution of health care can play in the prevention, detection, and intervention strategies that are presented to us.

Shelters and Other Social Service Agencies

One of the most important tools for interrupting intimate partner violence is the battered women's shelter. **Battered women's shelters** trace their history to the feminist consciousness-raising sessions of the early 1970s. As women, primarily in small, intimate support groups, began to disclose their own experiences with violence or those of their close family and friends, it became clear that there was a need for temporary shelter for women who lacked the assets to leave abusive relationships. The reader will recall, as we discussed at length in Chapter 8, that one of the biggest barriers to leaving that is faced by victims of intimate partner violence is the lack of resources that would facilitate an escape: namely, the money to rent a hotel room, finance travel out of town, and so forth. Thus, early on in the "shelter movement" (Garcia and McManimon 2010), women began to open up their own homes to provide temporary shelter for women and their children who were attempting to escape abusive partners.

By the mid-1970s, with the vision of some very strong women as well as their financial backing and support, shelters began to pop up around the country, first in urban areas like New York and Chicago and much later in suburban and rural areas, where unfortunately, they are still relatively rare. In fact, most people are surprised to learn that although there are 1,200 shelters for battered women, there are 3,600 shelters for abandoned animals. This partly reflects a lack of financial support for battered women and victims of violence in general, as well as a lack of understanding of the need that battered women and their children face. Most Americans grossly underestimate the level of intimate partner violence in their communities and thus are not compelled to support the building and maintenance of shelters in their own communities. This is particularly problematic in suburban areas where myths about "middle-class" people and in tight-knit rural communities where everyone knows each other exacerbate this tendency to underestimate the need for shelters.

Shelters fill a critical niche in the network of resources that many battered women and their children need in order to leave their abusive households successfully. In addition to providing a temporary place to live, shelters often provide opportunities for therapy for the women as well as their children, help in navigating other social services such as "welfare," and help in navigating the criminal justice system and the protection it can provide, including obtaining restraining orders and even the filing of separation and divorce papers. There is no doubt that many battered women would not have been able to successfully leave abusive relationships and establish independent lives for themselves and their children without a shelter.

That said, shelters are not able to meet all of the needs that battered women and their children face. In Chapter 11 we noted that victims of same-sex intimate partner violence often are unable to utilize all of the resources that shelters offer. For example, there are only a handful of shelters for male victims, including gay men. Lesbian victims may find that they are not secure and safe in shelters because shelter staff are not always able to distinguish victims from lesbian perpetrators who may present themselves as victims. Additionally, one problem that all mothers face is the fact that shelters often restrict the presence of young men over the age of twelve, as they may be perceived as threatening to the other victims who reside in the shelter. As a result, mothers with teenage sons may find that they either are prohibited from using shelters or may have to make alternative arrangements for their young sons, who themselves may be victims of violence at the hands of their fathers or stepfathers. Last, there are often significant time limits that shelters impose on residents; typically, these range from thirty to ninety days, depending on both the shelter's mission and available resources. The battered women's shelter in Winston-Salem, North Carolina, for example, restricts residents to a thirty-day stay. This restriction is based primarily on the fact that the shelter resources are stretched; each and every week, they have to turn desperate women away. Thus, they limit shelter stays in order to accommodate as many women and children for *temporary* housing as they can. Some shelters employ a holistic approach that involves more than just temporary housing and includes therapy, employment training or educational support, and programming for children. In these shelters, the length of the stay is often dictated by the therapy and training model more so than the need to continuously turn over beds. Either way, shelters are a temporary stop in the journey to leave abusive relationships. They fill a critical niche, but they are rarely a magic pill. Many battered women find that they turn to shelters more than once as they put their lives together and leave their abusive partners successfully.

As noted in Chapter 6, social service agencies, and Child Protective Services in particular, often become involved in cases of child abuse or neglect. In contrast to intimate partner violence cases in which women can and often do seek asylum in shelters, children under the age of eighteen are not capable or legally able to live on their own. As a result, in cases in which the violence or neglect has reached a certain level of severity, children are removed from their parent(s) and transferred temporarily to foster homes. We note that the decision to remove children from their homes and place them in even temporary—let alone permanent—custody of a nonrelative is a complex decision that often involves many different agencies and considerable time. For example, in a typical child abuse or neglect case, once the initial report has been made, usually to the Department of Child Protective Services, in the Division of Health and Human Services, an investigation is launched. This investigation will generally involve a site visit by a CPS staff member and interviews by CPS staff with the child, the parent(s), teachers, the child's physician if available, and other adults who have the opportunity to observe the child. Additionally, the court will generally appoint a **Guardian Ad Litem**, a volunteer with some paralegal training, who will interview the child and observe him or her in the home in order to make a recommendation to the judge regarding the ideal placement for the child. The GAL is an important "player" in the process because he or she is charged with evaluating only the best interests of the child. For a fictional account of the role of GAL, we recommend Jodi Picoult's book *My Sister's Keeper*, which follows the case of an adolescent girl who was conceived by her parents in order to be an organ donor for her older sister who has leukemia. The main character is suing for her right to make her own medical decisions—rather than allow her parents to make them—and a GAL is an important part of her case. If the court determines that the child would be better suited to live temporarily—in foster care—or permanently with other care providers, then the judge will order that the child be removed from the home, and if the placement is permanent, he or she will terminate the parental rights of the biological parent(s) and transfer custody to the legal guardian or adoptive parent. Thus, social services fills the "gap" in child abuse and neglect cases that shelters fill in cases of intimate partner violence.

As noted in Chapter 6, there are many problems associated with Child Protective Services and foster care as well—for example, the rate of juvenile detention is approximately seven times greater for children in foster care than for those living in a permanent home (Moarsh 2006; Pipher 1994). It is very difficult to determine when abuse or neglect is severe enough to remove a child, even temporarily, from his or her parent(s). Moreover, there is a great deal of controversy surrounding this determination. As noted above, these decisions are never made lightly. In some cases, where the CPS staff agree that the family has potential, they may choose to involve the family "as a whole" in counseling. The CPS staff at the Olmsted County Department of Social Services in Minnesota practices this approach. Operating under the assumption that most families have the potential to be healthy and safe if they are given the tools—education, resources—to do so, they take the entire family as their client and work with them to develop family "safety plans"; parents are required to attend parenting classes, children receive therapy, and social workers make regular home visits to ensure that the children are safe. Of course, the problem with this approach is when the decision to leave a family intact results in the further neglect, abuse, or even death of the child victim.

BOX 13.3   JOSHUA DESHANEY

Law: Poor Joshua!
Monday, March 6, 1989

Joshua DeShaney is paralyzed and profoundly retarded, the victim of brutal pummelings at age four by his father. Joshua, now nine, is also the victim of inaction by Wisconsin's Winnebago County department of social services. The agency failed to remove the child from his divorced father's custody despite continual reports of abuse for nearly two years, repeated hospitalizations for serious injuries, and regular observations by a caseworker of

continues

BOX 13.3   JOSHUA DESHANEY *continued*

suspicious bumps and lesions. Joshua's father was convicted of child abuse in 1984 and paroled from prison after less than two years. Last week, in a ruling that stunned children's rights advocates around the country, the U.S. Supreme Court voted 6 to 3 to absolve Winnebago County of constitutional responsibility for Joshua's fate.

"A state's failure to protect an individual against private violence," declared Chief Justice William Rehnquist, was not a denial of the victim's constitutional rights. "While the state may have been aware of the dangers that Joshua faced in the free world, it played no part in their creation, nor did it do anything to render him any more vulnerable to them." The majority's ruling provoked an emotional dissent from Justice Harry Blackmun. "Poor Joshua! Victim of repeated attacks by an irresponsible, bullying, cowardly and intemperate father, and abandoned by [county officials] who placed him in a dangerous predicament," he wrote. "It is a sad commentary upon American life and constitutional principles."

Government child-welfare agencies expressed relief over the decision. "A contrary ruling would have seriously affected programs and budgetary priorities," explained Benna Ruth Solomon of the State and Local Legal Center in Washington. For child advocates, the opinion was deeply troubling. Said James Weill of the Children's Defense Fund: "It's part of a line of decisions in which the court has indicated significant hostility to legal protections for children." Suits against agencies may still be filed in some state courts, but local laws often permit little or no recourse. In Joshua's case, a Wisconsin statute limits damages to $50,000—less than the cost of a year's medical care for the tragically battered youngster.

SOURCE: http://www.time.com/time/magazine/article/0,9171,957147,00.html.

We are not in a position to evaluate the various approaches to dealing with child abuse and neglect—ranging from removing children permanently from their parents' custody to working to keep families together—but we do note that underneath the controversy are advocates who care deeply about children and are seeking innovative ways in which to meet the needs of the children and keep families together, provided it will result in a safe environment.

In contrast to both intimate partner violence and child abuse and neglect, there are really no systems in place for providing temporary housing—shelter or foster care—for victims of elder abuse. Because a certain proportion of victims of elder abuse are already institutionalized and institutions are reluctant to identify their own faults when elder abuse or neglect is discovered, it is typically handled by the adult children who discover it. In most cases, the elderly parent is removed from the institution (or in cases of home care the home health care provider is fired), and in some cases, either civil lawsuits are filed or criminal complaints are taken out. Both of these approaches force the matter into the court system. It is more difficult to determine what happens when relatives are engaging in elder abuse and neglect. Unless it is reported to the police, we suspect that it is handled "within the family." As the reader will recall from our discussion in Chapter 5, when elder abuse or neglect is perpetrated by family members, stress is often the primary cause. Stuck in the sandwich generation, the typical caregiver is overburdened, and this leads to what we might consider situational abuse or neglect. Thus, if the abuse or neglect is discovered by family members, they take matters into their own hands and either remove the abusive care provider or begin to provide the support that relieves the abuser from the stress of the situation, and the abuse or neglect dissipates.

Intervention Programs

Whereas shelters provide an "intervention" for victims of family violence, the **intervention program**'s focus for dealing with the perpetrators is less often the removal of the offender and more often an intervention program designed to teach the individual alternative methods for discipline, childrearing, and dealing with marital or partner conflict other than violence. Interestingly, these programs are often administered by the same agencies that also provide services for victims. For example, in Winston-Salem, North Carolina, Family Services provides a domestic violence hotline, dispatches victim advocates when a woman is raped, conducts "safety checks" on families with known violence, administers the local battered women's shelter, and administers the local batterer intervention program. Family Services also provides the majority of the staff for the "Safe on Seven" program we will discuss in the next section. Family Services is essentially "one-stop shopping" for intimate partner violence.

The reader will recall that many communities approach child abuse and neglect through the utilization of social services programs, specifically CPS, and civil court—determining and arranging child custody—far more often than engaging the criminal justice system and prosecuting and detaining the abuser. The same is true for intimate partner violence. Batterer intervention programs—which comprise a variety of tools, including mandatory education classes, attendance at substance abuse programs, anger management, and even victim restitution, which we will discuss at length shortly—are the most common approach to dealing with the offenders in cases of IPV. In fact, they are not only the "go-to" model for social workers who are charged with assisting battered women and their children, but they are the "go-to" model even in criminal cases where the batterer is prosecuted. Mandatory attendance is the single most common *criminal* sentence for intimate partner violence cases. In a study of Winston-Salem, North Carolina, Harvey (2002) studied the previous five years of *criminal* cases of domestic violence and found that of those that resulted in a conviction, 75 percent were sentenced to attend the batterer intervention program at Family Services. Thus, it is important that we examine carefully the social service program that serves as the primary criminal justice response to intimate partner violence.

Batterer intervention programs vary, in part by whether they are administered by counselors in private practice or, as the Family Services program is, as sort of a hybrid social service and probation or parole program. There are at least three approaches to batterer intervention: feminist models (for example, Emerge), family systems–based programs, and counseling or psychologically based models that feature various aspects of counseling and behavior modification programs (Healey, Smith, and O'Sullivan 1998).

Feminist Models

- developed out of the feminist consciousness-raising movement that produced the shelter movement
- focuses on power and control as the cause of battering
- focuses on equality as the goal of treatment and reeducation

Family Systems Models

- are based on the assumption that intimate partner violence is a result of a dysfunctional family
- violence escalates as the result of the behavior of both people
- violence is the result of an interaction; it is not the problem of one person alone
- focus is on identifying problems in the interactions and teaching couples how to "solve" problems

Psychological Approaches

- focus on individual problems; a history of abuse or drug and alcohol addiction
- approach is psychotherapy (both group and individual)
- approach is cognitive behavior therapy (identifying "triggers" and learning alternative responses rather than violence)

Though all of these types of programs exist around the country, in their expansive examination of batterer intervention programs nationwide, Healey, Smith, and O'Sullivan (1998) note that the vast majority of programs have adopted what is referred to as the "Duluth Model," which is a psychological-counseling model that is deeply rooted in a feminist understanding of battering as an expression of power.

THE DULUTH CURRICULUM:
ISSUES OF POWER AND CONTROL AS PRIMARY TARGETS

Many batterer intervention programs adhere to, or borrow from, a psychoeducational and skills-building curriculum that is a component of the Duluth Model. Developed in the early 1980s by the Domestic Abuse Intervention Project (DAIP) of Duluth, Minnesota, the model emphasizes the importance of a coordinated community response to battering and places battering within a broader context of the range of controlling behaviors illustrated in the "Power and Control Wheel." The wheel depicts how physical violence is connected to male power and control through a number of "spokes" or control tactics: minimizing, denying, blaming, and using intimidation, emotional abuse, isolation, children, male privilege, economic abuse, and threats. According to the Duluth Model, the batterer maintains control over his partner through constant acts of coercion, intimidation, and isolation punctuated by periodic acts of violence.

The curriculum is taught in classes that emphasize the development of critical thinking skills around eight themes: nonviolence, nonthreatening behavior, respect, support and trust, honesty and accountability, sexual respect, partnership, and negotiation and fairness. Depending on the total length of the program, two or three sessions are devoted to each theme. The first session of each theme begins with a video vignette that demonstrates the controlling behavior from that portion of the wheel. Discussion revolves around the actions that the batterer in the story used to control his partner, the advantages he was trying to get out of the situation, the beliefs he expressed that supported his position, the feelings he was hiding through his behavior, and the means he used to minimize, deny, or blame the victim for his actions. At the close of each session, the men are given homework: to identify these same elements in an incident when they exhibited similar controlling behaviors. During subsequent sessions devoted to the theme, each group member describes his own use of the controlling behavior, why he used it, and what its effects were. Alternative behaviors that can build a healthier, egalitarian relationship are then explored.

Putting the Duluth curriculum into practice requires considerable skill on the part of group leaders. One group observed for this report strayed dramatically from the evening's agenda, as members succeeded in sidetracking the discussion away from their behavior into complaints about the curriculum and about their partners. Even when the agenda is adhered to, the classroom-style format can allow some members to sit back and not participate in discussions or even reflect on their behavior. Group leaders have to be vigilant against both the active and the passive ways batterers avoid taking responsibility for their abuse, both inside and outside of the group setting. Furthermore, directors of several programs noted that the tenor of the group intervention varies substantially depending on the style of the group leaders and how they view their role (e.g., as educators who teach new skills or as therapists who confront the men's inappropriate behavior).

352

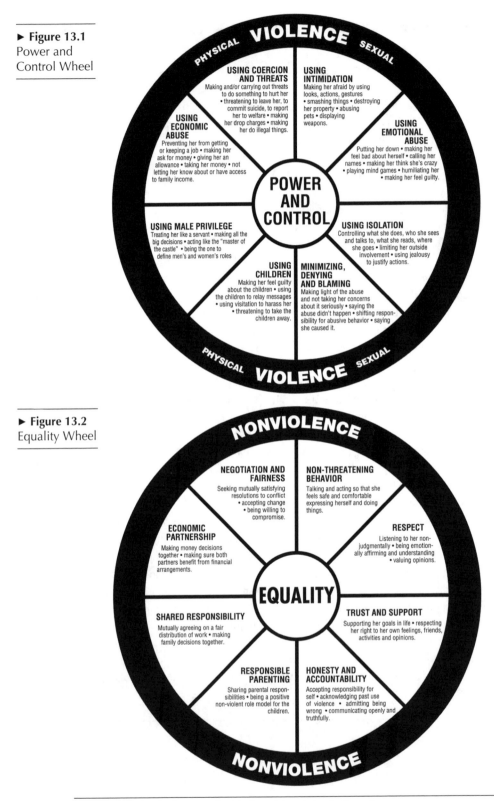

► **Figure 13.1**
Power and
Control Wheel

► **Figure 13.2**
Equality Wheel

Source: For both wheels, www.theduluthmodel.org/wheelgallery.php

Shortcomings of Batterer Intervention Programs

Perhaps the most extensive evaluation of batterer intervention programs is that conducted by Healey, Smith, and O'Sullivan (1998). They reviewed the models used in all fifty states and focused their analysis on several of what are considered by most practitioners to be the "model" programs, including Emerge in Boston— which is a program based on the psychological or counseling model that is also deeply rooted in the feminist understanding of family violence—and several programs that use the Duluth Model. In general, there are two key problems associated with batterer intervention programs: length and attendance. Several of the practitioners that Healey and colleagues cite note that many batterer intervention programs fail because they are not long enough. For example, the director of Emerge argues that any treatment that is less than four to six months will likely fail and result in recidivism because: "Many batterers, often known for being manipulative and intelligent, can readily adapt to a short-term intervention, quickly learning to 'talk the talk.' If the intervention is too short, it may end during this 'honeymoon' phase, leaving the provider satisfied with a job seemingly well done but with the abusive behavior fundamentally unchallenged and unchanged" (Healey, Smith, and O'Sullivan 1998, 47).

In contrast, a study by the CDC reported that length was not correlated with recidivism, noting that participants in a three-month program fared as well as those in a nine-month program after twelve months.

In general, our evaluation research of the Family Services program (conducted in 2005 and 2010) as well as the overall conclusions drawn by Healey, Smith, and O'Sullivan (1998) reveal that recidivism rates are quite high, but as is the case with other crimes, we would recommend researchers use a three-year window rather than twelve months to measure recidivism. As the director of Emerge noted, batterers can learn to talk the talk fairly easily—and our own interviews with batterers confirm this—and they are capable of making short-term changes in their behavior. Thus, a longer window to measure recidivism is more accurate in detecting true recidivism rates. We note that this does not mean that the intervention programs themselves should last three years; rather, the data all seem to indicate that programs that are between four and nine months are effective. What we do note is that in addition to a "honeymoon" period that may be experienced by a batterer who has been convicted on an assault charge, sentenced to an intervention program, and desires to reestablish his relationship with his partner, just like recidivism rates in other areas—drug abuse, property crimes, and so on—recidivism must be measured in a time frame that is sufficiently long to allow the everyday stresses of life, or in the case of batterers also their relationships, to emerge in order to determine if an individual will go back to his or her previous ways of coping or will have developed new and better ways of handling stress.

The second problem that batterer intervention programs face is attendance. For example, the evaluation research we conducted (Hattery, Williams, and Smith 2005) as well as that conducted by our colleague Lynn Harvey (2002) revealed that more than half of men (55 percent) court-ordered to attend Time Out (the local batterer intervention program) fail to complete the twenty-six sessions and that nearly half (45 percent) never attend a single session! How does this happen? In many counties like Forsyth County, NC, the offices of probation and parole have no jurisdiction over the Time Out program, and there is little coordinated effort between these offices. Thus, unlike court-ordered drug or alcohol treatment, which is highly monitored and if missed can be a reason to revoke probation and send the offender back to jail, there is no such accountability for batterers. This is troubling for two reasons. First, the court-ordered treatment is not received by the offender and thus he is more likely to recidivate, and, second, the complete lack of accountability likely empowers the offender to continue to engage in abusive behavior because there is no consequence for doing so!

Interestingly, in their review of batterer intervention programs Healey and colleagues identified programs that linked probation and parole with intervention services. They report, not surprisingly, that when batterers' attendance at court-ordered intervention programs is monitored, not only do they attend, but their recidivism rates go down. We suggest that this is likely for both of the reasons that nonsupervised interventions programs do not work: men who attend the program are receiving treatment, and there is a consequence associated with their battering—they are required to attend weekly sessions—and their recidivism is more likely to be detected by the probation or parole supervisor. Thus, we highly recommend that court-ordered batterer intervention programs be linked with probation services, as this combination seems to have the best chance of reducing recidivism.

THE CRIMINAL JUSTICE RESPONSE

The **criminal justice system** encompasses everything from law enforcement to corrections. For a variety of reasons, including the history of family violence, which we reviewed extensively in Chapter 2, and the overarching belief that family violence is a "family problem," for the most part, the only "units" of the criminal justice system that deal with family violence are law enforcement and the courts; unless the abuse results in significant injury or death, there is very seldom any sentencing of offenders other than to probation and possibly an intervention problem like those we reviewed above or an alcohol or drug treatment program. Thus, our focus in this section will be on law enforcement and the courts.

As noted earlier in this chapter as well as in our discussions of both elder and child abuse, neither child abuse nor elder abuse typically involves a 911 call and the arrival of a law enforcement agent on the scene. More likely, both child abuse and elder abuse cases make their way into the system because of either a report by someone concerned—a caregiver, parent, teacher, health care provider—or because the injuries sustained require the victim to be brought to the emergency room. Furthermore, in these situations, often the cases are referred to social services first, particularly when it is a case of child abuse, in which instance the matter is referred to Child Protective Services.

Thus, although occasionally law enforcement may respond to a call about elder abuse or child abuse, the typical call they respond to is one of domestic violence. As any police officer or deputy will tell you, domestic violence calls are the "worst"; they are dangerous, they are time-consuming, and they rarely result in an arrest. Thus, law enforcement agents are often reluctant to respond, if they respond at all. Countless battered women we have interviewed or seen interviewed for documentaries detail the fact that once their battering became chronic and they were known at the police department, even a 911 call rarely elicited a response.

When law enforcement officers do arrive on the scene of a domestic violence call, they typically have several difficult decisions to make: Who was the initiator? Should someone be arrested? And what other options might there be to defuse the situation? Of course, this is all on top of the fact that they have to assess their own safety as it is not uncommon for domestic violence incidents that result in a 911 call to include weapons. In fact, each year police officers are killed responding to domestic violence calls (for a detailed examination of officers killed in the line of duty and while responding to domestic violence calls, see the FBI's Uniform Crime Reports, which can be accessed at http://www.fbi.gov/about-us/cjis/ucr/ucr). A cursory Google search in May 2011 uncovered at least a dozen incidents just in the first four months of 2011.

Often the first decision that a responding officer must make is to determine, if possible, who initiated the violence and thus who is the perpetrator. Though the data on domestic violence all confirm that especially in cases of severe violence the vast majority involve a male perpetrator, it is not uncommon for both parties to be actively engaged in "fighting." Typically, the officer will deduce that the individual with the more severe injuries—perhaps the person who called 911—is the victim, but it is not always clear, and in some cases, as Garcia and McManimon (2010) note, officers will arrest both parties when they are unable to determine that one person initiated the violence.

Clearly, the primary decision a responding officer has to make is whether to make an arrest. In their extensive review of police departments, Townsend and her colleagues note first that although all departments have written protocols for responding to domestic violence, behaviors that they consider to constitute domestic violence vary: "All of the departments (99%) consider actual physical (non-sexual) assault as an act of domestic violence and 90% consider actual sexual assault domestic violence. Fewer departments consider violations of court protective orders (78%) or threatened physical (non-sexual) assault (78%) domestic violence; even fewer consider threatened sexual assault (65%), stalking (62%), verbal assault (50%), criminal trespass (46%), and property crime (43%) as domestic violence" (Townsend et al. 2006, 25). More troubling, their research reveals that even when there are protocols in place, the rate of following these protocols varies, as does the level of accountability for failing to do so. They suggest that failing to supervise officers' responses to domestic violence and hold them accountable for failing to follow procedures is a lost opportunity in terms of training officers in the most effective strategies for responding to these difficult calls.

One of the biggest changes in the policies and practices of law enforcement began in the mid-1980s and early 1990s with the Duluth Project. Historically, the law enforcement response to an incident of domestic violence was to defuse the situation by walking the man around the block, offering to take the victim to a friend's or family member's home or perhaps even the emergency room, in short to create distance between the individuals and give them both time to "cool off." Even when the victim demanded that the perpetrator be arrested, law enforcement agents were frequently reluctant to do so and often refused based on the grounds that they did not have probable cause: they did not "see him do anything." Countless interviews we have conducted, read about, or seen in documentaries illustrate this reality. Wearied by what they considered a lack of response, as well as a lack of accountability, feminist activists agitated for **mandatory arrest laws**. The theory behind mandatory arrest—which generally involves booking the perpetrator and holding him (or, rarely, her) for twenty-four or seventy-two hours or until they can be arraigned—is simply that in addition to creating space and a cooling-down period (though most men who are arrested rather than walked around the block become, understandably, more agitated, not less!), an arrest can provide a "wake-up" call that intimate violence will be taken seriously and has criminal consequences.

Beginning with the Duluth Project, the mandatory arrest movement slowly spread across the country so that by the end of the twentieth century, virtually every state had mandatory arrest laws. Interestingly, the most recent movement is the revocation of these laws as activists and practitioners seek noncriminal solutions to intimate partner violence. Mandatory arrest laws are quite effective in creating space between the couple. And in some cases, particularly when the arrest involves middle- and upper-middle-class white men who generally have not had any previous interaction with the criminal justice system, it does serve as an effective "wake-up" call. However, mandatory arrest has not been as successful as its advocates had hoped.

Both the research on mandatory arrest as well as anecdotal evidence provided by shelter staff and other practitioners who work with battered women reveal that there are some problems with mandatory arrest that in some jurisdictions have led to its suspension. One problem, identified by research relating mandatory arrest laws and intimate partner homicide, concludes that mandatory arrest laws suppress reporting incidents of IPV based on a fear of the arrest, and IPV that is significant enough to warrant an arrest instead goes unreported and undetected and ultimately escalates into homicide (Iyengar 2007).

- Because charges of domestic violence rarely end up in a conviction, the arrest, in addition to aggravating the batterer, may leave him empowered to engage in more violence and more severe violence because he learns there is no serious consequence for his behavior.

- For a variety of reasons, the women themselves often plead that the perpetrator not be arrested, or when he is they advocate for his release and provide the bail money. They may do this out of genuine fear that he will be even more abusive when he returns home, or because they feel guilty, or because they fear other consequences of his arrest such as lost wages if he misses work while he is on mandatory lockup, or, if he is a habitual offender they may worry that this will violate his parole or probation and send him back to prison. For whatever reason, this behavior discourages police officers from making an arrest and from even responding to domestic violence calls at all.

- Similarly, women may refuse to testify as witnesses in the rare instances when the cases go to trial. A victim's refusals may be for all the reasons stated above, as well as the fact that once some time has passed between the initial incident and the trial, she may have forgiven him, she may have reconciled with him, he may have stopped being abusive, and so forth, and thus they have lost the immediate need for a criminal justice intervention. This is similarly discouraging for police officers as well as detectives and prosecutors who have invested in bringing these cases, and it often negatively impacts their willingness to invest in other cases of domestic violence, which in part contributes to the low rate of prosecution.

- As noted in Chapter 11 (same-sex violence), mandatory arrest laws are often problematic when officers respond to an incident of same-sex intimate partner violence because the officers—seeing the world of crime through their cultural lens—assume that violence between two people of the same sex is not at all like violence between a male perpetrator and a female victim. As a result, they may be less or more likely to make an arrest based on their stereotypes about gay men as men and lesbians as victims or perpetrators.

- Similarly, mandatory arrest laws can be problematic in cases in which female victims are "fighting back" or engaging in self-defense. It is not uncommon for women in these cases to be arrested for domestic assault, when in fact they are simply responding to the violence being perpetrated against them.

In short, mandatory arrest laws have seen a cycle: they began slowly as a reaction to a lack of response on the part of law enforcement to intimate partner violence, they grew to be nearly universal, and there are now some jurisdictions repealing

BOX 13.4   RAINBOW RESPONSE

The Greater D.C. Coalition to Address Intimate Partner Violence in the LGBTQ Community

About Us

Rainbow Response is a grassroots coalition based in Washington DC that brings together organizations and leaders from the Lesbian, Gay, Bisexual, Transgender, and Questioning (LGBTQ) communities, along with traditional domestic violence service providers and government agencies, to increase the awareness about Intimate Partner Violence (IPV) amid the relationships of LGBTQ individuals. The Coalition works to promote education within the LGBTQ communities and beyond and identifies existing services that are provided in a manner respectful of the unique identities of LGBTQ survivors of IPV, as well as batterers.

Research and Education

Research indicates that intimate partner violence occurs at the same rate in heterosexual relationships as it does in LGBTQ relationships. In 2009, Rainbow Response released a groundbreaking report on IPV in the LGBTQ community based on surveys conducted over a year's time at various community events. This, the first report of its kind for the Washington D.C. metro area, confirmed what national research has shown: 28% of respondents self-identified as survivors of IPV. Emotional abuse, physical violence, and sexual violence were the most common types of abuse experienced. Rainbow Response continues its research endeavors to help bring light to the increased and urgent need for services for LGBTQ survivors.

Rainbow Response works to engage and educate the public through outreach on college campuses and at LGBTQ community events. LGBTQ Pride Season in the District is one of our busiest times of the year. The Coalition takes an interactive approach to community education; we use a Wheel-of-Fortune style game to teach people about the specifics of same-sex violence and we host town hall discussions where individuals can share their experiences and concerns. Rainbow Response also facilitates healthy relationship workshops where individuals or couples can discuss strategies to ensure that their relationships are healthy and loving.

Advocacy

Rainbow Response has written several testimonies advocating for the increased need of an educated response to victims of LGBTQ partner violence. Recently, Rainbow Re-

| BOX 13.4 | **RAINBOW RESPONSE** *continued* |

sponse has written to offer comments on the Office of Human Rights' proposed housing regulations to provide guidance concerning housing discrimination and protections for victims of Domestic Violence.

Technical Assistance Training

One of the first lifelines for those experiencing abuse is law enforcement. Rainbow Response, along with a coalition of other LGBTQ organizations, was successful in developing training modules and facilitating specialized, in-person trainings with both the Metropolitan Police Department and DC's Court Services and Offenders Supervision Agency. Additionally, in conjunction with the Mayor's Office and several other LGBTQ organizations, Rainbow Response participates in a critical incident task force with the Metropolitan Police Department to ensure that officers are well informed and able to provide culturally competent assistance the LGBTQ community.

SOURCE: www. rainbowresponse.org

them based on evidence that they may not always produce the best outcome. Additionally, as the movement toward handling minor cases of intimate partner violence focuses on social service interventions rather than a criminal justice response, we will likely continue to see a reduction in mandatory arrest with regards to intimate partner violence.

Restraining Orders

One of the most common criminal justice responses to intimate partner violence is the **restraining order**. Restraining orders vary by jurisdiction, and they come in both temporary and permanent forms. Typically, anyone who feels that they are being harassed and threatened by another person can go to court and seek a restraining order. In court, a judge will hear the "complaint" by the victim, and if he or she finds the evidence compelling enough, generally a temporary restraining order is granted. Temporary restraining orders are usually good for a matter of days or weeks—often thirty days—after which time the judge hears additional information from both parties and either issues a permanent restraining order that is generally good for a year or lifts the restraining order.

Restraining orders generally ban the parties from having any physical contact with each other as well as restricting the degree of proximity between the two parties; often they cannot come within fifty feet of each other. Restraining orders can also be tailored to specific circumstances, as is often the case when stalking or nonphysical harassment is involved. For example, the parties may be banned from phone or email contact, including text messaging.

Unfortunately, both the research and the anecdotal evidence reveals that for as common as they are, restraining orders are not very effective in preventing further violence (Garcia and McManimon 2010). For example, many battered women we have encountered reported that their partners knew exactly the distance at which the restraining order would be enforced and would position themselves just on the other side of the "line"—still able to harass but not violating the precise distance required in the restraining order. One woman we interviewed told of how her partner, who was also the father of her children, insisted that he would give her the child support check he owed her only if she would meet him in person. Desperate for the money, she did so. Upon her arrival at their agreed-upon meeting place, he called the police and had *her arrested* for violating the restraining order she took out on him! Another victim, a student in one of the classes taught by one of the authors, reported that her ex-husband, against whom she had a restraining order, would drive up and down her block waving a shotgun out the window, threatening to kill her. When she called the police she was told that they could not do anything because he was not violating the restraining order—he maintained the required physical distance mandated in the restraining order—and that she should call back if he shot the gun because then they could do something.

These examples illustrate the simple fact that restraining orders are only as valuable a tool as the willingness of the local law enforcement agents enforcing them. There are other problems associated with restraining orders as well. For example, they require that the victim appear in court and reveal very private information about him- or herself. This must be done at least twice. During the hearing for a permanent restraining order, the victim must repeat this kind of intimate information while facing the man (or woman) who is abusing her (or him). This can be a very intimidating process that is frequently a barrier to getting a restraining order. Additionally, restraining orders are not enforceable in certain circumstances. For example, on a college campus a restraining order between two students is not enforceable in the classroom. Let's consider the following scenario: If a female Wake Forest University student, we'll call her Mary, has a restraining order against her ex-boyfriend, we'll call him Tom, who is also a student at Wake Forest, the university cannot enforce the restraining order in the classroom. Thus, Tom can obtain Mary's schedule and register for all the same classes and sit in the same classroom—no matter how small—with her. Not only have we been made aware of these cases in our own classrooms by the university dean of students, but he confirms that every year he is faced with multiple cases of student domestic violence about which he must inform the faculty who have these students—the victim and the offender—in their classes.

THE CRIMINAL JUSTICE RESPONSE

Finally, we note that because restraining orders are civil documents rather than criminal orders, research shows that they are not a powerful tool in the war to protect women from violence. For example, Tjaden and Thoennes (2000) report that more than 50 percent of restraining orders are violated. Additionally, "There is growing evidence that abusers are becoming increasingly aware that they can avoid the service of orders of protection. The orders are civil documents and do not allow officers to enter the premises to force the person to accept these documents absent a court order. As a result, orders of protection go un-served for long period of time" (Garcia and McManimon 2010, 132).

That said, restraining orders, though they are controversial in terms of their effectiveness, remain a common tool for interrupting IPV and hopefully preventing it in the future. In Forsyth County, North Carolina, the domestic violence social service agency, Family Services, has established a unique program called "Safe on Seven" that involves staffing an office on the seventh floor of the courthouse where victims file the paperwork to take out restraining orders. What makes this program unique is that staff trained in dealing with both the victims and the perpetrators of domestic violence are there to assist the victim in filing the paperwork, but they are also there to make the process less intimidating; to create a safe environment for the victim, protecting her from the harassment of the offender who may also be present; and to offer her referrals into other programs that she may need, including a shelter, support groups, and social services where she can apply for welfare.

BOX 13.5   SAFE ON SEVEN

Safe on Seven (SOS)
Forsyth County Domestic Violence Center

Safe on Seven: Forsyth County Domestic Violence Center (SOS) is a multi-agency service center for victims of domestic violence. The Center is located on the seventh floor of the **Forsyth County Hall of Justice** at 200 N. Main Street in Winston-Salem, N.C.

The Center provides a "one stop shop" by bringing together key service providers, such as law enforcement, victim advocates, legal advocates and social services.

In 2005, Forsyth County received a grant from the US Dept. of Justice, Office of Violence Against Women, to create an integrated team for the prosecution of criminal and civil domestic violence cases and improve victims' access to community services. Previously, victims had to seek out services at multiple locations throughout the community. The Center helps minimize the difficulties victims face as they navigate the legal system. The overriding focus of the Center is victim safety and offender accountability. The US Dept. of Justice,

continues

| BOX 13.5 | **SAFE ON SEVEN** *continued* |

Office of Violence Against Women, the North Carolina Governor's Crime Commission, and Forsyth County have provided grant funds to support the continued work at Safe on Seven.

Clients of the Center are able to obtain legal advice, advocacy, referrals and protective orders as well as information concerning their court cases. The on site partners include the District Attorney's Office, Family Services, Clerk of Court, FC Sheriff's Office, the Legal Aid of N.C., the Department of Social Services, Winston-Salem Police Department and the Winston-Salem State University Center for Community Safety.

SOS's Hours of Operation
Monday through Friday
8:00 AM–12:30 PM and 2:00 PM–5:00 PM
Screening for 50B:
8:30–12:30 and 2:00–3:30

PARTNER AGENCIES SERVICES DESCRIPTION

DISTRICT ATTORNEY'S OFFICE DOMESTIC VIOLENCE UNIT:
Assists in preparing victims of domestic violence for appearance in criminal court and serves as liaison to the prosecutor.

LEGAL AID OF NORTH CAROLINA, Inc:
Assists with the court process involving requests for civil restraining/protective orders (50B) and accepts requests for possible legal representation at civil restraining/ protective order hearings.

CLERK OF COURT:
Assists with the court process involving requests for civil restraining/protective orders and processing these requests through the court system.

FAMILY SERVICES:
Provides assistance with risk assessment, safety planning, advocacy, and referrals for additional services.

DEPARTMENT OF SOCIAL SERVICES:
Provides assistance with the application process for services such as Work First, Food Stamps, Medicaid, Child Support Enforcement and Childcare

CENTER FOR COMMUNITY SAFETY:
Provides research and analysis of the Safe on Seven project.

FORSYTH COUNTY SHERIFF'S OFFICE:
Provides information to clients on service of the restraining/protective orders and domestic violence related law enforcement issues. Serves as the liaison between the District Attorney's Office and the Sheriff.

BOX 13.5	**SAFE ON SEVEN** *continued*

WINSTON-SALEM POLICE DEPARTMENT:

Provides follow up information and any further investigation that may be necessary about domestic violence incidents. They provide victim advocacy services through information, emotional support and referral.

KERNERSVILLE POLICE DEPARTMENT:

Provides initial and follow up investigation and information regarding domestic violence incidents. May assist the victim with transportation, domestic stand-bys, and referral to community resources.

COMMUNITY CORRECTIONS:

Specialized probation officers work closely with all members of Safe on Seven agencies to ensure accountability with domestic violence offenders.

CHILDREN'S LAW CENTER:

Provides quality legal representation and advocacy for children in legal and administrative proceedings

SAFETY TIPS WHEN DOMESTIC VIOLENCE OCCURS:

- Plan an emergency escape
- Keep money hidden to get away quickly
- Make extra keys to the car and house. Leave them in a safe and secret place
- Keep a list of emergency phone numbers in a safe place
- Keep extra clothing for yourself and children at the house of a friend, relative or neighbor
- Know someone you can tell about the violence and who will call the police if they hear suspicious noises coming from your house.
- Teach your children how to dial 911
- Develop a code word for use with your children and friends so they will know to call for help.

SOURCE: Family Services of Forsyth County, North Carolina, http://www.familyserv.org/.

As noted, research on restraining orders indicates that even when they are filed, they are violated more than 50 percent of the time, and a good number of them are never even served (Tjaden and Thoennes 2000). Thus, the restraining order can create a false sense of safety on the part of the victim and may actually result in increased violence or even homicide.

BOX 13.6	LACOLE HINES

A Deadly Mistake in Prince George's
Thursday, August 19, 2010

A young woman was murdered last week, an apparent victim of domestic violence and an unforgivable bureaucratic error.

Prince George's County police say that LaCole Hines, 17, was shot in the head Aug. 9 by Marcus D. Shipman, her 23-year-old boyfriend. Ms. Hines was in a Landover liquor store when Mr. Shipman allegedly walked in, shot her and sped away in a waiting car driven by a 16-year-old accomplice. Mr. Shipman and the teenager were arrested after they crashed the car. Ms. Hines died at an area hospital late last week.

What makes this heinous act all the more tragic is that it might have been prevented. Two weeks before the shooting, police issued an arrest warrant for Mr. Shipman after he threatened Ms. Hines with a gun—a felony, first-degree assault. But he was never arrested because the Prince George's Sheriff's Office, which has primary responsibility for serving most of the warrants issued in the county, misfiled the document, the sheriff's office said. Instead of being handled on a priority basis, it was stashed away among misdemeanor warrants.

The employee responsible for the alleged mistake faces disciplinary action, the sheriff's office said, and the office has instituted a process by which the classification of warrants will be doubled-checked—something that was apparently not being done before the Shipman mistake. "My heart goes out to the 17-year-old girl," Sheriff Michael A. Jackson said in a statement. Mr. Jackson, a Democrat who is running for county executive, labeled the incident "a very serious lapse in my agency." (Readers should know that The Post has endorsed one of Mr. Jackson's opponents, Rushern L. Baker III, in the Sept. 14 primary election for county executive.)

Mr. Jackson said that this lapse was an "isolated incident." But how can he know that this was an aberration? For years, the sheriff's office has had severe problems carrying out its duty to serve warrants in a timely fashion. In 2002, when Mr. Jackson was first elected, the office had a backlog of 30,000 unserved warrants. This was a major campaign issue for Mr. Jackson, who used it as an argument for unseating the incumbent sheriff.

Yet now he won't or can't provide even a ballpark figure of outstanding warrants. His spokesman asserts that the office "has no backlog," but that is only because the office now refuses to use that term; the backlog has become a "structural inventory." Rafael Hylton, a member of the sheriff's office who is running to replace Mr. Jackson, puts the backlog at 48,000 warrants. Mr. Hylton told the Gazette newspaper that shrinking the backlog will be a priority if he is elected.

Backlogs and errors are almost inevitable when dealing with the thousands of warrants that sheriffs' offices are asked to serve each year. But Mr. Jackson's apparent failure to control the problem and his unwillingness now even to acknowledge it all but guarantee mistakes. In the case of LaCole Hines, the carelessness proved fatal.

Source: http://www.washingtonpost.com/wp-dyn/content/article/2010/08/18/AR201008 1805284.html?wpisrc=nl_cuzhead.

Prosecution

All forms of family violence have the potential to intersect with the criminal justice system through prosecution. As noted, with regards to both child abuse and elder abuse, cases are very rarely prosecuted unless (1) they involve a perpetrator who is a nonfamily member, for example, in cases of child abduction or child sexual abuse or paid caregivers for the elderly; (2) the violence is heinous; (3) the violence is sexual; (4) the neglect is life-threatening; and/or (5) the abuse or neglect takes place over a long period of time and there is a solid body of evidence for prosecution. Of course, the number-one barrier to prosecuting perpetrators of either child or elder abuse is reporting. If the abuse is handled within the family or within a social service agency such as Child Protective Services, it may not be prosecuted, especially if solutions that protect the victim and stop the abuse can be identified and implemented.

Thus, our primary focus with regards to prosecution is on intimate partner violence. The first factor that shapes the probability for prosecution is whether the law enforcement agent makes an arrest. In states with mandatory arrest laws this is a moot point, generally speaking, but as noted above, with a great deal of subjectivity and discretion given to law enforcement officers even in states with mandatory arrest laws, a major barrier to prosecution is the failure to make an arrest.

Prosecutors have similar discretion; the decision to prosecute rests *exclusively* with them. Research on prosecution rates varies across time and place, but the overarching conclusion we can draw is that cases of intimate partner violence are rarely prosecuted, with prosecution rates ranging from 2 percent to 21 percent (Garcia and McManimon 2010, 118). Barriers to prosecution include:

- a lack of physical evidence. As reluctant as law enforcement agents are to respond to a domestic violence call, they are also reluctant to return to the scene and collect evidence.
- a lack of medical evidence. As with rape cases, emergency room staff and physicians are primarily concerned with treating the injuries as quickly as possible. Thus, unless a victim advocate accompanies a woman through her emergency room experience, it is unlikely that forensic photographs and other medical evidence will be collected (see especially Martin 2005).
- reluctance of victims to testify. As noted previously, it is very common for victims in intimate partner violence cases to be unwilling to testify. For a variety of reasons including fear of the perpetrator, fear or guilt of his (or her) incarceration, a genuine desire for reconciliation and change, and the simple passage of time that can numb and lessen the reaction to the violence, prosecutors find that when the time comes for a trial, few victims are willing to testify. This is such a serious dilemma that some jurisdictions have experimented

with evidence-based rather than witness-based prosecution. This approach allows district attorneys to prosecute cases based on the physical and medical evidence without the testimony of the victim. As the reader can imagine, this approach is highly controversial primarily because although it may be successful in gaining a conviction, it disregards the desire of the victim, usually a woman, and may in short add to her feelings of victimization. If she is unable to control the prosecution of the case, she may feel that the state has not worked in her best interest even if the prosecutor believes he or she has. Additionally, if the sentence is not long, there is a danger of exposing her to more violence, that is, even if she refused to testify, the man is furious after being prosecuted and beats her more severely.

Domestic Violence Courts

In response to all of the shortcomings and problems associated with the prosecution of cases of intimate partner violence, some jurisdictions have experimented with **domestic violence courts**. Building on specialized drug courts as their model, domestic violence courts—which can be housed in either criminal court or family court (which is a civil court handling such things as divorce, child custody, child support, and so on)—domestic violence courts focus on therapy, intervention, treatment, and restoration. Advocates who practice in domestic violence courts—attorneys as well as judges—understand that the relationships and circumstances of intimate partner violence are complex and that in many cases the desires of the victim are twofold: getting the violence and abuse to stop and, if possible, reconciliation. Thus, the approach in domestic violence courts is getting both the victim and the perpetrator the help they need, be it drug and alcohol treatment, entrance into a successful batterer intervention program, therapy and income support for the victim while the perpetrator is completing treatment, and ultimately a safe reconciliation, if that is desired. Domestic violence courts are also based on the principle of **restorative justice**. Just because they eschew jail or prison as punishment does not mean they ignore the pain and damage done by the perpetrator. Thus, they often employ a model of restorative justice that provides an opportunity to "right the wrong" and create accountability on the part of the perpetrator. One common strategy is to require the perpetrator to listen to the victim describe the violence and abuse from her (or his) perspective. This is often very painful for the perpetrator and often very cathartic for the victim. Additionally, some research on battering indicates that it is a result of an inability of the batterer to "take the role of the other," or in other words walk in the shoes of the victim. In short, he (or she) has not developed an ability to empathize. If empathy can be built through a process of restorative justice, some research suggests that the possibility of successfully treating the batterer and ending the abuse permanently is significantly higher (Goodrum, Umberson, and Anderson 2001).

CONCLUSIONS

In this chapter, our goal has been to review and explore the various responses to family violence by various institutions in our culture. We examined the role of health care providers, the role of social service agencies (including CPS), the role of law enforcement, and the role of the courts. Overall, we noted that the institution *least likely* to have any significant response to family violence, and this is especially the case with child abuse and elder abuse, is the criminal justice system. For the most part, child abuse is primarily dealt with through health care providers and social services, particularly Child Protective Services. Often child abuse is detected during hospital and clinic visits, and many health care providers have systematic programs focused on preventing child abuse. When child abuse does occur, it is typically handled through an investigation by Child Protective Services staff who determine if the child can remain in the home or if she or he must be removed and placed in foster care until the family situation is resolved. Additionally, Child Protective Services may partner with civil court judges to recommend or require that neglectful and abusive parents attend parenting classes—run by social services agencies such as ExchangeSCAN—as part of the process of regaining custody of their children.

Elder care is rarely addressed by *any* institution. It is not a priority or even a focus for any of the institutions we have researched and discussed in this chapter. Unless the abuse takes place by a nonfamily member, it rarely reaches the point of institutional intervention. Even in cases where the abuse is perpetrated by a nonfamily member, such as by a home health care provider who may be physically, emotionally, sexually, or financially abusing an elder person, often the adult children will simply fire that person rather than bring the case to the authorities. Sadly, there has been very little to say about the institutional response to elder abuse.

Thus, most of the chapter has been devoted to understanding the role that various institutions play in dealing with intimate partner violence. As with other forms of family violence, we noted that the majority of the "response" is by social service agencies, namely, shelters that house battered women and intervention programs that attempt to treat batterers. Unlike the case with child abuse, there is very little involvement by health care providers, which is a major missed opportunity for both prevention and intervention.

Furthermore, although we praise the social service providers who work diligently and in many cases devote their lives to the treatment and prevention of intimate partner violence, we note that at every turn there are serious shortcomings that result in gaps in service and populations that remain unserved or underserved, and unfortunately for both victims and offenders, the probability of success—defined as leaving an abusive relationship, reducing recidivism, or reconciling into healthy relationships—is limited. In the final chapter, we explore possibilities for the future.

RECOMMENDED READINGS

Curry, Lynne. 2007. *The DeShaney Case: Child Abuse, Family Rights, and the Dilemma of State Intervention*. Lawrence: University Press of Kansas.

RECOMMENDED FILMS

The Burning Bed (HBO, 1984)
Defending Our Lives (Cambridge Documentary Films, 2007)
Sin by Silence (http://www.sinbysilence.com/)

BIBLIOGRAPHY

Garcia, V., and P. McManimon. 2010. *Gendered Justice: Intimate Partner Violence and the Criminal Justice System*. Lanham, MD: Rowman and Littlefield.

Goodrum, S., D. Umberson, and K. L. Anderson. 2001. "The Batterer's View of the Self and Others in Domestic Violence." *Sociological Inquiry* 71, no. 2: 221–231.

Harvey, L. K. 2002. *Domestic Violence in Winston-Salem/Forsyth County: A Study of Domestic Court Cases in 2001*. Winston-Salem, NC: Center for Community Safety, Winston-Salem State University.

Hattery, A. J. 2008. *Intimate Partner Violence*. Lanham, MD: Rowman and Littlefield.

Hattery, A., and E. Smith. 2007. *African American Families*. Thousand Oaks, CA: Sage.

Hattery, A., M. Williams, and E. Smith. 2005. *The Efficacy of the Time Out Intervention Program in Forsyth County*. Winston-Salem, NC: Wake Forest University.

Healey, K., C. Smith, and C. O'Sullivan. 1998. *Batterer Intervention: Program Approaches and Criminal Justice Strategies*. Washington, DC: National Institutes of Justice.

Iyengar, R. 2007. *Does the Certainty of Arrest Reduce Domestic Violence? Evidence from Mandatory and Recommended Arrest Laws*. Washington, DC: National Bureau of Economic Research.

Martin, P. Y. 2005. *Rape Work: Victims, Gender, and Emotions in Organization and Community Context*. New York: Routledge.

Moarsh, M. 2006. *Understanding Gender, Crime, and Justice*. Thousand Oaks, CA: Sage.

Pager, D. 2003. "The Mark of a Criminal Record." *American Journal of Sociology* 108: 937–975.

Pipher, M. B. 1994. *Reviving Ophelia: Saving the Selves of Adolescent Girls*. New York: Putnam Press.

Rhodes, K. V., C. L. Kothari, C. Cerulli, J. Wiley, and S. Marcus. 2011. "Intimate Partner Violence Identification and Response: Time for a Change in Strategy." *Journal of General Internal Medicine*: 1662–1664.

Tjaden, P., and N. Thoennes. 2000. *Full Report of the Prevalence, Incidence, and Consequences of Violence Against Women: Findings from the National Violence Against Women Survey*. Washington, DC: US Department of Justice.

Townsend, M., D. Hunt, S. Kuck, and C. Baxter. 2006. *Law Enforcement Response to Domestic Violence Calls for Service*. Washington, DC: US Department of Justice.

14 Where Do We Go from Here?

In total these acts of violence are like a ritualized acting out of our social relations of power: the dominant and the weaker, the powerful and the powerless, the passive . . . the masculine and the feminine.

—MICHAEL KAUFMAN,
"The Construction of Masculinity and the Triad of Men's Violence"

The final chapter of the book will first provide a summary of what we have covered so far and then proceed into a carefully laid-out prescription—based on the data presented in each chapter—for the prevention of all forms of family violence. Our proposals will include suggestions for modifying the criminal justice approach, as well as suggestions for the development of more successful prevention and, when necessary, intervention programs. Unlike many texts on this topic, we will also provide suggestions for the ways in which reductions in inequalities—race and ethnicity, social class, sexuality, and particularly gender—will likely lead to reductions in the levels of all forms of family violence. We will conclude by providing the reader with suggestions for future research.

OBJECTIVES

- To provide the reader with a brief summary of the history of various forms of family violence, the theories used to explain family violence, and the most common responses to it
- Based on our discussion of the responses to family violence, we will lay out a series of prescriptions for improved response—highlighting what works and what does not—as well as suggestions for both prevention and intervention
- We will conclude by offering the reader a perspective on the ways in which reductions in social inequalities of gender, race and ethnicity, sexuality, age, and so on would inevitably produce reductions in family violence

KEY TERMS

corporal punishment

family theories

environmental and contextual
   explanations

feminist theories and power theories

Conflict Tactics Scale

intergenerational transmission of
   violence theory

restorative justice models

Family and Medical Leave Act

INTRODUCTION

We began this book by arguing that families—in the United States and around the world—are complex and when taken together form a complex institution that is both thriving and evolving in response to changing requirements, expectations, and shifts in other institutions and social structures, including the economy and the legal system. At the time of the writing of this book, Judge Vaughn Walker ruled in the potentially landmark "gay marriage/Proposition 8" case in California that marriage is genderless; in other words, this ruling legalized marriage between two men or two women. Though controversial and not likely settled yet, most analysts believe the case will end up in the US Supreme Court; the legalization of gay marriage—which parallels the state-by-state legalization of interracial marriage—is yet another example of the changing state of the institution of the family in response to changing societal norms.

This book does not address the issue of the changing composition of the institution of families, but rather focuses on the dark side of family life: violence. Regardless of the social changes that contribute to different forms of family violence, family violence is never okay. It is never a "healthy" or "reasonable" adaptation, and it is never a solution.

SOCIAL CHANGES

There have been a variety of societal changes that have shaped family violence. As we discussed at length in Chapter 2, though there are differences in the emergence of different forms of family violence in US history, one commonality is the awareness of family violence. Prior to the mid-twentieth century, there was a high tolerance for responding to "undesirable" behavior with **corporal punishment**, and men—fathers and husbands—who were charged with the moral development of their children and wives, were allowed to engage in physical violence in order to achieve this. As such, unless children or wives were murdered or severely injured, their physical abuse was not only not defined as problematic or "abuse," but was fully legally and tacitly sanctioned by society. Social workers began to raise concerns about child abuse and neglect during the Great Depression, when many single mothers struggled even to provide food and shelter for their children. It was not until the second-wave feminist movement of the 1960s and 1970s that any attention was placed on spousal abuse, and this attention generated more focus on other forms of power-related abuse, including child abuse and elder abuse. Thus, family violence has largely been an area of concern and study for only forty years or so.

Elder abuse was also largely shaped by the societal changes that impacted the ways in which we, as a culture, defined abuse and the degree to which we considered it a concern. Additionally, as noted in Chapter 2, elder abuse was also impacted by an additional societal change: specifically, the changes in life expectancy across the twentieth century. At the turn of the twentieth century, the average life expectancy, though it varied by race and gender, was in the midforties. Few people lived long enough to become "elderly," and thus the incidence of elder abuse was limited. Across the twentieth century life expectancy soared to the midseventies, again, with variations by race and gender, and as a result people not only lived long enough to become "elderly" but lived long enough to develop a series of chronic and debilitating diseases—such as diabetes, cancer, and especially Alzheimer's disease—that resulted in their need for living assistance and even institutionalization, which contributed significantly to the increased risk the elderly face for experiencing all forms of abuse.

In the previous twenty years or so, largely as a result of the work of feminist activists and scholars, definitions of abuse were also expanded. By focusing attention on the power that exists in abusive relationships, feminist scholars illuminated the importance of expanding definitions of abuse to include emotional abuse, psychological abuse, sexual abuse, and even financial abuse and neglect. Today, it is widely accepted by scholars, activists, and practitioners that some abusive relationships may never involve physical violence, yet the impact of other forms of abuse may be just as severe, or even more severe; additionally, it is not uncommon for abusive relationships to incorporate multiple forms of abuse. This recognition shapes our response to abusive relationships as well as our approaches to prevention.

THEORIES AND METHODS

In Chapters 3 and 4 we explored both the theories and the methods that are used by scientists who study family violence to understand, explain, and predict various forms of family violence. In sum, there are three key theoretical approaches utilized by scholars of family violence: family theories, environmental and contextual theories, and feminist and power theories.

1. **Family theories** focus on the family as a unit that is composed of a set of complex relationships. Families experience conflict, and when they do,

lacking other skills, individuals may turn to violence as a mechanism for resolving conflict or solving problems. Furthermore, as noted above, roles inside of families often involve requirements of socializing or providing care for other members. In this capacity, some members of a family may employ violence or other abusive behaviors, believing that these strategies are necessary—the corporal punishment of children—or they may result from the intense pressures to accomplish socialization or caregiving. Last, family violence theorists acknowledge that abuse tends to follow patterns of power: those with more power abusing those with less power because "they can" and because "it works." In other words, parents may physically punish children or husbands may batter wives in response to a behavior they do not like, and it generally has the desired effect: the behavior ceases. Practitioners who subscribe to the family violence paradigm focus on interventions that involve the entire family; for example, family therapy may be used to address domestic violence or parenting classes may be used as a tool to reduce child abuse and neglect.

2. **Environmental and contextual explanations** do not constitute a separate theoretical paradigm but rather are subsumed into other theoretical frameworks, including family theory, criminology theories, and even some aspects of feminist theory. Environmental and contextual explanations focus on the role that environmental stressors and context play in producing family violence. For example, research on child abuse reveals that parents of children with special needs, parents with an above-average number of children, and single parents are at greater risk for engaging in child abuse and neglect. Similarly, elder-care givers who are part of the "sandwich" generation—caring for both aging parents and children simultaneously—are at greater risk for engaging in elder abuse and neglect. Recognizing the role that environmental stressors and context play in producing family violence results in intervention and prevention strategies that focus primarily on the factors that put families at risk for abuse.

3. **Feminist theories and power theories** of violence focus on the role that power and privilege play in producing family violence. Feminist scholars argue that abuse almost always follows the same pattern: abuse is perpetrated by individuals who occupy positions of higher status, and the victims are always members of oppressed groups. For example, the vast majority of intimate partner violence involves men, who often hold positions of economic, as well as physical, power, abusing women; child abuse involves parents—who have every type of power—abusing children; and similarly elder abuse is predicated on the status hierarchy of age. Last, feminist theory shapes prevention and intervention by focusing on disrupting sys-

tems of power at the structural level and encouraging the acknowledgment of power and privilege at the individual level in ways that lead to greater awareness and a lesser likelihood of using that privilege in destructive ways.

In the case of family violence, data are collected in a variety of ways, including surveys, interviews, observations, and the reporting that is required of various agencies at the local, state, and federal levels. For example, the Bureau of Justice Statistics requires that all local law enforcement jurisdictions relate all crimes that are reported, investigated, and closed annually. National studies such as the National Crime Victimization Survey involve calling randomly selected individuals and surveying them about their experiences as victims of crimes. Both of these methods are used to create prevalence estimates for various types of crime in the United States. Additionally, scholars may conduct interviews, surveys, or observations among smaller populations in order to learn more about a particular aspect of crime. For example, we have interviewed nearly fifty men who either were court-ordered to a batterer intervention program or were required to work with CPS—because they had battered their female partners in front of their children—in order to learn more about the "triggers" men identify that lead them to engage in violence. These types of studies are especially useful for exploring family violence in special populations that may be less visible or even invisible in national studies; these studies are especially important in the case of marginalized populations, such as same-sex couples and immigrants. Last, we note that scholars of the family violence paradigm have designed survey tools, specifically the **Conflict Tactics Scale**, in order to explore the utility of family theory in explaining family violence. The reader will recall that the CTS has been administered dozens of times to dozens of different samples—both national samples and local samples. The primary contribution of the CTS is that it was developed based on the assumption that violence can be and often is perpetrated by both members of the couple, and thus it was the first tool capable of revealing the otherwise hidden phenomenon of "mutual combat."

DATA ON FAMILY VIOLENCE

Despite rigorous methods for identifying and measuring family violence, estimating the prevalence of various forms of family violence is difficult and likely to be subject to flaws that result, primarily, in underestimates. Family violence is largely underestimated because a certain amount of it goes unreported and undetected. Because developing statistical estimates of family violence requires some sort of reporting, national statistics are likely to underestimate the actual number of victims and incidents. Additionally, as noted above, though we now have social and legal definitions of abuse, reporting of abuse requires that the victim or perpetrator define the behavior as such, or it requires being witnessed by an outsider who labels it as abuse; because most family violence occurs inside the home, though, this is not common. In some cases, ideological beliefs will prevent accurate identification and intervention in abuse cases. For example, there remain large pockets of parents who believe that corporal punishment does not constitute abuse, despite social norms and even laws that label it as such. In many cases, a victim's own shame may prevent them from labeling their experiences as abuse and subsequently reporting them.

That said, unfortunately, family abuse is very common. Estimates by the CDC as well as reviews of medical records suggest that as many as 2.3 million Americans over the age of sixty experience some form of abuse—based on their age status—each year. The statistics on child abuse are even more startling. As many as 5.8 million children are the victims of child abuse each year, and tragically 1,800 children per year die as a result of the abuse or neglect. The most common form of family abuse is intimate partner violence; estimates are that at least one in four women will be in an abusive relationship in her lifetime, and as many as 50 percent of all women—including many who will never live in an abusive relationship—will experience *one abusive incident*. Why is intimate partner violence so much more prevalent than either elder or child abuse? We suspect that there are two key reasons: ideological and structural. Ideologically, as we have discussed at length in this book, the long history of tolerating gender-based violence coupled with a resurgence of cultural and religious supports for rigid, and inherently unequal, gender roles result in strongly held beliefs that tolerate if not promote the abuse of women by their intimate partners. Structurally, one of the key differences between intimate partner violence and either child or elder abuse is the probability that a woman will have many different partners across her lifetime, whereas children will likely have only one set of parents and parents only one set of children. Thus, in abusive households, the risk to children or elders is extremely high, but it is simultaneously extremely low in households that are free from abuse. In contrast, a woman may have eight to ten intimate relationships in her lifetime, including serious dating relationships, cohabiting relationships, and marriages, and with each subsequent partner, her risk for being abused "resets." This increased exposure to different potential abusers, which is more or less unique to women and occurs only rarely in the cases of children and elders, results in significantly higher rates of intimate partner violence than either elder or child abuse. That said, despite the fact that we know battered women have a very difficult time leaving abusive relationships, children and elder victims have almost no chance unless the abuse or neglect is detected. Thus, for those children or elders living with abuse, the likelihood that it will be severe and long lasting is high. Intimate partner violence may constitute a single incident after which a woman leaves the abusive relationship, or it may last her entire lifetime.

NEGATIVE CONSEQUENCES ASSOCIATED WITH IPV

We devoted the second half of this book to an extensive and multichapter discussion of intimate partner violence, and in these discussions we documented the negative outcomes associated with IPV. These range from physical injury, emotional hurt and pain, and billions of dollars in health care costs to untold losses in economic productivity, the costs of services for battered women and their children, and finally the costs associated with the criminal justice system: responding to domestic calls, detaining batterers, and adjudicating the cases.

But the biggest negative consequences associated with IPV are not the economic costs born by a variety of institutions, but rather the costs to families in the contemporary United States. Most individuals who end up in violent relationships never intended for their relationships to go this way. As we noted in Chapter 7, many of the women we interviewed, and in fact *all* of the African American women we interviewed, experienced sexual abuse or had premature, "consensual" sexual relationships—we refer to this as premature sex engagement—that left them impaired in their abilities to deal with romantic partners (Hattery 2009). Many of the women and men we interviewed witnessed violence in the families in which they grew up. Many of the men, and this was especially true for African Americans, witnessed severe violence, even gun murders of parents in their homes. Many men vowed that they would never treat their romantic partners and their children this way. Yet they did.

But I still look at it like this. I think as far, you know, young men we come up and we gonna see our mothers and our fathers together, you know we come up and we that get that thing going on, you know, like my moms was married to my real dad, I did see him slam her head on the car, I was in the car, I did see that one, so you know, I think I think these young men when we see that when we children and as we grow up we like I'd never do that when I get married. I get married I never do that, I ain't gonna say this, I ain't gonna do that to my wife, but when we grow up, you know what I'm sayin', not knowin', you know what I'm sayin', in our mind, that's what we really been taught to do, that how we been taught to deal with things, you know, moms say something she smack in the mouth or somethin' like that, that kind a stick with guys you know, well guys say I ain't gonna do this, I ain't gonna do that, but when they get in the situation that do exactly that, you know.

Manny, twentysomething African American man, North Carolina

The primary negative outcome of IPV is that it ruins individual lives, and it ruins families. Boys who grow up *witnessing* violence in their homes have triple the risk for becoming physically violent with their own romantic partners than boys who do not (Ehrensaft and Cohen 2003). Boys who grow up in families in which their fathers (or father figures) beat their mothers learn an important lesson: that women have no value and that women's self-interests are not linked with their own. This is similar to the findings of Scully's (1990) interviews with convicted rapists who reported that "rape" was when they decided they forced a woman to have sex, not when the woman herself made the same claim.

Living with IPV is stressful at its minimum and lethal at its most severe. For women, living with IPV can mean having to learn to apply makeup to cover cuts and bruises, learning to scream into a pillow so that the children will not hear, choosing homelessness, or living in a shelter in a new city or state or region of the country in order to survive. For men who are abusive, the outcomes of violence include living with someone who is afraid of you, often being separated from your children, and in some cases may include being arrested, charged with a crime, and some sort of punishment, ranging from attending an intervention program to incarceration.

So often scholars of IPV, and we as a culture, focus on the toll that IPV takes on its victims. But men who perpetrate this kind of violence lose as well. They lose the chance to have a loving, intimate relationship with another person. They often lose the chance to raise their children or have any sort of relationship with them. They lose the chance to fulfill that part of the American dream that includes making and raising a family. And they must live with the pain that they have hurt someone they claim to love and the guilt that they have created a toxic environment for their children. By exposing their children to violence, they are contributing to the intergenerational nature of this poisonous phenomenon. Men, too, are hurt by the violence they perpetrate. Therefore, it is in their self-interest to reduce the prevalence of this social ill.

The Intergenerational Transmission of Violence

Though most men who grow up in violent households do not become violent, nevertheless, those who do are at a significantly greater risk for becoming violent.

Intergenerational transmission of violence theory: the belief that the predilection to be violent and abusive, especially the likelihood of becoming a batterer, is inherited from one generation to another.

Will argues just that point. Although Will's adherence to this belief may in part be a mechanism to excuse his behavior, it is also clear that he understands something about the intergenerational transmission of violence in his own family history.

It's heredity, but I think some people take it a different way by heredity, you know, how they pick it up. One way I think the main way, that I see it as, from seeing it. From you seeing it. It's not in your blood. It's actually from seeing it.

Will, fiftysomething African American men, Minnesota

We argue that we need to further explore the mechanism for intergenerational transmission. Unlike many aspects of socialization and social learning, we do not believe it is as simple as boys learning by watching their fathers. Rather, we learned a great deal about a possible mechanism for transmission when we asked the men we interviewed what advice they would give their sons. Their responses fell primarily into two categories: do not get hooked up with a bad woman, and do not get played.

Analyzing the advice these men gave or planned to give their sons, we would argue that what gets passed on in the intergenerational transmission are beliefs about men and women: beliefs about gender. Men intend to teach their sons how to be masculine. They may not teach them explicitly that they should hit their romantic partners, but they teach them how to be the "man of the house," how to be in control, how to require certain behavior from their romantic partners. Furthermore, they teach their sons lessons about women. For example, they teach their sons about appropriate roles for women, about behaviors that are common in women, and about the ways in which women will try to manipulate and control them. In essence, they need not explicitly teach their sons to hit women, as partner violence, especially verbal abuse, will be a logical outgrowth of their general lessons about the way women are, what it means to be a man, and the roles of men and women in a relationship. If boys learn that they are the ones in charge, that women are out to manipulate them, and that *real men* keep their women in line, then it is quite likely that these boys will grow up to be perpetrators of IPV, even if they are bound and determined not to become batterers like their fathers.

As far as my son goes, I'm gonna teach him to stand up for himself, not to let anybody run over him. Just to really be cautious about who he deals with, um, to really, really get to know the person, not just having sex with them and stuff like that, to really get to know someone before you get involved with them, 'cause there's so many diseases, it's, uh, you have some . . . out there and so he just really needs to be aware of what that person likes and dislikes and see if it matches up with some of the stuff he likes and dislikes before he gets involved with her and makes a mistake.

Ward, thirtysomething African American man, North Carolina

PROPOSALS FOR CHANGE

In the following section, we begin with specific recommendations that could be implemented by various institutions, and we conclude with musings about the relationship between reducing inequalities and reductions in various forms of family abuse.

Criminal Justice System

As we discussed at length in Chapter 13, there are a variety of interventions into family violence by the criminal justice system; the success of the criminal justice system in intervening in family violence is variable, however. As we argued in Chapter 13, there are seldom law enforcement or legal interventions in child abuse or elder abuse cases for a variety of reasons, most notably because the victims in these cases differ in one significant way: the victims are unable or extremely unlikely to report the abuse or call the police. In the next section, we will discuss other potential "sites" for intervention that may be more successful. With regards to the occasions when someone reports the abuse or calls 911, which is most likely to happen in cases of intimate partner violence, there are a number of issues that need to be addressed:

- Ideological constructs constrain responders' ability to identify abuse. As noted in both our discussion of history and our discussion of "responses," part of what limits appropriate law enforcement and criminal justice responses to family violence is the long-held and intractable beliefs about punishment. As noted earlier, beliefs about child discipline and appropriate gender roles often prohibit responders from identifying abuse and intervening appropriately.
- In many cases, perpetrators have established a high level of control through using terroristic strategies; when confronted, a victim may be too afraid to admit that abuse is occurring or may refuse to press charges or testify.
- In some cases, especially cases of IPV in which victims are fighting back, responders report that they "have trouble" determining which person initiated the violence and is thus the perpetrator and which person is the victim. Research indicates that this problem is cited frequently in cases of same-sex couple violence.
- Law enforcement personnel do not like dealing with family violence, and as noted in Chapter 13, one of the major impediments to preventing and interrupting IPV is the unwillingness of law enforcement agents to serve and enforce protective orders.

- For many of the above reasons, prosecutors are often reluctant to pursue abuse cases, and judges are often reluctant to impose sentences that include incarceration or, for that matter, any level of accountability.
- Because some components of IPV are civil rather than criminal matters, judges rarely if ever impose sanctions on perpetrators that hold them accountable. In cases that land in criminal court, abusers may be sentenced, for example, to an intervention program that is not required to report attendance to the court or a probation officer.

Considering each of these shortcomings of the criminal justice system, we propose the following recommendations:

- Educate, educate, educate! All professionals who have the slightest possibility of interacting with victims of any form of family violence must be educated about the nuances of the offender-victim relationship so that they can more accurately identify abuse and respond appropriately to it. Beginning with some basic principles such as it is never okay to hit another person or to deny him or her access to the basics in terms of food, housing, and sanitation, law enforcement and criminal justice staff must be educated about the realities of family violence and myths must be debunked. As our colleague Patricia Yancey Martin (2005) demonstrated, when this type of education is employed by rape crisis centers, the interventions are perceived as being more fair and appropriate by both the victim and the offender.
- Incarcerate when necessary. Incarceration can serve several functions, including punishment, deterrence, and public safety. Although it has not been shown to be much of a deterrent on precriminal populations, it may serve a deterrent function for future violence among perpetrators of some forms of family violence. And while incarceration is not likely to be effective for sexually abusive perpetrators, it may be for those who engage in physical violence and financial abuse. Last, incarceration can be a way to ensure the future safety of the victims, be they children, a spouse, or an elderly parent.
- Alternatives to incarceration. Despite the potential that incarceration has to meet several important needs when we as a society respond to family violence, it may not always be the ideal response. Specifically in cases in which the abuse is not severe or long-term, it may be possible to treat individuals who have engaged in abuse so that they can become contributing members of society. Additionally, depending upon the severity and types of abuse, there may be both a desire and advantages associated with reconciliation, if and only if the perpetrator can be successfully treated and rehabilitated. Many victims of IPV hope to reconcile with their abusive partners, and many

children could benefit from ongoing relationships with their parents, provided they can be educated and supported in nonabusive parenting techniques. Additionally, in cases of both IPV and child abuse, incarcerating the perpetrator prevents him (or her) from working and thus providing income for the family, which is generally never in the best interest of the victims.

We suggest that in some cases, perhaps most that involve early intervention, alternatives to incarceration would be most effective in responding to family violence. Let us be clear; we believe accountability must be required. Connecting intervention programs with probation and parole services, as is the practice with substance-abuse treatment programs, would provide that accountability, ensure the completion of the reeducation programs, and allow the batterer to remain employed and contributing financially to his family. We can imagine a similar model for parents who engage in child abuse. Given the high cost and other negative consequences associated with foster care, even a small probability for success of this type of model makes it worth trying.

As noted in Chapter 13, another attempt to achieve better outcomes while ensuring accountability is being explored through domestic violence courts that utilize restorative justice models. **Restorative justice models** are built on the assumption that families will try to stay together or reunite if they have the freedom to do so as well, and thus the resocialization of perpetrators will ultimately be in the best interest of all parties, even if the family members choose to separate. We remind the reader that this model can and often does provide not only accountability but also higher rates of "reeducation" and a higher probability for reunification and a cessation of violence. We suggest that more jurisdictions explore domestic violence courts based in restorative justice models as alternatives to incarceration.

PREVENTION AND INTERVENTION

We must begin thinking of prevention and early intervention of family abuse just as we do with regards to many health issues, including regular visits to the dentist, cancer screening such as mammography, and health screenings for conditions such as high blood pressure and diabetes. These prevention and early intervention strategies save numerous lives and save our health care system and government billions of dollars per year. Thus, we strongly advocate a significantly greater investment in both prevention and early intervention programs, for which there are many models that could be adopted at relatively low cost and a high payoff.

Given the prevalence of the early warning signs in actual cases of IPV (see Chapter 12), and given the relative ease in teaching about both the early warning signs as well as strategies for developing healthy relationships rather than potentially predatory ones, we feel strongly that well-developed and extensively integrated prevention programs could be pivotal in reducing IPV, especially dating violence among young people. Prevention programs could be built into many already existing institutions and curricula. For example, Family Services in Forsyth County, North Carolina, has developed a teen program geared toward addressing all aspects of healthy relationships, including when and how to make decisions about sexual activity, reproductive health, and of course dating violence. Though this program is currently only voluntary, the staff hope to get permission from the school board to provide the healthy-relationships curriculum to the local high school health educators. Based on successful programs, "healthy relationship" units that focus on preventing dating violence while promoting healthy relationships based on partnership rather than traditional gender roles that promote male dominance and female submission could be routinely added to the health classes that all students in public high schools take in the ninth and tenth grades. These units would fit comfortably alongside already existing units on sex education, nutrition and fitness, and drug and alcohol education. We believe these types of programs hold tremendous promise for reducing the most common types of IPV—those based on the cultural norms derived from traditional gender roles. Last, we note that these programs could be developed in ways that are not "sexuality specific" such that they would prevent IPV in both heterosexual and same-sex relationships.

Both child abuse prevention programs and elder abuse prevention programs could be targeted toward those individuals who are preparing for and in the early stages of either parenting or caregiving for an elder. Identifying new parents is far easier than elder caregivers, primarily because parenting begins at a certain moment that typically is initiated in a hospital, whereas elder caregiving may begin slowly and intermittently and without a specific starting point. That said, we believe that models for preventing child abuse could be modified to address elder abuse.

We would recommend that a variety of parenting programs and child prevention programs be implemented routinely beginning with the initial prenatal examination and extending through childhood and the teenage years. One approach that we have seen is the monthly newsletter that many hospitals send to new parents. Each monthly installment describes the typical development that parents can expect at each month as well as the challenges that parents might face. For example, because colic often begins in the third month, the third installment often carries a discussion of colic, how to recognize it, and tips for dealing with it. As the child ages, these newsletters could be reduced to twice per year and include discussions of appropriate discipline, and for preteens and teenagers the newsletter would likely include suggestions for boundary setting and materials that would guide discussions about sexuality, drugs and alcohol, driving safety, and so forth. Once a child enters school, these newsletters could be disseminated by the school district but include health information generated by the local pediatrics department. This type of newsletter would likely have some impact on reducing child abuse as well as improving health outcomes for children.

BOX 14.1 **UNIVERSITY OF WISCONSIN**

University of Wisconsin-Extension ■ Cooperative Extension ■ B3790

Parenting the First Year

MONTH 1

What is baby like?

If your baby doesn't have much hair, has short arms and legs, and has a head that looks too big, your baby looks pretty normal! Baby might not be what you expected, though.

Maybe you didn't get the boy or girl you wanted, or maybe the baby just doesn't fit the picture of the "dream baby" you thought about during pregnancy or saw in magazines and on television.

It can take time to get used to your baby. Some parents love their new arrival right away; others have to get to know the baby better. That's normal.

It may be a little bit scary at first to care for a tiny infant. But you'll gain confidence with time.

Do yourself a favor...

Becoming a parent is an exciting change, but it will take time to feel comfortable in your new roles. Parents and babies learn together. Don't expect to know how to do everything overnight.

During the first weeks after your baby is born, you may be surprised by your strong feelings. You may feel down or on the verge of tears for seemingly no reason. For mothers, these feelings may come from the changes your body undergoes to return to normal. You may also feel thrilled and proud.

For the time being, keep your days as simple as possible. When you are having a rough time, talk with someone close to you.

Baby's states

Every 3 to 4 hours baby may move between these six states:

- **deep sleep** — breathing is deep and regular
- **light sleep** — baby's eyelids flutter, breathing is shallower, baby may startle or move
- **drowsiness** — baby may fuss, eyes sleepily open, may wake more fully or fall back to sleep

- **awake alert** — baby is most responsive, body and eyes seem more focused
- **fussy alert** — baby seems over-stimulated, fusses, turns away, thrashes
- **crying** — baby cries, gets parents' attention, with soothing may sleep or return to alert state

Watch how your baby moves from one state to another. This will help you learn your baby's unique behavior.

Your baby wants you to know:

- I like to look at your face the most, but also like bright colors, mirrors, and patterns.
- I feel comforted when you hold me and talk to me.
- I stare at things, but I don't grab for them yet.
- Loud noise, bright light, and rough handling scare me. Handle me gently.
- I may quiet when someone picks me up and cuddles me.
- Please change my position sometimes so I can look at different things.
- When you move me, I like your hand behind my neck, so my head doesn't flop over.

A similar model could be developed and designed to prevent elder abuse. The primary challenges would be identifying who needs the information and disseminating it at the right time. Because elder caregiving, as noted, may begin slowly and intermittently, it may not be possible to identify appropriate recipients of the newsletters until families engage an institution such as their health care provider, home health care system, or residential programs. That said, in all cases in which an adult child accompanies their parent to a health care appointment, screening for caregiving could begin. Both the adult child and the senior could be offered information regarding the early stages of caregiving, including discussions of expectations and challenges. Regular newsletters (or other forms of contact, such as e-notes) could follow, with each installment addressing different issues, including hiring care providers and handling finances as well as a discussion of the kinds of physical and mental decline that can be expected. These programs are built on the assumption that in cases of both child abuse and elder abuse, lack of information, lack of understanding about what to expect, and feelings of being overwhelmed are causes of the majority of both child and elder abuse. Thus, in a best-case scenario, this approach would reduce a majority of cases of both child and elder abuse.

Education programs such as these, however, primarily address neglect; unfortunately, much child and elder abuse takes the form of physical abuse and sexual abuse. We believe that there is very little that programming can do to prevent these types of abuse. Thus, we address the issue of intervention. Clearly, intervention is important in all cases, not just those involving severe abuse, neglect, or sexual abuse. As we noted in Chapters 5 and 6, there are a variety of forces that reduce the likelihood of intervention. With regards to child and elder abuse, one of the key barriers is the small probability that the victim will report the abuse or call 911. Thus, the thrust of interventions will have to be located in institutions, including the health care system, schools, and senior day programs, where the abuse can be recognized and detected without the victim having to report it directly. Though abuse is more often identified and reported in emergency room cases, we strongly recommend that routine screening for child abuse and elder abuse be developed and implemented among family physicians and internists who see patients for their routine and nonemergency care. As was the case with law enforcement and the criminal justice system, we begin by noting that physicians and other health care staff need to be educated about child abuse and elder abuse. They must be trained to recognize less severe violence, abuse in its early stages, and symptoms of nonphysical abuse, namely, emotional or psychological abuse and sexual abuse. Additionally, we must develop reporting mechanisms and protocols that are "easy," not time-consuming, and otherwise not prohibitive; for example, health care providers should never worry that reporting possible abuse would in any way damage their reputations or leave them open for lawsuits. Simultaneously, we should consider developing sanctions for failing to report abuse that could reasonably be identified by a group of one's peers; these could be developed similarly to the way in which medical malpractice standards are established. These strategies would move us significantly forward in terms of intervening in both child and elder abuse. One example of this is provided by the Texas State Department of Health and Human Services.

| **BOX 14.2** | **TEXAS SEXUAL ABUSE OF A CHILD STANDARD** |

Texas Family Code on Child Abuse

The Family Code requires that you not knowingly fail to report any case where a child may be adversely affected by abuse. In particular, there have been some misunderstanding of the criminal laws relating to offenses against children. Sexual abuse, including sexual assault and indecency with a child, can occur even when there is no force, duress, or coercion; in other words when the minor and his or her partner are both willing sexual partners. Your own attorney can explain these criminal laws to you *so that you can then report when required by law.*

Source: Texas Department of State Health Services (http://www.dshs.state.tx.us/child abusereporting/default.shtm)

Similarly, education programs that are required for all teachers and senior day programming staff should focus on recognizing the early signs of all forms of abuse. Because teachers and day programming staff are likely to have the most regular contact of any nonfamily member, with potential victims, the educating of these staff has the potential to be *even more powerful* in successful intervention approaches. As with health care providers, we must develop mechanisms that are "easy" and not time-consuming and ensure the professional and personal safety of the reporter. For example, the Texas Department of Health and Human Services allows for reports of child abuse to be made online. Their department website is careful to point out that they are mandated to investigate any report that reasonably suggests abuse might have taken place. As noted in the previous text box, the department also makes clear that failure to knowingly report the presence of abuse is an actionable offense. Furthermore, the department website makes clear that a report need only indicate the child about whom one is suspicious. Any other information—such as the name of the suspected abuser or addresses for the child or abuser—is helpful but not required. These types of mechanisms—such as online reporting and requiring only the name of the child—tend to streamline the process and if implemented widely would likely increase dramatically the number of cases that would be investigated in the early stages before greater harm has been done to the victims and more severe consequences face the perpetrator. Early intervention improves the likelihood of rehabilitation and reconciliation, both of which are often desirable for both victims and offenders. We turn now to a larger and more esoteric discussion of the types of broader social changes that would likely result in decreases in all forms of family violence.

THE BIG PICTURE: REDUCTIONS IN INEQUALITY

Our analysis and framework for understanding family violence are based on the express assumption that all forms of family violence are outgrowths of inequalities, both inequalities of status, such as gender, race, age, or sexuality, as well as inequalities within individual relationships. Based on these assumptions we would expect family violence to follow general patterns: IPV will generally involve men perpetrating abuse against their female partners, child abuse will involve parents and stepparents abusing children as well as older siblings abusing younger siblings, and elder abuse will involve adult children abusing their vulnerable parents. The explanation for these patterns is that individuals hold social power imbued to them via systems of domination—patriarchy, age, and so forth—and this power can be abused by engaging in violence against the person with less access to social power. At the individual level, we see the interaction of these systems of domination vis-à-vis individual access to power, such that IPV often takes the form it does because men typically earn more money than their female partners, and this leaves women dependent upon their male partners to meet their basic needs and thus vulnerable to IPV. Similarly, children and older adults are vulnerable to abuse because they are dependent economically and in so many other ways on the people who care for them. Of course, part of what becomes interesting is when abuse follows the societal patterns but defies the actual individual situation. For example, as we discussed extensively in Chapter 8, when men are unemployed and find themselves economically dependent on their female partners, this creates a climate ripe for intimate partner violence. Thus, the inability to remain dominant at the individual level—as the breadwinner—often leads men to turn to the social power imbued to them by patriarchy in order to reestablish their dominance in their relationship, and this reassertion of dominance is often accomplished through the use of violence.

PRESCRIPTIONS FOR PREVENTING AND INTERRUPTING
FAMILY VIOLENCE: DISRUPTING INEQUALITIES

As we have argued, much abuse is an outgrowth of social inequalities and inequalities in individual families. Thus, here we offer societal-level approaches to reducing inequality and thus reducing all forms of family violence. Though there are differences that characterize the various forms of family violence—for example, the elderly are the most vulnerable to economic or financial abuse, whereas young girls are the most vulnerable to sexual abuse—we believe that our overall argument can be and should be extended to all forms of family violence. In short, as long as some people are relegated to the status of second-class citizens while others occupy positions of power and privilege, all forms of family violence will be present in numbers that impact millions of Americans and adversely affect our social world.

Economic Reform

One of the constant themes throughout our discussions has been the issue of economics, finances, and money. As we noted in Chapter 9, dominant ideologies of masculinity prescribe that men take on the role of "breadwinner." Moreover, many if not most women expect that their male partners will contribute significantly to the economy of the household (Bianchi, Robinson, and Milkie 2007). When men are unable to meet the economic needs of the family, they often report being nagged by their female partners, and they often feel their masculinity threatened. In fact, scholars and family therapists alike agree that one of the most common sources of couple arguments is money: how much the family needs, who is going to earn it, how much needs to be saved, and how it is going to be spent.

We argue that most men (and women) should be contributing economically to their households unless they are incapable of doing so—perhaps they are disabled—or unless they are "stay-at-home" dads, which remains relatively rare in the United States. According to the most recent 2010 census, the percentage of men who are stay-at-home dads continues to lag below the 10 percent mark. Additionally, many men need to take more economic responsibility for their families than they do, a problem we encountered in our interviews and an issue that is significantly increasing as a result of the current economic climate. However, we argue that in order to make serious headway on the problem of IPV as it is associated with economics, we need to demand serious economic reform. The truth of the matter is that even in the best-case scenario, where a hardworking man is working full-time, year-round, he will have to make at least nine dollars an hour in order to keep his family above the federally established poverty line. As most poverty experts note, though, living above the poverty line does not mean that you are "making ends meet" (see Edin and Lein 1997). We suspect that over time, we would see a decline in IPV if we returned to an economy that offered a living wage to all employees, not just those with special skills and advanced education (Ehrenreich 2001). Although the recession is too "new" for there to be any solid data on its correlation with IPV and child abuse, we can speculate with a great degree of certainty that the economic recession that began in late 2007 and early 2008 has increased the rate of both IPV and child abuse. Anecdotally, we know from speaking with colleagues who run battered women's shelters that calls to domestic violence hotlines and requests for shelter stays have increased significantly since the fall of 2007. We can also anticipate that the downturn in the economy has made the elderly more vulnerable. As their retirement and 401k accounts were pummeled by the huge drops in the stock market as well as financial crimes such as those perpetrated by scam artists like Bernie Madoff and the Enron scandal, they inevitably became more dependent upon their children to assist them in meeting their daily needs. In some cases, this may result in an elderly person finding him- or herself no longer able to pay for home health care or institutionalized care and having to move in with one of his or her children. As we discussed extensively in Chapter 5, this creates an environment ripe for the stresses that lead to elder abuse.

Economic reform that provides a living wage to men is not the only key to disrupting IPV. As discussed at length in Chapter 8, women are vulnerable to IPV because of the economic oppression they suffer. As long as women continue to earn only a portion of men's wages—currently, women earn seventy-one cents on the male dollar, a ratio that has remained relatively stable for the past twenty years—they will be dependent on men in order to provide economic stability for their families. The outcome of the gendered wage gap is, according to Rich (1980), compulsory heterosexuality or, as we argued in Chapter 8, compulsory partnership. Battered women stay in abusive relationships because they cannot leave *and* feed their children. Battered women who do leave often jump quickly into relationships with men they barely know out of sheer economic need. They need someone to help pay the rent and fill the refrigerator. And the men with whom they jump into relationships often become abusive. Thus, economic reform that provides a livable wage to all workers and reform that will address the gendered wage gap are critical in that these reforms will result in women being less economically vulnerable to their male partners, and thus IPV will be reduced.

GENDER EQUALITY AND DISMANTLING PATRIARCHY

In Chapter 9 we argued that IPV is a "logical" by-product of patriarchy. Inside a system of male domination, in which men are defined as superior and women inferior, in which men have social, political, and economic power and women have little to none (see Zweigenhaft and Domhoff 1998), the prevailing model of gender relations is one of domination, power, and control. Acker (2006) describes this as a *gender inequality regime*. In a system designed around oppression and inequality, it is not surprising that the dominant group uses a variety of means to control the subordinate group—in fact, one would *expect* them to do so. Clearly, not all men are batterers, but as Andrea Dworkin argued, all heterosexual relationships contain the elements necessary for IPV. What is remarkable, frankly, is when some men *choose not to* exercise the power and control they have that is bestowed on them by patriarchy; it is in fact *truly remarkable that the majority of men do not engage in violence against their female partners, even if they grew up witnessing it in their own families.*

Patriarchy is, at its most fundamental level, a system of privilege. Part of the privilege is, as noted, the power to choose when and how to exercise power. Another and equally important aspect of the privilege is the ability to render women and women's "interests" invisible. Scully's study of convicted rapists provides insight into this aspect of privilege: "Since patriarchal societies produce men whose frame of reference excludes women's perspectives, men are able to ignore sexual violence, especially since their culture provides them with such a convenient array of justifications. . . . *Indeed, it appears that . . . a man rapes because his value system provides no compelling reason for him not to do so*" (1990, 116).

We could easily replace "sexual violence" with "intimate partner violence," and it would accurately reflect what men who batter report. The structural rendering of the "victim" or "oppressed" as invisible allows the oppressor to feel justified in his or her behavior.[1] Men batter because they can get away with it and because they do not see the interests of their partners as inextricably tied up with their own.

In examining the relationships of these men and women living with violence, several patterns emerged. As we discussed at length in Chapter 9, many men identify a similar trigger to their violence: their inability to meet the demands as a breadwinner. One of the traps of any system of domination, and patriarchy is no exception, is that it defines very rigid roles for both men and women. Women are relegated to the status of second-class citizen, with little power and few choices. Men are also relegated to a narrow set of available roles: the primary role being that of economic provider. Furthermore, this rigid role assignment is strictly enforced. How do we know? Despite the fact that men, as well as women, are eligible for the provisions of the **Family and Medical Leave Act**, allowing them time off from work when they have a new baby—or adopt or have a sick family member who needs to be cared for—fewer than 10 percent of men take advantage of it, and some report they are not given "permission" by employers to take advantage of this provision to which they are legally entitled (see Hattery 2001). The ranks of the stay-at-home father, though growing, are relatively small, at about 8 percent (nationally). As we noted in other research, when men do stay at home, they incur a great deal of negative feedback for this decision (see Hattery 2001).

Another distinct pattern that emerges in these couples is that men's attempts to control their female partners and their use of violence are often triggered when their female partners engage in behaviors that are perceived *by them* as uppity. In short, women are verbally berated, beaten, and abused when they are *acting as if they are free*.[2]

Women are abused and beaten when they take too long on an errand or return home later than expected. They are abused and beaten when they have lunch with a coworker their partner does not like—which he may define as any man besides himself. They are abused and beaten when they decide they are not going to clean up after their male partners and especially if this involves cleaning up or preparing food for their partners' male friends as they watch sports events, like football or boxing. They are abused and beaten when they decide to change the dinner menu or the time the meal is served. And, mostly, women are abused and beaten when they talk to or express any interest in a man other than their male partner, even though the expression may simply be of the friendship or collegial variety. When women exercise agency, engage in their own decision making, or attempt to wield power, they are verbally berated, beaten, and sexually assaulted. In other words, IPV is a form not only of "rule" enforcement (or discipline) but also of "role" enforcement; women need to know their place. This pattern of violence can only be explained as part of a larger system that is designed to keep women in their "rightful" place, as second-class citizens, on this earth to serve the needs of their male partners. The greatest risk factor for becoming a battered woman is simply being a woman.

THE FINAL WORD: RELATIONSHIPS AS PARTNERSHIPS

Understanding *family violence* requires that we see systems of domination and the ways that they are interconnected. Family violence is a logical outcome of patriarchy, but it is reinforced by other systems of domination, such as class exploitation and racial domination. Fighting the epidemic of family violence means dismantling patriarchy so as to empower women, but it also means that roles for men must be expanded as well. When men are boxed into evaluating themselves within a narrow framework of masculinity, they will almost always fail. Thus, revising our constructions of masculinity (as well as femininity) will offer men more opportunities for success, but also a richer life experience. What does this mean? Practically, it can mean things like associating masculinity with being a "good dad." Being a supportive partner can be defined as being a "real man." It means transforming heterosexual relationships into partnerships. Referring back to our discussion in Chapter 9, this would mean defining both men and women in relation to their intimate relationship and in relation to the labor market. As long as we continue to define men primarily by their relationship to the labor market (I am a plumber or I am a banker) and women primarily by their relationship to men (Tom's wife), we will be unable to transform heterosexual relationships into true partnerships.[3]

Destroying the notion that men must be breadwinners and women must be restricted to the role of "support" (taking care of the home and the children, being supportive of her man) and replacing it with a notion that men and women in heterosexual (or same-sex) relationships are in partnerships would have many positive outcomes. The notion of partnership suggests equality and interdependence. If one is interdependent on one's partner, then it would be totally against one's self-interest to sabotage or harm that partner. If men and women identified their self-interests as interconnected, then the result would be healthier, happier, more fulfilling relationships for all of us. And violence would become a rare event.

Dismantling patriarchy, however, means more than simply creating new constructions of masculinity and femininity and new norms around gender relations in relationships—both heterosexual and same sex. For true equality to arise and for a serious reduction in IPV, women must be given access to real social, political, and economic power. Women must be paid a fair wage, women must have the opportunity for political leadership, and women must have access to social leadership as well. The same holds true with regards to sexuality. Both gay men and lesbians, who also build relationships that can be constrained by traditional stereotypes about gender and masculinity and femininity, need to have real access to social, political, and economic power as well. Only when they have access to these sources of power and can live as citizens of the "first world" will they be able to build meaningful relationships free of the negative trappings of heterosexual relationships and thus free of violence. For this to be effective, however, disrupting systems of gender domination will also *require* the simultaneous dismantling of racial domination, heterosexual domination, and reformation of the economy.

In order for men and women to live healthy, productive lives in relationships with each other, both men *and* women need to be freed from the severe economic exploitation that currently exists in the political economy of the United States. The rich continue to get rich by stealing the labor of the poor. Every time a worker is paid less than he or she is worth, the net gain goes to the business owner. Only when men and women are paid a fair and living wage for their work, only when they are all offered opportunities for economic advancement based on fair principles, not the exploitation of others, will they be able to live in healthy relationships with each other, relationships that are free of violence. This is particularly important for lesbians, who because of the gendered wage gap typically have lower overall household earnings than their straight counterparts. Indeed, as D'Emilio (1983) notes, economic freedom is essential not only to healthy gay and lesbian partnerships but to their very existence!

Finally, as we noted above, minority men must not be treated as second-class citizens in economic, political, or social life—and especially in the criminal justice system—if they are to develop a healthy masculine self-identity. Similarly, we cannot justify the battering of minority women by invoking a system that devalues them and their bodies. True equality for men and women is tied to equality for *all* men and *all* women, regardless of race or ethnicity (see Davis 1983). Moreover, *gender equality* is interwoven intimately with equality for children and the elderly, especially because it is women who are most often the caregivers for their children and their aging parents. Thus, the struggle for *gender equality* has the potential to transform all human relationships and reduce all forms of family violence.

NOTES

1. This argument can be applied to other systems of domination such as racial superiority or economic exploitation.

2. See Auerbach 2004, an op-ed in the *Washington Post*, for a good explanation of the interlocking web of violence, HIV/AIDS, and IPV.

3. We should note here that the same concern can be expressed about same-sex couples, though, as discussed in Chapter 11, there are obviously no gender differences present. We hope that when gay marriage is finally legalized across the United States that gay couples will not succumb to the same tendencies heterosexual couples have of living in anything but true partnerships. That said, we know, based on research about internalized homophobia, that at least some gay couples will attempt to mimic or copy heterosexual marriages, and this could be devastating to them individually and to the institution of gay marriage more broadly.

BIBLIOGRAPHY

Acker, J. 2006. *Class Questions, Feminist Answers*. New York: Routledge.

Auerbach, Judith. 2004. "The Overlooked Victims of AIDS." *Washington Post*, October 14.

Bianchi, S., J. P. Robinson, and M. A. Milkie. 2007. *Changing Rhythms of American Family Life*. New York: Russell Sage Foundation.

Davis, A. Y. 1983. *Women, Race, and Class*. 1st Vintage Books ed. New York: Vintage Books.

D'Emilio, J. 1983. "Capitalism and Gay Identity." In *Powers of Desire: The Politics of Sexuality*, edited by A. Snitow, C. Stansell, and S. Thompson. New York: New Feminist Library Series.

Edin, K., and L. Lein. 1997. *Making Ends Meet: How Single Mothers Survive Welfare and Low Wage Work*. New York: Russell Sage Foundation.

Ehrenreich, B. 2001. *Nickel and Dimed: On (Not) Getting by in America*. New York: Owl Books.

Ehrensaft, M., and P. Cohen. 2003. "Intergenerational Transmission of Partner Violence: A 20-Year Prospective Study." *Journal of Consulting and Clinical Psychology* 7: 741–753.

Hattery, A. 2001. *Women, Work, and Family: Balancing and Weaving*. Thousand Oaks, CA: Sage.

———. 2009. "Sexual Abuse in Childhood and Adolescence and Intimate Partner Violence in Adulthood Among African American and White Women." *Race, Gender, and Class* 15, no. 2: 79–97.

Hattery, A. J., and E. Smith. 2007. *African American Families*. Thousand Oaks, CA: Sage.

———. 2010. *Prisoner Reentry and Social Capital: The Long Road to Reintegration*. Lanham, MD: Lexington Books.

Kaufman, M. 1992. "The Construction of Masculinity and the Triad of Men's Violence." In *Men's Lives*, edited by Michael Kimmel and Michael Messner, 28–50. New York: Macmillan.

Martin, P. Y. 2005. *Rape Work: Victims, Gender, and Emotions in Organization and Community Context*. New York: Routledge.

Rich, A. 1980. "Compulsory Heterosexuality and Lesbian Existence." *Signs* 5: 631–660.

Scully, D. 1990. *Understanding Sexual Violence: A Study of Convicted Rapists*. Boston: Unwin Hyman.

Travis, J., and M. Waul. 2003. *Prisoners Once Removed*. Washington, DC: Urban Institute Press.

Zweigenhaft, R. L., and G. W. Domhoff. 1998. *Diversity in the Power Elite*. New Haven: Yale University Press.

Appendix

Data Sources

As noted in Chapter 4, there are a variety of data sources available for secondary analysis. Here we provide an overview of each, we review each, and then we provide the source. Generally, qualitative data are not available for secondary analysis because the researchers' investment and involvement in the data collection are so expensive and time intensive that these data are generally not made available for secondary analysis by others. For some excellent books based on qualitative research, we provide a list at the end of the Appendix.

National Violence Against Women Survey: As noted in Chapter 4, the NVAW Survey is a large-scale survey that was conducted with a randomly generated sample of people living in the United States. It was available in both English and Spanish. Developed by Patricia Tjaden and Nancy Thoennes, the survey was completed by more than eight thousand men and eight thousand women over the age of eighteen. The following is a summary of the variables:

Respondents to the NVAW Survey were queried about the following: (1) their general fear of violence and the ways in which they managed their fears, (2) emotional abuse they had experienced by marital and cohabiting partners, (3) physical assault they had experienced as children by adult caretakers, (4) physical assault they had experienced as adults by any type of perpetrator, (5) forcible rape or stalking they had experienced by any type of perpetrator, and (6) incidents of threatened violence they had experienced by any type of perpetrator. Respondents disclosing victimization were asked detailed questions about the characteristics and consequences of victimization as they experienced it, including injuries sustained and use of medical services. Incidents were recorded that had occurred at any time during the respondent's lifetime and also those that occurred within the twelve months prior to the interview. Data were gathered on both male-to-female and female-to-male intimate partner victimization as well as abuse by same-sex partners. Due to the sensitive nature of the survey, female respondents were interviewed by female interviewers. The questionnaires contained fourteen sections, each covering a different topic, as follows:

- Section A: Respondents' fears of different types of violence and behaviors they had adopted to accommodate those fears.
- Section B: Respondent demographics and household characteristics.
- Section C: The number of current and past marital and opposite-sex and same-sex cohabiting relationships of the respondent.
- Section D: Characteristics of the respondent's current relationship and the demographics and other characteristics of their spouse or partner.
- Section E: Power, control, and emotional abuse by each spouse or partner.
- Sections F–I: Screening for incidents of rape, physical assault, stalking, and threat victimization, respectively.
- Sections J–M: Detailed information on each incident of rape, physical assault, stalking, and threat victimization, respectively, reported by the respondent for each type of perpetrator identified in the victimization screening section.
- Section N: Violence in the respondent's current relationship, including steps taken because of violence in the relationship and whether the violent behavior had stopped. The section concluded with items to assess if the respondent had symptoms associated with post-traumatic stress disorder.

Other variables in the data included interviewer gender, respondent gender, number of adult women and adult men in the household, number of different telephones in the household, and region code.

This data set has not been used as extensively by other researchers, though we employed it for an analysis of interracial and intraracial intimate partner violence (Smith and Hattery 2009) and found not only that it is relatively easy to manipulate, but one strength of the data set is that both men and women are queried and the sample is diverse racially and ethnically, making analysis of intimate partner violence by race and gender feasible. The analysis performed by the scholars who developed the survey and received the funding to conduct it is outstanding and is cited by virtually everyone researching intimate partner violence. The report can be found at Tjaden and Thoennes 1999. Last, another aspect to the survey that we found useful is that it includes both physical and sexual victimization in childhood and adulthood. As we discussed in Chapter 7, this allowed us to test for a relationship for both men and women between childhood experiences with violence and adult domestic violence. The data are available at the Inter-University Consortium for Political and Social Research (ICPSR) and can be analyzed by students and faculty interested in conducting secondary analysis. We highly recommend this site and this particular data set. For a listing of all available data sets and guides for analysis, visit the ICPSR home page: http://www.icpsr.umich.edu/icpsrweb/ICPSR/index.jsp.

The Conflict Tactics Scale: We remind the reader that we reviewed the Conflict Tactics Scale at length in Chapter 4 and recommend that the reader return to that discussion before exploring this data set. The CTS is available at the following website: http://www.friendsnrc.org/download/outcomeresources/toolkit/annot/conts.pdf.

Crime Surveys: As we discussed in Chapter 4, an additional source of information regarding all forms of family violence comes from the variety of surveys that are conducted by the various local, statewide, and federal agencies charged with tracking crime. All of these agencies publish their data as reports that are available to the public. For all of their shortcomings, they are an excellent source for the most recent data on a variety of types of family violence. Compared with both the NVAW and CTS surveys that often take years to collect, analyze, and write up, law enforcement surveys are compiled annually, with some data reported on a quarterly basis, and thus they are frequently the best source we have for recent data. As noted, the primary limitations include underreporting—obviously, incidents that are never reported to the police are never counted in several of these databases—as well as the underreporting that is a by-product of the requirement of the victim to identify the incident as a crime; even if an incident is never reported, it will be captured in the NCVS. That said, these sources remain some of the best for obtaining the most recent data on family violence.

National Crime Victimization Survey: The NCVS is conducted annually by the National Institute of Justice, part of the Bureau of Justice Statistics. This survey of approximately one hundred thousand individuals over the age of twelve captures data on all different types of victimization, including domestic violence, violence by ex-spouses, child abuse (abuse by a parent), elder abuse (abuse by a child), and victimization by other relatives. The survey is also designed to collect demographic data on victims and offenders, including race and ethnicity, gender, relationship between the perpetrator and the victim, and, for the victims, income and educational attainment. Homicide data are not reported in the NCVS. The data from the NCVS are also housed in an archive at the ICPSR and can be accessed—without an institutional account—examined, and downloaded for secondary analysis. The website also includes links to other sources of data as well as online access to papers and reports that have been published using these data. See http://www.icpsr.umich.edu/NACJD/NCVS/.

The Bureau of Justice Statistics, the federal agency charged with compiling all of the data with regards to crime, victimization, law enforcement, and corrections, also contains data on several different forms of family violence. The data on domestic violence and violence against women are particularly good. As with the NCVS, the interested student or scholar can access prepared reports, prepared tables, or raw data that can be downloaded and reconfigured and analyzed. As researchers who regularly rely on sources such as the Bureau of Justice Statistics to obtain the latest data on intimate partner violence as well as data on trends in incarceration—race, gender, crime committed, and so forth—we can assure the reader that the data available through the BJS are substantial. However, the website is not always easy to navigate, and often the data are not compiled in the precise format we need. Thus, parties interested in truly using sources such as these will frequently find that they need to download a variety of both databases and data tables and transfer only the relevant data to another program (Excel, SPSS) or in some cases to handwritten tables for manual calculation. Thus, though one can find easily the number of homicides last year, identifying the number of domestic violence homicides—because they are not tracked and categorized separately—is more time-consuming and complex because it will require the student or scholar to combine data from different sources in the BJS. That said, the BJS remains the best source for this type of data.

The Bureau of Justice Statistics is also an excellent source for data on corrections. As we discussed in the later chapters of the book, very few perpetrators of any type of family abuse serve any significant time in jail or prison. Thus, there is little to be learned about individuals convicted of family violence charges in the corrections data. However, a little-known nugget in these data is the results of the annual *Survey of Inmates in State and Federal Corrections Facilities*. The results of this survey—which can be downloaded—are summarized in reports by BJS statisticians. Their analysis provides insight into some of the differences between intimate partner violence, for example, and other interpersonal violence. For example, though most of the inmates incarcerated for violence are men, those incarcerated for "family violence" almost always assaulted a woman, whereas those incarcerated for "nonfamily violence" almost always assaulted another man. Similarly, the vast majority of female victims of homicide were killed by their intimate or ex-intimate partners, whereas the vast majority of male homicide victims were murdered by a nonrelative male. Last, the interviews with female inmates reveal very high rates of victimization by male partners prior to their incarceration; more than half of all women incarcerated for property and financial crimes (forging checks, larceny) were living with men who battered them at the time they committed the crime. Thus, these data can provide a rich source of data for students and scholars interested in family violence as a predictor of other criminal behavior. The Bureau of Justice Statistics website can be accessed at the following address: http://bjs.ojp.usdoj.gov/.

The Uniform Crime Reports: The UCR are the result of data compiled by the FBI as part of the mandatory reporting by law enforcement agencies in local districts. Each month every police department and sheriff's office must submit a form to the FBI detailing crimes that were reported, crimes that were investigated, and outcomes of these processes. Because these data include crimes that were reported but not necessarily solved or resolved, they provide another opportunity to estimate the prevalence of certain types of family violence that become criminalized. As one can imagine, the level of violence that is necessary in order for one to report the crime, to call the police, and to have the offender arrested is generally fairly high. Thus, as noted, these data are likely to severely underreport all forms of family violence, as most family violence does not escalate to the point of an arrest. That said, the UCR are probably the best source for data on the most severe forms of family violence: homicide of children, parents, and intimate partners. As noted previously, because domestic violence homicide is not tracked separately from all other homicides, the student or scholar interested in estimating domestic violence homicides—and there more than 1,500 per year—will have to compile data from a variety of tables in order to cross-check; the UCR are an excellent source with which to begin. The UCR data are available at the FBI website: http://www.fbi .gov/ucr/ucr.htm.

LIST OF QUALITATIVE BOOKS ON FAMILY VIOLENCE

Browne, A. 1989. *When Battered Women Kill*. New York: Free Press.

Hattery, A. 2008. *Intimate Partner Violence*. Lanham, MD: Rowman and Littlefield.

Pipher, M. B. 1994. *Reviving Ophelia: Saving the Selves of Adolescent Girls*. New York: Putnam Press.

Raphael, J. 2004. *Listening to Olivia: Violence, Poverty, and Prostitution*. Boston: Northeastern University Press.

Smith, Earl, and Angela Hattery. 2009. *Interracial Relationships in the 21st Century*. Durham, NC: Carolina Academic Press.

Tjaden, Patricia, and Nancy Thoennes. 1999. *Violence and Threats of Violence Against Women and Men in the United States, 1994–1996* [computer file]. ICPSR02566-v1. Denver: Center for Policy Research [producer], 1998. Ann Arbor, MI: Interuniversity Consortium for Political and Social Research [distributor].

Weitzman, Susan. 2001. *Not to People Like Us: Hidden Abuse in Upscale Marriages*. New York: Basic Books.

Acknowledgments

Any book, no matter how it is authored, is the work of many people. We want to publicly recognize the input of our original acquisitions editor, Alex Masulis, as well as Evan Carver who took over the project midstream and shepherded it through the review process and into production. Evan's insight into some of the more complex reviews helped us to write what we believe is the strongest text on family violence on the market today. We are indebted to the many production staff who have helped us manage copy editing, visual art that is included in the book, cover design, and all of the other work that is always behind the scenes but without which the book would be nothing more than manuscript pages typed on our computers. We are grateful to the many agencies and experts who contributed their knowledge, especially Dr. Tom Nakagawa, Wake Forest University School of Medicine, who worked with us to understand the complex and controversial issue of shaken baby syndrome. We would like to acknowledge the support of the staff of the Women and Gender Studies Program at George Mason University, Suzanne Scott and Christine Hernandez, and the work of the students enrolled in Women and Gender Studies 100 for their contributions to the course website materials, especially the chapter PowerPoint slides: Amanda Annatone, Devin Dowd, Jessica Gibbs, Sara Mallick, Ashley Parker, Abigail Price, Taylor Strang. As always, we are grateful to the men and women whose lives we were allowed to peek into. Their experiences with the pain and trauma of child physical abuse, domestic violence, and child sexual abuse are the cornerstone and driving force of this work. Without them, there would be no book. That said, any errors that remain are ours alone.

Winston-Salem, NC
September 2011

Index